Ida McKinley

Ida McKinley

The Turn-of-the-Century First Lady through War, Assassination, and Secret Disability

Carl Sferrazza Anthony

The Kent State University Press
Kent, Ohio

Published in cooperation with the National First Ladies' Library

Library of Congress Cataloging-in-Publication Data
Anthony, Carl Sferrazza.
Ida McKinley : the turn-of-the-century first lady through war, assassination, and secret
disability / Carl Sferrazza Anthony.
pages cm
Includes bibliographical references.
ISBN 978-1-60635-152-9 (hardcover) ∞
1. McKinley, Ida Saxton, 1847–1907. 2. Presidents' spouses—United States—Biography.
I. Title.
E711.95.A57 2013
973.88092—dc23
[B]
2013012413

17 16 15 14 13   5 4 3 2 1

To Martha whose fortitude helped me brace the rewriting of the lost Spanish-American War chapters, Pat whose resourcefulness rescued the lost pictures in the eleventh hour, and Mary whose faith in the value of this story never wavered.

God gives us love. Something to love
He gives us; but when love is grown
To ripeness, that on which it throve
Falls off, and love is left alone.

Sleep sweetly, tender heart, in peace!
Sleep, holy spirit; blessed soul,
While the stars burn, the moon increase,
And the great ages onward roll.

Sleep till the end, true soul and sweet!
Nothing comes to thee new or strange.
Sleep full of rest from head to feet;
Lie still, dry dust, secure of change.

—Alfred Lord Tennyson, "To J. S."

(Ida Saxton McKinley's favorite poem)

Contents

Acknowledgments

FOR THEIR WORK in helping to produce *Ida McKinley,* I would like to thank Mary Regula, Martha Regula, and Pat Krider of the National First Ladies Library, independent researcher Craig Schermer, Janet Metzger formerly of the McKinley Presidential Museum, Nan Card of the Hayes Presidential Center, members of the board of the National Epilepsy Foundation who reveiwed text related to seizure disorder, Joyce Harrison, Christine Brooks, Susan Cash, Mary Young, and Will Underwood of the Kent State University Press, and copyeditor Valerie Ahwee.

The Red Room, 1899

IT WAS, SAID Miss Pauline Robinson of New York, "like a mandate from Windsor," as if she were being presented to old Queen Victoria herself. A member of the wealthy, powerful, and socially elite DuPont family, at seventeen years old Pauline had already enjoyed privileges most Americans could not even imagine, yet she had "never been so excited" as when her closed coach "drove in the White House gate." Along with another young debutante, a Miss Lee, and the wife and daughter of Washington's Episcopal bishop, Pauline had been granted a "private audience" with the nation's First Lady on Saturday, May 6, 1899.

Ascending the white marble North Portico steps and slipping into the old mansion's entrance lobby, they were met in front of a garish wall of Tiffany glass by George Cortelyou, the president's efficient secretary. Each handed this man with a mustache and monocle her engraved calling card. While he delivered their cards to the First Lady, they retreated to a dressing room to ensure that their appearance was meticulous, for even though the evening social call was designated "*en famille*," it demanded strict adherence to a dress code. Miss Robinson wore a silk pink blouse, white skirt with tulle bow, a pink hat, and long white gloves. These times called for rigorous adherence to rituals of protocol, dictating matters like formal dress codes, intended to command respect for the ruling class of executive branch officials and ensure an equality of status among them with king, prime minister, or pasha. It was the dawn of the so-called "American Empire."

Returning to retrieve the women, Cortelyou now escorted them down the gloomy, columned hall to the door of the Red Room. "We were all announced in a loud tone of voice," Pauline reported in a letter to her mother two days later, and each then "went up separately." As the women entered, "two gentleman of the War Department" immediately rose in attention and abruptly silenced whatever they had been discussing with the First Lady. Their presence, however, was not incidental to the drama that was unfolding in a private room right above them, which resulted in politics that would reverberate across the globe.

"When my turn came, I put into practice the Dodworth curtsy," Pauline recounted, referring to a formal and proper manner of kneeling before royalty. "It was quite effective and you know I did so because I saw at once Mrs. McKinley liked pomp and flattery. She was reclining in a chair, dressed in pale blue satin, her favorite color, and knitting slippers."

Reclining and knitting. Both "activities" were practically all the public had expected of Ida McKinley three years earlier during her husband's presidential campaign, the result of his crafting her persona, which both affirmed him as a martyr to her "invalidism" and prevented the truth about her "nervous" disability from being disclosed. Despite the greater understanding of neurological disorders at that time, a vast percentage of the general public would have ignorantly judged Mrs. McKinley to be better suited for an institution than the White House had they known she lived with epilepsy.

Keeping secret his own medicating of Ida and his perpetual search for a cure that did not exist, McKinley had little choice but to frame the reality of her unpredictable symptoms as a chivalrous matter of preserving the sanctity of her privacy. He cast her as so utterly dependent on his support, and the legend of his sacrifice so romantically played to the Victorian imagination, however, that not even newspaper articles reporting her activities that proved her strength and independence during the first half of her tenure as First Lady could counteract it.

From the moment she arrived in Washington, when she refused the use of a wheelchair and strode through the train station, Ida McKinley defied expectations. While acknowledging her chronically recurring immobility without shame, she sacrificed none of the traditional First Lady duties but rather adapted her condition to it, hosting weekly receptions, welcoming visiting delegations, attending state dinners, stopping to speak with tourists. Unable to tour welfare institutions, she delivered lavish bouquets from the presidential greenhouse and made hefty financial contributions. Her inability to headline fund-raising events was circumvented by donating personally knitted items for sale or auction. That evening in the Red Room, even Pauline Robinson was made to realize just how genuinely committed Ida McKinley was to this work. "She told me with evident pride that she had made 4,000 pairs," the young woman wrote, "and one pair brought 300 dollars for a fair last year."

In deeds both large and small, Ida McKinley impressed her personality on the public, whether it was ignoring pressure from the temperance movement and deciding to serve alcohol to guests or refusing to attend church on Sunday with her husband to instead indulge her passion for theatrical comedies with friends. Not only did she travel extensively with the president around the nation, she left him in Washington to make excursions on her own. In fact, Ida McKinley would become the first incumbent First Lady to break custom and briefly travel to another country.

Never interested in the domestic tasks women were expected to manage, she worked to help secure employment for unmarried women who had to support themselves. She not only went public with her support of a woman's right to vote but to higher education as well. She proved her belief that racial equality would be achieved through education by committing to underwrite the private school costs for a family of several children.

While Mrs. McKinley was certainly vulnerable to persoanl flattery, she was remarkably indifferent to how the general public perceived her. She sought only to glorify the president's image, even at the cost of her own. "Look here," she told her young visitors, opening her bag of wool to show them a picture of her husband inside it, which she could always see while knitting. "I am never idle," she quipped, "and this is a great incentive to work. There is only one Major McKinley in the world for me."

All the while she was holding court, the First Lady seemed more conscious of young Pauline than Miss Lee and the bishop's daughter, who had sat on either side of her. "I noticed Mrs. McKinley looked over in my direction once or twice," the nervous New York girl recalled. "My dear, draw your chair up closer to me," the First Lady abruptly instructed her. Miss Robinson did as told, and Mrs. McKinley then asked, "Are you as much interested in us?"

Pauline suddenly remembered the bishop's daughter's advice that "Mrs. McKinley liked compliments." A bit tense, the teenager blurted out that she was "so pleased and considered it such a privilege to meet her."

"My dear," replied the First Lady, "wait till you meet the President—then I shall consider you to have been truly honored." She then began regaling them all with stories about her beloved "Major," the same sort one read in the papers; Cabinet members knew better than to change that subject. Even at those times when she had been sedated with bromides to prevent her from having a seizure, she could acutely detect the patronizing subtext of politely veiled chatter around her and silence the room by sharply calling it out. Bored by the First Lady's tales of the Major or overly eager to impress her, Miss Lee learned her lesson fast after interposing, "Oh, I have heard about that . . ." one too many times.

"Finally," Pauline reported, "Mrs. McKinley turned around to me." As if Miss Robinson was somehow suddenly her familiar confidante, the First Lady put the other outspoken girl in her place: "There is no use telling anything to Miss Lee. She knows it all."

With the sense of dramatic timing that was naturally his, the president suddenly materialized to rescue an unwitting victim of his wife's arch opinions. William McKinley wasn't as devoted to theater as was his Ida, but after nearly a quarter of a century of strangers scrutinizing them, they'd produced their own fine-tuned performance tableau. Whether it was arranging her shawl or opening her parasol, the president's demonstrations were all variations on the same theme: an attentive husband indulging a loving wife. It was played out in the Red Room. "When the President first came in he brought Mrs. McKinley a bouquet of her favorite flowers, lilies of the valley," Pauline recorded. "It was so sweet of him and she seemed delighted."

If the president's solicitousness at times seemed rehearsed, it was inspired by a deep, abiding trust, tempered by tragedy and loss and a daily renewal of committed support. Though forged by his necessary preparedness for the unpredictable but inevitable recurrence of her chronic disabilities, his attentive care misled many to presume that she was incapable of caring for herself.

In fact, over the course of the past year, it had been Ida's presence that proved his only relief from the killing toil of preparing the nation for international war, although he ignored her fear of assassination attempts on his life.

He trusted her belief in Lt. Col. Theodore Roosevelt's leadership and complied with her request that his "Rough Rider" cavalry be permitted to proceed to Cuba and liberate it from Spain's tyranny.

A number of intimates believed that the president, having invited her opinion as he composed his policy initiatives, had come to recognize the value of her peculiarly emotional reasoning for retaining the Philippine Islands as an American colony.

This unexpected and intense Filipino "insurrection" against the American military presence had also begun to affect the McKinleys individually and as a couple. Just five weeks after Miss Robinson's call, a moment that would prove to be the halfway point of the McKinley Administration, the Major's methodical positioning for another term as president and Ida's nuanced resistance to it would set her on a course of such rapid decline that she would soon be confined to a wheelchair and provide history with those stories that would forever caricature her as an invalid.

As it happened, Pauline's chatty letter to her mother about her visit to the McKinleys would provide an innocent glimpse of the subtle tensions marking this shift. The Major could hardly fail to notice Ida's reluctance to let Miss Robinson leave. Instead of employing one of his courtly tactics to move her along, however, this time he curtly challenged his wife. "You don't look very much pleased," he cracked, adding that a Lutheran church leader was waiting for a scheduled meeting.

"That makes no difference to me," she shot right back. "Does it to you?"

McKinley knew how unpredictably Ida could escalate a minor disagreement into a contentious battle. Wisely avoiding a conflict with guests present, he tried to artfully diffuse her frustration with a bit of witty repartee, which she usually loved. Lutherans might not matter, he suggested, but he liked Methodists and Episcopalians well enough. She was not amused.

"At this Mrs. McKinley seemed piqued," Pauline observed. "What about Presbyterians!" she said sharply (being one herself).

"Why my dear *of course* I like Presbyterians," he rushed to assure her, reverting to his familiar acquiescence. After all, Ida had so grandly praised and professed her love for him to the guests. Having reaffirmed his loyalty to her, however, "Mrs. McKinley was satisfied," Pauline wrote. The president, however, had wordlessly won his point. It was time for the next appointment.

The women rose to depart, but Mrs. McKinley singled out Miss Robinson with an impulsive act of generosity. "Here is the young lady whose first visit it is to Washington. I want her to remember it," Ida effused. Pauline was overcome, writing that, "[A]nd with that she actually handed me the bouquet the President had given her!! Everyone seemed to think that quite an unusual thing for Mrs. McKinley to do."

Miss Robinson never learned why she had become the focus of the First Lady's continuing attention that evening, and with such a growing sense of familiarity, as if there was something she recognized about the young woman's soul.

If the Major was foremost in her heart, someone else had never left her mind. More than two decades had passed since Katie McKinley's life had ended. To her mother, however, she not only continued to live on and even mature in some mystical realm but, as she had come to hope, may have also by now returned to earth in the form of another young woman.

Even the remotest possibility of this was sometimes just enough to keep Ida McKinley living on.

∗{ 1 }∗

A Daughter Studies

HISTORY WOULD JUDGE HER as the wife of a United States president, but Ida Saxton McKinley defined a sense of purpose to her life by living closely with those she loved.

From her parents to her brother and sister, her father's father and mother's mother, nieces and nephews, uncles and aunts, first and second cousins, Ida was bound tightly to her closely knit clan and was blessed that it valued daughters as equally as sons. Although of German, Irish, Scottish, and English ancestry, her identity was *Cantonian*. She was born in what began as a small village established with help from her grandfathers and would die in what became an industrial center propelled by her father and husband. From Ida's first breath at its south end to her last gasp farther north, from the scent of its summer red roses to the grime of its winter chimney soot, Canton infused her very being.

John Saxton, her father's father, was the eldest of eleven, a native Pennsylvanian and War of 1812 veteran. He'd been a *Huntingdon Gazette* printing apprentice before arriving in 1814 in a small settlement he had read about in Ohio, a state only since 1803. Named after the Chinese city of Canton, wood buildings were being raised on surveyed plots by a diversity of ambitious men: three German brothers from Philadelphia who operated a gristmill, a Frenchman with a medical practice, and an Irishman starting a produce business. "Four farm wagons at one time have just pulled into the [town] Square," Saxton wrote his father upon arrival. Days later, on July 23, he circulated a prospectus soliciting interest in a newspaper. Determining it was feasible to start a weekly paper based on annual $2 subscriptions, he returned to Pennsylvania to purchase and transport a bulky printing press by ox team to Canton. The first issue of his *Ohio Repository* was issued on

March 30, 1815. Once established, he married his childhood sweetheart Margaret Laird, daughter of Scottish immigrants. Canton was his place of "beautiful eminence."

Within four years, the newspaper, which focused on national as well as local stories, was successful enough for Saxton to buy a building to house its offices and printing plant. Among those reporters he mentored was Joseph Medill, from the nearby town of Massillon, later the famous *Chicago Tribune* editor. Content was driven by Saxton's rabid commitment to abolition of African American slavery and education for women. Through him Ida was introduced to abolitionist and *New York Tribune* publisher Horace Greeley and once asserted herself to secure a front-row seat to hear him lecture in Canton. The one-time Whig Party presidential candidate often stayed with the Saxtons during his trips to the region, an abolition stronghold.

As municipality president, township trustee, county treasurer, and public school founder, Saxton's civic duty also included charitable work as a First Presbyterian church elder. Few in Canton were ill, indigent, or struggled in any way for long before Saxton discreetly called, providing a food parcel, envelope of cash, or simply companionship. This left a deep impression on Ida, who developed a lifelong commitment to aid those who were suffering, even strangers, wherever she lived. She even continued her grandfather's work after he became frail and deaf. If, during periods of disability, she was unable to make visits, Ida drew up lists of food, flowers, or cash for delivery by messengers to those she knew needed attention or support.[1]

John and Margaret Saxton raised six sons and one daughter in a brick house they built on the south end of Canton's main thoroughfare, Market Avenue. Their first child, born May 1, 1816, was Ida's father, James Ashbaugh. Privately tutored, he had his father's sense of balance, was shrewd yet honest, gentle yet disciplined. Among her uncles, Ida was closest to her Uncle Joe and, later, to his son Sam, who, at twenty-three years her junior, became like a son. She also developed a lifelong friendship with her cousin Mary, daughter of her Aunt Hannah. Ida was the fifth of twenty-one Saxton cousins.

Thirteen years before Ida was born, eighteen-year-old James Saxton began a hardware business, and by the time she was nine, he had sold it to Uncle Joe. Among the generations of her father and grandfather, members of the Saxton clan often pursued businesses together and sold interests among themselves. John and two brothers had helped their father establish a nail factory. When one of them pursued scientific engineering to eventually develop the nation's first measuring weight system and camera, his brothers invested in his endeavor. Another brother, Joshua, first worked as *Repository* printer, and then became copublisher. In later years, John sold the paper to his nephew Thomas.[2]

Her mother's family was small but also entrepreneurial. Five years before James Saxton had even arrived in Canton, the Spread Eagle Tavern, built and owned by Ida's maternal great-grandparents Philip and Eva Dewalt, was thriving. There they hosted Lutheran services on Sunday and served the home-brewed beer of their native Germany the rest of the week. In 1829 their son George, one of five adult children, bought the tavern with his wife, Christiana Harter, also from a German immigrant family. Ida's mother Catharine (always called "Kate") was born on August 18, 1827, the third child of George and Christiana; Kate had a brother John and a sister Harriet. After attending Emmetsburg Female Seminary in Maryland, Kate was sent to a second boarding school, Linden Hall Seminary in Lilitz, Pennsylvania. Her father asked the school principal that his daughter's course of study be "kept economical" with a "regular English Education" and music. George Dewalt believed that Kate's education should result in "usefulness," rather than the "mere show" of the fine arts usually emphasized for girls.[3]

The same year Kate began at Linden Hall, her parents and siblings moved into a large Federal-style house on the southwest corner of what was then 8th Street and Market Avenue South. It is likely that a reception was held there following the August 20, 1846, First Presbyterian Church wedding of Kate Dewalt to James Saxton, who moved into the Dewalt House with her and her parents, sister, and brother. Within a month, Kate was pregnant with her first child.

Kate Saxton's baby was delivered in the Dewalt House on June 8, 1847, by Canton's most prominent physician, Lorenzo Whiting. Why the girl was called Ida is unknown, but the choice bucked a family tradition of using the same names in succeeding generations. Family letters disprove later claims that Ida Saxton was a sickly child. The only story to endure from what was her otherwise conventional development from infant to toddler was Ida's unusually intense attachment to her "affectionate, kind, sympathetic mother." Even into adulthood, Ida was with Kate so frequently that people assumed she was a "younger sister rather than a daughter."

The bond with her daughter reflected Kate's closeness to her own mother Christiana, and both women became strong role models for Ida, establishing in her a belief that such generational links not only entrench family commitment but were central to the value of a woman's life, a view that would dramatically impact her life. As Kate prepared for the birth of her second child Mary in December 1848 and then cared for the infant, Ida had the full attention of her grandmother, which intensified all the more her affection for Christiana, as if she were a second mother. When the young family moved in 1850 from the Dewalt House to one next door, separation from her grandmother was apparently difficult for three-year-old Ida. Kate, pregnant with her third child at the time of the move, nevertheless felt it was important for a young family to establish its own household. James Saxton was also financially stable enough to do this; an 1850 census showed they had three servants by then, likely a nurse for the baby, a cook, and a maid.

Kate Saxton gave birth to her third child just two days after the shock of her father's sudden death on October 29, 1850. She named the baby boy George in his honor. By then, Kate's brother John had moved to Indiana and within two years, her twenty-year-old sister Harriet died, thus leaving Christiana to live alone in the Dewalt House. For both emotional and practical reasons, James and Kate Saxton and their three children returned to live with her there. Saxton's business success also allowed him to share the cost of maintaining the large house.[4]

By the time he sold his hardware business and then a "fancy goods" store, Saxton was already in banking, announcing in the June 21, 1854, *Repository* that, as founder and president of the new Stark County Bank, he would begin accepting deposits up to $500. Drawn into aspects of civic development, he became a trustee of the new Canton Union School, which had been approved by local vote in 1848 to offer public education. Little is known of Ida's early life in the house. Her childhood piano, which survives, attests to a later claim that she was an "enthusiastic musician." The object she most cherished and kept within her sight in any home she lived in for the rest of her life was a small rocking chair, given to her as a Christmas gift when she was a child.

In September 1853, six-year-old Ida began her formal education at the two-story brick Union School, among the first generation of Canton children to do so. By 1855, she was one of five hundred students taught mathematics, English, elementary science, vocal music, and drawing over the course of eight years of primary and grammar school. More than any subject, however, what most endured from her education was the influence of a principal whose reputation had preceded her.

By the time Betsy Mix Cowles was working at the Union School, she had earned a national reputation as founder of the Ohio Women's Rights Association and the Women's Anti-Slavery Society. One of Oberlin College's first graduates and founder of a girls' academy "for intellectual im-

provement," Cowles was highly respected by school trustees James Saxton
and Lorenzo Whiting. In 1850, the trio organized the Stark County Common School Association. Saxton even influenced her to join the Presbyterian church and attend services with his family. Ida Saxton's attachment to
Cowles was stronger than that of other students. Her motivation to excel
in math in particular, for example, can be attributed to the fact that Cowles
believed it important for girls to learn. Cowles also shared the Saxton values.
James, a strong abolitionist like his father, joined the Canton Anti-Slavery
Society, founded by Whiting with Cowles's aid, and the local Republican
Party, becoming a supporter of Abraham Lincoln for president in 1860.[5]

Two months after the Civil War began, Ida Saxton completed middle
school. Because of uncertainty about how the war might affect the family's finances, her further education was delayed until 1862, and instead Ida
began work in support of the Union Army. Accounts of her as a "school-
girl in the civil war" detailed that Ida spent "many an hour outside of
study . . . devoted to the preparing of lint and bandages for the wounded
soldiers at the front." In being what one source called "a leader among the
patriotic girls of Canton in every work for the comfort and relief of sick
and wounded soldiers," she directly emulated her mother, who was now
working as the Canton Soldiers Relief Association treasurer and hosting
meetings in the Dewalt House.

Even though Cowles had left Canton in 1857, Ida's memory of her mentor remained strong enough to motivate her to leave the haven of home
to resume studying under Cowles at Delhi Academy in Clinton County,
New York. Contemporaries asserted that Ida was "gifted as a scholar" and
"an apt learner," enough so that James Saxton believed her "advancement
speedily warranted the superior advantages" of private boarding school.
Already with more formal education than most of her peers, Ida's training
included math, which was intended to prepare her for professional work.
James Saxton's bank thrived not only through honesty and caution but also
through his ongoing "study of monetary questions" and familiarity with
"every phase of finance, theoretical and practical. . . ." He was confident
Ida could also do so, writing Cowles on March 14, 1862: "I commit Ida
to your care. I trust you will take the same charge of her that you would
if she was your own. I want her education to be more practical than
ornamental & particularly want her to pay attention to bookkeeping &
branches connected with it."

Boarding at Delhi Academy, however, left both student and teacher on
edge. They both quickly discovered that their abolitionist Republicanism
was an unpopular view in the solidly Democratic town. The one highlight

Cowles recalled of their time there was news of the Emancipation Proclamation. A final indication of Ida's solidarity with her teacher is that when
Cowles left Delhi after the 1863 spring term, so did Ida, having completed
three semesters there.

Ida resumed her education that fall at the Cleveland Female Seminary,
renamed the Sanford School during her first semester when it was purchased by the new principal, Solomon N. Sanford. He taught students natural and moral sciences, and his wife and vice principal, Louise, instructed
students on hygiene and "domestic economy." A bonus to this school was
that, just outside its gates, the sixteen-year-old could catch the Kinsman
Street omnibus to the Cleveland depot and take the railroad to Canton on
weekends.

Ida apparently carried a rigorous course load. She took advanced mathematics, grammar, geography, penmanship, and history. She also had the
choice of electives in French literature, instrumental music, singing, drawing, painting, and sculpture. Almost certainly she continued her piano
instruction in twice-daily classes. Marking her first sustained exposure to
foreign languages, Ida excelled in French, Latin, and Greek. The incident
that eclipsed all others during her two years at Sanford School took place
in her last term. She heard a chilling eyewitness account from classmate
and native Indianan Harriet Sherman. In Washington over Easter break,
Sherman was thrilled to discover, as she took her seat to watch a come-
dic play, that the president was also in Ford's Theater to see *Our American
Cousin*. She recounted being startled to hear gunfire, then was bewildered
when the famous actor John Wilkes Booth jumped on stage and ran off.
More disturbing was Harriet Sherman's description of the next moments
as she stood near the doors and watched the bloodied and unconscious
Abraham Lincoln being carried out, the first president to be assassinated.[6]

Ida graduated from Sanford School two months later and began her last
three years of education that fall at Brooke Hall Female Seminary in Media,
Pennsylvania. It was a commanding three-story building with a covered
piazza running the full length along one side. Its founder and principal
Maria Lee Eastman ruled the finishing school with propriety. The school,
which opened in 1856 with students drawn from elite mid-Atlantic families,
placed a decidedly untraditional emphasis on developing physical strength
and athleticism in the girls.

Led by the friendliest of teachers, Harriet "Hettie" Gault, the students
began each day with a vigorous walk into town and around the courthouse
square. James McKnitt, the school's young groundskeeper, recalled how

Miss Saxton took to the new exercise immediately. Yet even when it wasn't part of a formal regimen, Ida felt compelled to walk. She was known for leading friends on hikes through the nearby woods, across a footbridge, to the rail station, and back. Other times she challenged herself by running slowly down a steep incline, then vigorously climbing back up again. Even when it rained, she maintained her rigorous exercise with laps of fast-walking, up and down the full length of Brooke Hall's enclosed front porch.

McKnitt also remembered Ida attending Friday night dances in the school's large hall and Sunday morning services in the town's United Church of Christ. She often spent Saturdays in nearby Philadelphia, shopping and then attending the opera, theater, or concerts. On weeknights, she played piano and learned card and parlor games, her favorite being euchre.

During the school day, one source noted, "quickness kept her at the head of her classes, while she spent less time in study than any of the others." Although Miss Eastman confessed to being "more severe with her than any other," she later claimed it was to disguise her favoritism for Ida whose intelligence made her stand out. It may have also been to keep her influence and antics in check. "She led the other girls in their enterprises, sometimes mischievous ones," a later vague account ran. Ida's empathic individuality, combined with her overtly generous warmth, made her a role model for more insecure students like Louise Deshong, whose growing confidence would lead her to pursue a career in photography. Ida never used her biting wit and worldly sarcasm to embarrass others. Her appreciation of fellow students for who they were was especially appreciated by daughters of public officials like Gen. Daniel Sickles or Maryland Congressman John Findlay.

Graduating in 1867, Ida Saxton returned to Canton confident and curious. Whether voicing her opinion during a game of cards, walking around town for exercise, or engaging prominent speakers on lecture tours, Ida Saxton, as a local reporter put it, "left the stamp of her personality. That is what she does everywhere."[7]

⤜ 2 ⤛

The Well-Employed Belle

IDA SAXTON'S SUN-KISSED CHEEKS and well-toned physique were the result of walking great lengths at a rapid clip, but her upright posture indicated inner discipline and assuredness. Her large dark blue eyes sized men up directly. Beneath a glossy chestnut-colored coiffure piled high and elaborately twisted, she smiled wryly, sensuality radiating from even the static duo-tone of a Victorian photograph.

A large number of Canton's upper-class college boys and young professionals began asking her if they could visit her in the Dewalt House parlor. Sensing that their ulterior motive was to gain favor with her powerful father, Ida took few of them seriously and just enjoyed flirting with them. "Every man in town promised to be a brother to me," she quipped, "And, oh! I did have such a good time." James Saxton, "well aware of the attentions," it was euphemistically put, "dreaded losing her to some unwelcome suitor." With his intense loyalty to the Union, the "unwelcome suitor" was worse than a mere opportunist; he was a former Confederate Army major.[1]

Six years Ida's senior, native Marylander John W. Wright had supported Southern secession on principle, not as a slave-owner. After the war, he worked for a Little Rock, Arkansas, newspaper before earning a law degree. He likely met Ida while providing legal advice to her father on the side while employed at Canton's E. Ball & Company.

James Saxton earned $53,340 in 1869, which was more than anyone else in Canton earned—except Cornelius Aultman.[2] Saxton was consolidating his wealth and power. By 1868 he was on the city council and invested widely not only in Canton property but farm acreage in the outlaying Minerva, and even in Nevada silver mines. As his attention was increasingly diverted from the bank, he needed trustworthy help there, so he hired Ida.

Having Canton's leading belle working in the bank, presumably without salary, was so unconventional that many locals assumed it meant Saxton was suffering hard financial times. One local insisted he hired his daughter because he "did not believe in girls doing nothing between the graduation day and the marriage day," while others said it was to make up for the lost time of her company when she was away at school. All theories shared the misperception that Ida simply did as she was told. In fact, Saxton respected her enough to first propose the idea to her, which she "strongly supported." Ida later quoted her father's rather feminist reasoning: "I have seen enough girls left stranded by sudden losses of means and I don't intend that this shall ever happen to my daughter. She can be taken care of at home now, but I may be poor someday. Nobody ever knows what is going to happen. I want her to be able to support herself if trouble ever comes her way. Above all, I don't want her to have to marry solely to be supported, as I have seen plenty of girls do. I want her to marry because and whom she wants to."

When the bank was open to the public, Ida interacted with customers from a barred teller's window, but numerous accounts that claimed she had been hired to "learn something of the banking business," such as determining dividends, compounding variable-rate loan interest, and reporting methods, place her in more than a clerical position. She worked for two years after her June 1867 graduation, took six months off to travel, and returned in January 1870 for another year. Her employment caused "something of a commotion" among those who believed banking was inappropriate work for a woman and the unfortunate result of women pursuing higher education. Ida defended herself, only agitating critics further by quipping that her skill in finance was indeed proof that she had pursued a rigorous education to learn more than just "a little Latin." Canton native, reporter S. F. Call, recorded that "Through all the flutter that her presence caused in the place of business, Miss Saxton preserved a businesslike calm. She worked diligently and learned the business thoroughly. She was accurate, quick, and reliable, and she had the equipment to take her place in the business world and hold her own with men." Her ability, another contemporary further suggested, "qualified her to hold a position in a much larger establishment." For making her a "practical woman of experience," Ida later told a reporter, she "never ceased to be grateful for this training."[3]

Being able to interact with such an attractive woman drew more men into the bank, including many who frequently returned if they missed Miss Saxton during their visit.

Ida, the star among her circle of cousins, always stood out at the suppers, ice cream socials, and other fund-raising events then being held to underwrite the construction of a new First Presbyterian church, the effort led by patriarch John Saxton. At a March 1868 Schaefer's Opera House benefit variety show, Ida made rapid costume changes for her appearance in a series of posed fantasy tableaux, set to music, including "Descent of the Fairies," "the Little Pilgrim," and "the Ten Virgins." The audience of twelve hundred voted her the "best actress" prize.

Ida could not be missed in a crowd while gallivanting on surrey rides, waltzing at dances, or promenading the storefronts. As 1868's blooming dogwoods gave way to thickening shade trees, she found relief from stifling humidity at Meyers Lake, two miles outside town. During most summer weekends in the years after the war, a young social crowd swarmed the sleepy lakeside inn, which was famous for its creamed chicken on waffles. Although most couples sought some privacy by slipping off on rented rowboats and canoes, Ida Saxton and her boyfriend John Wright lingered with the crowd at the inn's picnic tables where she couldn't help eclipsing him.

If beauty, intelligence, wealth, and compassion weren't enough to set Canton's only bank lady apart, her behavior did. However feminine in appearance and manner, Ida ignored the etiquette code. Showing an appetite was masculine, one dictum declared, and women must consume just part of a meal in public, and then only with hesitance. One afternoon in the summer of 1868, Miss Saxton consumed her creamed chicken on waffle with gusto.

The sight of Miss Saxton eating chicken both confused and amused a twenty-four-year-old attorney who loved recalling that moment for the rest of his life. He never mentioned her boyfriend John Wright, the Confederate Army major, but any jealousy he may have felt would be understandable, especially since he himself was a Union Army major. The attorney, who had been in Canton for less than two years, lived in a rented room. His sister Anna was a Union schoolteacher. Anna, accompanied by her brother, came over to say hello to Ida. After the brief introduction, the giddy belle in summer white never suggested to the somber teacher and lawyer, in black mourning for their sister, that they get better acquainted. Not long after, in fact, when Ida ran into one of his friends, she remembered nothing about the man in black, except his military status, so she called him "the Major." Observing their introduction, however, her friend Catherine Meyer saw that it had been "love at first sight" for William McKinley.

Even if William McKinley had been a customer at Stark County Bank instead of First National Bank, however, Ida was unavailable. In her shimmering red foil costume as the "Queen of Hearts," Miss Saxton made more of a statement by entering Schaefer's Halloween Ball in October on the arm of her Confederate major, John Wright. To the elite of Canton, dressed as Scottish laddies, Chinese dancers, shepherds, and tambourine girls at the invitation-only ball, the first formal social event John and Ida attended together as a couple practically announced their engagement—even if James Saxton did not. A photograph of Ida's sister Mary, wearing a giant poster-board, was on the front page of the *Repository*. She appeared with her genial fiancé Marshall C. Barber, who was from a Canton founding family. Mary, or "Pina" (a Spanish nickname for "little one"), had become Ida's confidante while living with her during her last year at Brooke Hall.

Knowing that marriage would inevitably alter their relationship, the sisters decided to take a six-month exploration of Europe, beginning in June 1869. Planning a budget in the months preceding the trip helped to distract Ida while John was temporarily relocated to Louisville as a Ball Company regional sales agent. Between his returns to Canton, they kept in touch by letter, and Ida promised to buy him a special gift during her impending adventure.[4]

As the Saxton sisters traveled through England, Scotland, Ireland, France, Germany, Italy, Belgium, Holland, Austria, and Switzerland, they were taken to cathedrals, castles, museums, galleries, natural wonders, and street markets by Jeanette Alexander, a Canton teacher who had previously guided a tour group through Europe. Before the *City of Antwerp* had even set sail, she insulted Ida's intelligence. To James Saxton, Miss Alexander claimed her exorbitant fee was due to the travel expense and professional services of her brother, who would manage the group's money. Ida insisted she was more than capable of handling not just her and Pina's budget but that of the whole group, which would reduce the cost. Implying that women were incapable of handling money, Miss Alexander snapped that Ida didn't want Jeanette's brother to accompany them because he didn't fawn over Ida. Ida didn't back down and instead of potentially losing two clients, Jeanette agreed to drop her brother from the trip and assume control of costs and appropriations. Ida, suspecting that Jeanette padded expenses, kept a careful account of the small amounts of money she turned over, asked to see the bills, and then checked for accuracy. Daily, for six months, she also calculated and compared the costs of goods, lodging, transportation, and purchases in each country, finding Europe costlier than she expected. Still, she insisted that she and Pina live within their overall $2,000 budget. Whenever they arrived in a new city, Ida went to a designated bank to withdraw cash from her prearranged "letters of credit" and retrieve any waiting mail.

From the moment they parted, she and John exchanged love letters, and he vowed to wait at the pier when her ship returned home. In a letter to her mother, Ida asked anxiously when the new church building would be complete, suggesting she was already thinking of her wedding there. Four days before landing in Cork Harbor at Cobh, Ireland, Ida turned twenty-two years old.[5]

The moment she landed, Ida embraced new experiences and interests. In Ireland, she got on a horse for the first time and just took off. In Scotland, her lifelong love of Robert Burns's poetry began after they visited his historic home. On the Continent, Ida got her ears pierced and began drinking. Pina told their parents, "Sunday, Ida and I had a bottle of wine for dinner and today Ida, Effie and I had a bottle. . . ." In Frankfort, Ida admitted it "seems dreadful to be attending the Opera [on] Sunday night but we were told the music was much finer than any other night. . . . Do not tell any person at home about it." At a Baden-Baden casino, the sisters were "so interested in the gambling."

Pina also tattled about a male friend, who "comes into our bedroom lots of times, [and] it seemed very strange at first but we are all used to it now." While Ida felt the need to assure her parents that the man "watches us girls as close as if he was our brother," it horrified Miss Alexander, who was further scandalized when Ida slipped off "with some gentleman" in Paris. Ida made no apology for enjoying evening dates with different men, assuring her parents about a Chicagoan she stepped out with in London: "I do not like him very well. . . ." She held her own against James Webb, a persistent middle-aged doctor, who bragged about being the brother-in-law of Ohio's new governor. Learning she was from Canton, Webb mentioned a war comrade, a major, who settled there. Ida wrote her father to ask the "Major" about Webb's reputation. Her father forgot to do so and it wasn't important enough to Ida to remind her father to ask again about Webb's war comrade, who was William McKinley.

Ida and Major Wright faithfully kept in touch. In early August, he returned to Canton from a sales trip feeling ill, but sensing that it had more to do with his spirits, Ida implored her mother to look after him: "Ma, Mr. Wright is not very sick I think, but I want you to show him very marked attention, and do all you can to make his stay in Canton pleasant, write and tell me every word he says." Other than John and her parents, Ida rarely asked about anyone else in Canton as she was then so engrossed in meeting people from cultures and classes that were different than her own.

When she first arrived in France, with "crucifixes on each side of the harbor," Ida first expressed what would be a lifelong antipathy toward Catholicism:" . . . we are now in a Catholic country so attended that church, it seemed more like a show than anything I could think of, the way they were all dressed and the parade they went through with, I could scarcely believe I was in a church. . . . The form and ceremony was too much." Veiled and feeling "about sixty-five" for a ceremonial meeting in Rome with Pius IX, she "bowed before him and kissed his hand not because he is the Pope," she wrote her parents, "but such a nice old man." She found familiarity in Scotland: "I am really in love with the Scotch, they seemed to be a good deal like our people . . . this is Presbyterian country." She also recognized Europe's institutionalized anti-Semitism. Shocked by Prague's refusal to maintain sanitation in the Jewish quarter, she feared its residents "will all die of the cholera."

Perhaps the most poignant moment of her journey came when she encountered a painter in an Amsterdam gallery who had either lost or been born without his arms, and painted with his feet. "It was very unpleasant for me to look at him at first, but after that feeling passed away, I was very much interested," she recorded. Rather than stare or ignore him, Ida engaged the artist, Charles Felir. He demonstrated how he mixed paint on a palette and applied a fine brush to canvas with his feet. When she wondered how he was able to function daily, he told her how "he shaves himself, cuts his meat, dresses, does everything for himself." After Ida promised that she would keep in touch with him, Felir further amazed her by writing his address on a card for her in his beautiful penmanship. The encounter uplifted her. "I think it was wonderful," she wrote. "I did not believe such a thing could be done until I saw it myself."

Ida also grew aware of how privileged her life was at home as she witnessed the stark reality of poverty. After crossing through rural Switzerland, she wrote, "It is terrible the way some of the poor people live, having the cows and sheep in the same house or close by, and the dirt. . . ." As she traversed Belgian farmlands, she "saw the women in the field working as hard as the men and in some instances harder," but seemed even more shocked at the working conditions of young female lace-makers in Brussels and the paltry wages their work yielded. "The girls work from six in the morning until eight at night and are paid 2 francs and 2½ francs a day," she reported, stunned to learn that one lace handkerchief took three months, yet the crafters barely survived with their wages. Age offered no relief from such conditions. Ida commented again in Switzerland that "some of the poor old women are bent almost double carrying such heavy things on their backs. I would not like to live in Switzerland and work as some of the women do." At Brieg, her indignation rose to anger. "The women are made slaves of in this country," she told her parents. Her Saxton egalitarianism also emerged. Shakespeare's humble birthplace proved to her that "it does not require a palace to produce brains." After viewing separate morgues in Munich for the rich and poor, she concluded, "I did not see any difference." She found compensation for failing to spot any British royalty by seeing the wax figure of President Grant "having a little conversation" with his political antagonist President Andrew Johnson at Madame Tussaud's wax museum.

Ida's experimental midnight gastronomy and laughter about her poor French came to an abrupt halt as the party arrived in Geneva on September 25. Instead of joining Pina for an early dinner, Ida eagerly retrieved their cash and waiting letters at the bank. The day before, she had received another love letter from John and bought him an engraved silver card case. On returning to their suite after her meal, Pina saw her weeping on the terrace. Ida bluntly told her the news in a letter from home: "Mr. Wright was dead."

The next morning, Pina reported to her parents about the effect of the traumatic news on Ida: "Ida looked pale and feels very badly. She did not eat any breakfast. . . . It was a fearful shock to her. I was very glad that Ida was not at home when Mr. Wright died and I think she was glad but she never said so." Ida admitted that she struggled to ward off the resulting depression: "I know I should not feel so, but I cannot help it." She was "very glad to leave" Geneva.

The next leg of their trip at least gave Ida a chance to pursue her favorite sport of hiking, at Montanvert, Switzerland, overlooking the Chamonix Valley. "At least the natural scenery has surpassed anything we have seen in our travels," she commented. After a four-and-a-half-hour climb up Rigi Kuhm, Ida reflected, "Its beauty compensated for the fatigue."

Hiking had become a mainstay of Ida's life at Brooke Hall, but it was all the more exhilarating when she hiked in a new landscape and was exposed to the elements. After putting cold cream on the previous day's sunburn, she eagerly headed out for another lengthy climb, inspired by the air and the atmosphere. "When I first woke up this morning," she wrote, "the sky looked beautiful. I never saw anything grander[.] The heavens seemed to be all on fire. I never saw such glorious light in the sky." Soon enough, a steady rain began, but in their rubber shoes, pinned-up skirts, and hooded cloaks, with a climbing staff in one hand and an umbrella in the other, the sisters were prepared and, Ida joked, made "a very good appearance." Natural beauty vitalized her. "It is hard to tell about," she concluded of this leg of the journey, "yet it is something we will always remember. I am charmed with Switzerland, the beautiful lakes, the grand mountains, and the fresh air makes us all feel real good. . . ." She also expressed her frustration in remaining uncertain about the circumstances of John's death:

> Mr. Wright spoke in his last letter he would be either in Canton or New York to meet me. Only think that now he is dead, and buried. I cannot realize it. The next place we have letters sent it will [be] hard not to find any from Mr. Wright. I have felt all the time that perhaps I would receive one more letter before he was taken so very sick. I am so anxious to hear all the particulars, how long he was sick? If he suffered? Who took care of him? I think I could ask a thousand questions if I saw any person who knew. I suppose I must wait until I get home, which seems a long way off.

Learning that that he had died on September 2 of meningitis, she obliquely referred to their dashed future plans: "Things will be very different from what I expected when I get home."

Renewed antagonism with Miss Alexander served to further distract Ida, who called her "very self-willed." Ida and Pina had planned to save time by driving to Lake Como, but Jeannette argued they must cross it by boat. "Miss A does not like to have us suggest anything that would be an improvement on her plans," Ida wrote exasperated, and "it was quite a while before she would give up her way of doing it." The group went by carriages as the Saxtons wished.

Italy failed to meet Ida's romantic illusions of it, and she found that the "beautiful Italian sky" was cloudy, the language "not as musical as I thought it would be," and the roasting chestnuts in Milan, Venice, Florence, Pisa, Fiesole, and Rome were no different than those in New York. Still, she found it "a pleasant kind of country to be in without a gentleman." From Naples they went to Nice and Marseilles, and then back to Paris, the end of their sojourn.

Unlike Pina, who was eager to be reunited with her beau Marsh Bar-ber, Ida admitted, "I would like to stay in Europe with some nice French family, study French and music." She also hinted that she needed "several months" to truly explore Italy. Beyond John Wright's death, however, the enduring reason for Ida's often more solemn mood through the latter part of her trip was separation from Kate. "I never go to the stores but I wish you were with me Ma," she wrote her mother from Brussels, suggesting to both parents that "If you could only make up your minds to cross the ocean you would be a thousand times paid by seeing all that is on this side. . . ." Quipping that she had become as "large as Ma" in Europe, Ida underlined their closeness by remarking that "people will really mistake me for Ma," a reference to how similar people already thought they were. While her father is often credited with Ida's development, a family friend later remarked that Kate, as a "woman of cultivation," had taken "great pains with her daughter's education."

"I have thought of you a great many times, my dear," Ida wrote her spoiled and disengaged twenty-year-old brother George in one of many letters to which he never responded. She listed all the places they had vis-ited in an effort to inspire him to read about them so that when he heard her stories about Europe, he "will enjoy it so much more." He did no such thing. Pina bluntly asserted that George had no "value of money."

That Christmas, the sisters presented the gifts they brought back from Europe, but Ida returned with the greatest gift for herself, wanderlust. "I am up every morning between six and half past," she wrote one day from Europe, "and by seven am ready to read up my guide book . . . about what we are going to see that day." Never having been "half so busy before in my life," she wished she could have back "the time I used to idle away. . . ." Most days in Europe, she walked about ten miles, sometimes upwards of twenty.

Recognizing the value of time only confirmed her impulse to stop expending it to write how she'd spent it. Initially she claimed she didn't like composing letters because she was unable to first "correct mistakes" before mailing them, but even at boarding school, with ample time for this, Ida had avoided sharing her thoughts, reminding Kate that, "you know my aversion to writing letters. . . ." It was no accident that Ida left questions about her unanswered, maintaining her privacy even with fam-ily, once adamantly warning George, "I do not want any of my letters shown to any person while I am gone."[6]

Ida Saxton came back to work in the new year enthused, her "one ambition" being to "master the intricacies of finance." More often she now spent most of the day in the back office, wearing white paper cuffs to protect her sleeves from ink and pencil shavings as she drew up farm mortgages, reviewed loan applications, checked interest statements, and prepared payment contracts. As her father, the bank president, focused on diversifying his business endeavors, Ida went from being his aide to his substitute, one customer recalling that "so well did she learn to fill it that at times she performed her father's duties when he was away," and was often "running the bank." Some articles during her lifetime reported her title as being assistant bank manager.

Saxton worked primarily on his other business from his bank office. That past November, he was added as a defendant to a party of five in a complex case filed against them by three plaintiffs. The original defendants had already engaged a team of attorneys, who then also represented him, an opportunity that would give a member of this legal defense team access to Saxton's daughter when she returned from Europe, which he had been determined to have for over a year. In fact, after the defendants were rendered a favorable judgment with compensation, this attorney hand-delivered Saxton's check to the office he shared with Ida. The incident forced father and daughter to finally take notice of Maj. William McKinley.

Saxton had known of McKinley even before his election as Stark County prosecuting attorney a year earlier. In 1867, when the attorney first got to Canton, he lost no time discovering its leaders and then convinced an associate of Mr. Saxton to recommend him as legal counsel to the bank president. McKinley's ingratiation failed. Saxton knew this type and, perhaps in reference to John Wright, snapped, "No, I have had enough of these young lawyers. I give them an excuse to come here on business, and then they get to running with the girls, and that is the end of it." Now, as McKinley handed Saxton his check, the banker praised him. Perhaps a bit unctuously the Major claimed that this was his "proudest moment" since coming to Canton.

A tale that McKinley made deposits at Saxton's bank to swoon over the "coquettish" teller belied the facts that he banked at First National, which was a floor below his office, and that by 1870, Ida was manager, not a teller. It was while attending a lecture by Horace Greeley, sponsored by the YMCA, that she first focused on McKinley, the organization's new president, while he eloquently introduced her grandfather's friend.[7]

Few imagined them together. Ida was worldly and educated. The Major's limited schooling kept him provincial and reliant on a remarkable intuition. She smiled and laughed easily. His politeness was excessive, seeming rehearsed. Ida was impulsively expressive, with an earthy wit. The formal Major was restrained by prudish rectitude. She was sunny both at heart and on the surface. Behind the Major's intense stare was a grave solemnity that challenged an essential optimism, the result of familial security repeatedly upset by deprivation.

The seventh of eight children, William McKinley was born in rural Niles, Ohio, on January 29, 1843, but was abruptly uprooted to Poland when that village offered the only work his father could find. Illness interrupted his time at Alleghany College, and family debt prevented his return. He had worked as a schoolteacher and a postal clerk. Along with his brothers James and David, who worked in California, and unmarried schoolteacher sisters Anna and Helen, McKinley helped support their parents and young brother Abner. (Sarah, their married sister in Cleveland, had her own family to provide for.) Their father was largely absent, toiling amid the grime of iron-production furnaces as a manager of manual laborers, barely keeping up financially. A dutiful son, the Major always used "junior" on legal documents, careful to avoid being mistaken for his father.

Unlike Ida, he needed to prove himself to advance in the world. While she was practicing math in quiet Delphi, he was a volunteer in the Ohio 23rd Infantry, demonstrating battlefield valor and rising through the ranks. As Miss Saxton strode the streets of Philadelphia shopping, he was so reduced in financial means that he had to quit Albany Law School and prepare on his own to pass the Ohio bar. While she posed on the Brooke Hall lawn with other daughters of privilege, the Major was pounding the Canton pavement, soliciting legal work. He talked himself into a prestigious law practice by promising to carry all of the workload but share all of the profits. To those with wealth and power, it looked like groveling, but it linked him to the respected Judge George Belden. As his biographer Margaret Leech put it, "There was no sham in his virtue and only one touch of subtlety—he precisely understood its usefulness to the advancement on which he was determined."

By the time he was pursing Ida Saxton, McKinley had committed himself to Canton and its population of nearly nine thousand. He bought a home with his unmarried sisters, but as he was earning just $1,000 as a prosecuting attorney and drew no salary as the local Republican Committee chairman, he had to borrow from a cousin for his share of the house purchase. William McKinley knew he could go only so far in politics without a larger income of his own or wealthy patrons.

For his own business purposes, James Saxton pragmatically saw McKinley as an asset worthy of investment. While this likely encouraged Ida to pursue a mutual romance with McKinley, it was not the incentive. She hadn't had her father's blessing when she dated John Wright, and she didn't need it to believe William McKinley possessed personal qualities she valued. His thoughtfulness was obvious to those who saw the gentle manner in which he helped the elderly "Mother McKinley" in and out of their buggy every Sunday at church and the sweetness of his voice in speaking to her. His loyalty to fellow Union veterans and to his mentor and wartime commander Rutherford Hayes, now Ohio's governor, was poignant and unshakeable. He made a strong defense for women's suffrage during a YMCA debate and for African American former slaves' right to vote during Hayes's 1867 campaign. He was so "devoid of bigotry," his most assiduous Canton biographer noted, that he had "as a grace of his nature the tolerance that is unconscious of its own virtue."[8]

Whether invited by father or daughter, McKinley soon frequented Dewalt House parties. In 1865, the house had been enlarged to three floors, with a wide porch wrapping around it and an Empire-style mansard roof. The top floor had a spacious ballroom. Even though Ida's grandmother Christiana Dewalt still owned it and lived there, its new appearance and the prominence of her son-in-law soon had Canton calling it the "Saxton House." One guest, Charles Klein, vividly recalled his impressions of McKinley there:

A favorite place for holding dance parties was the commodious top floor of the old James Saxton residence . . . scene of many brilliant social gatherings. . . . [McKinley's] affable manner soon gained him admission to the upper crust of Canton society. I well remember how the splendid personality and carriage of Major McKinley on the dance floor of the old Saxton residence impressed my youthful imagination. I thought he was the most handsome, dignified and graceful human being I had ever seen as he led the grand march around the ball room, curtsied to the ladies, or acknowledged a salute with his most fascinating smile. His appearance at that time, neatly dressed, full chested with the customary standing collar and black tie. . . .[9]

What "Mother McKinley," the pious Nancy Allison McKinley, thought about her son's dancing she left unsaid. The Major, more attached to her than anyone, emulated her sanctity. At ten years old he "witnessed" her

Methodist faith in a tent revival meeting. He was notably deferential to her on Sunday, always driving her to church and sitting beside her in the pew. He passively ignored the religious restrictions she wanted him to follow. She was displeased when he enlisted in the killing business of war. While living with him, Anna, Helen, and Abner in Canton, Mrs. McKinley was wise to the pleasure her son found in the cigars he picked up at political meetings. She was proud when he prosecuted local saloon owners who violated Stark County's alcohol sale regulations but frowned when he sipped wine. Despite these lapses, he embodied her enduring lessons of humility, living by Christ's principles rather than espousing biblical literalism.

Although John Saxton never dictated doctrine to his granddaughter Ida, his devotion to his church continued to be impressed upon her each Sunday during and after services, when he hosted an open house for his extended family. Since her return to Canton after graduating in 1868, Ida taught Sunday school, and one of her pupils recalled the "healthy bloom" of her face as she focused attention on each student, which forecasted a lifelong empathy for children. While in Europe, she bought gifts for each child and worried about who was substituting for her. She asked her mother to "find out how many scholars come regularly. I would like to know who all are in my class now." Ida instructed the children on the Westminster Confession of Faith and made them memorize the Shorter Catechism. Though Ida never relied on Scripture, she had been fully inculcated in Presbyterianism's primary tenet that God predestined the fate of every individual.

She liked teaching Sunday school for another reason. As she walked to her class, she often crossed paths with Major McKinley, who was on his way to the Methodist church. "I do not like this separation every Sunday, you going one way, and I another. Suppose after this we always go the same way," he quipped one week. She beamed and replied, "I think so too." She confessed to delaying her arrival at Sunday school to wait for and walk with McKinley.[10]

He soon tried impressing Ida with chivalry as she worked as a waitress at a church lunch. With her own quick rhythm, she scooped pink ice cream into bowls, loaded them on trays, and dashed out from the kitchen to serve them. The Major gallantly slipped in, declaring she worked too hard. Ida kept at it, just fine. While trying to pull the tray from her hands, he overturned the ice cream on her white dress. He was mortified, but she laughed.

Soon enough, townspeople noticed the orange tip of a lit cigar floating down Market Avenue at night toward Saxton House, a sure sign that

McKinley was calling. Sometimes he came by a second time, to wish her good night, while nosey neighbors watched through the vine-covered porch trellis. When the Saxton coachman George Fagan took Ida out for errands, she frequently asked him to stop at First National Bank, which provoked gossip since it was a rival of her father's bank. Ida, however, walked through the lobby to ascend the stairs and visit the Major in the law office he shared there with his brother Abner. Herman Kuhns didn't keep the secret for long that Ida and the Major paid him to deliver their love notes.

Having endured the loss of John Wright, Ida Saxton resisted romanticizing the Major. When others later assumed that she and the Major had been young sweethearts, Ida cut them off with "Not at all." There's also a suggestion that not until she felt his partnership with Belden was secure did she fully commit herself to him. "After he began his law practice at Canton, why, my other wooers dropped off one by one," she later pointed out subtly. Once committed, however, a fear of losing him to some threat overwhelmed her, perhaps a residual reaction of the trauma of losing John Wright. When the Major was late for a party at her Uncle Joe's, Ida was beset with panic, asking other guests, "Have you see the Major? Do you imagine the Major is sick? Has the Major been called to the city?"

One day that fall, as they drove over a hill from Massillon, the Major overcame his fear of talking about the future, asked Ida to marry him, and, as he recalled, "my fate was settled."

She accepted. When he asked Ida's father for permission to marry her, the banker's eyes welled as he told him, "You are the only man I have ever known to whom I would entrust my daughter." Although she liked recalling her father's words, Ida also made clear that *she* made her own decision, and that McKinley was the suitor about whom she and her father "*both* agreed."[11]

Knowing her love for unique jewelry, McKinley asked his brother David in San Francisco to order a wedding ring made of California gold, with diamonds around a ruby. "It is now settled that Miss Saxton and I will unite our fortunes," he informed Governor Hayes and his wife, "I think I am doing a good thing. Miss S. is everything I could hope for."[12]

Although the Presbyterian church was not entirely finished, the ceremony took place there on January 25, 1871, but with seating for only seven hundred, its lobby and steps were packed with some three hundred other guests. Ida, in an ivory satin gown, was escorted down the aisle by her father; they were attended by Pina in pink, Ida's friend Amelia Bockius, the Major's brother Abner and cousin William Osborne. The ceremony was conducted by both a Presbyterian and a Methodist minister. *Repository* reporter Josiah Hartzell covered it all in detail.

A wedding reception was held in the Saxton House ballroom after the ceremony, but mixed with happy chatter about the couple's future was Ida's grief for her grandmother. In November, Christiana Dewalt had died suddenly in the house that she had willed to her daughter Kate.

To guests who didn't know about the financial strain on the groom's family, it was more difficult to explain why William McKinley senior wasn't at the wedding. It would be another five years before the Major's father would be able to cease the toil of managing his Michigan pig-iron furnaces, when he was financially supported by his children's pooled resources. Ida wisely intuited that he was less influential over the Major than his mentor Governor Hayes whose praise of "unsurpassed capacity" and "executive ability" raised the younger man's confidence. "That was the bond between them," Ida pointed out. Still, she agreed with her father-in-law's view that the Major was wrong in considering a return to the army as a career officer. "The army is no place for a young man in time of peace," was the unwelcome advice from senior to junior. Ida "sided with the father." As a Washington reporter later put it, "Mrs. McKinley was ever proud of the influence she had in turning her husband's mind toward the paths of peace. . . ."

After the reception, the newlyweds caught a night train to begin a three-week honeymoon. In New York, they posed for separate pictures, their oval images framed together. In Washington, D.C., McKinley apparently revealed to her his plan to follow Governor Hayes into politics, ignoring his mentor's warning that "a man sacrifices independence to ambition. . . ." While marriage meant that Ida would sacrifice her independence for a life calculated by her judicious new husband, he often acquiesced to her wishes. On their return to Canton on Valentine's Day, the new Ida McKinley was "so pleased with the trip that she then declared her husband would some day be president of the United States." Friends found the bride's outlandish insistence endearing. Ida, however, was serious. As time went on, "she always clung to this belief and repeatedly declared it. . . ."[13]

⋅≼ 3 ≽⋅

Birth and Death

JUST AS IDA'S JANUARY WEDDING had been overshadowed by her grand-mother's death, the joyful news in March that she was pregnant with her first child was darkened by the death of her grandfather on April 16. Ida's wedding was the last time most people had seen John Saxton. He died just seven days before his new church was dedicated, an event he had been determined to see. Having been so "closely associated with these old people," according to an account based on her sister's recollections, Ida McKinley "felt their loss keenly."[1]

The newlyweds lived in the residential St. Cloud Hotel until they leased a home owned by James Saxton. On April 24, James bought a five-year-old wood house on the corner of Market and Elizabeth Street from George Harter for $7,800, twelve blocks north of Saxton House. James had initially wanted Ida and her husband to live in Saxton House, but Ida's mother had declared, "No young woman does as well as under her own roof." Despite Ida's proximity to her friends Amelia Bockius and Kitty Endsley (whose sister Annie would marry the Major's brother Abner), Ida spent most of the summer and fall of 1871 in Saxton House with her mother while awaiting the birth of her first child.[2]

Ida named her baby daughter, born on Christmas Day, after her mother. Some weeks later, the Major reported to Kate's brother, John Dewalt in Il-linois, that "Ida and the baby are well." Healthy and, by all accounts, happy and curious, the child was always called Katie. She became the center of Ida's world and so occupied the Major that he seemed untroubled by his failed re-election bid as county prosecuting attorney to his friend William A. Lynch.[3]

By the following summer, Ida began circulating again in Canton. Although maintaining membership in the Presbyterian Church's Ladies Aid Society, she joined the Major's Methodist church, where Katie was baptized. The couple's closeness was uninterrupted by parental responsibilities; they took a daily drive together, and Ida often joined the Major at his numerous civic appearances, such as placing flowers on the graves of Union soldiers on Decoration Day and attending a YMCA fund-raiser to sample the food made by various church women. It was a busy and happy time that proved brief; in retrospect, it was the last period of her life when she felt truly hopeful about the future. Just after Labor Day, she simultaneously learned that she was pregnant again and that her mother was terminally ill and unlikely to live long enough to see her second grandchild.[4]

Judging from the rapid progression and "protracted and intense sufferings" that Kate endured from her unspecified illness, it was likely cancer. Raised as a German Lutheran, Kate felt compelled to be baptized in her husband's faith, having attended his family's Presbyterian church for years. In early autumn, she was "scarcely able to be taken to the Sanctuary" for the religious ceremony, and only "strong purpose nerved her." Her pain was so intense that, despite Ida's powerful emotional support during this period, Kate "often expressed the desire, if it were the will of God, to be released from her earthly sufferings."

That year, Christmas was bittersweet for the pregnant Ida as it would be the last with her mother, the first with her daughter, and the only one all three would spend together. On this day, which was both Katie's first birthday and first Christmas, her parents gave her a small rocking chair. Placed beside the one that Ida had been given as a child, Katie's rocking chair would always remain significant.

Ida was riddled with anxiety for nearly the entire term of her pregnancy as she watched her mother descend into pain and a "weakened condition" by the time she died on March 14, 1873, in Saxton House. Kate was buried at Westlake Cemetery.[5]

McKinley's first biographer, Charles Olcott, aided by the family reminiscences of Pina Saxton, recalled that Ida had "lived in such intimate companionship" with their mother that the realization she would never see her again was traumatic, and "the shock was too great for her to bear. Her nervous system was nearly wrecked." This trauma, which surely affected the unborn child's well-being, was in addition to the nervousness Ida felt about her second childbirth.

Two weeks and four days after Kate's death, the birth of the McKinleys' second child on April 1, 1873, was described as "difficult." The infant girl, named for her mother, joined a family unable to joyously welcome her. Intense grief over a lost loved one, even in combination with postpartum depression, is typically temporary. From all accounts, there was no birth defect affecting Little Ida other than being what was termed "sickly." While this left her vulnerable, there was also a chance for the child's survival and, along with sixteen-month-old Katie, the prospect that the McKinleys would be a thriving family of four. Such hope faded when Little Ida died of cholera after living four months and two weeks.

For the couple, the period between Ida's mother's death on March 14 and their infant's death on August 20 marked what Olcott called "the beginning of the great sorrow that was to hover like a cloud over the remainder of their lives." While Ida McKinley was affected by physical problems that would, over time, also lead to psychological ones, it was the Major who, in reaction to his wife's deteriorating health, was initially affected emotionally and eventually physically as well.[6]

Ida McKinley's invalidism was not hypochondria but a complex series of related and unrelated medical crises. In a brief six months, she was beset by chronic disabilities, from reports of spinal injury and immobility of one leg to sudden convulsions and blinding headaches to vulnerability to infections that proved nearly fatal. With often little more than vague anecdotal reports, attempts to delineate her symptoms and precisely discern the onset of illnesses and disabilities along a documented timeline proved impossible. Similarities in contemporary accounts and some records of medical treatment provide informed impressions, but the true nature of Ida's health problems can rest only on supposition and ultimately remain speculative.

Her immune system was compromised while carrying a baby who was dependent on Ida's own health during the seven months preceding Kate's death. It left both Ida and the child she was carrying vulnerable to infection from routine viruses and bacteria that, had she been healthy, she would have withstood with perhaps nothing more than a cold. With what would become a lifetime of rapidly contracting fevers and infections in her sinuses, lungs, stomach, and extremities, Ida was likely exposed during this period to some outside agent that permanently compromised her immune system. It was likely why Little Ida was weak upon birth.

Whether it was due to general weakness or a limb swollen by infection, Ida also suffered some type of traumatic fall, just before or after Little Ida's birth, perhaps while climbing the high steps of a carriage. As Edward T. Heald learned in the 1940s from those who, as children, or whose parents had known Ida McKinley in the 1870s, "Something had happened to her spine that made her bedridden much of the time in the first years. Neighbors noticed that McKinley almost had to carry her to the carriage and lift her into it." Beatrice Blake recalled how "She slumped when he was not holding her; he had to hold her to keep her from falling. There must have been a weakness in her spine." Another local said, "After the birth of the last child Mrs. McKinley was told that she might never be able to walk again. She was very young, and hope is buoyant then and sees beyond any tragedy, but the doctor's prophecies were true. . . ."

Lower spinal injury in the lumbar section can result in nerve damage to the legs; depending on the severity, such nerve damage can cause permanent loss of mobility or inflamed muscle and scar tissue that chronically pinches a nerve, leaving the leg numb or painful. The latter scenario seems more likely in Ida McKinley's case since years later she was able to walk alone, if only for a short distance. Once when she rose to greet a reporter, she took several steps using both legs, then suddenly needed her cane. "My husband's right arm has so taken the place of my foot," she pointed out, "that I have never been deprived of any enjoyment in life because of my lameness." This is supported by a contemporary account that "partial paralysis of one leg made it difficult, although not painful, for her to be upon her feet, and this inability for exercise in turn had a serious effect upon her health."

Other observers deduced that her loss of mobility was due to phlebitis, a deep vein clot that slows or blocks blood flow to the leg. Pregnancy predisposes some women to thrombophlebitis; those recovering from childbirth with prolonged bed rest are frequently affected, and assuming a sedentary life can chronically perpetuate it. Ida's immobility, whether it was largely neurological or vascular in nature, is what led to the public's perception of her as an invalid. As her close friend Mary Logan affirmed of the spring and summer of 1873, Ida McKinley's "actual invalidism dates from this period."[7]

As the circle of those familiar with McKinley widened, references to his wife's fevers and colds or reliance on a cane readily explained her "invalidism" and helped avoid disclosure of the more baffling disability she manifested in 1873. Firsthand accounts of Mrs. McKinley's symptoms referred to her having a "fit," "paroxysm," or "convulsion." Her condition, which was shrouded in mystery and ignorantly stigmatized as a form of insanity, was not accurately stated for the public record until after her death, when her last physician finally described it in unequivocal professional terminology as "epilepsy" (in the twenty-first century, the condition is termed "seizure disorder"). In two surviving letters McKinley wrote, one to his father-in-law and another to his brother, and numerous checks he made out to her doctors, the Major confirmed this. It was for good reason that he disclosed the facts only to those two men and Ida's sister and kept his contact with medical consultants about the matter private.

By 1873, the biblical claim that epilepsy was a supernatural hold on a person's faculties still persisted. By the time Ida Saxton was born, the medical profession had classified epilepsy as a psychiatric disorder, which led to the misperception of it as a type of insanity. State laws forbade "epileptics" from marrying since experts claimed that children could inherit the disorder, and those whose symptoms were manifested in brief, aberrant behavior were socially shunned. Patients without caretakers ended up living in isolated colonies or in prisons for the criminally insane, where their throats were choked by chains to flush blood into the brain. Shortly after Ida McKinley's first seizure, hundreds of poor or working-class Ohio women with "fits," unable to find steady work, were abandoned at the new Athens Lunatics Asylum, located 150 miles from Canton.

That same year, London neurologist John Hughlings Jackson discovered that the disorder was provoked by electrical and chemical mischarges in the brain, its symptoms related to the affected parts, which dictated different functions. Among potential causes of new-onset epilepsy are head trauma and postnatal complications. Other than her difficult childbirth, various accounts consistently suggest that Ida's seizures began as a result of her injurious fall, which led to a permanent condition beyond head and back trauma: " . . . her nervous system shocked to a point of despair . . . ," "Her nervous system was nearly wrecked. . . ," and "Nerve specialists were called but could do nothing."

Ida, enduring what was described as the "long and severe illness, and a resultant prostration of health and strength," was cared for by her father's physician, Dr. Whitney, a general practitioner. He apparently first suggested that Ida may have begun suffering from epilepsy, but could not make a clinical diagnosis without consulting a neurologist. From what can be extrapolated from her treatment history, Whitney ordered complete rest since the length and severity of seizures could be affected by physical agitation, emotional stress, hunger, and fatigue. He may have initially given her arsenic, which was believed to reduce convulsions. By the time her younger daughter died in August, Ida remained too debilitated to care for her older one.[8]

As if fate yet again insisted on linking momentous, happy occasions with a mournful ending, her sister's long-planned wedding took place two days after Little Ida unexpectedly died. Even if she had the stamina to attend Pina's wedding to Marshall C. Barber, Ida's spirit was too broken for her to appear at the event. Pina's immediate move to her own home also left James Saxton in anguish. Not yet six months since his wife's death, he was now living only with twenty-three-year-old George. Having his family who, until recently, had been so close but were now apart was intolerable for Saxton; within days of Pina's wedding, he suggested that the three McKinleys come to live at Saxton House.

Ida and the Major accepted with alacrity, fleeing the leased North Market Avenue house. Saxton sold that house back to Harter just ten days after Little Ida's death there. Although Pina and Marsh moved into their own home, she was at Saxton House caring for Katie until Ida recovered somewhat. Two years later, the couple moved permanently to Saxton House, initially living on a $9,000 gift from her father before Marsh began to work managing Saxton properties. McKinley also soon benefited from Saxton's prosperity.[9]

That fall, Saxton, who served as executor of an estate that owned the large multi-lot commercial building across from his home, recognized its potential and coaxed Ida and the Major to purchase it by lending them the down payment. The long three-story structure became known as the "McKinley block." Saxton soon convinced the Major and his brother Abner to move their joint law office there, giving McKinley convenient proximity to Ida at home across the street. Much of McKinley's legal business came either directly or through reference from his father-in-law. In 1874, he represented Ida's father as plaintiff in two cases of unpaid claims and her uncle in a similar case. He won all three. Finally, Saxton moved his bank into the building; while in New York restructuring a friend's business, he asked the Major, instead of his son, to become bank manager. Saxton said that his son "wouldn't do." The Major gratefully agreed, though he hardly had a choice, so deeply indebted was he to Saxton.

While Ida "never entirely recovered," as her sister pointed out, her six months of complete rest at Saxton House enabled her to recuperate until she was able to make her first public outing at a private party hosted by Judge Frease on March 13, 1874. Ida's appearance without the Major at a party where liquor flowed freely put her at odds with her husband's defense of prohibition advocates in a case against saloons that violated local liquor sale and consumption laws. Publicity about the case turned McKinley into a reluctant temperance leader. Having enjoyed wine with dinner since her trip to Europe, Ida was not among the many women who supported McKinley at temperance rallies. Some later claimed McKinley's ill-considered foray into the prohibition issue was due to Ida's "prodding"; in fact, as one chronicler correctly wrote, "it was Ida who toned down his hard-line approach."

Despite his considerable responsibilities, McKinley was increasing his political activities. Having campaigned for local Republicans as well as Ulysses S. Grant's presidential campaigns since 1868, McKinley was elected in May 1875 as Stark County's delegate to the State Convention, to be held in Columbus on June 2. While his occasional overnight trips away from Canton suggest that Ida's condition had stabilized, he was riddled with anxiety when a legal case delayed his expected return by several days, as evidenced in his earliest surviving letter to her, on May 12:

> I received your precious letter a moment or two ago and it fell on me like sunlight in a dark day. It is a beautiful rainbow in my sky, giving me courage, hope, love and promise. I am sorry you are staying up so late and I don't want you to do so for the purpose of writing me. Your health is dearer to me than your letter written at the hazard of the former. I found upon looking for paper to write you—that I had left it at home, but I managed to hunt some up. I just telegraphed your father that if he would come tomorrow night [to Canton] he could be in time [to care for you] as it is about absolutely certain that the case will not be reached before Friday morning which will take us the balance of the week, possibly Monday of the [next] week. The contemplation is awful. I can hardly control myself to remain so long, indeed. I feel like flying for home in the morning but then I could only get there before I must return. Accept much love for yourself & Katie.[10]

McKinley adored his daughter, whose golden locks were styled in curls for her first photograph in a Canton studio, her blue eyes focused directly into the camera, her face as cherubic as those on a Victorian Valentine's Day card. Having lost Little Ida less than two years earlier, Ida McKinley was obsessively protective of her remaining child. Of his sister-in-law, Abner McKinley recalled to his friend Bill Beer, "She would sit for hours in a darkened room, holding Katie on her lap, weeping in silence. Katie was not allowed out of her sight, unless the Major took the child for a drive. . . ." Once, spying his niece in front of Saxton House, Abner dashed across the street from his law office to invite her for a walk. "No, I mustn't go out of the yard," three-and-a-half-year-old Katie replied in obedience to Ida's rule, "or God will punish mamma some more."

There was also a happier memory of the child, recalled by the Major's eldest niece in San Francisco. To her friend, *San Francisco Call* reporter Sarah Comstock, she later provided the only known details about the maturing personality of Katie McKinley and even some impressions of Little Ida McKinley:

> . . . it is said by those who saw her that [Little Ida] seemed more like a Christmas angel, come to earth for only a little while, than a real child of this earth. . . . Somehow, those who saw her could never quite believe that she was meant to be kept here, frail thing that she was. . . . Katie, a more vigorous child, and one in whom the hopes of all who loved her centered . . . had almost reached the age of four proud years. She was growing stronger and merrier every day. She was already making her own small place in society. Having her little friends who came to see her and whose calls she returned, with the delight in sociability . . . [s]he was full of lively childish interests—in her dolls, in her games, in her pets.

In mid-May, the Major returned home, relieved to find Ida and Katie well and, assured in that knowledge, left two weeks later for the Columbus state convention. Named chairman of resolutions, he had cachet through his close association with Hayes, who was unanimously renominated as governor. The Major had a lighthearted confidence in his future when he came home, only to find that Ida's greatest nightmare had come true. Katie lay in bed, delirious with scarlet fever. On June 25, 1875, with "heart disease" listed as the cause, Katie McKinley succumbed to death.[11]

If Little Ida's death broke her mother's health, Katie's death crushed her soul. Ida prayed fervently for her own death. While accounts from those close to her are purposefully vague, Olcott later learned from Pina that the "black pall of grief which enveloped her," a nervous breakdown, "came near ending the mother's life." While there was no suicide attempt, she almost died by the more passive method of starvation, although it is unclear if this was due to a refusal to eat or a complete lack of appetite, which is symptomatic of severe depression. "Ida would have died years ago," a Canton friend later stated, "but William would just not let her go."

In less than three years, Ida McKinley had not only lost her grand-mother, mother, and two daughters but control of how her body now re-acted to her mind. Depending on what part of her brain had been initially affected, the severity and frequency of unpredictable seizures, preceded or followed by depression, may have only been further induced by the degree of emotional stress she experienced. If a seizure emanated from the brain's emotional center, mood disorder could also have been triggered. Thus, the more fearful Ida McKinley might have been about these new, unsettling sensations in her body, the deeper and longer the seizures would become. For Ida, the vicious circle of this new reality was confusing, depressing, and overwhelming.

Unlike women typical of her background and faith, Ida McKinley found no solace in God. Beyond the guilt typically felt by parents who survived the loss of young children, Ida's grief was worsened by an odd incident a year later during McKinley's legal defense of striking miners. A deranged woman, believing that God had foreseen McKinley's abetting what she perceived as the immorality of the strikers, spluttered at Ida that, in "anger with the Major," the Creator "had punished her some more" by taking Ka-tie, the fifth family member in as many years. To Ida, with her Presbyterian belief that God had taken them from her for some predestined reason while refusing her plea to join them, the idea that God had abandoned her made sense. On only several occasions did she ever go to church again.

With the passage of time, Ida McKinley restored her sense of personal pride, realizing that confining herself to Saxton House only confirmed town gossip that she had "a deeper mental illness," as a McKinley biog-rapher later put it. Although Ida was socialized to believe that a woman's primary sense of purpose was motherhood, she still lacked a child on whom to focus her attention, which would have aided her long-term recovery. Though still able to conceive, the unfounded fear of "passing" epilepsy to a child was the likely reason the couple "knew that with their lost ones was buried all hope of again hearing the voice of a child of their own in their home."[12]

Knowing that a continued state of depression would eventually dete-riorate the Major's optimism and their marriage is what most motivated Ida's recovery. At a time when she saw no value in her life, he had. He never expressed disappointment that her disabilities would prevent them from having a traditional household. Desperate to halt her morbid spiral, he sought any means to motivate her "interest in existence" and was even willing to sacrifice his plan for a political career. In perhaps their most serious marital discussion, he asserted to Ida that "If you would suffer by the circumstances surrounding me in a competition for public station, I will devote my ambition to success in private life."

Throughout all the frightening instability Ida endured in just over two years, the only constant had been her husband's devotion. The McKinleys' family of four proved sadly brief. It was no less a family, however, with just the two of them. If fate denied her a chance to nurture growing children, Ida McKinley would nurture the maturing career of her husband. "Your ambitions are mine," she responded to his offer. "I have no fear that your choice in life will leave you as you are in the things that make you dear to me."

The marriage thrived by daily acts of love. Ida was deeply empathic when public events left the Major worried and doubtful about his political future, even during those times when she was unable or unwilling to help herself. She sustained him with approval and adoration that was, at times, so intense that it appeared cloying to observers. When they argued, they kept the details to themselves. Any discord was implied only when they praised each other, like the time Ida confessed to a reporter that although she could be excessively needy, her husband remained "so patient."

Neither denied that she or he had been forever changed. While her "mind remained strong," as one source put it, after 1875, Ida's sensitivity to motion, light, and sound could easily rattle her into a fragile state. As for the Major, his assiduous Canton chronicler Timothy Heald observed: "There was never a working moment from this time [1875] on that McKinley was free from anxiety regarding his wife's condition. His patience and care for her became a household legend. This zero hour was the turning point of McKinley's life. . . . He accepted, without bitterness, this distress as part of God's plan. His first consideration was to soften the blow for Ida as far as he could. His devotion to her grew with her dependence on him."

Ida was so sure of his intentions that she entrusted her entire medical care to the Major, knowing less about it than he did. Such dependency, McKinley's scholarly biographer Wayne Morgan believed, "fulfilled his basic need to be loved, and that mattered most." Once this "martyr" role rooted into his identity and served a political purpose, however, McKinley so stringently refused to relinquish the perception of his own indispensability that he failed to see how it began, ironically, to endanger Ida. In time, no matter how lovingly he sought assurances that she was doing well in letters and telegrams he penned to her during his absences, she grew hostile to his devotion to politics. At the start of this dynamic, however, when the opportunity to gain wider recognition by joining Governor

Hayes on his re-election tour arose just eight weeks after Katie's death, the Major first gained Ida's approval before setting out for an August 18 event in Massillon and overnight trip to New Milan the following morning.

Whatever regrets McKinley may have felt about how he had to function now as caregiver and politician, he "concealed them from Ida and friends alike." He did suggest that he managed to fulfill both roles with a bit of acting: "You know Mrs. McKinley has been an invalid. It has always been my practice when arriving home, no matter what cares or problems I might have been facing, to greet Mrs. McKinley with the cheerful attitude that everything was right with the world, and my affairs were going just as I ordered them." Employing this benevolent image enabled McKinley to become expert at disguising the ruthlessness often required for political success. As Heald put it, "Under his pleasant and gentle manner lay this iron determination."[13]

Both McKinleys remained haunted by the loss of Katie. For Ida, no matter how affectionately she held a little girl visitor, once the room was silent, her mind went to Katie—what she might be saying or doing, how she would look, what she would be studying or wearing. In her imagination, Ida willed Katie to stay alive, maturing through the passing years. To ensure that her memory of Katie would never fade, she displayed the girl's first-birthday rocking chair next to the one from her own childhood, when she'd literally been Little Ida; it came to represent her namesake second daughter, known only abstractly to the McKinleys as an infant. On the chairs, she also sometimes displayed clothes that Katie and Little Ida had worn. Wherever she lived, these items were not only within Ida's sight but seemingly Katie's as well. The couple kept her small original studio picture framed on a bedroom table; an enlargement, painted to give her pink cheeks, red lips, blue eyes, and yellow curls, was hung high on the parlor wall, near her clothes and chair. McKinley reminisced about her as each year neared its end, calling her his "Christmas present born on that day." The closest he came to revealing the grief her death caused him was in a formal note to a friend whose adult son died from an accidental fall: "Only those who have suffered in a similar way can appreciate the keenness of such affliction."[14]

The burden thrust on Ida McKinley in just over two years wasn't resolved by processing grief for lost loved ones or using the cane she now kept within reach. However bravely she tried new treatments or accepted the fact that, five years after hiking the Alps, she was an invalid at twenty-eight, Ida could not escape the realization that, even with the Major's love, life guaranteed no stability. Learning that she must find it by how she perceived life became her daily challenge.

☙ 4 ❧

The Active Invalid

As AMERICANS BY THE THOUSANDS poured into Philadelphia for the Centennial Exposition during the summer of 1876, Ida McKinley stayed at home alone. Months after Hayes's second gubernatorial victory, he was running for president, and McKinley, hoping to ride his coattails, ran as the Republican candidate for the U.S. congressional representative of Ohio's eighteenth district. During the campaign against Democrat Leslie L. Sanborn, Ida made only one appearance, at a massive picnic in the town of Freeburg.

Following McKinley's election that fall, Ida's life assumed a familiar rhythm over the next fifteen years. The Major conducted not only his local business but also eight consecutive congressional campaigns (one of which was successfully contested by his opponent, another which he lost) from a large office he established on the top floor of Saxton House. This was a spacious area that had served as a ballroom in Ida's youth but was now where they lived. In fact, this two-room Saxton House suite was their residence of longest occupancy, the larger space serving as both bedroom and parlor. Working just on the other side of the door and knowing that Ida was within reach if she needed him allowed the Major to work for hours without worry. Ida's father, who closed his bank by 1876 to start one of Canton's first gaslight companies, also moved his office into the house, on a lower floor. Pina and Marsh Barber, with the first two of their eventual seven children, two-year-old James and nine-month-old Mary, also moved in.

In Washington and later Columbus, the McKinleys rented residential hotel suites with comparable configurations, taking meals in the hotel dining rooms and living with compact efficiency. During McKinley's congressional career, they resided at Ebbitt House. Its two-block proximity to the White House allowed Ida and the Major to socialize easily with Rutherford Hayes and his family once they assumed occupancy of it following Hayes's inauguration on March 4, 1877. Ida McKinley did not join her husband for those festivities, however. She was then in Philadelphia under the professional medical care of Silas Weir Mitchell, one of the nation's leading neurologists, at the Orthopedic Hospital and Infirmary for Nervous Diseases.[1]

Founder and first president of the American Neurological Association, the forty-nine-year-old Mitchell's groundbreaking *Injuries of Nerves and Their Consequences* had been published a year before the onset of Ida's seizures. He was among the first to integrate a regimented treatment for ailments with clinical psychology to deal with the emotional issues he believed were related to physical symptoms like seizures. By then, Mitchell had developed his famous "rest cure" to treat the era's epidemic number of "hysterical women." As the subject of his second book, *Fat and Blood*, published the year Ida came under his care, the "cure" consisted not just of special diets and body massage but lengthy bed rest and social isolation, which was intended to quiet patients' minds. Mitchell, who believed that men's brains were larger and more capable than those of women, based his "rest cure" on his theory that female nervous systems broke if they assumed complexities he claimed that only men could process. As his patient, the future author Charlotte Perkins Gilman recalled that he told women to "live as domestic a life as possible" and have "but two hours intelligent life a day."

Ida McKinley, who was a voracious reader without any typical domestic responsibilities, was the least ideal candidate to benefit from Mitchell's care. The excessive bed rest he ordered for patients would have only worsened her mobility problem. When journalist Murat Halstead later found Ida reading one of Mitchell's novels, "she mentioned that she had been for some time under the professional care of the author," but focused on her more pleasant memory that "all the time she spent as his patient in Philadelphia her husband wrote her three letters a day."[2]

How long she endured Mitchell's treatment is unclear. During the Major's public appearances in Canton that spring and summer, from a rowboat race to a wedding anniversary party, Ida appeared in the record only during an August camping trip made with family and friends. Canton native William Kuhns's childhood memory of an incident at the campsite marks the earliest firsthand account related to her seizure disorder. When several young boys began playing a serenade on makeshift musical instruments, the Major dashed out in a panic from the tent where Ida was suffering from a torturous headache, suggesting that even the slightest noise would greatly worsen her condition. Her headaches did not necessarily indicate the onset of seizures, but they made even talking painful. Even the tiny hairpins used to hold up her elaborate Victorian coiffure put pressure on her skull, so Ida consequently cropped her hair into a short style with bangs.

Just a week or so after the camping trip, another incident served as evidence that Ida McKinley's seizures were highly unpredictable. On September 7, she had no problem in hosting an open house "parlor concert" of Mendelssohn, Schumann, Chopin, and Liszt piano pieces that were far louder than the young boys' band music. Printed handbills distributed through Canton inviting citizens to "the residence of Mrs. Wm. McKinley, Jr." counteracted gossip that the new congressman's wife was unwell. While never denying that she had disabilities, Ida McKinley was determined to be an active invalid. An October 12 *Repository* squib also served notice that she, along with the Major, would "be glad to see the citizens of Ohio generally, and of his district specifically, when they have occasion to visit Washington."[3]

Washington, D.C., was no longer the pastoral backwater it had been before the Civil War. Muddy streets were now covered by wooden planks, horse-drawn streetcars provided mass transportation, and plumbing and sewage systems made the city more sanitary. There were now cement and brick sidewalks for those walking to the Corcoran Gallery, which opened that year. Ida McKinley's new life in the capital city, however, centered on the most prestigious spot there, the Executive Mansion, as the White House was officially called. The McKinleys were quickly incorporated into the First Family's circle of visiting relatives, friends, and colleagues, invited to informal weekday suppers and Sunday hymn-singing gatherings around the piano. Ida formed a permanent friendship with the president's son Webb, and ten-year-old Fanny Hayes was always "quite thrilled" to ride the Ebbitt House elevator during her frequent visits to Ida's hotel suite.

McKinley, having known the First Lady since her days as a Civil War nurse in his regiment's encampments, escorted Lucy Hayes to public events when the president was away. On at least two known occasions, Ida lunched alone with Lucy in the White House, suggesting that the First Lady had been alerted to the possibility that Mrs. McKinley might have seizures and was prepared to ensure proper care if necessary. The Hayes

Administration's detailed social records disprove Ida's later exaggeration that she was hostess in Mrs. Hayes's absence, but she did stand with the president and First Lady as their "social aide," along with other women close to the family, in the receiving line to welcome guests. After befriending Emily Platt, the president's niece and a fellow social aide, Ida frequently invited her to the McKinley suite for lunch and card games, then fostered a romance between the young woman and the Major's wartime comrade, Gen. Russell Hastings. The relationship, allowed to flourish without press notice, resulted in a White House wedding on June 19, 1878, with Ida McKinley a "conspicuous figure" among the guests.

No single honor by the First Family, however, elevated her confidence more than being invited by the president to be his escort at the February 26, 1879, diplomatic corps reception. As Hayes recorded in his diary, he "promenaded" the state rooms with Mrs. McKinley, who became the focus of attention of hundreds of executive department, legislative, judiciary, and military leaders at the event. That spring, the McKinleys shared three private dinners with the president and were guests at two state dinners, but the social pinnacle came when Hayes hosted a dinner party to mark Ida's thirty-second birthday, knowing how much the annual occasion meant to her.[4]

Engaging with some of the nation's most powerful and interesting people seemed to enable Ida to recover some of her natural sociability. There was a dash up to New York during its busy opera and concert season. She joined the Ladies Aid Society, affiliated with the Major's Methodist church in Washington, and worked to have nourishing foods, fresh flowers, and reading material contributed and dispersed among the city's impoverished residents or those isolated in hospitals. Reporters soon recognized her. On April 19, the *Washington Post* listed "Mrs. McKinley of Ohio" among the "politically eminent" engrossed by House debates. When she left an entourage of train guests travelling with Hayes before it continued on to tour the upper Midwest, the September 19, 1879, *Cleveland Herald* declared that "The presidential party lost one of its brightest attractions in Mrs. McKinley's absence. Her pleasant conversational powers and winning manners had been an excellent feature of the Presidential festivities." That autumn, she renewed a friendship with Brooke Hall classmate Rosalie Bates, who also lived at Ebbitt House, and formed a new one with Sue Rand, both of whom were married to naval officers. One December day she both lunched and dined at the White House.

The next month, the first of the new decade, she was back there for dinner three weeks in a row. After such an astonishing period of activity, her visiting brother-in-law David McKinley was able to report in February that "but for a very bad cold, she would be very well."[5]

Unfortunately, given the complexity of her multiple conditions, if Ida McKinley experienced a rise in body temperature along with a "very bad cold," it may well have been what triggered an onset of her dreaded seizures. About two weeks after David McKinley's observation about her health, the congressman's wife was brought to New York and placed under the care of Meredith Clymer. The sixty-three-year-old pioneer neurologist was not only president of the New York Society of Neurology but also an Albany Medical College professor on mental and nervous diseases. As a specialist in spinal injury cases, he was also then treating Abner McKinley's daughter Mabel, who had advanced scoliosis. Clymer's book, *The Mental State of Epileptics and Its Medico-Legal Relations,* was published in 1870, and was followed four years later by *The Legitimate Influence of Epilepsy on Criminal Responsibility.* While his conclusion that many "epileptics" met a "sad fate" by being institutionalized, Clymer adamantly defended his correct belief that seizures were a brain dysfunction, not a type of mental illness.

The first documentation in William McKinley's hand related to Ida's health was the check he wrote to Clymer for his treatment of her, along with a March 12, 1880, message informing the neurologist that Ida was "much better." He also noted that a "plaster came this morning," a reference to the thick adhesive bandage with a mustard seed paste, which was applied to injured or nerve-damaged bodily areas, its natural heat intended to help relax affected muscle and tissue by increasing blood flow to them. His check of $693.67, roughly equivalent to $19,000 in the early twenty-first century, must have covered more than mustard plasters. It is difficult to ascertain whether he treated Ida for just leg immobility or for seizures as well. Unfortunately, it is the most obscure episode of her medical treatment.

The initial suggestion by Canton's Dr. Whitney, the Saxton family physician, that Ida had epilepsy was never confirmed by a specialist, and the family remained unsure of the accuracy of Whitney's diagnosis. Her father discussed the theory with a Dr. Wellington with whom he was acquainted. As Saxton reported to the Major, Wellington was "not so sure that Dr. W[hitney] is correct in his theory of Ida's case." Since he was now working with Clymer, McKinley prodded the expert neurologist to consult in writing with the Saxton family doctor: "Have you written to Doctor Whitney?"[6]

Clymer's final report on Ida McKinley's case is missing. Shortly after asking Clymer to consult with Whitney and to deliver his expert analysis, the Major wrote a March 17 letter that uses medical terminology related to epileptic symptoms, making clear that Clymer confirmed Ida McKinley's seizure disorder. The letter contains two specific references: "I suppose from the tone of your letter you are either unwell or *expecting to be.*" This describes Ida experiencing what is called an "aura," a foreboding sensation of imminent seizures, which itself is a simple partial seizure that may spread to involve more of the brain. His second reference was in writing to her, "I hope you are safe though, if not take three doses of Bromide, during that period." In this sentence, McKinley is referring to her prescription for bromide salts, in use since 1857 as the only medicine to prevent or reduce detectable seizures.

Before leaving Canton, the Major put Ida in her father's care. Ida did not feel that her aura warranted concern, so she initially ignored her bromide regimen. When she had a sudden onset of seizures, she wired the Major in alarm, unsure of the proper dosage. "Have your Father telegraph for the Bromide prescription, taking no [directions?] from the bottle." James Saxton was persistent in seeking answers about his daughter's condition. Several years later, for example, he reported a friend's "temporary trouble" with severe memory lapses, which one doctor termed "nervous prostration," suggesting to the Major that perhaps Ida endured similar symptoms.

Auras and memory lapses were but two symptoms attributed to Ida McKinley's epilepsy by many different individuals during her life. There were also eyewitness recollections of her loss of motor skills, falling off chairs, the need to be "bandaged" due to bruising, the twitching and convulsing of facial muscles, bodily stiffening, and hissing. It is often difficult to determine the true nature of these symptoms. She often resumed her conversations right after a seizure, so it was never certain whether she was aware or not that she had just experienced one, or was consciously ignoring it, a differentiation helpful in determining the seizure type. So-called "partial seizures" can often manifest in purposeful, repetitive behavior, like buttoning or unbuttoning a shirt or the rapid, constant knitting for which she became famous. Without a clinical record, no definitive seizure classification can accurately be made. Uninterested in details about her disabilities but confident in the Major's management of her care, Ida steadied herself by focusing on his career.

When Ida feared that a contentious issue or political rival threatened her husband's career, he sought to reassure her. During the race for the

Republican nomination race for what he hoped would be his third congressional term, for example, he reported reactions to his appearances throughout the district to her.[7]

On March 8, he wrote that the largely Democratic Salinesville was "ours" after his speech there, claimed there was "nobody but McKinley men" in Hanover after hours of meetings, and thought that rival Laurin D. Woodworth "didn't look entirely confident" when they met in Wellsville. A month later, writing Ida from Youngstown, he declared, "The fight was a fierce one, but my friends were victorious and they are happy." He scratched out a tally of each township's delegate vote for her, showing his thirty-five trumping Woodworth's fourteen. While never known to offer tactical campaign advice, Ida McKinley did play a role in his 1880 election. While keeping her activities within the traditional realm of women, she helped increase his political prestige and value to his constituency, positioning him as an influential insider with access to Washington's most powerful leaders.[8]

In preparation for what would be the largest public gathering ever held in Canton, a September 1 reunion of Ohio's Civil War veterans expected to bring in some 60,000 visitors, Ida coordinated the effort to make Saxton House the event's central focus point. While others fund-raised for the parade, fairgrounds luncheon, and rest stations, Ida reconfigured Saxton House rooms into guest suites and entertaining spaces, supervised landscaping so the grounds could accommodate crowds, and planned an evening reception for several hundred. She gave the building the bunting and ornamentation to appear as the official welcome center for visiting dignitaries and as the temporary residence of President Hayes and Republican presidential candidate James Garfield. Welcomed by Congressman McKinley, the Hayeses and Garfields led a parade down to Saxton House, where thousands waited for their arrival beneath the massive flag and "Welcome" sign Ida had ordered hung. The next day, following the reunion at the fairgrounds, Mrs. McKinley hosted an evening reception for the comrades of the Major's 23rd regiment and their spouses. In appreciation, the 23rd passed a resolution of thanks to "the esteemed wife of the gallant Major." The event was widely covered not only by the Ohio press but the national press, and the sudden rise in McKinley's prestige soon drew other high-profile celebrities, including Republican vice-presidential candidate Chester Arthur and legendary General Sherman. In executing her vision, Ida helped craft a tangible association between McKinley and Hayes and Garfield. The Major won his third term.[9]

During the March 1881 Garfield inauguration festivities, even among the "distinguished company assembled," the *Washington Post* reported, an effervescent Mrs. McKinley stood out at a reception in the mansion of Senator Pendleton, "brilliant last evening with light and flowers." A month later, seemingly "cured," Ida eagerly made a transcontinental trip by rail to the Golden State with the Major for their tenth wedding anniversary, visiting his brother David in San Francisco and exploring the foothills of the Sierra Mountains. The presumption that Ida was permanently immobile because she was seated for their San Francisco photo portrait was dramatically discounted by another photograph taken weeks later that showed her standing on a boulder in the Sierras, holding a walking staff, as were the Major and another couple. Their trip to California was lighthearted and joyous, with McKinley writing a colleague that they were "having a delightful time here." On returning east with David, when their train pulled into Chicago, they learned that President Garfield had been shot. They reached Canton on July 4.[10]

Perhaps provoked by the shock of Garfield's assassination, Ida had a sudden onset of severe seizures and, in accordance with the Mitchell "rest cure," was confined to rest in Saxton House. After enjoying her freedom in California's fresh air, Ida felt that her life had shut down, leaving her feeling sensitive and isolated. As business drew the Major away from home, Ida "thought herself neglected," Abner recalled. Her frustration burst in a tirade, in which she accused the Major of conducting a furtive romance, and culminated in "a frantic scene." Days later, McKinley, David, and Abner were walking to Saxton House when a female constituent approached the Major. "Please," he whispered to her, "don't walk into the yard with me. Ida might see you." While her seizures continued into September, Garfield died, and McKinley was among the few officials chosen to serve as honorary escort of his funeral train from Washington to Cleveland. These factors converged to first put McKinley's duties in conflict with his care of Ida, but as former President Hayes recorded in a September 22 note, "McKinley could not come on account of his wife's sickness." The Major's brothers cared for her when he attended the Cleveland funeral four days later, and when McKinley casually mentioned seeing "a handsome lady" there, a second jealous outburst from Ida violently escalated until it was "cut short by an epileptic attack."

However, Ida's outburst, rather than jealousy over some attraction the Major may have secretly felt for another woman, was more likely about losing a freedom that her husband continued to enjoy. Any anger she felt about her helplessness would have been all the more intense given her need to internalize it, knowing that rising stress could worsen her seizures. Even those who knew that Ida had seizures failed to appreciate how the disorder dictated her existence, unless they witnessed her enduring one. Saxton maid Amelia Jansen never forgot the moment she realized this. "Mrs. McKinley fell off her chair in an epileptic fit," she recalled. "When she came to she couldn't remember what happened." McKinley's political associates, with no knowledge of what was "wearying" him, began to resent Ida, one harshly declaring that she was a "burden, wasting his time, [and] hurting his health." That attitude is what led to a "cloud of sympathy" for him that would grow to become politically advantageous, but it also meant a lack of empathy for Ida.

Only the Major truly grasped the depth of Ida's struggle, so he was understanding and forgiving, but he was also the one person on whom she could unleash her frustration without irreparably harming their relationship. After some four months of recurrent seizures, the Major was relieved to report to Abner on January 13, 1882, that "Ida is growing stronger and better. She was five days without any fainting attacks and they have been less frequent on other days."[11]

When Ida emerged again in Washington, she found it had irreparably changed. With Garfield's death, Republican power shifted to the New York "Stalwart" wing of his successor, Chester Arthur. At one of the new president's receptions, Ida wistfully studied Lucy Hayes's portrait. "She misses Mrs. Hayes and yourself every day," the Major wrote the former president in February 1882. After five years of living in Washington from mid-autumn to mid-spring, the couple increasingly confined themselves to suite 2465 at Ebbitt House, where they shared a large pink-silk canopy bed. From his office in their suite, the Major routinely sent out copies of his speeches. On the advice of Hayes, McKinley had worked to become an expert on the issue of foreign trade, particularly the tariff on imported goods, initially in protection of northern Ohio's steel and iron industries. The McKinleys enjoyed dressing for dinner in Ebbitt's residential dining room and joining in stimulating conversation with fellow boarders, including the librarian of Congress. They entertained at dinners in a private parlor, a March 1884 bill showing that they offered wines to their guests and also had bottles sent upstairs for themselves. When breakfasting in their suite, the couple frequently ordered corned beef hash; a recipe for chicken croquettes that she submitted for a congressional cookbook suggests Ida's only other known food preference.

Ida traveled around in a hotel carriage, rented at a dollar per ride, venturing out quite often—eight times in one month—to personally deliver her own unique gift of charity to friends and strangers alike. Though she did not regain the vigor she had in California the year before, by March 1882, the Major happily reported to Abner that "Ida is improving." Instead of ruminating during those periods when she was immobile, by the spring of 1882, Ida had already become expert at knitting, turning out thousands of pairs of wool bedroom slippers, with cork soles and ribbons to lace them. What began as a pastime quickly evolved into Ida McKinley's mission to provide a pair of the warm, comfortable slippers to anyone who was suffering, whether she knew them or not. Names of individual children in orphanages, indigents in poorhouses, and patients in hospitals given to Ida by the Major's constituents, congressional spouses, and Ebbitt House neighbors kept her constantly at work. If time permitted, she also sought to match some aspect of the person to the color of the wool of the slippers they would get, such as gray for Southerners (the Confederate uniform color) or purple for those in mourning. She took special joy in delivering the slippers, although she usually remained in her carriage while a coachman carried the gift into the building. Eventually demand for Mrs. McKinley's slippers was great, as charitable organizations sought a pair to auction at fund-raisers, some fetching astronomical amounts.

As Ida sat knitting, she was enveloped by the scent of her favorite freshly cut June roses or flowering plants, bought from hothouse florists. With the radiator on full blast and flowers overflowing from vases and shallow dishes on windowsills, tabletops, mantels, even the floor, her room simulated a greenhouse. While Congress was in session, the Major worked out of his Capitol Hill office from early morning until sometimes past midnight while Ida was content to glimpse his large enameled picture at the bottom of her yarn bag. He was concerned that she should never be left alone. Since Ida suffered from a type of seizure that could result in injury if she fell or briefly lost consciousness, the Major ensured that Ida was never alone, and a secretary-aide by the name of Miss Poor kept her company in his absence.[12]

Ida's first winter in Washington as an invalid was brightened by the presence of her namesake niece-by-marriage, David McKinley's daughter, Miss Ida. The visit was the result of a compromise Ida had suggested after an argument she witnessed in San Francisco between the teenager and her father. Miss Ida wanted to marry her poor and equally young boyfriend, George Morse, but, as David McKinley explained to his sister-in-law, he refused to consent because "I want her to marry a man who is able to support her and one she can look up to. Not a mere boy." He hadn't counted on Ida urging the girl to persist in her desire to marry for love, as she herself had.

Ida became especially animated whenever she was around a niece who was about the same age Katie would have been had she lived. Her closest bond was to Abner's daughter Mabel, whose spinal injury also left her disabled, but Ida most often insisted on Mary Barber's presence. When Pina resisted having her eldest daughter uprooted from home, the Major gently pleaded with the girl's father and promised that another niece would also be invited to give the girl someone her age for companionship. "Ida and I have thought it would be awfully sweet if Mary could come and spend a couple of weeks," he wrote, for example, in 1887. "We will ask Grace McKinley to come also. They ought to come now before it gets too warm. We have a bedroom adjoining our parlor which we can give them, so that they will be near us. It would be a nice thing for them to come." Months later, when Ida again wanted twelve-year-old Mary's company, he suggested to Marsh that their second daughter join her this time. "I suppose Pina will say they can't leave school," he admitted. "To that I say a week or two will make no difference in a lifetime."

There is a strong indication that the visits weren't always pleasant for the teenage girls, especially if Ida was enduring an episode of seizures, and they often sought escape from the apartment by gallivanting around Washington. "We would have enjoyed it more if our Canton nieces could have dropped in upon us everyday," the Major wrote a bit unappreciatively after a recent visit by the two older Barber girls. Understanding why they didn't want to spend their entire time in Washington cooped up in the apartment, he sought to lure them back by assuring them that "Ida is herself again." Reading between the lines, however, it seems to have been less a matter of Ida being selfish than his compensating for guilt at being away from Ida all day long. "My good husband's time is all occupied," she wrote in one note, "so that I see but little of him."

The need for visits from their nieces became moot by Memorial Day in 1884 when the Major's 1882 fourth-term victory by a mere eight votes was successfully challenged. Returning to Canton earlier than expected, the McKinleys found Saxton House full of visitors, including the brothers of Mary and Ida, ten-year-old James, six-year-old George, five-year-old John, and one-year-old William. Before year's end, Pina also gave birth to her seventh and last child. The baby girl may have been named for her late grandmother, but her name and date of birth couldn't help but evoke another strong emotional meaning for Pina and Ida. Katie Barber was born nearly thirteen years to the day after Katie McKinley.

Another change in Saxton House was the frequent absence of James Saxton, who, following his July 29, 1882, wedding to fifty-year-old widow Hester B. Medill, spent summer and fall at her Potsdam, New York, home. No longer assigned tasks by his father, thirty-one-year-old George's only interest among the many family enterprises was tapping maple trees at their Minerva farm. Otherwise, he focused on Canton Bicycle Club activities and, recalled an adolescent Emil Kauffman, sitting "in a big armchair on the front porch, watching the girls go by." The extent of his work as manager of his father's multi-use commercial building was leasing space and collecting rent. After renting an apartment there to a "remarkably handsome" seamstress from nearby Columbiana County, her husband, and two sons, George set up a private office there for himself, where, neighbors noticed, he seemed to spend all his time. The woman's name was Anna George, and after she modeled a fur that George Saxton had asked her to alter, he declared it looked so beautiful on her that she must keep it. It was the first of many extravagant gifts the aging bachelor pressed on the young mother.

The Major worked in his office on the top floor of Saxton House while Ida was in the adjoining room, and the couple's Canton life was blissfully isolated from whatever affected the rest of the family on the floors below. As Bill Beer related to his son, because of the uncertainty of Ida's health, the Major had become a "soft-spoken, watchful nurse in his own house, and a worried guest if he was in company without his charge." Even though she had her hands full, Pina could be counted on to look after Ida for several hours or several days if the Major had to leave the house. Winning back his congressional seat, however, returned them to Washington in the winter of 1885. Work increasingly required him to be out on the road.[13]

"I hope you will not feel disappointed at my not reaching home as soon as you expected. I know you can not fret more than I do," he wrote her with an alarmed guilt for being separated from her longer than anticipated. "There seemed to be a necessity (as they put it to me) for my remaining and so I thought under all the circumstances I had better." On another occasion, he feared he had incurred her disapproval for being away: "I got your precious letter today and it was so welcome. I feel so much the better from having got it. I was afraid you had stopped writing and this made me all the more gratified to get the letter."

It was not entirely the Major's imagination that Ida might emotionally manipulate him for his absences. However unsteady her penmanship, she capably composed brief notes and telegram messages to him when they were separated; when they were reunited, however, she became suddenly incapable of even signing her name. When the Stark County Horticultural Society asked her to obtain one of former First Lady Lucy Hayes's "handsome dinner bouquets," it was the Major who had to write the request for it. He also felt the need to explain this odd arrangement, once writing her niece, "your Aunt Ida, you know, writes but little."

McKinley's legendary devotion to Ida increased. He always made at least a passing reference to her even in business meetings, and above his desk hung a massive photograph of her that dominated the room. However genuine his devotion, it also provided a tactical advantage over the lobbyists, journalists, and politicos who came to question or negotiate with him, lowering their guard and making them less likely to exploit such a gentle soul. At the least, it gave him a saintly persona.[14]

While there are no accounts of Ida McKinley's visits to her husband's Capitol Hill office, one from about 1885 describes her as being "able to be about" his Ebbitt House office. In both his offices, the door remained open "so she could hear the Major's voice" from her adjoining room. This had political implications. In hearing what others said to him, Ida was privy to whatever issue was under consideration. Her being witness to whatever McKinley stated also helped prevent anyone who might later challenge his version of what transpired. However subtle and unintentional, it was one way Ida McKinley helped serve her husband's political purposes.

Ida McKinley also assumed a more direct political role. By 1884, she was a confirmed advocate for a woman's right to work, regardless of age, race, or marital status. This belief was shared with her father and emerged from her defense of her right to work while employed in his bank. Ironically, the derivative power she gained through her marriage now enabled her to help other self-supporting women seeking employment. An example of an appeal from one such woman came to Ida on February 29, 1884, through her father: "I received a letter yesterday from Miss Ada Miller saying that she has been before the civil service commission and wanted a situation very badly and that everybody told her that you could [do] more to get her one than any other person and wanting me to write to you on her behalf. If you can get her a situation I wish you would do it. As I suppose it is true that she is very poor but competent."

Not long after her brother-in-law Abner McKinley married Miss Anna Ensley, Ida befriended her unmarried sister, Catherine "Kitty" Ensley, and helped launch her career as a stenographer and secretary. Although Kitty's prior employment is unclear, she asked Ida for help in finding work in Stark County shortly after the Major was elected to Congress. While he would have felt obligated to help Abner's sister-in-law regardless, Kitty pursued the issue through Ida, who kept the matter in front of the Major. Ten years later, she helped Kitty Ensley find work in Washington, first in a private office and then in a federal government job and, over the years, Kitty had numerous promotions. Poet Mary E. Kail met the congress-man's wife while living either in Leesburg, Ohio (once part of McKinley's frequently gerrymandered district), or after she returned to her home city of Washington, D.C. Kail, who was lyricist of the 1876 Hayes campaign song and author of "Crown Our Heroes," a poem often read at events honoring Union Army veterans, sought Ida's help sometime before 1883 in securing a federal job through the Major's political patronage. Two years later, when the new Cleveland Administration replaced patronage positions with Democrats, Kail faced an impoverished retirement until she was introduced, almost certainly, again by Ida McKinley to Jane Stan-ford, the wealthy wife of California's U.S. senator, who underwrote the publication of her poetry, and allowed her to live without worry. When she died, Ida and the Major provided a floral tribute for her funeral.[15]

When her own father died on May 16, 1887, at age seventy-one, Ida reacted with greater calm than she had when she suffered other traumatic losses a decade earlier. James Saxton had left his mark on Canton, helping it develop into a vital industrial city, and his was the largest private funeral the city had ever seen. Although he had been dispensing gifts of his as-sets to his children while alive, in death he left them all wealthier. Once the Major had processed Saxton's will, Ida, Pina, and George were joint owners of the large working farm in Minerva, silver mines in Nevada, numerous rental properties in Canton, and mineral-rich lands in the area. Proud of the Major's public service, Saxton died just before McKinley's dramatic rise in national prominence.[16]

Throughout the summer and fall months of the congressional recess in 1887, McKinley worked intensely in his Saxton House office, drafting the tariff speech that would prompt powerful political and business leaders to begin thinking of his presidential potential. He was able to continue monitoring Ida, who was just a room away. Returning to Washington at the end of the year, Ida continued to enjoy another long stretch of such excellent health that when she needed to return to Canton early in 1888, she insisted on making the train trip alone. Although her health remained the Major's priority, he didn't have to sacrifice focusing on his career at this critical juncture as long as they were together. The ensuing anxiety provoked by their separation was evident in his March 17 telegram to her in Canton: "My darling wife, I am quite solicitous to know how you are. The telephone is out of order. I hope you are feeling better. Please send me a line saying how you feel. Accept a full heart of love."

"Received your telegram," she responded, "Delighted you're well. Am comfortable[,] but homesick." The brief words revealed a defining truth about how Ida McKinley perceived her life. Her concept of "home" was not bound to location, but to him. His telegrams and notes were more than of informational importance to her, and she anticipated them with equal passion. As the *Washington Post* later reported, the Ebbitt House staff was amazed at "how precise and prompt she was in calculating the hour when he would reach the designated cities and when she would receive a message from him." When a friend asked what McKinley could possibly express in such telegrams that were of such value to her, Ida snapped, "He can say he loves me."

Once Ida returned to Washington in early April, however, the inherent conflict between his dual devotion to his wife and his career emerged more sharply for the Major. While cognizant of how his absence for a single vote could adversely affect his political record and also working on the final edits of his long-anticipated tariff speech, he was nevertheless extremely anxious about Ida waiting up late for him to return to their apartment. Confined to his congressional office and able to catch only a few hours of sleep on his black leather couch there, he dispatched a messenger with a note to her at Ebbitt House: "I do not know how long we will yet remain but it looks as if we could be here for the night. . . . I hope you will not worry about me, but have a good nice night's rest & I will try & breakfast with you in the morning if I do not get to you earlier. God bless and keep you. Accept a full heart of love and a thousand kisses." A week later, he apologized for again sleeping at the office, due to a floor debate preceding a vote: "The opposition seems determined to suit out and nothing remains for us but to stay with them which we will do unless later on we can take a recess. . . . Receive my evening benediction of love. . . . I will be with you sometime in the morning. Goodnight and may the good angels guard you."[17]

On May 18, William McKinley finally delivered his tariff speech, a convincing yet eloquent argument that the monetary value of products manufactured in the United States must not only be raised but protected by the rates of what were exported and imported to ensure a stabilized national economy. In that presidential election year, the Republican National Committee printed and distributed millions of copies of the speech for national, state, and local races, thrusting the name of William McKinley into the country's consciousness.

One of her rare handwritten letters indicates that Ida McKinley played something of a role in attempting to further raise the Major's national profile in connection with tariff. It was she who granted approval to a manufacturer of a set of souvenir cutlery being imprinted with his image and was overt in both her promotion of the tariff and concern for his overtaxing work schedule: "[The] Major is working very hard, to protect our home industries just now & I do not think is looking well. I hope, however, the hardest part will soon be over." In observing that "Mrs. McKinley's illness never interfered with her lively interest in public affairs and in the part that her husband took in them," reporter Alexander McClure accurately concluded that Ida McKinley perceived all political issues through the prism of how it affected her "dearest." She believed no public servant more diligently studied issues and was thus more honest in his view of them than was her Major.[18]

Ida McKinley's pride in the public's reaction to her husband's tariff speech was increased further by the response he received after another incident that garnered him national attention at the June 1888 National Republican Convention in Chicago. Accompanying him while staying at the comfortable home of her cousin Mary McWilliams, Ida again perceived what was a tactical political move as a natural aspect of his character. When it became clear that Ohio's U.S. Sen. John Sherman, whom McKinley endorsed, couldn't clinch the nomination, delegates who knew Ohio was key to winning the general election began to spontaneously declare for McKinley during the roll call. With every eye in the convention hall upon him, McKinley summoned his theatrical talents to stand on a chair and halt the roll call. He humbly pleaded that there be no further declarations of support for him, not wishing his fidelity to Sherman to be tainted. Startled by this unexpected act of political humility, delegates fell into reverential silence. It made the presidential nomination of Indiana Sen. Benjamin Harrison rather anticlimactic.

Witnessing this bit of drama unfold left Sherman's campaign manager and financier, Cleveland industrialist Mark Hanna, dumbstruck, and determined to "no longer to put his money on the wrong horse," as his brother-in-law put it, Hanna kept his eye on McKinley.

No matter how well McKinley was received in Chicago, it was their homecoming to Canton on June 28 that was most gratifying to Ida. As word of their return circulated, a crowd began clustering around Saxton House and calling for him. Stepping out to the "scene of an ovation," McKinley was especially moved by the large presence of Democrats, making it less a partisan celebration than one for him. In the next day's *Canton Repository* story, Saxton House was rechristened and referred to for the first time as "the McKinley residence."

Only two weeks to the day later, while the Major perspired in the torpid Washington summer, focused on the tedium of tariff rates, Ida McKinley's fate yet again radically turned in Canton. McKinley, when handed a telegram while on the House floor, bolted from the Capitol Building to catch the next train to Pittsburgh. When he arrived, a *Pittsburgh Chronicle* reporter, who recognized him as he waited for the train to Canton, recounted that the Major was in "one of those expansive moods," optimistically predicting that Harrison would take Ohio and bust the Democratic hold on the southern states. It was a command performance by McKinley, conjured with the disciplined self-control he had learned to maintain after nearly two decades of hiding any concern about Ida. At that very moment, she lay in bed burning with fever, unconscious and dying.

Ida was especially susceptible to infection because of her compromised immune system, and whether it was bacterial or viral in nature, her body worked to kill it, reacting with a raging fever that left her delirious and in danger of dysentery. When his train pulled into Canton, McKinley flew into a waiting carriage, which sped to Saxton House. He dashed up the three flights of winding stairs to their bedroom, and gently slipped his hands into Ida's, calmly murmuring, "Ida, it is I." As Pina later told McKinley's biographer, the house was filled with distraught family members and a doctor who insisted that if measures failed to sweat the infection from her system, it would mean her recovery was unlikely. McKinley sat with her throughout the night until morning, calmly reassuring her. The next day, she weakly managed to open her eyes and whisper, "I knew you'd come." She regained consciousness and her temperature decreased, but the fever had taken a toll. McKinley reported two months later that Ida "continues extremely ill." A month later, on September 21, she was only "improving slowly."[19]

With warranted fear about her, the Major requested an indefinite leave of absence from Congress in August, which was granted. Vanishing suddenly after just getting national acclaim required an explanation, especially to party bosses who intended him to campaign for their candidates. For the first time in McKinley's career, Ida was a political topic. "Major McKinley!" a facile editorial ran, "Everybody wants him. And nobody is getting him. Of course he has the heartfelt sympathy of everybody in the sickness of his wife, whom he has been so devotedly attending, but his absence in the campaign has been so universally regretted." Individual political figures barely veiled their frustration. As a member of the Ohio State Republican Committee explained, "Of course we are hoping his wife's convalescence may continue at such a rate that he will be able to take the stump later, as we are confident it is a double affliction for him to feel that he cannot help increase the big Republican victory for the American eagle this fall."

None of the reports hinted at the nature of Ida's illness, and McKinley offered no details about the nature of what kept him off the campaign trail, but several factors converge to suggest that Ida McKinley may also have served as a convenient excuse to cover another intention. Whether or not candidates lost elections that fall because McKinley didn't stump for them, the Major's absence didn't harm the race most important of all to him—his election to a seventh term. If it was true that Ida's convalescence necessitated their being isolated together, it was equally true that he needed to work uninterrupted to finalize the details of his pending tariff bill and thus solidify his acclaim. He simply transferred this process to Washington when Congress convened in December, Ida being well enough to go with him there. Except for brief hours when he needed to be on Capitol Hill, he remained with Ida, working at Ebbitt House. Colleagues, lobbyists, and trade advisers who came to confer on the bill also met Ida, often for the first time, and witnessed McKinley's solicitous care of her. Hearing about this, a reporter called to interview them.

The public got its first impression of Mrs. McKinley in a *Home Magazine* article about her that was reprinted in newspapers, like the March 1, 1889, *Repository.* While pointing out how committed she was to his political rise, the article praised McKinley for "his entire consecration to his invalid wife." While it marked the first time Ida was referred to as an "invalid" in print, it offered no suggestion as to what ailed her, but it did affirm her "fine mental attributes."[20]

When McKinley, who was long a member of the Appropriations Committee, began his seventh term in Congress in 1889, he was named chairman of the Ways and Means Committee. The position brought funding for an "assistant clerk," and he hired twenty-three-year-old typist and stenographer Charles M. Bawsel, who was soon invited to share evenings, weekends, and holidays with Ida as well. She came to trust him to sign her name to her mail and even matched him with Mina Danner, a distant relative, whom he married. Bawsel fearlessly incurred her wrath and provoked her laughter, and she loved how he loved the Major. "It is nip and tuck between Mrs. McKinley and I as to who adores him the more," he wrote his aunt. Charlie was trusted so quickly that the Major rented a room for him in Canton that summer so he could look after Ida while he campaigned. When former President Hayes invited the McKinleys to the memorial service for his beloved Lucy, Ida responded with a hasty telegram in her husband's absence, explaining that "Major cannot meet his political engagements and accompany me, and I am not strong enough to come alone." The Major winced at the telegram's suggestion of insensitivity. To avoid any other such incidents, by the fall he had entrusted Charlie to escort Ida to important events.

When the McKinleys returned to Washington in November 1889, Ida's stamina had returned while the Major's began to weaken. Except for a recuperative break in February at Old Point Comfort, Virginia, however, he resumed a grueling schedule, challenged by the imminent gerrymandering of his district by Democrats who now controlled the statehouse and sought to make his district their own. Two moments of glory came on April 16, when the "McKinley Bill" was introduced, and October 6, when it was signed by President Harrison. Ida was so proud that the name McKinley was attached to the bill that she failed to realize that in raising tariff rates by nearly fifty percent, the bill immediately resulted in more expensive household items.[21]

That year, she was unwittingly made the subject of a paid political advertisement placed in the November 3, 1890, *Canton Repository* by Texan David A. Murphy. "An Appeal for McKinley" had one simple, direct message: "McKinley, the man whose constancy and devotion to an invalid wife not only endears him to every family in Ohio, but commends him as being 'the model husband' to every household in America. Vote for McKinley." If it was the first time that Ida McKinley's public persona as an "invalid" was exploited for political purposes, it was the last time it was done without her own complicity. It did not, however, have the intended effect. Because Ida had "gotten nervous about the election," the Major joined her instead of his supporters on election night 1890, which he lost. With Democrats gerrymandering his district in their favor came the charge of "defeat by fraud," which increased McKinley's reputation for honesty. As he wrote Mark Hanna, "I agree with you that defeat under the circumstances was for the best."[22]

After a final congressional tour of Tennessee battlefields, the couple went home in April 1891, where Saxton House had become a focal point for those curious to catch a glimpse of McKinley. He could be found most days in town, attending civic meetings or conferring with legal clients. Ida was less accessible. As a "fervent patroness" of the Canton Flower Mission Guild, the members of which visited the hospitalized and housebound with flowers, she made large financial contributions and signed her nieces up as volunteers but never managed to attend meetings. When five teenage girls from Massillon founded what would become the national Daughters of Union Veterans to honor their fathers, they paid tribute to Ida by naming the first of many local divisions the "Mrs. Major McKinley Tent," tents being the name for regional branches. She, however, barely acknowledged the group. If she ventured out alone, gossip inevitably stirred. When Ida brought jewelry to be repaired at a local watch shop, the jeweler's daughter, Estella Dueber, complained that her father was always expected to leave his shop and go "around to the back," where Ida "insisted" on remaining in her carriage to conduct business, suggesting it was a peculiarity rather than her inability to exit the vehicle without help. Abner McKinley told Bill Beer that despite the affection she showered on them, the "children of Canton told each other, across fences, that Mrs. McKinley had fits."

This attitude wasn't exclusive to Canton. While lunching with the couple, ex-congressman John Wise referred to "when Wallace turned [you] out," a shorthand reference to McKinley's 1882 contested election. At this, "Mrs. McKinley interrupted by inquiring something, with a surprised look, which implied that she did not altogether understand what I meant when I spoke of Wallace." Wise condescendingly assumed that "she had never been allowed to hear or see [read] of his defeat." He believed that his former colleague's wife, who spent her days listening to his political business, wouldn't question the abrupt end of his congressional term because Ida McKinley was a "sweet, pathetic little invalid."[23]

There proved to be little opportunity in Canton to determine what was wrong with Ida McKinley in 1891. They were barely home before plans began to send them to Columbus as Ohio's next governor and First Lady, and Ida McKinley spent her forty-fifth birthday in Cleveland as she and the Major met with financier Mark Hanna to plan the campaign. Hanna learned fast that Ida was the surest way to win over McKinley after he invited him to an important dinner earlier that year, a command opportunity for anyone hoping to continue rising in politics. The Major turned down the invitation but promised to visit at a time "arranged with Mrs. McKinley." When Hanna discovered how much Ida loved flowers, he invited her to join the Major so she could enjoy the garden "in the glory of early summer." While her impression of the political boss went unrecorded, Ida would approve any role Hanna played if it helped her husband.

Weeks later, after McKinley's nomination for governor, Hanna took charge of financing and organizing his campaign, which kicked off with a parade in the Major's birthplace, Niles, Ohio. It included the Ida McKinley Club, a group of women in red dresses, carrying blue umbrellas. Hanna recognized how well Ida responded to flattery. Beyond winning the governorship, there was a greater significance to the Major's victory that fall. "Won't McKinley be an important factor in the Presidential election? He is ambitious for it," former presidential candidate James G. Blaine wrote Gen. Russell Alger, an associate of the new governor-elect. The Major wasn't the only ambitious one. As a congressional wife, driving around Washington with friends one afternoon, Ida McKinley pointed out the Executive Mansion and casually remarked, "I will live there some day."[24]

❧ 5 ❧

"Tremendous Leverage"

SHORTLY INTO HIS FIRST TERM, the tale of Governor McKinley's ritual feat of devotion to his wife had spread so quickly that tourists began to gather at just the right time on the state Capitol Building plaza to watch him. Since there was no official residence provided for governors, the McKinleys lived in the residential Chittenden Hotel, directly facing the Capitol Building.

Each morning after leaving the Chittenden and walking across the street, the Major turned and paused on the same spot on the front steps of the Capitol, then removed and waved his top hat up at a window in their suite. There, Ida would reciprocate, fluttering a handkerchief. At precisely three o'clock in the afternoon, without regard for business, the governor stepped outside to the same spot, and doffed his hat. Ida would respond with another wave of her handkerchief. It was their way of checking in on one another, but the busy governor's steadfast gesture so fulfilled some romantic Victorian ideal that the Capitol's legislators and clerks, hotel residents and tourists could not help watching with admiration this private moment acted out on the open-air stage of the plaza.

The public seemed to expect little but symbolism from the new governor's wife, having witnessed at the inaugural ceremonies her obvious disability as she sat throughout McKinley's January 1892 swearing-in ceremony and the reception that followed as guests streamed by a receiving line. Ida appeared at dinner parties, but the governor arranged them. Although one source claimed that Mrs. McKinley had particular concern for "motherless children" and that "many an orphan has had occasion to love her for untiring deeds of kindness and an unflagging interest in its

welfare," there is no record that she did work for any of the state's orphanages, like the famous Sailors' and Soldiers' Orphans Home in Xenia.[1]

Typically, Ida focused on individuals rather than institutions, eager to
knit slippers for those in need rather than the charities that helped them.
As the governor's wife, she prompted a public search for the identity of
an eleven-year-old Ohio girl so she could be properly awarded France's
Legion of Honor award for bravery after the child signaled an engineer
to stop a train full of French citizens, thus averting a disaster. After learning about a local three-year-old singing sensation, Ida invited the child to
perform for her and the governor. Their patronage attracted newspapers'
attention and led to bookings that launched the girl's stage career as the
famous Elsie Janis. When Kitty Ensley lost her job, Ida again helped the
"splendid stenographer" and "careful industrious woman" by having the
Major urge a former congressional colleague to hire her.[2]

Ida was most animated at night. Charlie Bawsel, who now worked as
McKinley's chief executive clerk, recorded that after dinner together, the
governor sat

> . . . reading to his wife extracts from his partially prepared speech, and
> as Mrs. McKinley's white fingers fly over the slipper she is crocheting
> she nods her approval of this point or that. Friends drop in during the
> course of the evening—lots of them, also callers, perhaps to see the
> Governor on business. As a rule they are alike received in the parlor.
> To be sure the Governor has an office in connection with his rooms
> where he can smoke, talk politics and plan. But a conference must be of
> the most pressing nature to detain him long from Mrs. McKinley's side.
> Her husband is absent from her all day, and his evenings belong wholly
> to her. This, the little lady insists upon.

The governor's private secretary James Boyle, stenographer Opha Moore,
speech and correspondence writer Joe Smith, and Cleveland banker Myron Herrick, who served as an unofficial adviser, recognized how important Ida was to the Major, but only Charlie seemed to realize the reverse
was also true, commenting that "Mrs. McKinley's whole being is wrapped
up in her distinguished husband, and with an almost idolatrous love she
clings to him—even as a tender vine to a stalwart oak. . . ."[3]

Popular among Republican leaders, Governor McKinley was besieged
with requests to address the party faithful during legislative breaks and recesses. He was eager to comply, especially since the stimulation of travel

seemed to help Ida's health flourish. In February, they were in Pittsburgh and Chicago; in March, Cleveland, Providence and Pawtucket, Rhode Island, Boston, and New York. After some 2,000 miles of travel in one week, Ida McKinley was noted as "looking well and hearty." In May they went to Ann Arbor, Michigan, and took a brief vacation at Elberon, New Jersey. In June, the governor was the star attraction at the National Republican Convention in Minneapolis, although Ida stayed in Chicago with her cousin. From there until mid-August, they went to the Black Hills of South Dakota, then to Beatrice, Lincoln, and Omaha, Nebraska; then Denver and Colorado Springs, Colorado. They were in Vermont the last eight days of August. By mid-September, Ida took a break, resting at the Somerset, Pennsylvania, summer home of Abner and Annie McKinley, while the Major spoke in Indianapolis. From the end of the month into October, they went to Philadelphia, Washington, West Virginia, Missouri, and Michigan. Despite seeing so many places for the first time, what most permanently impressed Ida was the Chicago World's Fair, where the Major dedicated the Ohio Building before they returned to Columbus for the start of the legislative season. She called it "the greatest exhibition the world has ever witnessed and nobody who can do so should miss it." From then on, Ida McKinley was eager to see world's fairs wherever they took place.

When McKinley returned without Ida to Canton in November for his father's funeral, he did not stay at their suite in Saxton House but rather with his widowed mother. In fact, just after he became governor, when he began coming home to Canton every Sunday just so he could escort his mother to church on Sunday, not only did Ida remain in Columbus but McKinley began staying in his mother's house rather than with his in-laws. Beyond keeping Nancy McKinley company, however, there was another reason the governor chose to stay in the smaller house, now crowded with his orphaned niece and nephew, teenagers James and Grace, children of the Major's brother James, who died two years earlier. The governor and his wife thus avoided having to share a roof with her now publicly disgraced brother. A month after McKinley's inauguration, Sample C. George sued George Saxton for $20,000 in damages, blaming the latter for his wife Anna's "alienation of affections." Despite this, Saxton brazenly continued the embarrassing drama for six years. The suit was withdrawn and reinstated, and Saxton directed Anna to obtain a divorce by establishing South Dakota residency and promised to marry her if she did so. Anna did as he told her, only to return to Canton to find him pursuing a rich widow, and then sued him for $30,000 for breach of promise.

He would counter-sue and seek a restraining order to keep Anna away from Saxton House and his office in the McKinley Building, where she knew he indulged in more than business.[4]

Although reluctant to share a household with George, the McKinleys remained engaged in the lives of Pina's children, especially the two older girls, Mary, sixteen, and Ida, eleven. As Charlie recalled, "They want many Barbers to visit them." When Ida was in Canton without the governor, she continued to stay at Saxton House.

As evidence of just how much improved her health had become, on one occasion, she traveled alone from Canton to Columbus. Failing to first alert anyone in the governor's office to retrieve her at the train depot when she arrived, she had to arrange her own transportation home. Although it proved her complete capability in looking after herself when she was well, she was not pleased about having to do so. When she arrived back at the McKinleys' suite, she complained about being neglected. Charlie, however, put her in her place: "No one knew of her coming. Consequently no one was at the depot to meet her—a truly dreadful thing! I understand she was quite 'huffy'; and after office hours went down to see her and told her we're not gifted with the power of second sight, etc." He also detected an emerging streak of vanity in the governor's wife, writing, "Mrs. McKinley was highly indignant because I did not at once notice an elegant new gown she had on. . . ."[5]

Whether Ida was combative or charming, her health was enjoying a period of stabilization. Taking advantage of this, the Major thought it an opportune time to again attempt to "cure" her epilepsy and decided to consult yet another medical specialist. It was likely either a Columbus physician or osteopath Albert Fischer (who felt his field was too experimental yet to be helpful) who referred McKinley to Joseph Norton Bishop in New York, a successful specialist in "nervous diseases and troubles of women." By early February 1893, the Major placed Ida McKinley in Bishop's care while he returned to Columbus.

Going to Bishop suggested that the McKinleys were seeking some other type of medication to treat Ida's seizures. Bishop, an 1876 graduate of Long Island College Hospital in Brooklyn, was best known for his use of experimental pharmacology to treat neurological disorders. By 1884 he was listed as a botanist in the *Drugs and Medicines of North America* quarterly and opened his practice three years later with his office and residential suites for longer-term patients at Fifth Avenue and 38th Street. With large muttonchop whiskers and a florid face, he was said to have both a "commanding personality" and a "genial disposition." Three years Ida's senior, Bishop would play a crucial role in her life.

Among the city's elite, Bishop voyaged annually by luxury liner to remote parts of the globe, summered in Newport, wintered in Florida, and underwrote the esoteric effort to recreate Robert Fulton's *Clermont* steamboat. During a sojourn in fashionable Colorado Springs, Bishop was enlisted to join the Reception Committee for President Harrison's visit. His political loyalty was not irrelevant; Bishop was entrusted with the secret of Mrs. McKinley's epilepsy, delicate personal information that could be scurrilously exploited to destroy McKinley's career. Even the fact that Ida was seeking medical care now merited a squib of news. "I suppose you have seen by the papers rumors of Mrs. McKinley's illness in New York," Charlie wrote to a relative, "It is not serious, however." During a brief exchange with a *New York Times* reporter at the Windsor Hotel (where the McKinleys maintained a suite, courtesy of Abner, an investor there), the Major's remark that Ida was "improving" was his first public reference to her health. On his way to Ohio, he planned to return to New York within days to deliver a scheduled speech.[6]

On Thursday, February 16, McKinley was on his way back to New York when his train stopped at Dunkirk, New York. An urgent telegram was rushed to him on the train from the station manager, wired by his political aide Myron Herrick. McKinley was being held liable for a debt that would be assessed at over $100,000 by the time the dust settled. Fearing that this meant the end of his political ambitions, he did not continue on to New York to pick up Ida but instead asked his brother to do so while he bolted back to Ohio.

Seven years earlier, McKinley had signed promissory notes for his boyhood friend Robert L. Walker, a successful entrepreneur with coal mining, stonework, and printing ventures. Walker raised his capital to make his investments by obtaining bank credit that required him to sign notes holding him liable for the loans. To protect themselves against potential default, the banks required these loans to be signed by a second person, who would be held equally liable for the loans. McKinley cosigned for Walker on mutual trust, who lent him $2,000 for each congressional campaign. Walker continued his enterprises by using credit extensions, and when he implied a need to refinance to tide him over, the Major cosigned his second batch of bank notes. In reality, Walker was going bankrupt and left McKinley legally liable for the debt. The story broke on Friday, and that night, McKinley met with Walker in Youngstown, Ohio, and issued a

press statement: "I will pay every note of Mr. Walker's on which I am en-
dorser. . . . I must understand the situation before I can rest for my whole
future, politically and financially, is involved in this." His anger faded and
he forgave Walker.

Meanwhile, banker Myron Herrick convinced McKinley to then come
to his Cleveland mansion to confer with a circle of political and business
advisers and telegraphed Ida McKinley to join them, assuring her, "Do
not worry over the Walker matter. Your husband has friends who will see
that every obligation bearing his name will be paid and no stain will blot
his fair name."

Escorted by Abner from a buggy cab through New York's Pennsylvania
Station to her train, the forty-seven-year-old governor's wife determinedly
made her way to Ohio alone. It would not be his friends but his wife who
would save the Major. As the view of grimy cities gave way to the darken-
ing winter landscape of central Pennsylvania, Ida McKinley formulated a
financial bailout plan. The woman who arrived at the Herrick house on
Saturday morning had none of the fretful anxiety the men waiting had
expected her to feel.

With flinty practicality not seen since her days in Europe, Ida put up all
she owned to pay the debt, drawing on five asset groups. There was her
personal property, including her valuable diamond collection, real estate
given her outright by her father, and her stocks. She and the Major co-
owned the McKinley Block Building, a lucrative piece of commercial
real estate. The largest portion of her assets was her one-third share of
inherited real-estate properties that were leased for residences and businesses, Canton's Grand Opera House (opened in 1890 and managed by
Marsh Barber); the Minerva farm, which yielded substantial apple, potato,
and syrup produce sold to area venues; the Nevada silver mine; and Saxton House. Ida was fetched from the Cleveland depot by a coachman and
immediately announced her decision to Herrick upon her arrival. The
New York Times reported days later that "Her friends have urged her to
retain an interest in the property, but she has steadfastly refused to listen
to any argument. . . ." Whether her "friends" were, in fact, her brother and
sister, with whom she had to consult regarding their joint assets, was not
disclosed, but George and Pina would have had to buy out her share.

Meanwhile, the governor's friends and admirers wired offers of support. Most persistent was Herman H. Kohlsaat of Chicago, an acquaintance since 1876. With an ear for a good story and a genius at public
relations, he was then half-owner of the *Chicago Inter Ocean,* an interest

he sold to then buy outright the *Chicago Times-Herald* and the *Evening Post* in 1895. From Chicago, he wired the Major: "Have just read of your misfortune. My purse is open." McKinley asked him to Herrick's. Also coming to the Sunday meeting were the couple's Canton attorney William R. Day, the Major's wartime comrade Russell Hastings, and three others who could muster legal, political, and financial help: Thomas McDougall, a Cincinnati attorney; John Tod, the wealthy son of a former Ohio governor; and businessman James H. Hoyt.

Although McKinley could manipulate scenarios to serve his interests, he was scrupulous about money; his $130,000 liability was "in excess of anything I dreamed of." He was so stunned that an old chum could deceive him that he became uncharacteristically indecisive. This aberration, however, only drew out a decisive impulse in Ida, and in commandeering the response to the crisis, she exercised her greatest degree of power on behalf of McKinley's career.

Into Sunday afternoon, Ida McKinley sat in a ground-floor sitting room conferring with the men. After accounting which assets she held apart from her husband, they arrived at an estimated value of $75,000. In affirming her decision to liquidate assets and advance the proceeds toward McKinley's debt, Ida sparked a confrontation with several men who argued against her actions. "My husband has done everything for me all my life," she finally snapped in anger. "Do you mean to deny me the privilege of doing as I please with my own property to help him now?"

The Major, who was averse to conflict, took Ida upstairs as the debate continued. "Because McKinley has made a fool of himself, why should Mrs. McKinley be a pauper?" Tod growled. Kohlsaat disagreed on tactical grounds: "Because if McKinley is to stay in politics he must show clean hands and not be open to the charge he has put his property in his wife's name." McDougall made the strongest case to defy her decision. "What Mrs. McKinley has is her own," he said, adding she would need it if she was widowed. He pointed out that the Major hadn't been granted "credit or trusted him on the faith of her property." In "stripping this matter of all needless sentiment," he adamantly opposed "any conveyance of any interest of hers to . . . pay his debts. . . ."

Evidencing none of the idealized submissiveness of the Victorian woman, Ida McKinley held her ground against the men, and they made "little progress" with her. They finally compromised by agreeing to let her assign all her assets to Herrick, Day, Kohlsaat, and the absent Hanna as trustees.

This pleased Ida, but gave the Major sudden pause. They conferred alone. "Your name shall not be tarnished," she told him. "If you will give up your property, I will give up mine." His view of her offer was never made public, but a remark she made to him suggests that he initially resisted it. McKinley decided that Hanna must be consulted before a final course was followed. Her fiercely protective instinct downstairs had shifted her marriage's balance of power, proving that she could be relied on when well. "Mrs. McKinley takes it very calmly," Charlie Bawsel reported of Ida, "and is better than she has been for some time. . . ." It was Ida McKinley's finest hour.

The Major conferred with Hanna in Chicago the next day and the upshot, as reported in the February 22 *New York Times* was that Ida's assets were separated from those of her husband and placed in a trusteeship that Hanna would manage, but that she "refused to any arrangement that would leave her a dollar as long as there was a dollar owing on the Governor's debts." Her heroic intentions were somewhat eroded, however, by the Major's protective instinct. He and Hanna agreed to a "private understanding" that her assets would be used "if needed," and a legal provision ensured that if they were used, any funds extracted from Walker would be first applied to Ida's account. But even with their combined assets, there was still an outstanding debt of $40,000.

Hanna also realized that even if the debt were paid, the scandal would still undermine the governor's renomination that June and his shot at the presidential nomination in three years. When McKinley understood this, he agreed to let the trustees acquire the debt and manage his assets, and they seemingly acquiesced to his insistence that he would pay them back. In reality, this generated the next phase of the plan, which was to rapidly pay off the debt without touching any McKinley assets. Contributions would be collected with finesse just short of solicitation, in small amounts donated by a public sympathetic with the perception of the story as shaped by Kohlsaat and large amounts from wealthy industrialists, cultivated by Herrick and Hanna. While the plan enacted by these men would require diminishing Ida McKinley's political influence in public, in private they never attempted to diminish her power over the Major.

Kohlsaat rapidly arranged the facts of how the Major was victimized by "aggravated treachery" into a breathless narrative intended for sentimental Victorian consumption. His first bit of melodrama was disclosing that McKinley's one indulgence was insisting that the trustees now in control of his finances continue to pay out a small annuity to Ida's widowed Aunt

Maria, proving his unselfishness. Leaking details of the Sunday conference, Kohlsaat decided he must "tell the story" and broke it in his Chicago paper, making Mrs. McKinley the focus: "She is an invalid, and her fortune came as a legacy from her father. . . . Thus the two may become penniless. They will lose their Canton home and all their household goods. Mrs. McKinley's farms and all will go so that in poverty they begin life again."

Of course, the McKinleys owned no "Canton home." Among the several farm properties left to the three Saxton siblings, Ida owned a half-share of one of them. And the McKinley marriage had not begun in anything close to poverty. Kohlsaat then made as strong a plea for donations as he could just short of begging: "The Governor will turn over every penny he has, but this will only be a drop compared with the aggregated liabilities. He said his wife was thoroughly decided to help him out with her own means. . . . However all of it will not cover the debt. . . . The Governor will . . . make it his project in life to pay all that he had been dragged into owing. . . . The friends of Mrs. McKinley, heroic woman that she is, declare she must not put her fortune at the mercy of creditors. . . ." Ending his first report, distributed through his newspaper, Kohlsaat left audiences dangling as he asked, "Will the Governor resign? Well, it is hardly possible to see what else he can do."

The plan worked. As other newspapers reprinted and embellished Kohlsaat's story, the McKinleys returned to Columbus to find themselves flooded with letters "so full of comfort," not only from across Ohio but the nation. "My mail [is] overflowing with sympathy," the Major reported to Herrick, "and the most earnest protest against Mrs. McKinley turning over her property." He didn't exaggerate. A New York fur importer, C. C. Shayne, wrote the governor: "I do not believe your wife should use her private fortune to pay off your debts, yet everyone appreciates her motives," adding that McKinley was "making a mistake when you refuse the assistance of your friends." One James MacArthur sent his poem, "Tested," in tribute to McKinley's "noble, devoted wife." Many envelopes contained small donations, like that sent by W. J. Magee, Flour & Feed Dealer, to aid "such grand and noble characters." A Democrat from Tennessee congratulated McKinley for having "a true wife, true and faithful," and sent $1 toward the debt, adding that the "estimation on which you and your noble wife are held today by all good men is worth many times more than all the wealth of Vanderbilts and Goulds."

In his next story, Kohlsaat quoted the Major telling the trustees, "I am no beggar" and could not assent to a public debt-relief fund. Rather than discouraging further donations from citizens, Judge Day pointed out, the statement yielded more. Meanwhile, allegedly unbeknownst to McKinley, Herrick drew up a cautious form letter to leading Republicans and capitalists, praising McKinley's partisan loyalty and pointing out how he had helped industry while in Congress, and hinting that he now needed help. Hanna and Kohlsaat discreetly made the same case in person, with great success. The Illinois Steel Company donated $10,000. Along with Hanna, Kohlsaat, and McDougall, the millionaires Bellamy Storer, John Hay, Andrew Carnegie, George Pullman, and Philip Armour each gave $5,000; most of the prominent Ohio, New York, and Pennsylvania industrialists, party bosses, and businessmen gave in the range of $1,000 to $2,000. Herrick pressured banks that held the notes to reduce the amount by 10 percent as a form of contribution. As was already the McKinley custom, there was no paper trail of promises or deals while Hanna publicly declared that donations were accepted only from those "who give from *proper motives.*" Within weeks the money was raised, and the McKinleys' assets remained their own.

Editorials in the leading national newspapers universally praised not just McKinley's honesty but Ida McKinley's heroism. As the *New York Times* put it, "In surrendering her private inheritance to meet the demands made upon her husband's signature, Mrs. McKinley withstood the remonstrance of almost all her near friends and relatives. Both Gov. and Mrs. McKinley felt relieved after they had done everything in their power to meet the obligations incurred. . . ."

It was only many years later that Kohlsaat revealed a larger but unstated purpose of the organized effort to defuse the Walker scandal. As he wrote, "the organization to nominate McKinley in 1896 was actively at work. The most minute detail was not neglected. Each man who declared himself favorable to McKinley's nomination was enrolled alphabetically under Mr. Hanna's supervision." He would also disclose that contrary to the perception that McKinley had humbly placed his fate in the hands of his advisers, he was "in constant touch with the situation. . . ." Finally, in conducting his masterful public relations approach to the crisis, Kohlsaat acknowledged that he, Hanna, Herrick, and Day owed much of the success to Ida. "I think that all the gentlemen connected with this affair," he wrote Herrick in a private note, "will appreciate the tremendous leverage we have received by Mrs. McKinley's act."[7]

Those who encountered her privately respected Ida's freedom to voice her opinions frankly. Author Mary Terhune recounted an afternoon drive with the couple. She recalled that Ida launched into effusive praise of her husband for writing her twice daily when they were apart. McKinley, feeling uncomfortable, changed the subject by pointing out sights along the way, but Ida "resumed the topic," the author recalled, going on, point by point, about "his unwearied regard for her health, his tender solicitude, his skill as a nurse, and similar themes. . . ." Finally, the embarrassed Major "checked her," remarking, "*Ida,* my dear!"

After discussing this conversation with an old friend of the McKinleys, Terhune confirmed her suspicion that Ida's monologue was rehearsed. "He owes more to her than the public will ever suspect," the friend confided. "His wife was his guiding star, his right hand. She was, then, a woman of unusual personal and mental gifts, more ambitious for him than he was for himself."

That Ida had tactically focused on McKinley's political rise contradicted the public's perception of her as a woman who submissively sacrificed a quiet home life for her husband's career, an image McKinley had calculated to be so vital to the image he was burnishing for himself that he began staging it like a public performance. Having grown accustomed to the governor's daily ritual of waving from the Capitol plaza to Ida at the window of their hotel suite across the street, state legislators shared an inside joke about the "pose and a love of the dramatic in McKinley that few people realized." As future state senator and President Warren G. Harding later revealed, "This was a daily ritual with McKinley, but some observant persons noticed that this pleasing little exchange of salutation occurred even on days when Mrs. McKinley was known to be in her home in Canton."

McKinley soon adapted this ritual for audiences. Sensing the stare of neighbors, he acted it out in front of Saxton House. Dressmaker Lillie Herbst recalled how "he would stand at the carriage as he was leaving, look back, take off his tall silk hat, and give a courteous bow" to Ida at the window. His first performance of the ritual before a massive crowd was on June 1 on his return to the Ohio Building at the Chicago World's Fair. Governor McKinley began his speech from a podium on stage with Ida listening from a balcony seat, but then scribbled a note, which he then signaled a messenger to carry up to her. The messenger slipped Ida's return message to McKinley on stage. The press assumed that he did this to check if his wife felt too tired to stay when, in fact, nobody ever learned what he wrote. She stayed, but their message exchanges continued. The audience purred in admiration of this public display of private devotion. Just before the next speaker began, McKinley rose to fetch Ida and left with her, which suggested that her final return message indicated her need to leave, thus requiring no apology from him for his early departure. The tactic allowed McKinley to avoid hearing other speakers voice any political disagreement with his own views and the impression of conflict. Similarly, when people waited to have a word with him after a speech he made at the Union League Club, he shrugged and explained that Ida was in the hotel and had "prior claim" on his time, then slipped out without giving offense.

Ida McKinley's role in the Walker scandal had so raised her public profile that during McKinley's June 7 nomination for a second term as governor by the Republican State Convention in Columbus's Grand Opera House, she was honored with a prominent seat on stage, on the left side, surrounded by flowers. When McKinley concluded his acceptance speech, the chairman carried the rose bouquet from the speaker's stand to Ida, while the audience cheered wildly for her.[8]

During the Walker scandal, Ida accepted an invitation to stay for several weeks at the Herrick mansion, prompting her lifelong friendship with Herrick's wife, the former Carolyn Parmeley. Like Ida, she was born into wealth, studied music, toured Europe, and had a taste for luxury items. More importantly, however, both women regarded wealth as less important than love and had married men with lower social status. Carolyn had also bailed out Myron when he became mired in debt. Ida was also drawn to Carolyn by her skill in needlework, and soon she had the Major asking Mrs. Herrick to "crochet a little piece of stripe which she [Ida] can have before her as an object lesson," to "get her a half yard of linen cambric," and even to "buy [a] needle."

The bond with Carolyn grew so strong that she became the first person outside of the family and doctors to be told about Ida's epilepsy. When the Swiss maid Clara Tharin had to leave Ida's service after several years ("by all odds the best maid Mrs. McKinley has ever had," said the Major) to join her husband Charles in New York, Carolyn was enlisted to help find another woman able to fulfill the role of nurse when necessary. "Changing of maids is not pleasant and I hope to secure someone who will stay with me for years, of course this must be someone agreeable to me," Ida told Carolyn pointedly, "in every particular." McKinley was equally cryptic in reference to someone able to cope with Ida's seizures: "You know about what she has to do with Mrs. McKinley, the amount of work and the character of the work." None proved equal to Clara, who would return.

After the Walker scandal, the McKinleys spent an increasing amount of time in Cleveland as guests in the Herrick mansion, and both couples often dined at the mansion of Hanna and his wife Charlotte Rhodes. For several years, they formed a tight group. Like Ida and Carolyn, Charlotte had also helped establish Hanna when he assumed control of her late father's coal and iron business, one of the region's largest. He diversified, buying a Cleveland streetcar company, which he had electrified and expanded, and the lucrative Euclid Avenue Opera House. Gifted in raising money, Hanna formed the Businessman's Republican Campaign Club and successfully managed Joseph Foraker's 1885 election as governor. Three years later he befriended Herrick, who recalled that Hanna, "in his big, kind, domineering way, . . . bossed me around. . . ."

Ida, enjoying Carolyn's company as the first woman friend she made as an adult, was loath to end their visits. Just after Carolyn arrived home after a lengthy stay with Ida, for example, she found a note waiting for her, saying that Ida "wishes that you might have remained with her longer." On another occasion, when Ida cancelled a scheduled Cleveland visit due to freezing temperatures, she had the Major write Carolyn, "But Mrs. McKinley wants you to come down and pay her a visit," without regard that Carolyn would have to endure the bitter cold. Ida once invited herself and two nieces to Carolyn's, adding that if Myron was still convalescing from an illness, "we will go to the hotel." Ida loved the mansion less for its luxury than its warmth, calling it "the home you gave us. . . ." As the Major amplified on her behalf to Myron, "Your home has been so restful to us . . . that it was very hard to break away."

Some weeks before the fall election, Ida McKinley's personal needs began to conflict with her husband's political career. Living in their silk-wallpapered room at the Herrick mansion and supping in the oak-paneled Hanna dining room might comfort the governor's wife, but it would mean the governor would not be at the Cleveland hotel, where he registered as a guest for public record. "Instead of inviting the public to meet him occasionally at his room in the hotel, he goes bowling out Euclid Avenue behind a four-in-hand," a Cleveland newspaper criticized. The amount of time McKinley spent with Ida at the Herrick mansion had begun to worry Ohio Republican leaders, who feared it might affect the re-election. The paper continued, "There have been 'mutterings' and 'cuss words' in private over the unfortunate habits that the Governor has unwittingly gotten into. It is time to call his attention to the facts for his own good." Naming Herrick and Hanna as "bosses" who "shower attention on the Governor," the *New York Times* reported that "The cultivation of his rich friends is breeding trouble for Governor McKinley."

Publicly explaining that his fraternization with Hanna and Herrick was a part of his effort to make Ida's life comfortable might dovetail with the self-sacrificing image he had worked to create for himself, but doing so would also suggest his desire to distance himself from the wealthy contributors Hanna would soon need to curry for McKinley's next campaign. However slight that risk, McKinley was unwilling to test it. While it was an instance of his choosing to make Ida's well-being a priority over his political career, he also correctly appraised that it was a negligible threat to his ambitions and won gubernatorial re-election. Hanna suspended his business enterprises and began to coalesce political and financial support for McKinley's 1896 presidential nomination. Days after the election, the Major took Ida, Kohlsaat, and Myron and Carolyn Herrick to see the comedy *Charley's Aunt* at the Standard Theater in New York and met with National Republican Committee treasurer Cornelius Bliss.[9]

Ida McKinley did not appear at the Major's second gubernatorial swearing-in ceremony on January 8, 1894, although he moved it to the west terrace so she could watch it from their window across the street. Two days later, Bawsel reported she was "not at all well but stood the ordeal bravely." She was troubled, however, by more than a cold. "To her his public career has been a sacrifice," recalled her friend, editor Murat Halstead. "She has felt that he has given far more than he received." The day after the Major won his second gubernatorial election, someone congratulated Ida by saying that his next victory would be winning the presidential election. "She shook her head firmly and said he would not, that the Governorship was his last consent to stand for public office. She meant that," Halstead affirmed, "preferring all the while that he should be a private citizen."

No one incident sparked Ida McKinley's shift from her early ambition to see her Major rewarded with the high honor of the presidency. The recent negative publicity stemming from her friendship with Carolyn Herrick certainly served as a warning that her personal life would be exposed by a presidential campaign. There would be greater potential for the public to find out that she had epilepsy, which would lead to inevitable and unwelcome inquiry about it. Her brother's legal wrangling with his adulterous former mistress was public record and a scandal waiting to explode.[10]

Having survived the Walker scandal with their assets intact, Ida no longer wished to delay what she vaguely referred to as their "trip around the world," to show her husband the places she had seen, and to see for herself new lands. Ida was in awe of India's British viceroy's wife, Harriet Blackwood, known as Lady Dufferin, who led efforts to create professional medical care for India's women, largely through the first corps of professionally trained native women. Ida's interest had been truly captured, however, after attending a Columbus church lecture in 1892, an otherwise routine event that may have had dramatic consequences on world history.

Through a relative of his who was president of the Presbyterian Women's Board of Foreign Missions, Abner McKinley's friend Bill Beer later learned about the lecture. It focused on the Mission's work to alleviate poverty among India's women and children, obstacles to converting the majority Hindu population to Christianity, and the Hindu belief that when a human being dies, his or her spirit is "re-incarnated" into the body of a newborn. The lecturer, Mrs. T. L. Saxton, was a Presbyterian missionary and secretary of the Seward, Nebraska, branch. She was not related to Ida but had a tremendous effect on her.

"Mrs. McKinley seized upon her when she was through with her talk," Beer related, "and then insisting that the missionary come home with her to meet the Governor. She ended by dining with the two and telling them all about India." Mrs. Saxton later recalled the conversation: "It was a curious experience. They seemed positively fascinated by my stories. I have never been a good talker and have always known my deficiencies in conversation. It startled me to have them hanging on my account of my work in the hospitals. . . . Mrs. McKinley said, 'Oh, how wonderful to be like Lady Dufferin and help all those poor children and their mothers!' I did not know of her losses and did not understand how keenly my talks about the Indian children must have hurt her. . . . She began to cry when I left and begged me to come back some other day."

Based on later events influenced by the meeting with Mrs. Saxton, the theory of reincarnation seemed to have given Ida McKinley a newfound sense of hope that Katie and Little Ida might have already begun a new life or soon return somewhere in the world. Though it is impossible to determine to what degree, if at all, she believed in reincarnation, it did offer hope. Perhaps not coincidentally, immediately after Mrs. Saxton's lecture, there was an increasing number of recorded incidents of Ida McKinley calling babies, toddlers, and young children to her side to hug, kiss, dote upon, and comfort, while scrutinizing the children and asking them questions. She usually ended by telling the children about her two daughters, though what she hoped to hear in response cannot be known. Whether or not she was somehow searching to see if she might detect the spirits of Katie and Little Ida, the highly respected journalist Murat Halstead did notice over a period of years that Ida had become an especial "lover of little girls, those of about the age of her own Kate and Ida when they were taken." At least it indicated how traumatic her dual loss had been on Ida some two decades after their demise.[11]

Instead of seeing India in 1894, Ida went to Minnesota, joining the Major on a summer sailing excursion with financier Julius Seymour, his wife, and their little girl, which increased Ida's pleasure. It had been a hard spring as Ida was deathly ill with typhoid. "I fear she will never be the same again," Charlie wrote, adding that her "doctor thinks she will pull through." After a recurrence of seizures, Ida returned to Dr. Bishop's care in February. She remained largely confined to Canton, and by the fall, Ida had stabilized enough to travel.

The nationally popular McKinley strove to please all the state Republican committees that now demanded him as a speaker. Ida would not be left behind. The frenetic lifestyle engaged rather than overwhelmed her. Time and again, she became excited as others validated her frequent claim that McKinley was the greatest figure of their times, a view based as much on fact as adoration. As the nation endured economic depression under Democratic President Cleveland's second term, union strikes and violence among unemployed mobs rose. None offered a more hopeful path to stable employment and better wages than the master of the protective high tariff.

In the fall, McKinley toured sixteen states to deliver some four hundred speeches, and Ida listened to him intently, over and over again, from platform, theater box, or a nearby open window. She adapted to the growing crowds surrounding the Major, but became the center of attention during a March 1895 sojourn south. McKinley had valued Kohlsaat's handling of the press during the Walker scandal and enlisted him to manage the news about his southern tour. In order to disguise the purpose of the tour to mislead McKinley's potential presidential rivals, Kohlsaat again used Ida McKinley as a tactic, implying that her well-known "invalidism" was the reason for the trip, betting that the press would not be indiscreet by asking about specifics. When he left Columbus with them, Kohlsaat announced that the Major had "to take Mrs. McKinley away from the trying March winds of the Ohio climate." McKinley elaborated further, telling a supporter that it was a "little rest and outing." Then a suspicious *New York Times* reporter spoke to friends of Hanna. After "significant nods and winks," the truth "leaked out that the real purpose of the trip . . . was to bring McKinley in close touch with the Republican politicians of the Southern States, and pave the way for the capture of their delegates in the next National Republican Convention."

The speaking "visits" began on March 22 in Thomasville, Georgia, an elite winter colony where Hanna hosted the McKinleys for three weeks. The highlight for Ida was the presence of fellow guest *Chicago Tribune* publisher Joseph Medill, who had been mentored by her grandfather. Kohlsaat also arranged for her to join the Major in currying favor with *Atlanta Constitution* editor Clark Howell, whose critical editorials of McKinley soon turned perpetually kind. Ida effusively greeted one hundred guests at the Hanna welcoming party with "grace and ease" but refused to mingle at a packed reception held at the Mitchell House Hotel, choosing instead to wave to guests from the atrium above. She surely startled many of the white men hosting her husband when she insisted on remaining with the Major in the parlor of their suite so she could speak with African American men who had been chosen as delegates to the forthcoming Republican presidential convention, upsetting the understood social code of the Old South, which discouraged social interaction between white women and black men.

African American delegates from the southern states who were going to the 1896 Republican presidential convention had been chosen by a handful of wealthy and powerful white businessmen, who also determined which presidential candidate they would support. As they did with business and other transactions, these white gentlemen of the Old South brokered their political alliances in sociably hospitable settings like dinners and receptions, ideal venues for the courtly McKinley. As a biographer observed, "The social approach was not only ingratiating to the Southerners, but adapted to the wishes of the candidate."

In contrast, Ida McKinley made no effort to charm the Southerners. She was likely harboring some resentment toward the Major for being less than forthcoming about the real purpose of this sojourn. In fact, the closest McKinley came to doing so was to tell Col. J. F. Hanson of Macon, Georgia, that since "seeking to promote my personal interests is very distasteful to me," he avoided "seeming to seek an office."

McKinley had to confirm his plan to run for president with Hanna in order to solidify the process but not necessarily to Ida just yet. Journalist Victor Murdock, failing to confirm whether McKinley would be running for president, finally approached Mrs. McKinley for some insight, asking her, "Does the Major ever talk the presidency to you?" She replied with a deadpan look, then confessed, "He won't even talk to me about it. We'll have to join forces." Murdock wondered, "Do you suppose he talks to anybody about it?" Ida again looked hesitant before admitting "No, I don't." The Major had not technically misled her about the purpose of the southern trip for it was, in fact, also a rest for her. McKinley knew that her opposition to his becoming president was only a recent shift in her think-ing and that, given an incentive, she might quickly recover her previous and longtime enthusiasm. Consulting Ida before he publicly declared himself a candidate, however, could lead to conflict about it between them. Framing his decision to her as a duty to which he felt obligated but which he could not fulfill unless she gave him support and guidance would provide Ida with the incentive to accede to his ambitions. At some point, as their friend the journalist Halstead termed Ida's compromise, "she yielded to the exigencies of the situation, and as a good wife did what she could to aid him. . . ."[12]

McKinley did consult Ida about a Canton house for rent, which would meet her need for a private home and his for a campaign office. On the issue of space, she was accommodating; for all but their first two and half years together, they had functioned in two adjoining rooms without boundary between home and work. The McKinleys hesitated in signing the lease for this particular house, however, not because of its size or loca-tion, but because of its history. It was the North Market Avenue house in which they had begun their marriage in joy but later abandoned in grief. Nearly twenty-two years to the anniversary of Little Ida's death in the house, Charlie Bawsel wrote, "The McKinleys have not positively engaged that house but they have the [first right of] refusal of it and it is altogether likely they will engage it."

There is no indication of Ida's feelings about the house, but McKinley would never have rented it if she opposed living there. Perhaps return-ing was a victory over its dark associations, and Ida could cease roaming through hotel halls, at least for a year, and put the relics of Katie's rocking chair and Little Ida's infant dresses in the rooms their daughters once oc-cupied. Then, too, Ida may have repressed any fear she had in returning, not wanting to dampen her husband's enthusiasm. "We shall go to house-keeping in a very small home in Canton," the Major gushed to the press.

Their anticipated return on January 24 marked the day before their twenty-fifth wedding anniversary. Such rites of passage were important to both of them. In tribute to the mutual love that had sustained them through tragedy and illness, they planned to celebrate this milestone in the first home they had shared. Inevitably, the symbolism would be exploited for political purposes. From the start, the McKinley Silver Anniversary was planned as a semi-public event over two days. Guest lists were drawn not just from friends and family but wealthy and powerful business and political leaders from the state and the nation and several friendly reporters. Welcoming access and attention to McKinley's "invalid wife" in the "McKinley Home," as the press quickly labeled it, was a concerted effort to convey the message that, however unstated its nature, Ida's disability would not prevent her or distract her husband from fulfilling their official duties.[13]

Massive crowds marked McKinley's final public appearances as governor. Ida, accompanied by nieces Mary, Ida, and Grace, appeared healthy at these last speeches, for example, by not fainting in a sweltering Chautauqua tent packed with 10,000 listeners on August 24. She was oddly absent, however, from his last speech, in Alliance's Goddard Opera House, where he made an impassioned plea to voters to support his proposed funding increase for state institutions serving the orphaned, the aged, and the indigent. Ida sat alone in a private rail car that would take them to Cleveland and was nowhere to be seen when McKinley pointed out that the State Hospital for Epileptics was worthy of more funding. It is unclear if her absence was intentional.

McKinley became more sensitive about the public associating Ida's health problems with epilepsy the closer he came to running for president, even among family. When his sister Helen cautiously wrote him about a State Hospital for Epileptics patient, he did not write back, and his secretary responded instead ("under instructions from the Governor") only to say that McKinley was "very busy campaigning." Mentioning Ida's condition was verboten among her nieces, Mary admitting it was "not discussed," and Kate, a subsequent interviewer wrote, "did not suspect that her aunt was an epileptic, and resented the statement, when she heard it in later life, as a slander spread by the Democrats."

The most specific reference McKinley had put on paper was to Ida's "fainting attacks" over a dozen years earlier in a letter to Abner. Ida McKinley referred to herself as an "invalid," but was never known to say that she had "fits," "seizures," or "spells" in reference to her condition.

As long as Ida's seizures were not witnessed by the press, they would have no compelling reason to report it. There was a respected boundary around private medical details, even about public figures. While the *Washington Post* called her an "invalid," for example, it apologized for doing so, "almost a sacrilege to refer to it in a public print." There was no controlling what was said, however, by friends, neighbors, colleagues, staff, and others who saw Ida having a seizure. Even Amelia Waite, a justice's wife who befriended Ida in 1877, harshly described how spinal damage and seizures had turned Ida McKinley into a "fragile, nerveless creature" and "the wreck you see." There was concern that gossip by those who knew she had epilepsy could spread into "a whispering campaign," intended to emotionally influence voters, a rumor that would only be given credence if the McKinley campaign denied it or failed to address it in the newspapers.[14]

It was not paranoia or shame that drove McKinley to hide the reason for Ida's "fainting." The general public remained ignorant about epilepsy and new scientific findings, though significant, could not yet entirely change people's beliefs about it. Since women were generally expected to set the loftiest example of moral purity, those with epilepsy were judged especially harshly since it was widely believed that excessive masturbation was a cause. Even neurologist Frederick Peterson, who advanced understanding of the disorder, believed that there was a link between masturbation and criminality. By the end of the decade, dialogue about epilepsy became so open that mainstream *Harper's Bazaar* offered parents advice on emergency treatment of seizures in children. Yet two decades later, it was still believed, as Ohio doctor T. W. Shannon wrote, "Epilepsy is a terrible disease to look upon . . . liable to terminate in worse than death—in insanity. . . ."

The inaccurate, but prevailing belief that epilepsy was a form of insanity surely alarmed McKinley. People with a range of mental illness symptoms were classified as insane. Those showing aberrant behavior were deemed a menace and, at best, were institutionalized, derided, or seen as human curiosities. New York City's police commissioner said they should be euthanized. "[E]veryone would be better off if these incurable patients were put out of the way," said Theodore Roosevelt.

McKinley was concerned that the public might associate Ida's condition with insanity, which would emotionally wound her and damage his upcoming campaign. His worry was evidenced by his behavior one night at the theater. McKinley was unnerved by the subject explored in the play *Article Forty-Seven* and how Ida might be observed reacting to it. When he first attempted to escort her out as fake gunshots were fired on stage, Ida just "smiled up at him and kept shaking her head," the star Clara Morris observed. McKinley read the program, discovered it was about a woman's descent into insanity, jumped up in panic, and turned his back to the stage in an attempt to block Ida's view. As Morris recalled, "during all the scene of madness he never sat. Standing with his arm circling the top of her chair, his down-bent eyes never left her face for one moment, and when at the sound of the first gibbering laugh several women in front gave startled little cries, he stooped quickly and laid his hand on hers, though she had made no movement visible to me." At play's end, Ida was fine, but McKinley, mortified, "seized his wife's wrap quickly" and rushed her out, "carefully cloaking his wife."[15]

When the young McKinley first realized the need to ward off questions about Ida's health, he had to learn quickly to be evasive and simply say that Ida was "well," or "feeling better." After twenty years, McKinley prepared his responses to politely discourage further inquiries. Now that he was poised to run for president, their every move was reported in increasing detail. In April 1893, for example, it was printed that the Major brought Ida to New York to "seek an improvement in her health." Seven months later, in naming those who made a trip with the couple, the *New York Times* unwittingly suggested the nature of her disorder by noting that "Dr. Bishop . . . [was] to attend Mrs. McKinley. . . ."

No matter how smoothly McKinley denied the real cause of Ida's disorder, her health worsened. In spring 1894, Charlie Bawsel provided the first report of bandaging, which is indicative of unconscious loss of muscle control and subsequent falling. "You know she is suffering now from a dropsical trouble (confidentially)," he wrote to his aunt, "They keep her bandaged." A year later, McKinley wrote a $200 check to retain Bishop for "professional services and medicines" through at least March 1896. A month before he returned to Canton to begin his presidential campaign, there was a hint of anxiety in his note to the doctor, which enclosed a $150 check. "I wish you would forward to Mrs. McKinley by express a bottle of medicine," the Major wrote Bishop. "Mrs. McKinley is not getting on as well as I wish. She has her attacks, and I hope when I come down to New York to be able to see you."

The December 3, 1895, note, which was the first of several such exchanges between them over the coming months, provides a hint of something disturbing beyond a report of Ida's fluctuating condition. Successfully treating seizures with the salts of sodium, potassium, and ammonium bromide required vigilant observation of symptoms to determine the necessary and frequent adjustment of the powdered dosage. Casually sending the drugs to be used by a patient over several months without examining the patient to determine if the medications were being properly and safely given was negligent at best. Nothing in Bishop's professional history suggests that he was unethical. He was highly esteemed and one of the few physicians in the city whose profile was chosen for inclusion in the prestigious publication, *Representative Men of New York*. Listed as a botanist in the 1884 *Drugs and Medicines of North America* quarterly, Bishop may have overestimated his judgment of the necessary medications for a long-distance patient.

In his note to Bishop, McKinley did not ask the doctor to examine Ida, nor did the doctor suggest it. What they privately discussed is unknown, but Bishop's letters indicate there was an agreement for him to continue sending medication without an examination and for McKinley to send regular reports of Ida's symptoms. When the Major failed to do this as the campaign ensued, Bishop respectfully insisted that McKinley send reports but refrained from suggesting that he should go to examine Ida.

That McKinley did not want Bishop there during the six months before the nomination and the five months before the election might have been because the doctor's presence would have been widely noted. Since at least 1880, Bishop had given Ida bromides when seizures were imminent, and his actions show that he continued to dispense them without professional oversight. Bishop later expressed that he was honored for being entrusted with such a secret, but it was more about his service to the man he supported for president and with whose need for extreme secrecy he readily complied. While Bishop undermined his Hippocratic oath, the Major put his wife's health at risk in his pursuit of the presidency at the expense of Ida's care.

If Ida detected this, she said nothing. Instead, she strove to convince everyone that her happiness continued to be his priority. On January 18 the McKinleys led a parade in an open carriage to the ceremony that began Canton's welcoming festivities. Only the Major got out at the Court House. Ida returned home alone, leaving him to be serenaded by bands, praised in speeches, and celebrated by fireworks. In being "surrounded by many of the friends of their youth," Ida told the *Repository* editor George Frease, "she had never been happier in her life." Left unsaid was that the Major's sole purpose in returning Ida home to her beloved Canton was motivated by his political ambition of taking her away to Washington, fourteen months later.[16]

❧ 6 ❧

"At Home"

PART OF WILLIAM MCKINLEY's brilliance as his own presidential campaign manager was how he indelibly imprinted his persona on the public
and artfully turned the challenge of Ida McKinley's disability into an asset
rather than a hindrance. The first order of business was organizing the
setting for Ida McKinley to become the first presidential candidate's wife
to be deliberately used by a campaign. Carolyn Herrick, working with
the Cleveland purveyors Sterling & Welsh, was charged with acquiring
the basic furnishings of curtains, rugs, wall coverings, a dining room set,
and some parlor chairs. "You can do this," McKinley told her, "better than
we can." Ida and the Major would just "run in to give it . . . our approval."
Ida had no special requests except for their bedroom, asking that the window shades and Belgian lace curtains overlooking the back lawn be heavy
enough to keep out all light, in case she had one of her severe headaches,
and that the industrial odor of textiles be aired out. The room was dominated by a plump chaise lounge, upholstered in silk in her favorite color
of pale violet. French cretonne covered the walls. She bought her own
silver vanity set "at a fair price."

The primary focus was on "the Major's office," and "Ida's parlor," located on the main floor. While both spaces served those functions, their
greater purpose was to act as an event staging area and ceremonial site,
illustrating the McKinley story. Carolyn Herrick's task was to give these
public spaces the illusion of a private home as lines of supporters shuffled
along the main hall, looking into the Major's office and into Ida's parlor.
Both were stocked with items to symbolize their story, like props on a
political stage set. Along with a tangle of telephone and Western Union
wires to keep the candidate in touch with advisers and newswire services,

the Major's office contained props like law books; Civil War battle scene prints; an engraving of Lincoln, Hayes, and Grant; his congressional office's leather chaise ("which we prize very much," he wrote); and a table once displayed at the World's Fair Ohio Exhibition, made of wood inlays from different parts of the state.

The central focus of Ida's parlor was the bay window, where she liked to read, receive guests, and watch the street activity. Within reach were current journals and newspapers, and on small tables and a mantel were framed pictures of her parents, nieces, and nephews. Symbolizing her years as governor's wife when she suddenly increased her theater, opera, and concert attendance were autographed pictures of performers hung on the walls. The largest framed item, two inset pictures of President and Mrs. Hayes, was hung on a wall near the bay window, indicating its importance to Ida's story in recalling her years as a congressional wife. The Hayes picture is clearly visible in a widely distributed campaign postcard of Ida McKinley at her bay window, making her among the first political figures to employ the tactic of placing images of key figures within her own photo. No items were of more curiosity to the public and personal significance to the couple than Katie McKinley's portrait and rocking chair and Ida's own childhood one, though it was soon mistakenly reported as being Little Ida's chair, an error the McKinleys left uncorrected.

The entire house, the *Stark County Democrat* reported, was "so arranged" as to blend the public and private, political and personal. Even the dining room was furnished to serve political purposes. As much as Ida wished their evenings consisted only of supping with each other and, perhaps afterwards, having friends in for her favorite card games euchre or cribbage, the dining table always accommodated financiers, politicians, and journalists. "The family is two," their recently hired African American household manager Fred Floyd quipped, "but the table is set for twelve." Without irony for the fact that the building was furnished to serve more as campaign headquarters than a private home, the Major concluded, "We are looking forward with the greatest zest to our new experience in house-keeping." By mid-January, the last pieces were in place, and the McKinleys assumed occupancy, the Major writing Carolyn, "We got home just three hours ago and are so pleased with our new house." In appreciation, the Herricks were invited to join the family for the McKinleys' anniversary dinner.[1]

Weeks earlier, a thousand engraved invitations to the McKinley Silver Anniversary on Wednesday, February 5, were mailed for either the afternoon or evening reception. On the unseasonably mild day, Canton was animated with buggies conveying guests to the house. The McKinleys were "at home" to friends—and the nation. The front lawn was "brilliantly illuminated" by two locomotive headlights, the stone path to the front steps carpeted. "Thayer's Orchestra" of eight musicians played continuously while the dining room offered chicken salad, lobster salad, ham, olives, pickles, salted almonds, cucumbers, sherbet, petit fours, macaroons, and coffee. Ida, disappointing temperance advocates, had claret wine and an intoxicating "roman punch" available. Guests were directed to a second-floor coatcheck room by Fred Floyd. Downstairs, they fell into a line wending into Ida's parlor, received first not only by Ida's sister Pina and the Major's sister Helen, but also Hanna and Herrick, underlining the event's political purpose. *Repository* editor George Frease then led a few guests at a time to the bay window, where the couple sat encircled by roses and carnations, their favorite flowers; Ida was dressed in her wedding gown.

It was significant that as the February 6, 1896, *Repository* reported, "Each guest was warmly received with a kindly pressure of the hand by both Major McKinley and his lovable wife. . . ." To those who assumed that some unspecified malady was the reason why Ida sometimes did not shake hands, this greeting affirmed that whatever it was, it was neither severe nor permanent. Likewise, having the Major also seated to receive guests made it less obvious that Ida couldn't stand for long. When asked about her health, the Major repeated his practiced line that discouraged any further discussion of the matter: "She is ever happy when surrounded by friends, children and roses."[2]

After two decades of a largely solitary life, Ida was now surrounded by a staff. Local seamstress Julia McCormick was enlisted as her maid, keeping the bedroom tidy since Ida often let visitors peek in. A local catering crew was constantly at the back door, delivering food for receptions and dinners as arranged by Fred Floyd. Will and Margaret Heistand, McKinley's gubernatorial military aide and his wife, maintained the building and grounds. Charlie Bawsel was assigned to New York headquarters, but Ida was comfortable with the campaign staff who worked in the five bedrooms upstairs, which were converted for use as offices. Stenographer Russell Chase, on paid leave from the Massillon Sun Vapor Company, took shorthand notes, typed the Major's remarks to visiting delegations, and then ran them over to the *Repository* for inclusion in stories for the next morning's paper. From the governor's office, James Boyle continued as secretary, and Joe Smith, with his amazing recall of dates and data, handled correspondence. Typist Ada Miller, whom Ida had helped obtain her first job, was the sole woman on staff. Hanna and Herrick, the official campaign managers, often swept in from Cleveland.

On occasion, the campaign finance manager Charles G. Dawes, based in the Chicago headquarters, came to Canton for conferences. A gas industry executive from Evanston, the thirty-year-old had been awed by McKinley since his father had served with him in Congress. He had befriended Hanna in early 1895 and volunteered to help launch McKinley's candidacy, proving instrumental in securing Illinois for him. To enter the inner advisory circle, with access to the Major at home, Dawes first had to pass muster with Ida. McKinley took seriously her endorsement of those she determined were genuinely loyal. When Dawes learned that she shared his love of opera, he took her to see *The Magic Kiss* the day after Christmas. A pair of slippers sent to his wife Caro signaled Ida's acceptance of them both, and they grew close to her.

On at least two known occasions, Ida McKinley attended meetings of the campaign management in Canton and Cleveland, but what substantive role she may have played is hard to determine since she typically offered her opinions only to the Major. When a Chicago political operative sent recommendations to her while the Major was away, Ida reviewed the ideas, including one to hire "valuable allies" who could present the candidate's views among non-English-speaking voters in their native languages. In forwarding the proposals to the Major, she dictated her added suggestion that he "see the party while in Chicago." As one reporter put it, she was "always on the alert to further the political interests of her husband."

McKinley faced several formidable opponents for the Republican presidential nomination, including former Vice President and New York Gov. Levi P. Morton, House Speaker Thomas B. Reed of Maine, and Pennsylvania Sen. Matthew S. Quay. On March 10, the Ohio State Convention endorsed McKinley as its favorite son choice, and the Kansas delegation wired its support for him the same day. Nine days later, Oregon, Wisconsin, Nebraska, North Dakota, Vermont, Indiana, and Illinois followed suit. During the primary elections that would lead to the St. Louis National Republican Convention in June, he did not campaign nationally but shuttled to Cleveland or Chicago for conferences with his senior staff. Since these didn't include public appearances, which typically encouraged Ida's presence, she remained home. This proved fortuitous since after their anniversary, she became "afflicted with influenza." The February 18 *Canton Repository* reported, for example, it was "because of doctor's orders Mrs. McKinley could not attend" a lavish Massillon Club reception for McKinley. What persistently ailed Ida this time, however, proved to be more than the flu or even a period of renewed seizures.[3]

The necessity of focusing on the variables that could win him the nomination was one reason for McKinley's failure during the late winter and early spring of 1896 to keep Dr. Bishop carefully appraised of Ida's condition with frequent reports. His telegrams to Bishop are no longer extant, but the doctor's April 30 reply shows that Ida had an adverse reaction to the bromides he continued to prescribe without examining her:

Your telegram received and I write you the first opportunity to say that I think the last medicine sent to Mrs. McKinley was prepared as carefully and to as good an advantage as what has been sent before, excepting it did not have quite as much added to it to flavor it and to act as an alternative.

I have been working to a certain extent, in the dark, not knowing her true condition exactly, and for that reason, have had to keep as near as possible to the preparations that I have made for some time, hoping in this way, all would go well.

I have had fears that she might not keep as well as she has been because she is liable to have changes in her physical condition, or irregularity of the stomach and bowels, or other causes that would require a change in her medicine for the nervous system.

I have felt that as I received no word otherwise, that she was doing well, and the medicine agreed with her. I send you another bottle today. I have prepared it as I hope will do her great good. If there are any marked changes from what there has been, please give me a good full report, and tell me just how and in what way these changes have taken place, and then I can very quickly adapt her medicine and treatment accordingly.

I have given directions on the bottle sent today, to take as before directed, and that means in such dose as she needs, all depends on the condition of her nervous systems. She may need two or three doses a day, and these doses maybe be either 1 or 1½ teaspoonfuls. I assure you that I will be very glad to advise and direct in any way that I can, and prepare in my laboratory and send such medicines as I think she may need. Do not hesitate to command me.

Without knowledge of the composition and dosage of Bishop's most recent prescription or Ida McKinley's specific reaction to it, the new problems that began appearing in the spring of 1896 cannot be determined.

An educated guess, however, can be made based on findings from one of the first studies on the drug, conducted a dozen years after her death, and the patterns and known symptoms of Ida McKinley's seizure disorder. The effectiveness of bromides in reducing the frequency and severity of seizures diminished over a period of continual use, and a patient would periodically need to reduce or eliminate using the drug entirely for a time. Doing so, however, removed the block to the seizures, which would inevitably resume. In many instances when patients detected a reduction of the drug's effectiveness, they responded by increasing the dosage. This created its own problem, leading to the onset of a second, complicating condition known as "bromism" with symptoms difficult to attribute to the drug overuse unless a patient's condition was carefully monitored and studied. Some seizure symptoms could be briefly eliminated or reduced by other medications, but determining which drugs might affect which symptoms was a process of elimination requiring extreme regulation and careful observation.

The alternative to bromides as an attempt to control seizures was to follow a disciplined regimen of strictly scheduled rest, an absence of disturbances, and vigilant adherence to a bland diet. Reports of Ida McKinley frequently taking rest periods suggest she may have tried this non-medication method. Her determination to share the Major's public life precluded this as a viable option, and he was unable to supervise this regimen while conducting a presidential campaign, nor was he willing to have a nurse do so when he sought to convince the public that Ida was well enough. Yet with Ida exposed to the sensory overload of cheering crowds, blowing horns, and bursting firework displays, the threat that such stimulation might provoke seizures was great. The answer would be found in Bishop's medicine bag in the form of sedative pills in varying potencies.

That Bishop's letters weren't destroyed indicates just how distracted the Major was at the time. It is surprising, given his near obsession with not leaving a paper trail about anything personal. Among the thousands of his papers, only a very few to family members reflect his emotions. He had begun implementing a system to enforce secrecy, developed from working with Hanna. His assistant, J. B. Morrow, explicitly explained how the two men functioned:

> Mr. Hanna himself believed in messengers, rather than in letters. It was so in his business life. Mr. McKinley, after he became President, followed the same safe and cautious plan in his political business. During the campaign for the nomination in 1896 and earlier, Mr. Hanna went

to Canton and Mr. McKinley often visited Cleveland. All important communications were thus oral. After the nomination, Mr. McKinley and Mr. Hanna were connected by telephone. Such was the arrangement in 1896 and in 1900. Candidate and manager talked daily between Chicago and Canton or New York and Washington and Canton. Mr. McKinley was an adroit man. He has been known to have telephonic communications with him taken down in shorthand. . . . It might be said that Mr. McKinley was too crafty to put down in permanent form opinions and information which might arise to perplex him later on.[4]

Among journalists sympathetic to labor, McKinley's alliance with Hanna had already begun to develop conspiratorial overtones, the suggestion being that the candidate merely fronted Hanna's plan to guarantee greater business profits at the expense of the working man. Hanna did raise an unprecedented $7 million ($250,000 from Standard Oil alone) by suggesting that the greater a corporation's contribution, the more closely McKinley would heed its wishes and by depicting the Democratic candidate, messianic populist William Jennings Bryan, as anti-business, but nothing documents a quid pro quo. In contrast, Ida and the Major had refused Hanna's 1891 offer of $10,000 for their "personal expenses," which he had solicited for them as a note in his private papers revealed.

Selflessness was foundational to how McKinley presented his character to voters. As his contemporary Herbert Croly learned, Hanna decided that the best way to demonstrate this abstract concept was through Ida: "He was profoundly impressed by the unfailing patience, consideration and devotion which his friend had lavished on an ailing and difficult wife." In large measure, the way she was used in the handling of the Walker scandal had been a trial run.

Casting Ida as a Victorian invalid swooning on a fainting couch in order to garner sympathy for her husband for political advantage laid bare Hanna's cynicism, but it wouldn't have gone forward without the Major's complicity. While his publicly demonstrated rituals for Ida were stagey, his devotion was authentic. McKinley simply made practical use of his responsibilities, deriving benefit from his acts of love for Ida. Nor was Ida exploited; nobody more stridently publicized the Major's devotion, and it mitigated her guilt at being unable to help in a more active way.

The Ida McKinley story was the largest part of the Major's persona. If exaggerating his kindness was calculated to eclipse his ruthless drive, it was also testament to his genius for manipulating public opinion. Few felt his charm was feigned. "He shook hands with exactly the amount of cordiality and with precisely the lack of intimacy that deceived men into thinking well of him," observed *Kansas City Star* editor William Allen White.[5]

With its tale of disability and devotion, McKinley's marriage was lead witness to the candidate's character. The first sign of it came the week before the convention in a June 4, 1896, *New York Independent* editorial by Kohlsaat colleague Charles Emory Smith, himself editor of the *Philadelphia Press.* In listing the reasons why he predicted McKinley would win the nomination, along with his advocacy of the protectionist tariff and the gold standard without abandoning the silver standard, Smith named his "beautiful character . . . sweet and spotless life," elaborating that "His domestic life is a tender romance which touches every true heart. . . ."

Although Dawes noted that Ida was still unwell during a May 9 Canton meeting, two weeks before the convention, she made a startling public demonstration of her strength by striding two blocks down North Market Avenue on the Major's arm for an evening ice cream at McCoy's Confectionery. If this didn't reverse any Canton gossip about the true state of her health, the fact that she then insisted on climbing a flight of stairs to see the owner's newborn daughter certainly did. Learning the child was still unnamed, she piped up, "Then call her Ida Mae." It was the sort of anecdote locals were sure to share with national reporters about to swell Canton that summer for the intended front-porch campaign.

The McKinleys followed tradition by not appearing at the convention, which began on June 16. In closing his nominating speech for McKinley, chairman Joseph Foraker referenced the impact of their idealized marriage: "His personality will carry into the presidential chair the aspirations of voters of America, of the families of America, of the homes of America. . . ."[6]

The Major was awakened early on June 18 when the phone in their bedroom began ringing. It was Hanna calling on a direct line from the convention with the promising forecast. McKinley dressed and dashed to his office to check incoming newswire reports, humming the Scottish air "Bannockburn." He regaled relatives, advisers, neighbors, and friendly reporters who dropped in with anecdotes from past conventions, explaining the nomination process to his nieces. Sitting on the front porch, he saluted well-wishers who cheered him and jumped up to usher his sisters Helen and Sarah in when they arrived, asking, "Is mother coming today?"

Distracted, he had forgotten that his mother and wife were making a noontime appearance with the new Canton Relief Corps, a group of local volunteers organized to help the anticipated crowds that summer with housing, first aid, and dining needs. He was also too distracted to note Ida's upset mood as she walked up the path, carrying home a massive bouquet from the event.

Ida sat at the head of the table during two o'clock luncheon, next to reporter Murat Halstead. He found her "pensive," with what he gently termed a "pronounced personality." At some point during lunch, Ida let loose with her feelings to him: "She has not been in favor of the Presidential business. Of course, she wants her husband to win now, but she would rather he had not been drawn into the stream of events that is bearing him on to higher destinies, for the tendency of the great office will be to absorb the Major's attention, so that she can hardly, however great his devotion, have all the time in his society she would fondly claim as her own."

After lunch, when a friend made a religious reference with which she was unfamiliar, Ida had a Bible fetched, but when he cracked that the Major was "too busy a man to get acquainted with the inside," she humorlessly snapped back, "He does, indeed, know the inside of his Bible—no man better, I assure you and I speak that which I do know." Meanwhile, the Major was on the phone in his office, learning that he had been nominated on the first ballot with 661½ votes; Reed got 84½, Quay 61½ votes, and Morton 58 votes. He padded over to Ida's parlor, where she sat with his mother, bent over to kiss and tell her, "Ida, Ohio has just nominated me."

Within minutes, Cantonians rushed down to surround the McKinley house. They were soon joined by trainloads of nearby revelers, blowing whistles, throwing firecrackers, drinking beer, singing, and building bonfires as night set in. Rowdier crowds pressed up to look into the windows, destroying the flowerbeds and grass and breaking off bits of the picket fence for souvenirs. Surveying the wreck in the morning, Ida shrugged, "It will be either the poor house or the White House."[7]

Days later, Americans got to know Ida through her first extensive interview. A week before the convention, Charles Smith, the *Philadelphia Press* editor, in continuing his support of McKinley, assigned reporter Harriet Dell Hallmark to interview Ida. McKinley's formal greeting of Hallmark perhaps suggested the tone he assumed the interview would take. When she offered to wait until Ida was free of some visiting friends, he pontificated, "Then I very much fear you would never see her. It is the penalty of her geniality that she gladly pays."

Approaching Ida at her bay window, Hallmark was overcome by the scent of roses, massive arrangements that had been sent for Ida's birthday three days earlier. As the friends rose to leave, the Major lifted one of their children to kiss Ida. "[T]he children seem drawn to me because they know I love them so," she explained, making the point politically relevant by wittily using tariff jargon, "Reciprocity is great."

Silently dominating the room was the portrait of Katie, her angelic smile looking down on her mother. Though noting the two children's rocking chairs, Hallmark didn't get into the story of Ida's "lost girls," except as an aspect of the most detailed references Ida ever made to her disabilities.

Looking onto North Market Avenue from her window, Ida was distracted by passing bicyclists, but while expressing an interest in cycling, she admitted it was "quite beyond" her "as I can't even walk." The observation led to the interview's most sensitive discussion—her health. "Her physical weakness is no skeleton in a closet," Miss Hallmark decided, "She speaks of it to all. . . ." Ida demonstrated by rising, then hesitating and nodding for her nearby gold-topped mahogany walking stick. "You see," she said, "I am not strong." This was, to Miss Hallmark, "the only sign of invalidism." She related the explanation Ida provided, writing that the "muscles of her limbs are too weak to allow her to walk" and, following Little Ida's birth, "she has never stood upright or walked without assistance." Whether Hallmark misunderstood, or Ida exaggerated for a more dramatic account, it was untrue. There was no mention of neurological issues, the closest suggestion being Ida's frequently severe headaches and forthright explanation that she wore her hair short because she "did not feel quite strong enough to bear the hairpins."

Either Ida spoke off the record or others talked to the reporter about her political influence on the Major, for Hallmark depicted her as far more decisive than previously presumed, writing that McKinley relied on Ida's "sound judgment of wide-mindedness, of a good insight into men and affairs and the causes that condition both." She declared Ida to be "his confidante and helpmate," attributing her skill of analyzing political and business figures from years of overhearing them confer with the Major at home: "The advantages she has been given as a wife of a public man and the advantages fate gave her of remaining quiet . . . have developed that inborn trait to a wonderful degree—to an alarming degree, I should say, to the person who wished to gain by deceiving her. . . . The person worth observing is observed by Mrs. McKinley."

On the subject of how her disability might hinder her ability to host White House social events, Hallmark (or her sources) patently lied, claiming Ida was "accustomed . . . to constant entertaining. And her entertaining, mind you, is not confined to their Canton home. . . . [A]ll over America she has boundlessly entertained. . . ." In fact, the Major arranged any dinners they hosted in Washington and Columbus with their residential hotel kitchens. Easier to disprove was her exaggeration of once being a substitute First Lady: "I've tried that once and have ever since said I never wanted any longer duration of it. . . . I was Lady of the White House for two weeks during Mrs. Hayes's absence. Mrs. Hayes and I had always been on most cordial terms, and I was as often at the White House as she was at our hotel. So she persuaded me to stay there during a fortnight of unavoidable absence on her part during the [social] season."[8]

Ida's remarks to Hallmark about her husband were uniquely frank, even blunt. She stated that his early family life was not idyllic since "He ran away to the army when he was sixteen," and that his "strong bond" was with Hayes, not his own father. More startling was her remark that the Major was not the great love of her early years: "Not at all." Hallmark was struck by Ida's "common sense." Widely reprinted after appearing in the *Philadelphia Press,* the interview gave the public an unfiltered view of Ida McKinley that emphasized her independence rather than dependence, showing how she refused to be limited by her health problems. Hallmark concluded that Ida lived "singularly" and compared her to the feminist novelist Elizabeth Stuart Phelps. Mrs. McKinley's interview with Hallmark, however, may have been a bit too honest as she was not allowed to give any more interviews after that. After failing to secure an interview with Ida, Willa Cather of *Home Monthly* magazine had to sneak into a luncheon to speak directly with her. Ultimately, the real Ida was of less value to the campaign than the persona it shaped of her.[9]

Ever since Lincoln conducted his campaign from the front porch of his personal residence in 1860, numerous presidential candidates did likewise. None, however, outright refused to consider a speaking tour by whistle-stop train as did McKinley. Among Canton residents, the "favorite reason" for this was "his desire to be near Mrs. McKinley." Reporters concurred, the *Seattle Post-Intelligencer* explaining that "Mrs. McKinley is not adapted to days of handshaking nor to bows from car platforms." By never denying this was the reason, McKinley was yet again credited for putting his wife before his ambition and yet again, Ida served as his unassailable alibi. The real reason, McKinley told Hanna privately, was that he did not want to put his oratory skills on wide public display, knowing he would suffer in comparison to his emotive Democratic rival William Jennings Bryan. Even after Bryan gained on him, McKinley refused to whistle-stop, believing it "an acknowledgement of weakness." Adviser Julius Whiting especially supported his decision not to debate since "it would be absurd to give Bryan a chance at the women's crowds which would gather to hear McKinley." In fact, the "women's crowds" would come to gather at Canton in large part to see Ida McKinley, who was purposely used in direct appeal to them.[10]

While only women residents of Utah, Wyoming, and Colorado had been granted the right to vote, those without it still had an impact on shaping public discourse on election issues like alcohol temperance, public education, and racial equality, and most aligned with the Republican Party. It was the first to seat a woman as an "honorary delegate" at a presidential convention and elect a woman as an Electoral College member. In 1888, Hanna coalesced this support by funding the creation of the National Women's Republican Association, members of which, at the least, implored male relatives to vote for McKinley in 1896. As reported in the November 2, 1896, *Rock Springs Miner,* its president, Judith Ellen Foster, stumped for him in Wyoming, concluding, "McKinley is the embodiment of Americanism, and wears the white flower of a blameless life; is it any wonder women support such a party and such a man?"

Thousands of women in Republican clubs marched to the McKinley house that summer, and a ribbon badge with Ida McKinley's image was created to designate them as supporters. The first campaign event specifically organized to promote the candidate's wife was a reception given by 5,000 Stark County women to honor Ida and her mother-in-law. It was held in a vacant mansion, decorated with palms, ferns, flowers, and flags. Local writer Alice Danner Jones introduced the two Mrs. McKinleys and made the welcoming address from a balcony, remarking to Ida:

> He is bound to you by ties even closer than those which bind him to his country, and we believe he will say with us that the better part is of your making. . . . Mrs. McKinley, ever twenty-five years ago you prophesied Canton's future pride in Canton's young attorney. . . . [Y]ou linked your life with his. . . . Canton has been proud of you. . . . So purely womanly is your wifely devotion, so in sympathy with his every interest has your life always been. . . . Women such as you have given to our nation in the past. . . . Lucy Webb Hayes was her husband's truest helper; Jackson deferred to the opinions of his idolized wife. . . . We women believe that the importance of pure living is higher than all, and are satisfied that should you be called to preside over the destinies of the nation we shall have a man at the head with a character so pure. . . .

Inside, Ida sat on a raised platform inaccessible to handshakes as the line passed by.[11] She made three similar appearances through July, joining the Major on the front porch to welcome a delegation of Cleveland professional women. "We cannot all hope to win Presidents for husband," the group leader remarked in her speech to Ida, "but your example as a wife is before us." Ida joined former First Lady Lucretia Garfield two days later at the Cleveland Centennial Celebration's "Woman's Day," and then attended the "Notification Day" ceremony on her lawn the next day, the tradition in which candidates officially accepted the nomination after endless speeches. A luncheon, parade, and fireworks followed, setting the pattern for the front-porch campaign events. As usual, Ida was laden with rose bouquets.[12]

While known as a wise judge of political figures who entered her husband's sphere and of the content and flow of his speeches, Ida McKinley's interest in political issues was limited to how they affected the Major. There is no record, for example, of her addressing his initial support of the gold standard as a way of maintaining a higher value to the dollar. He also supported globally widening American markets, annexing the Hawaiian islands, building a canal in Central America, and achieving freedom for the oppressed people of the island of Cuba, a possession of a tyrannical Spain. Ida defended whatever his views were. "She is such a devoted wife," a friend told a reporter, "believing so completely that what her husband does is right, and encouraging him in doing so, that I am perfectly convinced that if the Major were to enunciate a doctrine of free trade, Mrs. McKinley would be his first convert."

Despite a pro-McKinley booklet's assertion that she was "reading the newspapers and keeping up with movements of the time," Ida's illness in the months leading up to the conventions had isolated her. When Missourian Richard Bland visited, she remembered him only as a congressional colleague of the Major, and he had to remind her that Bryan had recently defeated Bland for the Democratic nomination. Her privileged existence also contributed to her failure to grasp the reason why Bryan was so popular with the working class, who were then enduring a record 20 percent unemployment rate. A plea to her for help from a cousin whose son and his family were suffering due to his long-term unemployment was marked as having been read, but went unanswered.[13]

However, as a former bank manager, Ida did fully comprehend how the entire nation suffered under cost increases. With the price of wool especially high, she watched for sales before making purchases, asking Carolyn Herrick to stop at the Hoover Higbee Department Store to buy her "two

combination woolen suits of white underwear," since "I see by the paper
they are selling these very cheap." As the wife of a man who built his reputation on protecting American industry, she also fully comprehended the
economic and labor impact of foreign-trade imbalances and protectionist
tariff rates, a central campaign issue. To most women and men alike, tariff
increments of often a half-cent on raw materials remained abstract. To
help others grasp the issue, she had begun displaying practical American-
made household items in her living spaces since 1891, explaining underly-
ing manufacturing costs of each item in laypeople's terms.

L. W. Busbee was impressed after one such demonstration, reporting,
"She is heroic in her devotion to his work and her home has many tro-
phies of protection to American industries. There are vases and other
ornaments, the first products of American manufactories made possible by
the McKinley bill and everything about her room is American in manufacture. . . . [H]is wife believes in American industries and . . . give practical illustration of this by their own lives." It further illustrated how both
McKinleys used their private home for political purpose.[14]

Supporters visiting Canton who failed to gain entry into the house still
encountered Ida's Courtney Photographic Studio picture on cake plates,
jackknives, posters, paperweights, and tea towels, manufactured by Canton's
Novelty Cutlery Company and Bonnot Glass Company. Duebler Jewel-
ers crafted an Ida McKinley spoon, engraving the bowl with the White
House and the tip of the spoon handle with her face. A local confectioner
played on words under a picture of the front-porch house for its box of
"*McKinley Home*-Made Candy." Even the Sponge Crepon Company ran
a magazine ad with her maid claiming that Ida used its linen sleeve linings
in her own dresses.

The flow of humanity pouring into Canton on special-discounted
railroad rates arranged by Hanna glimpsed her when the Major gave one
of his speeches to various visiting groups, "an interested auditor of probably every speech that he made," the *Stark County Democrat* recounted. Ida
even became the first presidential candidate's spouse seen in a "moving
picture" newsreel. A Biograph Film Company employee, hand-cranking
a camera to capture the Major's walk to the lawn, caught Ida in the background, fanning herself on the porch.[15]

Although avoiding the largest delegations like the 25,000 who streamed
through the house to "call" on the Major on September 26, Ida made
appearances for groups that especially wished to meet her, such as the
Cleveland L'Overture Rifle, an African American militia, and a group

of women stenographers, who declared, "Mrs. McKinley, you are always mistress of our hearts. We want to see you mistress of the White House." Delegations invariably brought her massive floral arrangements, often using their state flowers, and presented them with a flourish of "best wishes for her health," as one Indiana group leader declared. The flowers, briefly displayed in the house, were then delivered to patients in area hospitals at her direction. She did keep for herself, however, hundreds of campaign buttons and ribbons. "The badges presented me are usually more elaborate than those worn by members of the visiting organizations," Ida told reporter Georgia Hopley. "They are made expressly for me as you see, are both elaborate and handsome, some are really valuable. . . . I shall put them away with other badges I have received during the public career of my husband. I have a number quite as handsome as these."[16]

No matter how crowded her home became, Ida was animated in the presence of little girls visiting with their parents. After a girl from Virginia recited some of the Major's speech she had heard that day, which Ida had missed, she awarded the child one of her prized campaign badges. Some observed how the sight of two sisters together, of any ages, especially captured her attention. Canton sisters Philippina and Louella Seesdorf always made a point of visiting Ida together, as did Emma and Gretchen Groetzinger. She was less enamored with boys. Listening from an open window as the Major spoke to McKinley Democrats, she spotted twin toddlers, but ignored the boy on his father's lap to focus on the girl, and "beckoned the mother to bring her up to the window," a *Repository* reporter noted. "She took the child in and caressed it, and pinned on its little coat a bright-colored little badge." Moses Belden, a local boy whose parents knew the McKinleys, never forgot her snapping when she saw him about: "Here's this Belden again!" She also was less patient with boys, chiding the unsure son of one distant relative, "Aren't you coming over to shake hands with your cousin?"

Living again in the house where Katie had been born and lived seemed to make Ida feel her presence all the more. During children's visits to the house, which Ida encouraged, she never failed to point out Katie's picture to them. Willa Cather reported in *Home Monthly,* "and then the children are all very quiet, for they know that that is the picture of Mrs. McKinley's own little girl who died a long time ago." Twenty-one summers after her death, it was as if Katie McKinley had resurrected on North Market Avenue. Ida eagerly permitted Katie's only picture to be used in press stories about the Major, and her image was soon mass-printed, sold on postcards in street turnstile racks. A Canton Novelty Company's composite postcard posed the girl between her parents, suggesting to thousands of visitors who didn't know better that Miss Katie might soon be First Daughter of the White House. Ida encouraged this. When showing off her most prized campaign badge, a two-sided image crafted especially for her, she bragged that it showed "my husband, and little girl," as if Katie were still alive.[17]

The more malicious elements opposing the Major, ignorant of the fact that Katie McKinley was dead, even tried to politically exploit her. The anti-papist American Protective Association, harboring a grudge against the former governor for his refusal to fire Catholic state prison guards, now declared that Katie and Little Ida McKinley were hidden in a convent, placed there by their secretly Catholic mother, which was ironic considering Ida's wariness of Catholicism. It was not the only whisper spread about Ida. "I think this low campaign against Mr. and Mrs. McKinley ought to be dealt with," wrote supporter Dudley Evans to Abner's friend Bill Beer. "The offices report that scandals are in circulation in Missouri and Kansas. Several men of some intelligence have asked me if it is true that Mrs. McKinley is an English spy. These reports prejudice a certain kind of second rate citizen intensely." Equally inexplicable was the gossip that Ida was of mixed race.

Evans and Beer were members of the McKinley League, a national network of powerful operatives that, among other forms of support, tried to track and thwart damaging whispering campaigns in different regions. Beer was on its organizational committee and though largely he solicited contributions, he proved so good a "confidential man" that "Mr. H[anna]" wanted to hire him as a private aide, according to Canton Leaguer Julius Whiting.

It was through Whiting that Beer had first alerted Canton headquarters to a rising "tale" about Ida McKinley among Westerners, which led them to ask, "[W]asn't there something funny about his [McKinley's] wife?" Whiting passed on the "entirely personal . . . things" being said about Ida to Hanna through an intermediary. He reported back to Beer that Hanna "seems quietly confident" that undecided voters would not vote against McKinley because of the rumors about his wife. Hanna's brother Melville confirmed this to finance director Cornelius Bliss: "We are all of the opinion that it would do harm to answer the slanders on Mrs. McKinley. My brother thinks it would make the matter worse." Given the sensitivity and personal nature of the issue, however, it was a higher authority than Mark Hanna who decided not to acknowledge "the scandal," but rather McKinley himself.[18]

The issue, however, was not limited to how distant voters perceived Ida's condition but also what the delegations coming to Canton saw of her and surmised. McKinley sought to prevent the possibility of Ida having a seizure in public by limiting her exposure. She always appeared before crowds from inside, positioned at an open window or on the porch, about two feet from the front door. According to Beer, visiting delegations' wish to witness McKinley's devotional ritual partially stemmed from a prurient desire to scrutinize Ida. "[A]lthough Mrs. McKinley was not displayed," he would relay to his son, "the curiosity of the deputations as to her health annoyed McKinley so acutely that several times he had her driven off to the farm" in Minerva, which she still owned with Pina and George. Her only other escape from the unrelenting scrutiny was attending small concerts in the private home of friends or those events she hosted. Within the guarded confines of home, however, guests might still see her endure a sudden seizure. Neighbor Frank Dannemiller witnessed one such incident in the house "when a seizure came on and McKinley threw a veil over her head, then removed it when the spell was over."[19]

Evidence that Ida McKinley's seizures had resumed by the fall campaign comes from Dr. Bishop's September 22 response to a call from the Major. Reference to her appetite indicates that McKinley had not complied with the physician's insistence on reports about her changing condition:

I have been anxious in regard to Mrs. McKinley, and how she would stand the great strain upon her nervous system, and the daily excitement of so many calling to see you and herself. If it were not for her great composure and control of her surroundings, I would have greater anxiety for her good health. I have decided to make a change in her medicine, and this change I hope, will help her to control and overcome the attacks that you tell me trouble her. I hope they are mild in their nature. I see her appetite is good, and I judge by this, that her physical condition is all that is desired.

Please favor me by noticing the results of the change I have made in the medicine, and if everything is not favorable, inform me at once. You are aware that no doctor can always tell what results will follow in giving any medicine until we watch the effects.

I will be pleased to learn all I can regarding her nervous condition, as this will help me to do for her the greatest good possible. It is not necessary for me to say that I am exceedingly anxious to do her great good, and in so doing, have her and your gratitude, and also the appreciation

of many thousands of good friends and well-wishers. Remember me
kindly to Mrs. McKinley, and I shall be anxious to hear again here long
how she is after taking the medicine I forward today.[20]

By Labor Day, McKinley realized that it was wiser for them to manage
a press release on the matter rather than risk having the media publish a
legitimate news story about the "whispering" and find the word "epileptic" in reference to Ida. He also recognized that a defensive press statement
might legitimize gossip or provoke further press inquiry and leave him in
the untenable position of either confirming the truth or lying about it.

Another concern was the information about her in magazine profiles
and various McKinley campaign biographies that appeared that fall. Some
accurately showed her as far from demure while others dismissed her disabilities; both images diminished the impression of McKinley as martyr.
Others went too far in declaring how desperately dependent she was on
him, and one came close to revealing the truth about her seizure disorder.

Their friend Murat Halstead's *Life and Distinguished Service of Honorable
William McKinley and the Great Issues of 1896* made Ida's immobility seem
like a pulled muscle. *Lives of William McKinley and Garrett Hobart,* by journalist Henry Russell, posed Ida as politically assertive: "From the beginning of his Congressional career to the present time, she has . . . aided him
by her practical advice . . . been of great assistance to her husband in his
political life. . . . She is, like her husband, a great reader of newspapers and
is a close student of them, and of public opinion as evidenced by them."
His assertion that she was "anything but the conventional invalid" was
correct, yet he flipped the truth by claiming the Major hadn't wanted to
run for president, and that "Mrs. McKinley did everything in her power
to overcome this reluctance."

Former reporter Robert Porter secured a book contract for *Life of William McKinley* after convincing the Major's aide James Boyle to lend his
name as coauthor, suggesting an exclusive. Porter wrote that while Ida
McKinley's "physical disability" didn't "interfere with her husband's career," she was a "nervous, high-strung woman." His effort to assure readers
that Ida had a normally functioning brain was clinical, based on his study
of her "remarkably well-shaped head" and face, although he said her eyes
were "underscored by dark shadows."[21]

Periodicals were no better. Their friend, *Repository* editor George
Frease, went so far in seeking to prove McKinley's devotion to Ida that
it suggested spousal duty would take priority over that to the presidency:

"No matter . . . how important the demands upon his time, the least call from Mrs. McKinley, indicative that his wife wanted his presence or was not properly attended instantly caused him to drop anything or everything under consideration and rush to her side." The pamphlet "One of the People" claimed Ida had been cured of her "serious physical ailment" and kept her hair short for a "girl-like appearance." *Demorest's Family Magazine* came close to describing her seizures, saying she suffered from "the continuing results of nervous shocks."[22]

Finally, McKinley decided that Ida's story would be told "officially" and authorized the publication of her biography, the first one written about a candidate's wife. Just after Labor Day, the Home Magazine Press released its booklet, "The Sketch of the Life of Mrs. William McKinley," spinning facts into Victorian euphemism. Its trusted author was former *Repository* editor Josiah Hartzell, a McKinley League member who had known Ida since childhood and reported her wedding for the paper. Pina was a likely source for facts and pictures, her daughter Mary then keeping company with Hartzell's son Ralph. The objective was to reinforce the Major's devotion as the bulwark of his character and to dispel the growing rumors about Ida's "nervous" ailment.

Most important, Hartzell confirmed her spinal damage and likely concussion from an accident, writing "she reeled and fell, it is true." To address her seizure disorder without using the word "epilepsy," he carefully chose qualifiers. Her "nervous system" was "almost" damaged, the "most eminent specialists" unable to revive "perfect" health. Her cognitive abilities were unharmed, since she "talks well and listens well." Whether Hartzell had delicately asked Pina what ailed her sister is unclear, but he reported, "There is no defined malady or disease." He used photos to discount previous written insinuations that her "personality" was affected by the nervous disorder: "It is true that certain writers endeavor, by printed words and phrasings, to depict her features and peculiarities. Such descriptions only leave a confused idea, or no idea at all of personal appearance, while photo-engravings, such as are found in these pages, speak so instantly and clearly to the eye as to leave nothing more or better to be desired."

Hartzell soaped his prose to suggest he would reveal what had been sacredly withheld until now, when the press and public had a right to know. "In all the annals of chivalry there is no more beautiful example of manly self-sacrifice and of womanly gratefulness," he went on in confessional style. "It was too sacred a thing, in anybody's case, to be bandied about in the public prints. Nevertheless, in these newspaper times, it was inevitable that it should get into print; but for the honor of the press it must be said that these things have only been alluded to with the greatest respect, even by Major McKinley's political opponents."[23]

Ida McKinley was genuinely indifferent toward any press about herself, as long as it did no harm to the Major's reputation. She expected no less from Hanna. Unknown is her reaction to a *New York Journal* story by Alfred Henry Lewis. In it he insinuated that Hanna had either duped her into giving him control of her assets during the Walker scandal (which Hanna still held) and thus kept McKinley beholden to him or, worse, that Ida's declaration that she would sacrifice her fortune to pay the Major's debts was just a ruse to win public sympathy and solicit contributions. Ida's opinion of Hanna is hard to discern but was perhaps suggested by the fact that among the select guests at his September 27 wedding anniversary dinner, the McKinleys were not on the list. Two weeks prior there was another clue. "She is more than ever interested in Mr. McKinley's speeches," the September 13 *Seattle Post-Intelligencer* suggestively reported, "and Mr. Hanna's maneuvers. . . ."

Among Lewis's greatest offenses was his October 24 editorial, "Who Is the Anarchist?" He ranted that if Hanna's corporatism helped elect McKinley, dark, reactive forces would be unleashed. "Does it occur to him that a calamity might happen more damaging to the cause of the Republicans than any of the unfortunate trials to which it has been subjected?" Lewis warned, "The murder of the martyred and beloved Lincoln . . . the assassination of Garfield. . . ."[24]

Ida McKinley suddenly fell ill the evening after the article appeared. The campaign may have taken its toll on her, a friend pointing out, "Even were Mrs. McKinley in vigorous health all this would have been considered most trying to patience, wearing to nerves and destruction of vital power." She was indisposed when the last Women's McKinley Club called on her October 27. As the hours before Election Day ticked away, what may have been the real reason for her resistance to the Major becoming president began to emerge. She had begun to fear his being elected just as subversive elements made good on their threat to assassinate world leaders, killing the French president, the Korean empress, and the Persian king in three successive years since 1894.

On Election Day, McKinley voted early and took a long walk. His victory confirmed, he took Ida to visit his mother, and the old woman knelt in prayer for them both. Ida McKinley, however, did not take comfort in a belief that God would answer her prayers. Friends saw how "greatly distressed" she was that night, one suggesting to reporter Edna Colman that Ida McKinley "never really knew peace of mind when he was out of her sight, for they were satisfied she had a premonition of his fate." McKinley put his arm around Ida. "This little woman is always afraid someone is going to harm her husband," he chuckled to their guests. "Oh, Major," Ida McKinley shot back at him in front of everyone, "they will kill you, they will kill you!"[25]

❧ 7 ❧

Silver Lights

Two weeks after the election, Ida McKinley proudly ventured out for her first carriage ride next to the president-elect. In the times ahead, she would relish daily rides not just as her sole outdoor exercise, but often because they were her only time alone with the Major. On Thanksgiving, he even rigged up his own buggy to drive her into the country. The campaign over, he was especially attentive to her again. Ida could have no idea that the beloved man seated beside her was actually endangering her.[1]

During her recent setback, the Major again ignored Dr. Bishop's warning that regular reports on Ida's condition were critical to her care. Only when she worsened after taking a new drug composition did McKinley contact Bishop in a panic. The usually pliant physician responded to the next president with polite exasperation:

> I am sorry that the last medicine sent does not seem to agree with Mrs. McKinley. I prepare and send some and send it just as near as possible to what she took formerly, and what she thinks agrees with her the best.
>
> Pardon me for saying that I feel I am treating her under a good many disadvantages, one of which is the lack of information that I have before me in regard to her physical and nervous condition. It is a great mistake for any patient to think that they can take one kind of medicine all the while and have good results follow. It is well known to every physician that certain medicines have to be changed according to conditions that may arise in the patient.
>
> I have been anxious to learn such information as I desire to help me in carrying out Mrs. McKinley's treatment successfully. I feel that some one should assume the responsibility of writing me from time to time,

98

and telling me how she is in regard to her appetite, how she sleeps, her general physical condition; also how much of the medicine she takes at each dose and how many doses each day, and inform me fully in regard to her nervous condition, and if her nervous troubles take on an aggravated form, tell me how often it occurs, and the nature of it and in this way, I could very quickly tell what would be the best medicine to send her, and what directions to give with the medicine.

I do not say this in any spirit of murmuring, but I say it because I feel that interest in her good health and future welfare; that I don't want anything neglected that will be for her good; and may I kindly ask that some one who has the time, and will take the interest to write me, and give me the information that I need and in this way, help me so I can help her. I do so hope this medicine I send her will have good results. Don't allow her or any one interested in her to feel that the medicine sent her are to be the same at all times, but are prepared according to the information received regarding her physical and nervous condition.[2]

Letters Ida received were considerably more pleasant. "We have looked, with reporters, after twilights into your windows and have seen you reclining on the lounge while your husband read aloud interesting letters. . . . Having reached the topmost round of success your daily life is food for comment by the daily press," a Colorado woman wrote. "We with your many friends are glad to know your health continues to improve and though for many years an invalid you have not been idle. I firmly believe that the love and faith and confidence in which you have held your husband has contributed as much as any other single influence to place him where he now stands." With more worry but no less affectionate was a letter from her old Brooke Hall teacher, Harriet Gault. "I have seen by the papers that you have been ill recently," she wrote. "I have been afraid that the tremendous excitement in which you have been placed might exhaust you." She also received a promise "to do all things for your comfort" from Jennie Hobart, wife of vice president-elect, New Jersey Gov. Garret Hobart.[3]

That every slight turn of her health now merited press coverage was just one part of a new reality for Ida. Ida, leaving for Chicago to stay with her cousin Mary McWilliams, was trailed by a band of reporters who discovered on the train that she intended to wear only American-made clothing as First Lady and would buy them all at Marshall Field Department Store. They failed to learn that it was because of huge discounts she would receive through McWilliams's husband, a store manager. The

Major, beset by separation anxiety, telegraphed her each morning, called each night, and wrote on her first day in Chicago. "This day has been very much like all the days since the election—many, many visitors . . . but you are greatly missed I assure you. I hope you will keep well & come back greatly benefited and have that part of your wardrobe provided which was your special mission."

Even in the privacy of the McWilliams home, however, Ida was confronted with the fact that she was a public figure in her own right. On her first night there, she was awakened by a midnight serenade of strangers. Days later, the doorbell was repeatedly rung by a steady stream of schoolgirls she felt compelled to welcome for two hours. Each time she left for a dress fitting, the press, who were keeping vigil across from the house, followed in hot pursuit. "I am sorry that you have been so besieged by newspaper people," the Major wrote her, "but congratulate you upon your wisdom in denying yourself to them. You will probably be let alone now."[4]

Ida McKinley had one of the happiest holiday seasons of her life that year, reveling in an overnight visit by Carolyn Herrick and having old friends from Congress stop in Canton on their way home from Washington. Ida breezed off alone to a card-party luncheon and dinner parties, made twice-daily drives with the Major, and was welcomed at friends' homes. At forty-nine years old, Ida was mistress of a household for the first time in her life and saw to every comfort of overnight guests, including her mother's brother from Indiana and the Major's niece and her husband from San Francisco. "Your kind treatment and loving welcome made us feel toward you as your own children," Ida Morse wrote her, "I hope Dear Aunt if I can be of service at any time you will call me as your own . . . to serve you."

On Christmas Eve, the Major surprised the Saxton sisters with a twilight sleigh ride over snowy hills into the woods. The next day, he and his three siblings, six nieces and nephews, and four spouses gathered for lunch at his mother's home. After looking through gifts sent them by the public, Ida and the Major hosted two dozen Saxton-McKinley family members for dinner, followed by singing around the piano. The lively day distracted Ida from the depression she annually experienced on Christmas; that year it would have been Katie McKinley's twenty-fifth birthday.

Ida McKinley felt so convivial that she decided to host a dinner dance, in honor of nieces Grace McKinley and Mary Barber, for one hundred young guests the night before New Year's Eve. With musicians and singers among the guests providing entertainment, the evening began with card games at round tables set up throughout the house. After a ten-thirty supper, Ida's parlor was cleared for dancing. The next day's *Repository* carried the startling news that "an old-fashioned cotillion was danced by Mr. and Mrs. McKinley. . . . [Y]ounger guests filled up the entrance to the room in their interest in the dance, and were delighted with the graceful ease with which Mrs. McKinley was able to go through the figure." Not since her days as Miss Saxton had Ida been known to dance. It was a triumphant end to a trying year.[5]

In the first weeks of 1897, Ida hosted a Brooke Hall reunion, posed for an Italian sculptor, and had her final Inaugural gown fitting. While in Chicago, she headlined a benefit performance of *The Coming Women* to help the University of Chicago and Presbyterian Hospital establish a kindergarten for the city's poor, largely immigrant population. The moment Ida took a mezzanine-level box seat, audience members began talking about and pointing at her and never stopped. She sat fuming, never removing her cape or hat, and was on the verge of leaving. The *Chicago Times-Herald* noted that patrons who bought the expensive tickets felt compelled to twist, turn, rise, and lean, even "take a chance at falling over the balcony railing," just to get a "much desired glimpse" of the next First Lady. Ida kept her gaze straight ahead on the show, a comedy set in the future of 1906 when women run the government and men perform domestic duties, but the actors were distracted by the rude audience. The paper said that while she "concealed annoyance," she was "painfully conscious of the fact that dozens were constantly gazing upon her."[6]

On her return home, Ida walked into a flurry of packing boxes, every item being sorted for storage in Canton or shipment to Washington. The house had already been rented for a three-year lease set to begin April 1, just thirty days after the McKinleys were scheduled to vacate and leave for Washington. More unsettling to her than the uproar at home, however, was the intrusion into her personal life, which came days later. Newspapers estimated that Ida's wardrobe for the Inauguration and her first social season as First Lady all cost $10,000, based only on the ten boxes of her new clothes. McKinley issued an indignant but vague denial, and Ida never confirmed how much she had spent. Being stared at in theaters and having the press print unconfirmed facts about personal matters like her wealth may have shocked Ida, but it would now be a regular part of her life. She had enjoyed the flatteries of the campaign, said *Repository* editor George Frease, but there was now "pathos in it all" for her. "It is no secret that the loving wife," he wrote, "has never been quite willingly surrendered to the highest public honors, which have now been given him."[7]

In the cold rain on the late afternoon of March 1, the Major emerged from the house in a tall silk hat, white cotton vest, and black Prince Albert coat, escorting Ida in her new emerald coat with purple piping, and hat decorated with satin violets. A roar went up as he slowly led her down the front walk to their coach, the white plumes on the heads of four white horses bobbing. McKinley nodded to the cheering crowds lining the route to the depot, and Ida waved her handkerchief. Family members who made the journey with him waited in the luxurious train cars of wood-paneled walls, full baths, silver and china service, even a roaring fireplace. Exiting first, the Major helped Ida from the coach and up the train steps into the parlor car, where she sat on a chaise. From the platform, he bid farewell to the crowd for them both, but kept the door open so Ida could watch and hear Canton's farewell. A cannon salute was fired, and the train pulled out, taking her away from home.[8]

An hour after noon the next day, they arrived in the nation's capital. Despite her pale face, which "bore the traces of the travel," Ida McKinley knew this was just the first of several tests over the next two days by which she would long be judged. Steeling herself, she insisted on walking independently without the Major's support. Her attempt, wrote *Repository* editor Frease, made it "quite evident that she is still the invalid." For Ida, however, it was triumph. She *did it,* a point noted by the hawk-eyed press corps. The *Chicago Record* left a detailed account: "Mrs. McKinley was quite worn out by the exertion walking through the long railway station to the carriage. There was an invalid's chair mentioned to the president-elect but it was less than one hundred yard to the carriage so she decided to walk. The distance proved two or three times as great as was expected and the family physician was much provoked when he learned his recently-discharged patient had been overtaxed."

Later in the day, the Chicago reporter caught up with Dr. Phillips and got a remark from him acknowledging his disapproved of her violating his order that she not walk on her own: "[I]n Mrs. McKinley's case any unusual exertion must not be undertaken. Her walk through the station this morning was extremely imprudent. If there is anything she ought not to do, it is to walk. She has a very good deal of the Major's temperament, and does not worry, and is, therefore, much more likely to make a speedy recovery from fatigue than many apparently stronger persons afflicted with nerves."[9]

Despite looking "tired and careworn" to one reporter, Ida did not wait for the Major to offer his arm when their carriage stopped at the familiar

Ebbitt House. Instead, while lugging a massive purple orchid bouquet given to her at the depot, she willed herself to walk alone through the entire length of the lobby to the elevator. On reaching their northwest corner suite, where a solitary hall guard kept the curious away, Ida sank into a sullen mood, resisting Pina's offer to join her for a carriage ride. While the Major immediately slipped into meetings with his Cabinet appointees who awaited final confirmation, Ida sent a messenger to the White House with word that she would not be joining the Major at the private dinner the Clevelands were hosting for them. The First Lady Frances Cleveland had a floral basket delivered to her. Ida never acknowledged it. Despite their partisan differences, the Major had an animated evening with the Clevelands, with the tall and attractive Frances delighting him with stories of her own mother's early years in Stark County. At the Ebbitt, Ida was awakened by an Ohio Republican League Club serenade.[10]

On Inaugural morning, Ida fortified herself with quail on toast, broiled chicken, porterhouse steak, hot rolls, Spanish omelet, wheat muffins, and coffee. As Clara helped her into a dark purple dress, the Major went by open coach to the White House to fetch Cleveland for the traditional ride together of the outgoing and incoming presidents to the Capitol. At the Ebbitt, Ida took the arm of an Inaugural chairman and, trailed by Pina and her youngest child Kate, was guided by McKinley's new private secretary Addison Porter into a closed carriage. Refusing to be separated from her sister and niece, Ida insisted that all five of them could squeeze in. They did.

At the Capitol Building, Ida took her first-row seat in the Senate chamber to watch Garret Hobart sworn in as vice president, then proceeded to the outdoor Inaugural stand at the Capitol's east front for the Major's presidential oath of office and Inaugural Address. As he spoke, Ida stared and listened intently, her focus only on him. While his speech went on, an increasing number of eyes shifted to Ida, especially those of the press. "Those who saw Mrs. McKinley during the inauguration ceremonies thought she was a stricken woman," Arthur Wallace Dunn reported. "Her chalky white face and general appearance of weakness showed so unmistakably her serious physical condition that no one would have been surprised if she had collapsed at any moment." She didn't.

Curiosity about Ida at the public ceremony was rivaled by the presence of "Queen Lil," the recently deposed Queen Liliuokalani of the Hawaiian Republic. Control of her government had been seized by U.S. military forces in Honolulu, prompted by American business interests there. Congress hadn't enacted Cleveland's provision to restore her sovereignty,

but she had hoped that McKinley would help. "We want no wars of conquest," McKinley declared in his Inaugural speech about colonialism, "[W]e
must avoid the temptation of territorial aggression. War should never be
entered upon until every agency of peace has failed; peace is preferable
to war in almost every contingency." The queen was there as the guest of
John Sherman, a senator from Ohio and McKinley's designated secretary
of state who supported Hawaiian sovereignty, but he would soon find
himself in conflict with the new president on the issue. McKinley had
chosen Sherman for his Cabinet only to remove him from it so Mark
Hanna could replace him. In defiance of Hanna, McKinley's Inaugural
Address also affirmed his support of civil service reform. Despite this, the
new First Lady was always able to secure federal appointments for qualified
friends and family, beginning with having a cousin designated collector of
the Port of New York.[11]

When the ceremony ended, Ida suddenly decided to attend the all-male
Capitol luncheon with the Major instead of proceeding to the White
House, where First Lady Frances Cleveland was waiting. Mrs. Cleveland
was delaying her own appearance at a luncheon being held in her honor,
which was tightly scheduled so that she could still catch the train with the
outgoing president, but she was "determined at any personal inconvenience
to welcome Mrs. McKinley." The press noted that Ida's "tedious delay"
of over an hour was "most embarrassing," but Frances proved "extremely
cordial" when Ida did arrive, offering her roses. A reporter pointed out that
Frances "had but a short time in which to cultivate the acquaintance of
Mrs. McKinley, but she made use of it so tactfully as to make Mrs. McKinley her warm friend at once." She took Ida inside, explained the room
layout, introduced the domestic staff, and offered "a good idea of the social
routine" before giving her "an affectionate farewell," and running to her
luncheon tribute where time now permitted her only to stop in to wave
goodbye, then catch her train. Ida offered no verbal or written apology.

One can only speculate as to why Ida McKinley seemed frosty toward
her predecessor, but it was not a matter of mere gossip, recorded in different
sources. The diary of a family friend of the Major documents a cutting
remark Ida made about Frances Cleveland and her husband profiting from
the sale of their home, which was hypocritical from one whose inherited
wealth came largely from real estate. A War Department official received a
letter from his wife, who said that Ida made her "nearly explode by calling
the Clevelands names." Ida criticized Frances Cleveland for arranging les-

sons and playtime for her two toddler daughters in a White House family room, snapping, "That woman kept a kindergarten class for her own."[12]

Once Mrs. Cleveland left, Ida was whisked up the elevator and brought to the designated McKinley bedroom, where a rose bouquet from Frances awaited her. Frances had also had the room freshly painted yellow, unaware that it was the one color Mrs. McKinley viscerally hated. Ida never entered it. After resting in another room, she joined the Major in a glass-enclosed stand to review the Inaugural parade, but felt weak and went back upstairs. By five-thirty, she was downstairs again, in the family dining room, where the extended Saxton and McKinley family members were eager to begin the delayed meal arranged by Mrs. Cleveland. Ida wouldn't permit dinner to begin until the Major arrived. The new president, however, took his time talking to former First Lady Julia Grant outside. Refusing to further delay supper, Ida would not go out to join him. As he finally entered the drafty lobby, Ida called out, "Major! Major, where are you? Oh! There you are! We'd better start now, the luncheon is announced, and all are ready." Only a First Lady could be so assertive with a president.[13]

Before long, the McKinleys were off to the Inaugural Ball in the cavernous Pension Building. Ida McKinley, the object of curious onlookers, decided to ascend the long marble staircase for a private reception, where she sat shaking hands for an hour. Guests focused their attention on her pale blue-and-silver-threaded dress. Some gasped at her hair. Despite the Audubon Society's plea that women stop using aigrette feathers because of the cruel way in which they were obtained—the feathers were pulled from live birds—she used some in her coiffure.

The McKinleys and Hobarts were soon led to a flag-draped balcony from which they waved like a royal family to the crush of humanity below. Frosted-glass electric bulbs hung from the soaring ceiling along the walls, casting silver lights across the massive marble columns that rose to the top. A reporter noticed that Ida "looked fatigued." There was one more event, a seated dinner, to test her. The challenge was in getting there. It meant a procession across the long hall through thousands of perspiring enthusiasts eager to scrutinize her as she passed within inches of them. Ida was determined to sail flawlessly through to the historic day's end. A wise committee man plowed through the crowd to open a passage, asking men along the way to link hands to form a cordon. "Through these lines of volunteers the President and his wife passed," writer Richard Harding Davis recalled. Moments into the presidential promenade came a wave of gasps and hundreds of people craned their heads, indicating that something had gone awry. Ida had stumbled. Whether she fainted from exhaustion or suffered a seizure, reporters either failed to learn or were too discreet to mention the incident. One chronicler later wrote simply that "in the excitement [she] lost her consciousness, which she soon recovered." Canton guest William T. Kuhns recalled that she was "gently hustled into the supper room and [was] seen no more that evening." By midnight Ida was safely transported to her new home as fireworks lit the winter sky.

Not everyone had been watching Ida McKinley at the ball. *McClure's Magazine* editor Ida Tarbell was startled when she learned that the War Department had placed undercover guards in the crowd of revelers after receiving the credible threat of "an attempt on McKinley's life." When she noticed that no one was protecting the Major, it dawned on Tarbell that "It would, of course, have been easy to assassinate the President and Vice President at the Ball."[14]

❧ 8 ❧

American Ida

NEWS THAT IDA MCKINLEY was in Garfield Hospital days after the Inauguration seemed only to confirm the narrative already set by the press: the new First Lady was an invalid, who had some disability too dreadful to name in polite society, and citizens must learn to patiently endure a tedious reign in deference to the fragile woman. In reality, the president's wife had only gone to the hospital to visit family friend Gen. Russell Hastings, who was hospitalized for a fractured leg. Ida, asserting her status as the president's personal representative, questioned, even peppered, doctors about the nature of Hastings's injury and the schedule for his release. She had come as the president's representative and wanted to return to him with specific answers.[1]

The small deed of a woman who was a self-acknowledged invalid assuming a task on behalf of her husband and offering support to a military man on behalf of her husband, along with other reports during her first weeks as First Lady, gave the public a more nuanced truth about Ida McKinley.

Americans had come to expect presidential wives to symbolize conventional feminine virtues, each fitting an archetype with influence at the national hearth: virginal bride Frances Cleveland transformed into the mother of toddlers; grandmotherly Caroline Harrison raised orchids and painted china; stoic Lucretia Garfield kept vigil, nursing her wounded husband; and moral Lucy Hayes refused to pollute guests with demon rum. In the imagination of Victorian Americans, an "invalid" was confined to her room with a nurse feeding her soothing broth and a minister calming her hysterics. Over time, emphasis on stories of Ida McKinley querulously insisting that the president push her in a wheelchair or snapping at guests seemed to confirm her as the quintessential invalid. It was a warped caricature, contradicted by studiously ignored facts. She would make public her views on controversial issues, demonstrating her opposition to prohibition by offering alcoholic beverages to guests, and her support of women's suffrage by warmly welcoming their most famous leader while refusing to receive those opposed to suffrage. She overtly exercised political patronage. She traveled thousands of miles by rail to meet the people of the country. She became the first incumbent First Lady to visit a foreign country. The press may have convinced the public that the often dependent yet never submissive Ida McKinley was an invalid, but she regularly contradicted that image.

On her first full day as First Lady, the *New York Times* conceded that Mrs. McKinley had "not been harmed" when she fainted at the Inaugural Ball and felt "no fatigue." She entertained a large group at lunch and joined her husband in welcoming his old wartime comrades, new Cabinet members, various governors, military leaders, immigration officials, congressmen, and senators, as well as some trusted journalists, like Murat Halstead. When the Major went out in the cold rain to hear several bands performing for the public, Ida located a good spot at an open window to watch, acknowledging those who called her name by bobbing her head while fluttering her handkerchief.

In their first month in the White House, Mrs. McKinley and the president entertained friends and relatives almost every night at cozy private dinners, often followed by a retreat to the Blue Room. They would call for "Sunbeam" (the Major's nickname for his niece Mabel) to sing and play the piano. Cynics who wondered about reports of Ida's energy level at private functions had their chance to watch her preside over the series of social season official dinners honoring the Diplomatic Corps, Supreme Court, Cabinet, House and Senate, Army and Navy. Interspersed with these were small receptions Ida hosted for women. Her first such endeavor two weeks after the Inauguration—for diplomats' wives—proved her entirely capable as a host without the Major.

Reporters, certain that the invalid aspect would be a narrative to count on for the next four years, seemed so eager to anticipate the first sign of illness that they rushed to report how she fainted and needed to be abruptly spirited away at a dinner following a grueling day of dedication events at Grant's Tomb on April 28. Later editions sheepishly corrected that it was the mayor's wife who fainted. As for Ida, she left early to catch a show at the Lyceum Theater. Finally, the *Washington Post* conceded that "Mrs. McKinley Disposes of Mooted Social Question," admitting that

"There has been a question in the minds of some as to who would be the lady to preside in Mrs. McKinley's place, it having been stated at various times that [she] was not physically able to cope with the social duties demanded in her position." Another paper noted how citizens during the election "and no small proportion of them men" wondered if a president could function with a disabled First Lady and gave "thought and talk" to it as a factor in their vote.

Ida's activity and visibility early on ended speculation, affirmed by an unnamed relative, likely Pina, who declared, "She loves Washington, has many pleasant associations with the city, and was extremely glad and happy when the time came to return here." As if to make it official, Ida McKinley "selected" the Blue Room on the state floor to host her own public events.[2]

A visiting teenager, Amelia Aiken, compared the McKinley family rooms to "a seven-room flat, tucked away in a corner of the massive structure like a cozy corner in a Turkish bazaar," with potted plants and cushioned divans scattered about. Among three guest suites, a dank, green-walled one with two brass-framed beds covered in plain white blankets, a reading lamp, and the First Lady's framed picture was for "the bravest heart." The First Lady's favored spot was a cushioned window seat in the West Sitting Hall, beneath the semicircular window looking west over the greenhouses. In a room dominated by a stuffed eagle with spread wings and Mother McKinley's portrait, Ida and the Major played euchre with friends in the evening or sang along as a visiting Mabel McKinley played the piano. The couple often dined alone in the Oval Library, which was adorned by a gold chrysanthemum-patterned wallpaper. Ida's gold-framed oval oil portrait hung here, and the Library's easy access to her bedroom across the hall made it an ideal place for her to receive callers and host smaller receptions.

To avoid the harsh afternoon glare, which could provoke her headaches and seizures, Ida chose a bedroom with windows facing north and had a small lavatory installed for her. The couple's two brass beds were placed side by side against the west wall, covered with blue satin bedspreads and Marseilles lace. The room held a massive mahogany dresser and an ebony wood cabinet. On the cherrywood table in the center, Ida placed her wool baskets, knitting accoutrements, and books. The mantel was covered with a silk covering that matched the pale violet wallpaper and carpeting. Amelia Aiken found it the "prettiest and most cheerful." In every room, on every surface, were overstuffed flower vases.[3]

The Major, like Ida, was a flower aficionado. He made the carnation boutonniere his trademark, removing it ceremoniously and presenting it to visiting children as a souvenir, a fact the Boston mayor's daughter Rose Fitzgerald would never forget as her sister received one while she did not. Ida had developed his knowledge of flowers—along with opera, theater, and poetry. Even his ubiquitous white vests were due to her influence.

Many afternoons, Ida leaned on her cane to walk a short length through the multi-structured greenhouse, watching various blooms and colors develop through the weeks. As Easter approached, she requested a large order of lilies to fill the house and to send to those confined to hospitals. According to one claim, a small bush of "American Beauty" roses was grafted to create the "American Ida" for her. A military aide later recalled Ida's one quirk about flowers: "Mrs. McKinley disliked yellow to such an extent that she would not have even yellow wild flowers around her. It was almost an obsession with her, it seems, and she liked blue as much as she disliked yellow. In consequence, the grounds were literally covered with blue flowers. Blue seemed to soothe her always, while yellow had the opposite effect. Strange, wasn't it?"[4]

Some fifteen workers serviced the greenhouses and gardens. Among lamplighter and laundrywomen, the domestic staff consisted of natives and immigrants, black and white. Doorkeeper William Pendel, electrician Ike Hoover, and accountant William Crook kept notes on the McKinleys for books they would later publish. William T. Sinclair, the first African American to hold the position of steward, was bonded for $20,000. Responsible for the mansion's valuables, Sinclair resisted lucrative offers from manufacturers seeking to advertise White House patronage. His integrity impressed Ida, and she implicitly trusted Sinclair to make purchases on her behalf as hostess. Sinclair passed on monthly, itemized invoices to paymaster Crook, who submitted these to the president for payment of food, liquor, train tickets, hotel bills, and other costs incurred by them and their guests. Herman Kohlsaat found the country-style menus prepared by African American cook May Benjamin like that "served in thousands of homes in the Middle West." Ida often asked for her peppery fried chicken and insisted on Alladio Royal California Cream Cheese, shipped from the San Francisco hotel that made it and that advertised its patronage "by our beloved President and Mrs. McKinley in the White House." The Major's only gripe was the custom that instead of the First Lady, the president was always to be served first, whether it was a family luncheon or state dinner.[5]

Despite the romantic notions about life in the Executive Mansion, it was, said one employee, "a poorly preserved and rat-infested old mansion." The elevator operated on water pressure, connected to a roof tank, but the pressure was often low, and the contraption couldn't be counted on, thus often hindering Ida's mobility. Though she was able to walk down the stairs with a cane, ascending them was exhausting; if the elevator was out, she had to be carried up. In some respects, the old technology limited her role as First Lady.

Whether she was going out or staying in, Ida McKinley was "fastidiously neat and particular about everything she does and what she wears," writer Gilson Willets observed. After Ida obtained a federal job for Clara Tharin's alcoholic husband Charles as a White House watchman, Clara returned to work as her maid. Clara kept order in the First Lady's dressing room, which adjoined the bedroom, storing all types of day and evening clothes and accessories with care. She even gave friends tours of the room to preview the eight new evening gowns Ida bought for each social season or to show off pieces of Ida's lace collection to be sewn on as cuffs and collars.

Ida had a sizable bonnet collection. Her obsession tested even the president's patience during one shopping trip, when her indecision delayed their schedule until he insisted that she just buy both so they could leave. While social commentator Harry March didn't know that Ida chose small bonnets to reduce head pressure, he editorialized that with the First Lady wearing "postage-stamp hats," a "precedent was set" that meant the demise of hats that blocked the view of theater patrons. Of her formidable jewelry collection, her favorite was a 210-diamond tiara from the Major. Willets further noted that "She rises very early and spends a long time in making her toilet, because of her dainty painstaking."[6]

After breakfast at eight-thirty with the Major, Mrs. McKinley spent most of her mornings "quietly whiling away the time knitting or engrossed in thoughts that were kept strictly to herself," recalled electrician Ike Hoover. She often began reading books she couldn't finish because the repeated view of two facing pages of double-columned text led to headaches, so she gravitated to monthly magazine articles or her favorite Alfred Tennyson and Robert Burns poetry as the print layout was easier on her eyes. One o'clock meant lunch with the Major and guests in the West Sitting Hall, followed by receiving individual callers or small delegations from various organizations in the Oval Library. She greeted larger groups in the Blue Room. The bright spot was her afternoon drive, hopefully with the Major, sometimes with a friend, but, Hoover recorded, "more often the maid would be her only companion." If he had the time, the Major liked to go beyond the city streets into sylvan Rock Creek Park. He liked the fresh air from an open carriage, but if it was cool, Ida insisted on a closed carriage as she was sensitive to lower temperatures. The doorkeeper recalled that Ida "always had to be assisted in going out or coming in," usually by footman Charles Reeder, a former Ebbitt House employee who was hired to work at the White House.

Dinners at six-thirty were held in the family dining room on the state floor if there were special guests, in the West Sitting Hall if it was with friends or family, or in the library if it was just the two of them. Their lifestyle was not lavish. For some fancier private dinner parties, they contracted the caterer Rauscher's and hired a professional to entertain after dinner, once inviting the famed singer Nordica to perform "Home Sweet Home." Although Ida's inherited wealth afforded their indulgences, the Major wrote the checks for everything, including Ida's purchases from Marshall Fields, B. Altman's, the Singer Company, and all of her medications.[7]

After dinner the couple loved playing cards, but whether players were Cabinet members or Canton neighbors, all adhered to one unwritten rule. Canton friend Darcy Lynch long recalled how, as the Major helped a mutual friend into a chair, he whispered into her ear, "Mrs. McKinley always wins." Many nights after dinner, Ida kissed the Major goodbye and dashed off without him to the theater. His later aide George Cortelyou recorded that McKinley "allowed nothing to interfere" with his waiting at the North Portico for her carriage to return and help her into the house.[8]

On those nights when Ida went to bed while the Major stayed up to work, his soothing voice as he read from the Bible calmed her into restful sleep. Among the multitude of reports about his devout Christianity, there is not even a vague anecdotal suggestion that Ida shared his religious devotion. She repeated prayers, believed in an afterlife, and found social identification as a Presbyterian, but she also incorporated elements of other faiths into her private belief system. On Sundays, the Major attended morning service at Metropolitan Methodist church. Ida stayed home. When he returned, he strolled with her outside through the flower beds. In the evenings, they revived the Hayes tradition of inviting friends for supper and singing hymns around the piano. John Fletcher Hurst recalled not only how Ida sang but that "occasionally Mrs. McKinley would play an accompaniment."[9]

Any changes to their living space that the McKinleys requested were submitted to the pompous Public Buildings Superintendent Theodore

Bingham for federal funding.[10] Ida approved his recommendation to permit historian Abby Gunn Baker to take inventory of uncatalogued historic
White House china, but when the First Lady, who was "very anxious" to
give Caro Dawes the prize gift of a piece of historic Lincoln china, Bingham prevented it by legal means and earned her permanent enmity.[11] Mrs.
McKinley had no interest in White House history. With her "preference
for new and modern furniture," according to the *Washington Post,* Ida "frequently ordered things sold that to her thinking were not in harmony with
their surroundings or were disagreeable in color." Her changes were limited
to reupholstering benches in gold satin for the East Room, acquiring a
gold mantel mirror and a Federal-era chair with a red-and-white-striped
cushion for the Red Room, and carpeting the family dining room. Finally,
as the *Philadelphia Times* reported, "She thought it the proper thing for the
pictures of husbands and wives to hang in the same room."[12]

Ida McKinley used the staterooms only for formal entertaining. Presidents traditionally escorted the highest-ranking woman down the grand
staircase to dinner or a receiving line, followed by the First Lady on the arm
of the highest-ranking male guest. Although he broke tradition at their first
dinner by escorting Ida, by their second dinner, they reverted to tradition.

The McKinleys took immediately to the empathetic vice president and
his wife, Garret and Jennie Hobart, whose twenty-year-old daughter Fan-
nie had died two years before. The Second Lady especially endeared herself
with her progressive attitude toward Ida's seizure disorder; trusting her with
the secret gave the Major some relief. At the first large state dinner, the
McKinleys followed protocol and sat across the table from each other. Jennie Hobart noticed that the Major "was anxious to the point of distraction
and never took his eyes from her" because if Ida had a seizure, she would
not be easily accessible. Fortunately, no such incident occurred, but he later
asked Mrs. Hobart, "Could it possibly offend anyone for me to have my
wife sit beside me?" As most of the guests were strangers to Ida, he was
equally worried "lest her illness cause embarrassment." Jennie not only assured him that a president had the right to alter protocol but that she would
always be on call for large events to help Ida or to assume any duty for her.
Mrs. Hobart never had to serve as substitute hostess, but McKinley did
change seating protocol so he could sit next to Ida. Even at a private dinner
for sixteen around an oval table that July, the McKinleys sat together. By the
next year's Diplomat Corps dinner for sixty-four at a massive rectangular
table in the long hallway, the change had become permanent, leaving one
magazine sniping that it made protocol "a difficult task."

Ida McKinley's disabilities were further integrated with tradition. As the president was "anxious that the First Lady should have the place of honor in the receiving line," she steeled herself to "stand with him," recalled Crook, "as long as her strength held out, after which she would sit down." Guests still wanted to shake hands even while she was ensconced in a large armchair. On Jennie's advice, Ida soon kept a bouquet on her lap to dissuade guests from reaching out to her. If they still did, Jennie stepped in and offered her hand for a shake. Contrary to popular belief, however, Ida avoided handshaking only to limit contracting any germs at the massive receptions, where as many as 3,000 members of the public lined up to meet her. At her first reception for invited guests in the fall of 1897, for example, it was noted that she "looked exceedingly well and smilingly greeted the last guest without the least show of fatigue, although she had shaken hands with several hundred people."[13]

Despite the new arrangements, the president could not protect Ida from those who scrutinized her to determine her mysterious malady. Eventually he had to dose her with sedatives to ensure that there would be no risk of a seizure in public. Eyewitness accounts document her seizures at private dinners; there is no record of any occurring at official public events. Instead, the public was left only to wonder over press reports of her appetite, likely affected by medication. "The present mistress of the White House does not partake of the series of courses set before the guests," *The Chautauquan* magazine reported. Despite her "most fitful of appetites," it added that "often her entire meal consists of a few crackers from the plate always placed at her side."

Of far greater political consequence was the question of what Ida McKinley permitted to be poured into the stemware. The day after the Inauguration, she hosted a dinner for young relatives and friends, and a *Washington Post* reporter cornered a nephew to find out about the new First Lady's temperance policy. "No, we didn't have a drop of wine," he responded. "You know, the Major and Mrs. McKinley never drink wine themselves and do not believe in setting a bad example for their young relatives or, in fact, for any one. I've never seen wine on their table, and I've eaten at their home hundreds of time." Prohibitionists seized on the story as proof that the First Lady supported temperance, a Women's Christian Temperance Union leader writing her: "Not only the Christian womanhood of Washington, but the Christian womanhood of the world will thank you for the stand you have taken on the temperance question at the White House. We are happy to know that at the beautiful entertainment which you gave at the Executive Mansion on Friday evening 'there were no wine glasses to pollute.' You and your husband deserve and will receive the thanks of a grateful people."

Before the White House could respond, the WCTU sent the press a copy of the letter, and within days it was nationally reported that Ida McKinley was reinstituting the Hayes ban on liquor. This led to a New York prohibitionist conference proposal of using the First Lady's name to further its agenda and a *Springfield [Illinois] Republican* editorial supporting the idea. One prohibitionist leader, a Dr. Buckley, finally warned that "there was no certain knowledge" she was on their side. The First Lady remained silent. When wine was served at Ida's first official dinner later that month, she was suddenly anathema to temperance leader Carrie Nation, who fanned her outrage upon discovering that one of the First Lady's Canton leased properties was a saloon, and provoked thousands of local WCTU protest petitions. The McKinleys drank wine only at private dinners and never dignified the WCTU attack. In thanking a McKinley friend for a gift of some spirits, his secretary added, "The President says he likes the taste of the wine very much."[14]

Ida McKinley became the first First Lady to provide musical entertainment after formal dinners, an unwitting innovation resulting from her wish to hear Ella Russell sing upon learning that the prima donna was scheduled to return from Europe. Ida, who was long a patron of all performing arts, followed the careers and tour schedules of certain actors and singers. With the privilege of her status, her wire to the young American opera singer requesting that she perform at the White House was practically a royal command. What made Russell's performance unique is that instead of being scheduled for a typical afternoon musicale, it followed the March 24 official Cabinet dinner of the formal social season. Accompanied by violinist Frank Wilczek, she sang arias from Liszt's *Lorley,* and ballads *Robin Adair* and *Within a Mile of Edinboro Town.*[15]

Ida continued the new custom, hosting post-dinner entertainment the following year, including the first piano trio performance with composer Ernest Lent and his wife playing his four-movement work on violin and piano, respectively, after the Supreme Court dinner. The most prominent African American among the year's performers was Boston Conservatory–trained violinist Joseph Douglass, grandson of legendary abolitionist Frederick Douglass. A grand piano donated by the Kimball Company proved more than decor for Mrs. McKinley.

By her patronage, Ida McKinley aided the careers of a variety of women performers, from Dutch opera soprano Mademoiselle Belinfante to American prima donna Geraldine Farrar, with ensuing newspaper notice of their

White House appearances lending them a prestige that no other public performance could. One of the more engaging friends Ida made as First Lady was with mezzo-soprano Hranoush Bey, the Imperial Ottoman ambassador's Turkish wife, who even obliged McKinley's request to travel with them to perform at an event. Ida also invited the now ten-year-old prodigy singer Elsie Janis to sing for a holiday Blue Room party and perform the melodramatic song, *Break the News to Mother.* Janis would credit the McKinleys' patronage of her since their Columbus days as crucial to launching her successful career.[16]

The First Lady also enjoyed showcasing popular music. In April, she hosted an evening East Room concert by the Yale Banjo Club and Glee Club, who performed contemporary college songs to which she "generously applauded the young men and expressed her delight," the *Washington Post* reported. A month later, she hosted perhaps the most unique of her musical showcases, a concert performed by the Mexican Army's Eight Cavalry Regiment in colorful state uniforms, consisting of native dance music and a march tribute to Ulysses Grant, composed by a Señor Morales. Ida continued to seek unusual music for her guests. Two years later she had the thirty-eight red-jacketed British Guards Band perform in the Red Room, their concert ending with *Nautical Fantasia,* which intertwined the *Star Spangled Banner* and *God Save the Queen.*

The First Lady also frequented the late Saturday afternoon public Marine Band concerts, which were held on the South Lawn in warm weather. Ida, seated on the portico with the president, became unusually animated, nodding her head or swaying her body to the music, and waving her handkerchief to the crowds. The band always included her favorite *Blue Danube Waltz* and *Swanee River.* Even if she was unwell and unable to appear, Ida insisted that the mostly working-class public who came not be denied what was often the only entertainment they had.

Although reports claimed that she "felt a craving for the old music of her girlhood days," and that "modern music did not satisfy her," the First Lady voiced no disapproval of the new "ragtime" sound when it was played for another unprecedented event that she and the president hosted—the first White House celebration of Valentine's Day. Since it fell on the same night as a scheduled Diplomatic Corps dinner, the First Lady lightened the after-dinner entertainment by hosting the only dance during the Administration, which was held in the State Dining Room. Guests did the "cakewalk" and "two-step" to the ragtime songs *Floradora, Goo-Goo Eyes, Whistling Rufus,*

Black America, and *Bunch o' Blackberries.* Rounding out the evening was *The Fortune Teller* by Ida's favorite contemporary composer, Victor Herbert.[17]

Unlike Frances Cleveland's open public receptions on Saturday afternoons for working-class women, entrée to one of Mrs. McKinley's small receptions was through a political or social connection. The only chance that ordinary citizens had to possibly meet her was at the annual New Year's Day Reception, but only two were held during the McKinley tenure, and at one Ida tired and left before the general public was admitted. Anticipating her first season of entertaining, Ida was anxious for her favorite niece, Mary Barber, to serve as her social aide and coaxed her to arrive early to "get acquainted with the White House." Other relatives served in this social aide role as well. Preceding Mary had been Ida's aunt Maria in the spring of 1897, followed by McKinley's San Francisco niece Ida Morse. Mary Barber would be followed by her sister Ida Barber, and then by the daughter of Mary McWilliams, the First Lady's cousin. The lifestyles of the young women sometimes irritated Ida. While some friends visited Mabel McKinley when she was social aide, the First Lady snapped to another guest, "Young people are always on the go, always out, always coming in late. What pleasure is there in that?"

As always, Pina had infinite patience in aiding her sister. She remained after the Inauguration to ensure that Ida's routine was set properly, knowing the president's time was limited. "I hope Aunt Ida is not as tired out and also that you have not been working too hard," Mary wrote her. Marsh also supported Pina, writing from Canton, "Don't hesitate to stay as long as Ida wants you. We will get along all right." Once back in Canton, the First Lady's sister had the thankless task of screening friends and relatives asking for White House invitations.[18]

The small number of guests who did get an invitation, however, received Ida's focused attention as she sat on a high-back wood chair lined with striped satin or a blue chaise lounge, the lights behind her to avoid triggering headaches. At her first Library reception, on St. Patrick's Day, a reporter found Ida's enthusiasm to be "magnetic." When someone tried to flatter her, she tapped the brooch pinned at her shoulder, a miniature of the Major, to remind them of the only reason she was there. She also welcomed organizational delegations and hosted artistic salons in the Blue Room. On February 17, 1899, for example, she held a performance of the actress Maude Adams reading from the book, *St. Hilda,* and later received the National Congress of Mothers. On another day, it was a dozen Native

American women teachers of the Seneca Nation. Ida especially enjoyed welcoming graduating classes. In one day, for example, she met with some 250 high school and college students from Maryland, Pennsylvania, Ohio, and North Carolina.[19]

Unless there was inclement weather, Ida kept the window open during her daily carriage ride and nodded or waved her kerchief to those who applauded her. She also entered and exited the mansion through the North Lobby, eager to greet any lingering tourists. When returning from her morning ride at about noon as tourists filed through the mansion, she made a point of entering through the lobby rather than a private entrance, so that they could see her. Her general inaccessibility, which was ensured by guards and staff, however, prevented Ida from engaging with those who sought her support on political issues that the president did not want either of them to be drawn into. Only by reading the paper, upstairs in her West Sitting Hall, did Ida learn how lawyer Mary Walker often lurked at the stairs leading to the executive offices with the hope of seeing her. Walker, an advocate for women's legal equality, wanted to enlist the First Lady's support after having been denied access to Ida's receptions. Similarly, deposed Hawaiian Queen Liliuokalani called daily at the White House for the First Lady, hoping to gain her sympathy in having the monarchy restored, but Ida was never given her card and was kept unaware of the woman's wish to see her.[20]

Mrs. McKinley committed herself to helping a number of charitable institutions, but her unpredictable mobility made her appearances at fund-raisers and bazaars impractical. Still, said Crook of the White House staff, "she felt that she could do something." Another example of how Ida adapted the First Lady's role to her disability was how she used her knitting skill to support charities. Hospitals, orphanages, homeless shelters, old-age homes, and other social welfare centers seeking her support invariably received a pair of her famous slippers to be auctioned. Amid the pressures of presidential life and yet a sedentary lifestyle, her work gave Ida a stabilizing focus and sense of purpose as she daily reviewed an unending list of organizations waiting to receive her handiwork. "This occupation is one of my greatest pleasures. It has relieved many hours," she explained in a rare interview with a reporter. "I gave a pair . . . as a prize at a fair in Paterson . . . my little gift had realized $50 for the funds." One reporter estimated that she made 4,000 pairs and spent nearly eight years of her life knitting. It creatively expanded her as well; she soon began designing and executing silk ties, steel-bead purses, and embroidered linens. "Her feeling was that these gifts had a personal significance such as would not have attached to things bought in the shops," the *Washington Post* chronicled. In one instance, she supplied an entire hospital ward with socks for the patients.[21]

Ida McKinley received what one paper termed an "enormous" amount of mail, which she liked to open herself, much of it from women asking her to intercede on behalf of male relatives condemned to death or imprisonment. "The pathetic appeals for pardons are very trying on her," journalist Henry Caldwell reported, "because she is compelled to decline to interfere in such matters." In a plea for her son, for example, one Lizzie Ramey wrote to the First Lady because, she explained, she didn't know "how else to reach your husband's kind heart." Ida was able to grant simple, personal requests, such as that of a ten-year-old who asked to attend one of her Library receptions, and the Chilean citizen who asked for her autograph.[22]

Some assumed that the Major forged Ida's signature on items, but her handwriting varied during her life due to occasional edema, which left her hands swollen. She most often hand-wrote letters to her nieces Mary and Ida in college, urging them to visit and often including cash gifts. Even to them, however, she sometimes reverted to dictating her letters to the Major. "Your Aunt Ida does not write letters you know," he wrote to Mary in one letter with his own signature, "and she has asked me to do this one for her." This was entirely impractical in answering the volume of public mail.[23]

President McKinley's secretary, Addison Porter, decided to assign federal clerk Ira Smith to process and answer her public mail, thus making Ida McKinley the first First Lady to have a federal employee work specifically for her. When asked by the Senate Appropriations Committee to justify Smith's salary increase, Porter made the case that Smith "answers a great many communications for Mrs. McKinley of a most delicate character, and he writes an excellent hand." Rather than type his responses, which didn't require her signature, Ida had Smith use his clear penmanship. He found her "gentle and kindly," and "enjoyed working with her."[24]

The innovations accommodating the First Lady obviously affected the tone of the new Administration. Navy Secretary John Long characterized both McKinleys as "gentle village people," but Ida was often bluntly honest about how her health limited her. When it was occasionally apparent to others that the First Lady was "physically unequal to the things she bravely was attempting to do," observed their friend, Senate wife Julia Foraker, the Major generated a "certain strain . . . masking his tender concern about his wife under a deferential solicitude for his guests." This opinion was seconded by Colonel Crook, who saw them daily. "There was little of real gayety in the White House during President McKinley's residence," he said, due not to Ida or her health but that the Major was "a grave, serious-minded man . . . for so much of his life that he had never cultivated the lighter side to any appreciable extent."[25]

Ida McKinley's early enthusiasm for her husband to become president died during his first term as governor after the crisis of the Walker scandal. Fear for his safety compounded her opposition to his pursuit of the presidency. Her hopes for their private life, however, were no match for his cautiously concealed ambition. He had successfully exploited her disabilities and his devotion to her to become president. As president, he now continued to dictate their public narrative by insisting she was a brilliant hostess. In fact, Ida McKinley's persistence in fulfilling a public role was an act of devotion for what he needed her to be. Not a whit of evidence shows that she pushed herself out of personal egotism. On Inauguration Day, Julia Foraker detected her "detached cool about it all." Ida's ambition for the future was revealed as they neared the White House, and she wittily quipped with ironic resignation that it was "almost another Canton."

Jennie Hobart later disclosed the desperate lengths the Major took to maintain his charade that it was the First Lady who planned and managed all of the White House entertaining, taking "no end of pains to give her the lion's share of the credit, even when none was due." One time, when Ida was exhausted, she suggested postponing a scheduled party. McKinley refused. Taking control, he "planned the menu, the entertainment, the flowers." When a little crowd gathered near her, the Major approached, bowed dramatically, and declared officiously for all to hear, "Madam, your party is a great success!"[26]

❖ 9 ❖

For the Sake of Appearances

"I SEE THAT MRS. McKINLEY has entered the room," noted Philadelphia Mayor Charles Warwick at the beginning of his speech at the banquet honoring the president. Then he continued with perhaps the most public acknowledgement yet of the expectations placed on a First Lady at the century's end:

> Madame, in our simple republican court the wife of our chief magistrate has precedence over all representative women in the land. She who most intimately promotes the comfort and happiness of the man whom our suffrages have put in charge of the nation, is entitled to our gratitude, as doing us all a service. We greet you thankfully. European nations boast the virtues of their queens. To the same qualities that honor them you add the graces of urbanity, sympathy with the people and accessibility, not common to crowned heads. As the most prominent of American women, we receive you to our hearts and say "God bless you."[1]

The mayor's mention of "accessibility" struck a sensitive chord, reflecting the idea of Ida being out among the masses. To do so, Ida would need attentive assistance beyond what the Major could now provide. If the president was making a speech at a New England fair, reviewing a parade in the South, or attending a Midwestern bankers' conference, he would find it difficult at best to just dash away if Ida suddenly experienced a seizure among strangers who would not know what was wrong with her.

Still, by June 3, when Ida appeared in Philadelphia, the public had no reason to suspect such problems. A story of her staying aboard the presidential yacht *Dolphin* instead of joining others ashore at Annapolis ended with news that on her return to the White House, she "appeared to be much stronger than when she left." That Mrs. McKinley declined Mrs. Cornelius Vanderbilt's dinner invitation in New York caused more amusement than alarm, especially when Mrs. Vanderbilt quickly accepted Mrs. McKinley's invitation to come see her instead.

The McKinleys knew that Ida's "attacks" might return at any moment. The staff was warned that during events on the state floor, a path must always be kept clear in case Ida had to be whisked to the elevator. Those familiar with her seizures were alert to any sign of onset. "Mrs. McKinley had one of her headaches," Charlie Bawsel wrote his wife cryptically after visiting Ida in mid-May, "and you know what that means for those around her."[2]

Seated beside Ida at the Philadelphia dinner was her old Brooke Hall school chum Rosalie Bache Bates and her husband Newton, the U.S. Navy surgeon the Major had just made White House physician. If Newton could be trusted to keep Ida's epilepsy secret and acquiesce to the Major's unregulated application of medications, the McKinleys, in turn, could be trusted with his secret. Newton L. Bates was terminally ill.[3]

For three months, the new First Lady was cosseted on yachts and hotel suites during three trips to nearby cities. During the summer season, when presidential families fled to the shore or hills to escape the heat, Ida would be exposed and examined by the public. McKinley, who controlled Ida's image more tightly than even his own, was less worried about those who might directly interact with her than about the masses who judged her based on what reporters wrote. Reporters would eavesdrop on her offhanded remarks and note every stumble. Accompanying the McKinleys on their first lengthy trip—to the Tennessee Centennial Exposition—were two dozen correspondents from New York, Washington, Baltimore, Philadelphia, Boston, Chicago, Canton, Cleveland, Cincinnati, and Louisville newspapers, as well as two from wire services who filed stories for smaller papers. Technology had increased the pressure. Ten years before, when Frances Cleveland visited Tennessee, *Leslie's Illustrated Weekly* depicted her call on her aged predecessor, Sarah Polk, in a pen sketch. Now there were photographers. Whether McKinley was capable of simultaneously taking care of the nation and his wife would be influenced by how the media cast the new First Lady.[4]

A First Lady's physical appearance was always a press obsession. With Ida McKinley, the focus was on her hairdo. A columnist's declaration that Ida's "shingle bob" had "set a fashion in hair dressing" was confirmed by a reporter, who noticed an increase in the style in Washington and a hairdresser who found it "decidedly unbecoming to the average woman" but conceded it "saves trouble." No press stories referenced Ida's 1896 remark that she wore her hair short to avoid head pressure, but one article used enlarged photos of her facial features to hint at a brain-related disability, concluding that her forehead proved that Ida was "more gifted temperamentally than mentally." W. M. R. French justified his offensive analysis, claiming that the "haze of vagueness" about the First Lady's disabilities "stimulate[d] a healthy curiosity" in her. More frivolously, reporters paid minute attention to the slightest change in her perpetually mentioned favorite shade, resulting in an avalanche of gifts from the public, like a handbag sent by a Lucia Evans "in your color . . . true blue."[5]

Ida McKinley drew comfort from her predecessors who filled the role of "First Lady," a title legitimized not by law but by *Leslie's.* In her first weeks at the White House, she invited Julia Grant and Lucretia Garfield together for dinner, who both proved especially supportive. Mrs. Grant sent frequent gifts and encouraging notes, and Mrs. Garfield called often, amused when she was once besieged by teachers who were invited to a reception with Ida. Harriet Lane, the niece of and the hostess for her bachelor uncle, President Buchanan, attended numerous state dinners, and elderly Letitia Tyler Semple, who had served as her father's hostess sixty years before, came to "every McKinley function."[6]

Like her predecessors, Ida McKinley was now the most famous woman in the nation—and the subject not only of gossip and speculation but grossly inaccurate news stories. It prompted Josiah Hartzell to update his campaign biography of Mrs. McKinley and include pictures of her healthy young nieces as her own version of Cabinet. Hartzell promised he would only be "culling out and fitting together incidents," but Ida was disturbed by his "unfounded exaggeration" of her vigor; it not only raised unrealistic expectations of her, it was dishonest. Once McKinley won the election, Ida "rigidly denied" press requests from reporters for interviews or to pose for photographs exclusively for any one publication, and Hartzell had to beg just for permission to include a photo of her in her Inaugural gown.[7]

Ida did cooperate with at least six photographers: Francis Benjamin Johnston, Louise Deslong Woodbridge, B. West Clinedinst, George Prince, T. Dinwiddie, and George W. Griffith. She posed in the greenhouse and mansion, standing and sitting. Employing the technique she had used during the campaign of posing with framed pictures of the Hayeses in the background, she now positioned the president's framed picture on a table next to her and Katie's portrait hung on the wall behind her. Johnston recalled

Ida sighing that she hoped "the morning's work would absolve her" of further sittings, but Clinedinst once caught her beaming off-camera, seeming to enjoy the process. The pictures were reproduced by the thousands as stereograph cards and in national newspapers and magazines, prompting an October 1897 issue of *Ladies Home Journal* to sell out completely. Ida McKinley even earned a footnote in photographic history as one of the first people captured in color, a three-separation positive Kromogram.[8]

McKinley knew the value of feeding the press harmless tidbits about her. A day before their Nashville trip began, for example, he thought about incidents from Ida's birthday dinner celebration hosted by the Hobarts and decided it was harmless to inform the press about the elaborate cake she took home, wisely withholding the fact that his gift to her was a diamond pendant, its $600 price tag exceeding most workers' annual salary. With similarly careful consideration, he arranged an extra precaution before the Nashville trip.[9]

As Dr. Bates's terminal illness made his presence on the trip uncertain, McKinley sought a substitute who might be willing to dispense medications for Ida. To circumvent notation on an official record, the drugs would not be requisitioned from military supply but brought from the doctor's personal dispensary. To avoid having to generate written documentation about Ida's illness or the drugs she required, McKinley would disclose the details verbally, in person. Thus, with circumspect reference to Ida McKinley as "the case in hand," U.S. Navy Commander B. P. Lamberton directed the second attending White House physician, U.S. Army Surgeon Col. Leonard Wood, to be on call in case Bates was unable to travel. "The President desired time to call on you to have a talk as to what you need to take on the trip to the South . . . I have some simple remedies on board suggested by Dr. Reilly but for the case in hand kindly bring your own medicines."

Bates made the trip. Colonel Wood, who stayed in Washington, accepted an invitation to join some military brass for dinner. The next morning, Assistant Navy Secretary Theodore Roosevelt wrote his wife about meeting the "very interesting Dr. Wood of the Army there," and how he had "been all through the last Apache campaign." The duo quickly forged a friendship, sharing a love of hunting and a conviction that the United States must "liberate" Cuba from Spain. Wood soon discovered that Roosevelt was as ambitious as he was.[10]

On June 9, the presidential train left Washington, wound through Virginia all day, and headed for Hot Springs, where the party of fifty spent

the night. As Ida played rounds of euchre and cribbage with War Secretary Russell Alger and his wife Annette, Secretary of State John Sherman,
Postmaster General James Gary, and Agriculture Secretary James Wilson,
nobody mentioned the controversy stirring in the paper about the speech
that Roosevelt had made days earlier, "To Be Prepared for War Is the
Most Effectual Means to Promote Peace."

Behind Roosevelt's argument that the United States must build twenty
battleships to "protect our interests" in foreign nations where American
manufacturers used natural resources and "protect our commerce" by
claiming the right to all oceanic shipping routes was his philosophy that
no "life is worth having if the Nation is not willing . . . to pour out its
blood . . . rather than submit to the loss of honor. . . ." His reference to
"cowards, or of those too feeble" to share his view was widely seen as a
reference to McKinley, intended to prompt him to act against Spain for its
presence in the American hemisphere and to liberate its possession, Cuba,
whose people it ruled with sadistic tyranny. Roosevelt privately derided
McKinley as a "jellyfish" for his cautiousness on the matter. McKinley,
however, had difficulty even finding someone for the thankless post of
American minister to Spain. Only on June 7 had he named Stewart
Woodford, who soon asserted that Spain must prove its promise to make
Cuba free by first withdrawing its troops from the island. If Spain refused,
McKinley vaguely threatened "further steps."[11]

Ida would have learned these details by reading the paper or overhearing murmurings between the Major and War Secretary Alger the next
morning, when they joined her at the viewing car's massive window to
take in the view of the Blue Ridge Mountains as the train chugged west.
During dinners over the past few months, Ida had come to know well the
individual Cabinet members and their wives, eventually feeling so relaxed
with her "official family" that she could be her real self.

As one of her later doctors told a friend, "when the social atmosphere
was unrestrained," Ida's "cleverness and wit was given free play, and she
proved a most interesting hostess." When a Cabinet wife who bragged of
her faith feared that an anonymous food basket she received might be poisoned, Ida teased her, "What are you afraid of? . . . Presbyterians believe that
nothing can harm one until the right time comes." She impersonated in
dialect some of the Major's zealous fans, like an Irish laundrywoman, who
bragged, "Sure and if the truth was known, me and the President is blood
kin, that we are! Me name is McKinney, and that's the same that his was before he got the stylish end hitched on to it." She even delighted in ribaldry.

"When I put Mr. McKinley to bed," she told the secretary of state's wife, "I go to bed with him." That Ida could be "light-hearted" was no surprise to a Canton friend, who believed her essential nature was "a very happy one." Even sardonic Thomas Beer conceded after his father's revelations about Ida that she had a "bright intelligence" and was "witty enough to amuse" some stiff egos. The Major especially appreciated it. "I'm tremendously glad that I married a woman with a sense of humor," he remarked.[12]

When they arrived in Nashville on June 11, the First Lady's entourage included her aunt-by-marriage Maria Saxton. Ida habitually brought a woman relative on long trips in case she needed a stand-in at events for any reason. The *New York Tribune* noted that when the public realized that Ida wouldn't join the procession through Nashville, there was "much disappointment" heard among the crowd. Typically, most of the citizens followed the president's carriage into town, and those more curious about Ida waited near the train until she emerged on an aide's arm to walk along a cleared path to her waiting carriage, nodding in response to applause she received. She would go to their hotel suite in the guest city, where she rested, changed, and then went on to the venue where the president was speaking. In Nashville, when Ida first arrived at the exposition grounds, she toured the Women's Building, which had home enterprise booths and civic group displays, but her auditorium entrance proved to be melodramatic, "one of the most delightful incidents of the trip."

As the governor of Tennessee spoke, his remarks were drowned out by a swell of applause from the back. "A moment later," the *Tribune* noted, "Mrs. McKinley appeared in the centre aisle" on the arm of a courtly Southerner. The governor "gracefully yielded the floor and the immense crowd were on its feet in a moment, cheering lustily" as she passed each row. The president then assumed his role, and rose from his seat on stage to gallantly dash to her. Ida raised her hands and he grasped them to lead her up a few steps and onto the stage. Like actors on opening night, they performed a last bit, the Major handing Ida a massive bouquet. She "bowed and smiled," and the audience "again broke into cheer."

Afterwards, Ida relieved an anxious women's committee by finally accepting their long-standing invitation to a reception, though she stayed only briefly. The party then left for Chattanooga, where, for the first of many times to come, the press reported that Ida did not attend church on Sunday. There were further stops in Knoxville, Tennessee, and Asheville, North Carolina. As she would at so many other times during the presidency, Ida McKinley served a symbolic but no less political purpose.

A primary objective of the former Union Army major, now president, was to convince the former Confederate states that they were part of the larger nation without disrespecting the South's culture from which it derived great identity. His larger vision was for nationalism to trump sectionalism, but it required the Southerners to trust his honor. Not only had staging his devotion to Ida in Nashville demonstrated to the Southerners the "knightly chivalry" they valued, but the *New York Times* suggested that white Southerners, having kept their pride through the indignities of Reconstruction, could relate to McKinley's "endurance that enables him to bear cheerfully the trials to which his nerves are necessarily subjected," a wordy euphemism for Ida.[13]

Upon their return from the South, Ida again belied the presumption that she was an invalid cut off from the real world. Reading in the *Washington Post* about its scheduled annual Pennsylvania Avenue parade of delivery boys, she immediately contacted the paper and asked for the parade route to be diverted onto the White House grounds, so she could show her respect for them. It was a touching little honor for the several hundred working-class boys of all races, some with disabilities, marching their banners beneath the North Portico to have the First Lady wave and cheer exuberantly to them from her window. Mrs. McKinley was less a maternal figure than she was an adult friend who respected children. She would stop her carriage to shout friendly questions or bid children to run over for a kiss. She coaxed them from crowds of White House tourists, and often took them upstairs to give them a gold coin. She was visibly hurt if they refused her gift of a flower or to speak with her, and worried about hurting them if she didn't immediately remember their names. When a visiting little boy asked her for toys to play with, Ida gleefully spilled a velvet pouch of her uncut jewels on the floor for him.

Children responded in kind. A demographic education study found that girl students with "high ambitions" considered Mrs. McKinley a role model "because she holds a high office." Some Milwaukee teachers arranged for students dressed in red, white, and blue clothes to stand in a flag formation along a presidential parade route for Ida—and she stopped the parade to speak with them. The First Lady even became a figure in the confession of a troubled child, who created a public embarrassment for her father after she claimed that Mrs. McKinley had visited her classroom and promised to obtain a federal job for him.

Her patience with little girls was boundless. She indulged her five-year-old great-niece Marjorie Morse for hours during her lengthy stay at the

White House, pretending to be frightened by the child's goblin tales and helping to arrange her dolls in the First Lady's bedroom. A great favorite was Grace Cortelyou, an executive clerk's daughter. If his wife was picking him up after work, Ida always asked her to bring Grace and let the child sit in Katie's rocking chair. Ida gave her a similar one on Katie's Christmas birthday. "It is as pathetic as it is beautiful," the *New York Tribune* observed, noting how children "appreciate that there is some special reason why they should be generous in returning the interest and affection. . . ." Ida gently but honestly told them why their visits meant so much to her, explaining to one, "You know I have no little girls of my own."[14]

Yet, by the persistence of her memory and the repetition of stories, Ida McKinley managed to carry the ghost of Katie McKinley into the White House some twenty-two years after the girl's death. If the toddler's portrait, clothes, and rocking chair did not make that clear, the artificial egg made of sugar, which the First Lady reverently showed guests as if it were a jeweled Fabergé egg, certainly did. A glimpse through the hole of the hand-crafted Easter gift presented a dioramic dreamscape of the White House lawn, with Katie and Little Ida playing on it.

In referring to her daughters so often and casually, as if they had simply left the room, Ida McKinley soon created a public familiarity with them. Mary Logan recalled how she "chatted lovingly of what might have been, if her own children had lived." A syndicated newspaper story, "The President's Children," melodramatically took it a step further: "There is an unspeakable, unfathomable depth of sorrow to the thought of what might have been Mrs. McKinley's happiness had her two daughters lived to see their mother in the White House. If living, they would now be young women, beloved and admired in the Washington circle of society. Alas!"

The "lost girls" tale gained momentum when the McKinleys made their first return to Canton as president and First Lady, on July 3, and visited Westlawn Cemetery to lay flowers on the "modest monuments" that rose "above each little mound" of Katie and Little Ida's burial plots. In an age preoccupied with mourning, it provoked something of a minor cult. After one reporter all but advertised the exact spot where Ida had "buried hope," tourists from as far away as California came to "see" the president's daughters, and souvenir postcards of their graves were sold. Even when Ida wasn't in Canton, she perpetuated public interest in her daughters, sending White House conservatory flowers weekly to Pina to place on the graves.[15]

Saxton House was chaotic when it became the presidential residence. Pina cleared rooms to accommodate the Major and his aides, entertained old friends of Ida who dropped in unannounced to see her, and endured Peeping Toms and serenades for the president. George Saxton's presence also gave the household a tense undercurrent. With George still unmarried and his love affair with Anna George over, his sisters were only slightly less humiliated by his slipping off to see the widow Eva Althouse. Managing all this while raising seven children made Pina practical. She dismissed the idea of Ida and the Major using the family-owned home behind hers, which was vacant when they first moved to the White House, as it would mean the loss of potential rental income.

While in Canton, Ida also finally convinced her niece Mary to take a year off from Smith College to be her companionate White House aide from November through the spring of 1898. Amused but unimpressed by Washington, the sincere, brown-haired student agreed out of duty to Pina. In a later interview with Margaret Leech, Mary affirmed that she "did not like to be with . . . Aunt Ida" without explaining why. Despite Ida's numerous other nieces, Leech noted that "no other was subject to the trying demands which Mrs. McKinley made on her favorite niece." Only by an embittered remark that Ida let slip during her last years was it clear that Mary was what she imagined Katie would have been like. The fantasy of a grown Katie, however, was not solely propagated by Ida. In fact, she was often more at peace with her loss than was the Major. After a friend once talked to the president about a debutante, he became strangely wistful, telling Ida how, if Katie had lived, "she would have resembled her." From her blue chaise, Ida took in his sadness, gestured him to her, and, using his family's name for him, said comfortingly, "God knew best, Will."[16]

During their stay in Canton, McKinley was reassured by the presence of physicians Thomas H. Phillips and F. E. O. Portman to attend to Ida if need be. When he returned to the White House on July 6 to prepare for their six-week vacation at Lake Champlain near New York's Adirondack Mountains, however, he had reason anew to worry. Dr. Bates was now too ill to accompany them. Perhaps because Dr. Wood had not yet seen the First Lady when she had a seizure, McKinley decided not to request his presence. Instead, within days of returning from Canton, he placed a rush order with Dr. Bishop, just as the physician was leaving New York for a lengthy trip to the remote country of Iceland. Bishop quickly prepared the compound and sent it by express. Not only was the First Lady's medicine delayed in arriving at the White House until July 14 but, as the president frantically wired Bishop's office hours later, "Bottle of medicine just received, not the same as the one preceding, please send the old medicine." Bishop's assistant,

M. E. T. Smith, was confused. Rather blithely, he responded to McKinley that Bishop "said it was the old medicine which Mrs. McKinley had been taking and that he desired her to continue the use of it until his return to New York. . . . I am sure it is the same old medicine which Mrs. McKinley has been taking for a long time. I will forward another supply, as you request, and trust that it may be satisfactory."[17]

When they entered the lobby of the Hotel Champlain, the Major signed the guest register as "William McKinley and wife, Canton," and Ida was flattered that their second-floor suite had been furnished in "my colors" of blue and white for her. The arrival of both Presidential Secretary Porter and War Secretary Alger, however, signaled that Ida would find herself competing for the Major's attention. The next morning, when five hundred blue-uniformed 21st Infantrymen from the Plattsburgh Barracks two miles away were seen approaching the hotel porch, it also became obvious that Ida would enjoy no ordinary vacation.

In honor of their commander-in-chief's presence, the Infantry began to stage marching maneuvers, a dress parade, and a regimental review on the hotel's large lawn. The manager had enclosed part of the porch with a flag to give the First Lady privacy, but the president ordered it removed, a reporter noting, "There had been a great deal of curiosity to see Mrs. McKinley, and this was now gratified." McKinley was praised for his "kindness." As a regimental band struck up a march, reporters, hotel guests, and the infantry saw McKinley lavish attention on Ida. She stared ahead at the Infantry, "apparently" interested, as one witness put it, "but she also seemed to be caring tenderly for the pretty daughter of Mr. and Mrs. Porter." If she intended to express displeasure about the sudden public intrusion, the president seemed unmoved. He declared, "Why, we ought to have this here every morning" and then went for a long walk with Alger, leaving Ida alone. That night, he hosted a reception for other hotel guests and several hundred locals. Ida sat watching, silently. The next day, he visited a local Catholic children's summer camp. Ida did not go. Two days later, the vice president arrived. Senator Fairbanks was expected days later. While he conferred for two hours with the vice president, war secretary, and U.S. ambassador to England, Ida stared out at the lake and mountains.

Even on their recreational outings, the president's priority was obvious. When they took a local train to pay respects at the grave of abolitionist John Brown, McKinley felt compelled to have it stop in every depot decorated with bunting, so he could shake hands with waiting crowds, like the 2,000 waiting for him at the Saranac Lake stop. A quiet dinner at the country home of Vermont Senator Proctor was cut short so he could make a spontaneous review of the Vermont National Guard.

As recorded in an editorial, the impression of one woman guest at the Lake Champlain Hotel who closely scrutinized the president's daily public rituals of devotion to Ida suggested that jealousy over other women he paid attention to contributed to Ida's miserable time. "Ever so much has been printed about the President's attention to his wife. I always thought it was greatly exaggerated. Not so," the unnamed guest offered. "Not that the President objects to a pretty girl. Oh, dear, no. I have watched him as he sat on the veranda. . . . When the girls looked up at him as they always did . . . he always smiled back at them as if he liked it, and not as if he was the President of the United States showing a favor." The editorial jumped to the rather harsh conclusion that while McKinley displayed "politeness and gentility," he was really "not . . . companionable at all" to his wife.

The only indication of Ida McKinley's mood was her refusal to even nod or smile, let alone speak when a flag was presented to the Infantry with an engraved plate indicating that it was a gift from her. Despite the Major's declaration that "Both Mrs. McKinley and I have improved in health," the press reported she was "much fatigued" and "very feeble." When Ida learned that the president had decided they would leave Lake Champlain so he could join a Grand Army of the Republic (GAR) parade in Troy, New York, she put her foot down. A press release reported that "Mrs. McKinley has often expressed a desire to visit Saratoga Springs, and in deference to her wish the entire party will leave here for that place. . . ." McKinley, however, wanted to join that parade and decided they would leave that night. While Ida was confined to the train, the Major joined the parade, unconcerned when a policeman shouted, "Anarchist to kill McKinley!" when he noticed a red flag in a tree and knew its significance. No credible threat was found, and the Major was eager to reach Buffalo, where the largest GAR gathering ever was underway. There was no further mention of "deference" to Ida's wish to visit Saratoga, and she never did.[18]

On August 25, McKinley led the parade in an open carriage and for six hours reviewed 45,000 marchers, watched by a crowd of half a million. It was rare for McKinley, who was generous by impulse, to enjoy being the center of attention so much that he seemed to make no effort to share the spotlight. Mrs. McKinley was expected at the parade, and her visit to the encampment of the Army Nurses Association was especially anticipated, but there was no sighting of her at all during the two days of festivities. She remained alone, in the private home of the Major's cousin George Miller, while the president greeted thousands at receptions in the Music Hall and the Buffalo Club for the Loyal Legion. During a midnight supper together, Mark Hanna convinced him to cancel a scheduled visit to Camp Jewett and instead take a cruise on his yacht *Comanche* across Lake Erie and stay at his Cleveland mansion. McKinley acquiesced. Porter explained the new itinerary to the press with the excuse that Ida had become "worn out."

Ida sat waiting for the Major on Hanna's yacht. McKinley decided to at least drive through Camp Jewett, followed by officials and reporters, but when his arrival was announced, a hostile policeman brusquely snapped, "I don't give a damn who it is, my orders are to let no one drive in here." Everyone watched for his reaction, but McKinley smilingly praised the man's sense of duty, even promising to reward him. It was too much for the *Washington Post,* which sarcastically recounted his "reputation for kindness, gentleness, tact, courage . . . upright and patriotic citizenship, the exemplar of simple, straightforward manliness, the illustration of a wise, conservative, and steadfast Americanism." While the paper hadn't before thought him a "poseur or any other kind of humbug," the editors concluded, "we can not imagine him in the role of even pretending to admire the ill-conditioned rowdy" with such "maudlin praise." The *Post* felt McKinley had gone too far in maintaining his image: "Too many demagogues have affected to extol it as rugged honesty in order to strike an attitude of greatness on their own behalf. But we hope and believe that Mr. McKinley will spare us an exhibition of this ridiculous and offensive hypocrisy by the President of the United States."

While the Major and Ida were still on vacation, there was a sharp rise in the number of reports from Cuba detailing the sequestering, torture, and starvation of its native women by Spain. Focusing on one account about a seventeen-year-old Cuban, Evangaline Cisnerous, who was starving in prison, Ohio Congressman S. S. Yoder drew ironic contrast to news stories of how protectively McKinley cared for Ida, suggesting that his silence about the atrocities raised questions about the sincerity of his concern for vulnerable women. As the McKinleys dined in the Hanna mansion, the new Women's National Cuban League began fund-raising for the Cuban women and called for the island's freedom from Spain. Former New York Congressman C. H. Turner pointedly quipped, "We hear that after his vacation our President will do something for the 100,000 persons who are starving in Cuba. God give him a short vacation."

On their return to Canton for the second time that summer, the McKinleys went their separate ways, she to Saxton House and he to his mother's home. Both found new concerns under each roof. In the brief weeks since Saxton House had served as the presidential residence, a warrant had been issued for the arrest of Anna George. Although the press withheld her name, it did report that in her letters to the president's brother-in-law, she threatened "to shoot, stab, or kill him." The press also reported her further threats to "his lady friends," and her breach of promise lawsuit against George Saxton. He went to the U.S. Marshal for protection, but because McKinley insisted that no Secret Service agents were needed to protect him, the prospect of a deranged Anna, gun in hand, at the "Canton White House" while the president was in residence had to be avoided.

Nancy McKinley's home, however, had its own tension. Like millions of Americans, the president's mother was outraged by the torture of Miss Cisnerous and attached her famous name to a petition-signing campaign begun by publisher William Randolph Hearst, demanding mercy for the girl from Spain's Queen Regent ("the first lady of Spain," former Confederate First Lady Varina Davis called her). Cisnerous was related to the would-be president of a liberated Cuban Republic, and Hearst cast her as a presidential daughter, thus enlisting the help of Julia Grant. He then asked Mrs. Grant to get the First Lady to join the cause. Ida, knowing that her public support would compromise the president's plan to avoid open conflict with Spain, resisted the plea.

The Major convinced Ida to leave Canton with him by suggesting a few days of peace at his brother Abner's rural estate in Somerset, Pennsylvania, but when he arranged a public reception and held meetings with the attorney general, the Maryland governor, a general, and a colonel in the house, his charade was called out. "Mr. McKinley's Holiday," announced another sarcastic *Washington Post* editorial, recounting how the "much-persecuted magistrate" fled "to a far-away retreat" in search of an "interval of peace," then reviewed "the quasi-royal bulletins" about "the receptions, the speech-makings, the civil and military ebullitions, the patient audiences and the poignant hand-shakings of which this exhausted President has been the victim." It harshly concluded that he had been deceptive about it all "from the very beginning."[19]

As Ida McKinley, leaning on her gold-headed cane, walked back into the White House on September 13, she could not have had any idea of the political consequence of the personal surprise that awaited her. Moments after she and the Major sat down for supper, Assistant Navy Secretary Roosevelt slipped into the hall adjoining their dining room, reminding an aide who was about to speak to the president to "keep the . . . secret." Just as she finished dessert, Ida heard the faint but unmistakable melody of *Home Again* and rose to find out where the music was coming from. Taking the Major's arm, she walked down the hallway and into the Blue Room, where the floor-length French windows opened onto the South Balcony. There she was greeted by Roosevelt—and the Marine Band. With his superior, Navy Secretary Long, out of town, Roosevelt had taken charge, arranging for the band to give the First Lady a private concert. Ida reacted with "intense delight" to a program that also featured not only the sentimental *Home Sweet Home* but the militaristic *Grand Army Patriot*.

Roosevelt's thoughtful yet politically deft move not only won over the First Lady but her husband too. The next day, September 14, McKinley invited him for a ride and praised his recently published pamphlet on the need to build a modern fleet of battleships. Roosevelt was pleased but cynical about the flattery. "Of course, the President is a bit of a jollier," he concluded. When Roosevelt then suggested intervention in Cuba, McKinley said that while he was "by no means sure that we shall not have trouble" with Spain, he intended to avoid war. Roosevelt boldly declared his every intention of fighting in a military uniform, a wish his wife couldn't even talk him out of. If it came to war, McKinley chuckled, Roosevelt could wear a uniform.

Three days later, Ida McKinley invited Roosevelt to dine at the White House with them and their guest, their personal lawyer, and the attorney general William Day, as if Roosevelt were under review. Ida's opinion of Roosevelt is unrecorded, but if she had raised any doubts about his loyalty or value to her husband, the Major would likely not have invited him for another carriage drive in public view just three days after that dinner. The day before, McKinley interacted with Roosevelt again—at a meeting with some of the Cabinet—but now the Major wanted to speak with him alone. In a span of seven days, the president, First Lady, and assistant secretary were together for five of them, cautiously engaged in a triangle of political courtship.

Roosevelt's thoughtfulness toward Ida had certainly prompted McKinley to focus more attention on this member of New York's elite class, whom he had previously perceived as being a bit distracted by his own ideas. During their third encounter, McKinley listened as Roosevelt outlined how placing naval ships in strategic positions off Key West for an easy blockade of Cuba and close enough to Manila Bay, foothold to Spain's possession of the Philippine Islands, would be key to victory in a potential war with Spain. Roosevelt was already developing this vision, pushing for a man who shared it, Commodore George Dewey, to head the U.S. Navy's Asiatic Squadron.[20]

Simultaneously, Ida McKinley unwittingly set in motion a shift in U.S. Army personnel that would soon provide momentum to Roosevelt's agenda. As Canton reporter F. B. Cass disclosed, Ida McKinley was "able to make herself felt, in a political way more than once since this Administration came in." When McKinley became president, James R. Tryon was serving as the U.S. naval surgeon general, and although his term expired in September 1897, he had no reason to doubt his automatic reappointment for a final two-year term and then retire on the generous pension. Just after Navy Secretary Long told Tryon that the president wanted to know the exact date his current term would expire, however, he ran into the terminally ill Dr. Bates, who told him bluntly, "Mrs. McKinley has promised my wife that I shall be appointed, and I suppose the appointment will be made." Although her action irritated top navy brass and even earned a veiled rebuke in the press, the First Lady's sole motive for having Bates named surgeon general was to ensure the financial security of his wife, her old friend. As his widow, Rosalie Bates would receive the large pension.

To override the First Lady's influence, Tryon went public, lobbying influential members of Congress and reporters to convince McKinley to retain him. A *New York Times* editorial about the pending Bates appointment even warned the president that naming an "intimate friend and family physician" would be a wrongful "slight." As reporter Cass chronicled, however, "it was of no avail against the wish of the President's wife." On September 21, just before the First Lady left with the president for a ten-day Massachusetts trip, Bates was named surgeon general.[21]

Despite the announcement that this autumn sojourn was for McKinley's "complete and undisturbed rest," Ida knew better. They were houseguests of his old friend William B. Plunkett, and McKinley so trusted his discretion that instead of having Ida struggle to climb to the second floor for the sake of appearances, the Major carried her and ascended the stairs. Unlike the Lake Champlain trip, the First Lady eagerly made public appearances. Plunkett led them through his Berkshire Cotton Factory and stopped the elevator and kept its door open on the floor where the milling machinery was running so Ida could glimpse how factory workers earned their living. The next day, as the McKinleys drove past Pittsfield high school in their open carriage, a few students, eager to shake the president's hand, leapt and held onto the side of the fast-moving carriage. Seeing that one teenage boy was losing his grip, Ida mustered a burst of sudden strength to pull him up to safety with her bare hands and was "obliged to hold him in," the papers reported. "He would have fallen under the wheels had it not been for her." Her act of spontaneous heroism dramatically contradicted the impression of a weak First Lady.

Equally startling, however, was the McKinley Administration's expanding narrative, introduced at the Hoosic Valley Agriculture Fair not by Cabinet members directing the nation's farms or factories but by its army and navy. With "factories again in motion," War Secretary Alger claimed that the United States was enjoying its era of greatest prosperity. After warning that the country would "defend its honor with the sword and the ship if need be," Navy Secretary Long declared that "in the hearts of the American people the name of William McKinley is becoming identical with peace and prosperity . . . and civilization." It was left to the president, himself, however, to link the nation's fate to "our Heavenly Father," assuredly in "His sacred keeping."

Although Long never mentioned Spain in his speech, that country's continued aggression in Cuba was never far from McKinley's thoughts during the Massachusetts trip. Days after the fair, he and Ida were honored dinner guests at the Lenox estate of John Sloane. Later accounts claimed that McKinley was anxious during the dinner because Ida had suffered a seizure. In truth, she was fine, and accounts detailed how happily she greeted guests who were invited to meet the McKinleys after the dinner. The president's tension was likely due to having to politely avoid the topic of Cuba, given the presence across the table of a fellow guest, the Spanish Ambassador Enrique Dupuy de Lôme.

While Ida did not have a seizure at the Sloane dinner, she did experience one at lunch the next day at the Stockbridge home of Republican supporter Joseph Choate. There, she experienced her first known seizure as First Lady in the presence of strangers. Choate's daughter recalled: "Suddenly in the middle of lunch the President rose from his chair, walked around the table and in the most dignified manner placed a napkin over the head of Mrs. McKinley (large napkins were then the fashion) and returned to his seat, saying "my dear wife is sometimes afflicted with seizures." The conversation was continued, and after a few minutes or so, Mr. McKinley got up once more, crossed the room and removed the napkin and Mrs. McKinley was herself again."[22]

That the First Lady's disability was revealed to strangers was mitigated by the fact that those who witnessed it kept it a secret. Except for a passing notice two days later that Ida had a "slight indisposition," the general public was never the wiser. Nor were there any such incidents when, shortly thereafter, she attended public concerts during a five-day trip to Ohio and Pennsylvania with the Major. By the time the First Lady was back at the White House, the public was told that "she looks like a different woman from the rather fragile person who went away. . . . She no longer walks with the assistance of a cane, and her step is quite elastic. Her color is greatly improved, her spirits have taken on greater vigor, and there is no longer any doubt of her being able to carry on all the requirements of her position. . . ."[23]

Three days after her departure for Cincinnati, the First Lady's doctor, Newton Bates, died. As more details emerged, the public learned that Ida had not only succeeded in arranging for him to briefly hold the status of surgeon general so his widow would receive his substantial pension but also prevented Dr. Tyron from being considered for reappointment to the post because he attempted to defy her wish by intimidating the president. The incident offered astonishing evidence of how, despite the presumption that she existed in languid passivity, Ida McKinley was often moved by a strong sense of purpose. From his observation of her behavior, White House aide Colonel Crook confirmed that by being "up and about," Ida was "doing her part, in every way desirous of aiding her husband so far as her physical disability would permit." In his 1897 book *The Sunny Life of Invalids,* which considered the impact of color on emotions, author Charles Howard Young used the First Lady's example of surrounding herself with the shade of "calming and cooling" pale blue as evidence of an unconscious inclination toward healing. In the popular magazine *Harper's Bazaar,* editor Elizabeth Jordan declared that, by refusing to passively assume the life of a shut-in, the First Lady was "an inspiration to all women" who "for one reason or another are hindered from playing a brilliant individual role in life."[24]

Despite periodic coverage that proved the First Lady was often independent and never entirely helpless, the nation's newspapers and magazines found more drama in portraying her as an invalid and defining her sole value as the Major's wife. In his essay "The Appeal of Frailty," prominent novelist and journalist Julian Hawthorne depicted her as a mere quivering vessel for the Major's godliness. To most men, he wrote, "such a wife would have become a burden," but for McKinley, Ida brought out "what was noblest and most generous." She became the Major's object of "special reverence as for something sacred and exquisitely beyond common humanity. . . ." Such maudlin pathos had popular appeal. Creswell McLaughlin, editor of a monthly teachers' magazine, suggested that the president's "gentle affection for his wife" should be "told to school boys" as a "pattern of knightly behavior." A hospitalized Pennsylvania woman wrote McKinley that his care for Ida "made thousands of women your devoted friends." After propagating a "weeping lantana" flower, commercial horticulturalists Conrad & Jones named the drooping flower "The Mrs. McKinley."[25]

Before she met the McKinleys, Marion Harland drew her perception of them from the popular image of the Major "tied to the arm-chair of a hopeless invalid." Once she came to know them, Harland recognized the tremendous degree to which Ida had been adapting and sacrificing her life on behalf of the Major's career, a point she emphasized whenever she encountered "contemptuous criticism" of Ida as a burden to him. One account made clear just how different Ida and the Major were from the prevailing assumptions made about each of them. As their train paused in a depot one afternoon, several dozen people surrounded it, hoping to catch a glimpse of the president and First Lady. McKinley ordered his window curtains closed, but then feared the public's reaction to this, so he directed Porter to tell the press, "While the President is thoroughly democratic and likes to talk and meet with people, he objects to being stared at, having unnecessary crowds about him and being regarded as an object of curiosity." Ida simply left her window open so the public could see her.

The First Lady was thoroughly unaffected. She spoke bluntly to reporters and the public, freely expressing joy or anger. She did likewise in reference to her fluctuating mobility problem. "I always forget that I cannot walk until someone reminds me of it," Ida McKinley had casually offered during the campaign. "My husband's right arm has so taken the place of my foot that I have never been deprived of any enjoyment in life because of my lameness." A tourist watching her exit the White House could see plainly that "She walked with a limp, as if in pain," but Ida used a cane or wheelchair if necessary without embarrassment. Her attitude made clear her belief that disability could be alleviated by challenging rather than succumbing to it. She did not reprimand her friend Mary Logan for publicly writing about the First Lady's physical condition, whether it was praise that "the effort she made was quite remarkable, in the face of her invalidism" or provocation of further curiosity by asserting that the medical details about it "can never be told." Nor did the White House reprimand newspapers that printed suppositions about her condition as conclusive facts, as when the *New York Tribune* emphatically declared that Mrs. McKinley suffered from "partial paralysis of one leg."[26]

The Major, however, remained in charge of Ida's medical care, even after naming Capt. Leonard Wood as the new White House physician. At times, Wood almost seemed more focused on where his high-profile appointment might lead than the fact that his knowledge of the First Lady's condition was limited by what the president chose to tell him. He had already proven himself adept at using social connections to gain greater status. Only two years before, Wood had coaxed his wife's uncle, a Supreme Court justice, to pressure President Cleveland's war secretary into naming him a U.S. Army Medical Corps assistant surgeon. Once he was on call for the Clevelands, it was just a matter of weeks before Wood's son was playing in the White House kindergarten with the president's daughters.

Soon enough, when Public Buildings Commissioner Theodore Bingham conspired to dishonestly use the First Lady as an excuse for his plan to reduce entertaining, Wood proved acquiescent. Bingham's press statement that "Mrs. McKinley, who is not sure that she will be able to endure the trying ordeal of the formal receptions, desired to have the number of guests at each restricted" was given credence by the additional fabrication that she did so at the "commands of her medical adviser." Dr. Wood had not, in fact, assumed such a prerogative. As for the advisability of continuing to dose Ida with Dr. Bishop's bromides, Wood either did not perceive the effect of the medication on her or did not question the president about it. Even just shortly after Wood became White House physician, McKinley sent yet another check for $250 to Bishop for more of his medicines.[27]

As the months ahead would prove, Wood was more focused on matters other than Ida McKinley. "Today I took a hard walk with Doctor Wood and we both discussed how we could get into the Army that would go to Cuba," Assistant Navy Secretary Roosevelt wrote his son. Whether Wood told him that Ida McKinley had seizure disorder is unclear, but when mere bravado failed to land him on the sands of Santiago Bay, this advocate for sterilizing the "feeble-minded" would realize Ida's power to thrust him into glory.[28]

⁕ 10 ⁙

In Time of War

IDA MCKINLEY HAD DEFIED public expectations by adapting the idealized First Lady's role to the reality of her life. Encouraged by the absence of any prolonged period of disability, she began to assume more trying responsibilities—as the attentive guardian of her husband's well-being, as a patriotic symbol during a national crisis, and as a political partner offering advice.

On New Year's Day 1898, she was spared the arduous task of greeting thousands of guests at the annual reception, which was cancelled since it fell within the mourning period for her mother-in-law, who had died at the end of 1897. Ida focused instead on the small debutante ball she would host for her niece Mary Barber in mid-January. In attendance was another winter houseguest, the president's niece Mabel McKinley, whose beautiful singing never failed to lift the spirits of the executive and domestic staffs. In this winter of content, the First Lady also indulged her passion for theatrical comedies, laughing uproariously in the presidential theater box many nights at *Beau Brummel, The Highwayman, Lord Chumley, Old Homestead, One Summer's Day,* and *Hotel Topsy Turvy.* "There is enough trouble in the world without seeing sad plays and reading sad books," Ida once explained, "One can't see much of life without laughing at it."[1]

Ida McKinley's compelling interest in theater soon led her to establish a new precedent among First Ladies, becoming the first to frequently invite actors to the Executive Mansion, an honor that gave credibility to a profession long scorned as disreputable. The night before taking her nieces to see Joe Jefferson in *Rip Van Winkle,* for example, Ida invited him to dinner so the girls could ask about the show, which he had made famous. Moved by *Way Down East,* Ida asked its lead, Phoebe Davies, to come discuss it with her at the White House. In the family quarters, Maggie Cline, the

"Irish Queen of Vaudeville," was impressed at how the First Lady "showed very much interest in my theatrical work, and asked me very many questions." In one of the first known instances of an actor entertaining in the White House, Mrs. McKinley arranged for an actress identified only as a "Miss Oliver" to perform some character monologues by playwrights Ian Maclarence and John Barrie (author of *Peter Pan*) for guests after a Blue Room reception. The event was so unique that it even prompted the president to slip down briefly from the Cabinet Room to watch.[2]

Undaunted by a heavy winter and spring entertaining schedule, Mrs. McKinley was fueled by an "elixir of ambition" fed to her most mornings by Dr. Wood. What he truly thought of her is hard to assess, but his authorized biographer and friend Herman Hagedorn ridiculed the First Lady as a "far-away creature, pathetic and unrestrained, who had . . . [no] hold on life or on herself." What the *New York Times* called his "tenderness with his patient" nevertheless served Wood well. Instead of dispensing medication, however, Wood's "stimulating" effect on Ida were his talks encouraging her to increase her activity while calming any anxiety resulting from it. There is no record of Ida enduring seizures while under Wood's care; his reduction of her stress may have helped her avoid these. While he preserved the record of awards and gifts given to him by the McKinleys, Wood left no documentation of his medical care for Ida and never acknowledged her seizure disorder. If Ida needed bromides, however, the Major usually dispensed them. Either way, the president quickly developed "unbounded appreciation" for Wood, and in less than six months, it was publicly reported that McKinley was "anxious to do anything to show his gratitude." McKinley knew, as *McClure's Magazine* would report, that "Wood's keenest ambition had always been to get into the line of the army and see active service."[3]

In addition to the scheduled season of White House dinners that winter, Ida and the Major hosted a unique one in January to honor Sanford Dole, the recently installed president of the Hawaiian Republic. Anticipating later official protocol, Mrs. McKinley first greeted his wife in the private quarters and was presented with a "state gift," a white bracelet from Hawaii with the native greeting "Aloha" in gold inlay. Ida never gave her opinion on the United States' annexation of the islands, but her presence in the Cabinet Room to witness McKinley signing the resolution signaled a tacit approval. Another McKinley innovation, introduced at the Dole dinner, underlined the growing sense of American global imperialism by military might—the playing of a martial air, *Ruffles and Flourishes,* to precede the traditional *Hail to the Chief,* which signaled the entrance of the American president. At the diplomatic reception a week earlier, not only did John Philip Sousa's tribute waltz to her, *The Lady of the White House,* premier, so too did *For Glory, Liberty, and Flag.*[4]

Two weeks later, on February 12, Ida and the Major hosted an official reception to honor the Diplomatic Corps. All eyes were on the regal Castilian wife of Spanish Ambassador de Lôme who, it was whispered, was guiding his "handling of the delicate Cuban problem." In her silver gown and diamond star pin, Señora de Lôme was received by the First Lady with the same neutral greeting she had offered at a reception four months earlier to the famed Evangeline Cisnerous, after the Cuban heroine was located in Havana, freed, and smuggled to the United States.[5]

Despite the dramatic rescue of Miss Cisnerous, tens of thousands of Cubans, charged with supporting rebel freedom fighters, continued to perish in concentration camps there. When Spain indicated that it would accede to McKinley's demand to remove its troops as a move toward Cuban self-determination, Spanish soldiers rioted in Havana and threatened retribution on U.S. sugar and other business properties there. In a move that the president claimed was intended to protect American interests in Cuba, he ordered the battleship *Maine* into Havana's harbor on January 25.

In reaction, de Lôme angrily vented in a private letter, saying that McKinley was a "low politician" catering to the "jingoes of his party," and that Spain didn't intend to honor its promise to him. Cuban freedom fighters intercepted and gave the letter to newspaper publisher William Randolph Hearst, whose publication of it incited outraged Americans to support war with Spain. Not even the First Lady was spared Hearst's "yellow journalism" tactics, such as printing rumor and sensationalizing facts. A story circulated that when Mrs. McKinley's Angora cat had given birth in 1897, she named two of them de Lôme and Weyler, the latter being Spain's ruler of Cuba. Once the de Lôme letter was published, the story claimed, she ordered the kittens to be drowned. Ida was surely outraged at de Lôme's insult of the Major, but the story was absurd for several reasons, not the least of which is that she never had a cat.

When Ida arose on Tuesday, February 16, the Major had already gone down the hall to the executive offices, where clerks were jammed into their small workrooms. On the state floor below, domestic staff moved furniture to prepare for the season's last reception scheduled that night, but before Ida finished breakfast, she got word that it was canceled. When Dr. Wood arrived, he went not to the First Lady but to the president to volunteer his military service. Ida was among the first to learn the stunning news that in the dark of early morning, just hours earlier, the *Maine* had exploded in an otherwise peaceful Havana harbor. Two hundred sixty-six sailors, most of them asleep at the time, were killed.

Most of the press, the public, and Congress presumed that Spain had blown up the *Maine* and demanded that McKinley declare war. Instead, he ordered an investigation and resisted war "until I am sure that God and man approve." It was not a game of bravado to him. "I have been through one war," he explained. "I have seen the dead piled up; and I do not want to see another." One morning, when Dr. Wood, who had come to see Ida, persistently advocated aggression, McKinley finally asked sarcastically, "Have you and Theodore declared war yet?" The quip was prescient. While the navy secretary was out of town, Commodore Dewey got an order, cabled by Roosevelt, to gather the navy's Asiatic Squadron at Hong Kong and prepare to advance on the Philippines.

McKinley's investigation committee did not find irrefutable proof that Spain had blown up the *Maine,* but its conclusion that it had likely mined the harbor was enough for most to raise the war flag. Not unlike the way McKinley used Ida to gain popular support, Sen. John M. Thurston of Nebraska made a "masterly" speech just after his wife's sudden death due to illness in Cuba, weeping as he invoked her dying request that the island be liberated. McKinley did finally request a $50 million defense appropriation, which Congress quickly approved, but he greatly feared that necessary preparations for conducting a U.S. war on foreign soil weren't in place.[6]

The prospect of impending war left the president with little sleep or regular meals, but only enervated the First Lady. Two weeks after the *Maine* tragedy, she was lead patron at a Washington concert fund-raiser to aid the widows and children of those killed on the ship. Three weeks after that, she went alone to Baltimore's Ford's Opera House to head a matinee benefit, which raised $5,000 for a monument to the sailors. On March 11, she hosted her first state dinner for a head of state, Belgium's Prince Albert, enlisting distinguished violinist Leo Stern to entertain guests afterwards. The long state floor hall was illuminated by red, white, and blue electric lights. For a dozen Canton friends who filled guestrooms to capacity, she held a reception and a luncheon for forty. "Are you not worried?" someone asked her. Ida gestured toward the executive offices. "Is not father there?" she quipped. "He will see that all comes right."[7]

On the morning of Thursday, April 21, the Major was helping Ida into their carriage under the North Portico, about to escort her, Mary, and Pina to the depot, where they would catch the train to New York. Suddenly,

Assistant Secretary of State William Day ran over from the adjacent State, War, and Navy Building, waving Spain's refusal to accept the terms of McKinley's ultimatum that it withdraw all its forces from Cuba. The Major kissed Ida, sent off her carriage, returned to his office, and had the news sent by messenger to the Senate Foreign Relations Committee. It signaled preparation for a declaration of war.[8]

Shortly after six that night, as Ida entered the Windsor Hotel in New York, a reporter noted that she was "looking very well," and indeed, as she told a friend, her "health is better than it has been for years." She turned down an offer to attend the meeting of a women's committee preparing to outfit a hospital ship to treat war wounded since she was in New York "privately." Ida McKinley quickly discovered that no matter what lines she drew for herself as a private citizen, to the nation she was always First Lady, an especially patriotic figure in wartime.

That night, the Windsor Hotel coaches dropped off Ida and her family at Daly's Theater as the orchestra struck up the overture to Oscar Hammerstein's comic opera *La Poupée*. The house lights were dim by the time Ida's party was seated in a central balcony box. The play's story of a determined but somberly religious young man who ends up marrying the "living doll" daughter of a wealthy man likely amused Ida, but as the intermission lights came on, she was thrust into her public role. As word spread that the First Lady was there, the band struck up the *Star Spangled Banner,* prompting the audience to rise and applaud. Press reports suggest that Ida was shocked, but nodded to the crowd. She had only witnessed this sort of public reaction when she was with her husband. Now this demonstration was for her.

The next day, when the manager of the Manhattan Theater learned that the First Lady was coming to see *Way Down East* there, he adorned her mezzanine box with evergreens, roses, and flag bunting. As the doors to the box opened and Ida walked in, thunderous applause rose from the audience as the orchestra burst into *Yankee Doodle.* This time, the First Lady waved her gloved hand and bowed until the lights dimmed and the show began. When the curtain opened on the second act, the audience saw that a picture of the president had been added to the set, and they spontaneously rose in ovation, staring up at Ida. She bowed again, more curtly.

As she was being hailed in New York, the president was ordering the blockade of Cuban ports and issuing an initial call for 125,000 volunteer soldiers. On Sunday, as she drove up to Grant's Tomb, he authorized Dewey's fleet to move into Manila Bay.[9]

On Monday, reporters noted that Ida received a parade of social callers and accepted an invitation to dine that night at the Mayor's home,
but knew nothing about the doctor who later slipped into her suite. Although he continued to send her medication to Washington, it had been
at least five months since Bishop had examined Ida. He wrote McKinley
that she was "well and happy," and he was pleased with "the good recovery she had made since I last saw her."[10]

Dr. Bishop would use well his renewed access, plying the White House
with unsolicited recommendations for political appointments of friends.
He wasn't the only one to benefit from rendering service to Mrs. McKinley. It had been twenty years since she was treated by Weir Mitchell, but
he successfully fished for invitations and wheedled a pair of her knitted
slippers for his Philadelphia church bazaar. None pulled as great a plum,
however, as Dr. Wood.[11]

In War Secretary Alger's authorization to increase the military establishment "in time of war," he included "regiments of cavalry . . . composed
exclusively of frontiersmen possessing special qualifications as horsemen
and marksmen." The idea had been approved by the president at Dr. Wood's
request. Each regiment would have one colonel and one lieutenant colonel.
Just days earlier, a frustrated Assistant Navy Secretary Roosevelt had been
ruminating, "I shall chafe my heart out if I am kept here instead of being
at the front, and I don't know how to get to the front." McKinley granted
Roosevelt's wish, offering to make him colonel of this new cavalry regiment. Roosevelt wisely took the lieutenant rank, urging Wood, an experienced soldier, to become colonel. By early May they were in San Antonio
training marksmen for their "Cowboy Cavalry," later famously known as
the Rough Riders.[12]

In New York, Ida McKinley kept abreast of the developing war, but
not through the papers alone. Upon arrival at the Windsor, the customary
telegram from the Major awaited her. Soon there was a phone call from
the White House, not from the Major but her young cousin Sam Saxton,
volunteering as an aide during the crisis. He reported that the president
was still "very tired and worn out." Ida immediately wired the president
back, less to assuage his worry for her than to express her worry for him:
"Arrived in good shape. Am well. Sam Saxton called. Do not expose
yourself or work too hard."[13]

Ida, still concerned about him, insisted that a direct connection be hooked
up between the Windsor and the White House, so she could speak to him

without going through the central exchange and risk having their talks transcribed for the yellow press. During her four days in New York, she called him twice a day. One bit did leak out: Ida encouraged him on Saturday, telling "of the enthusiastic support which the people of New York were giving to his policy in the present situation." Sometime on Monday afternoon, once Dr. Bishop had left her suite, she called her husband again. He told her the news. Spain had declared war against the United States the day before, so he had called a special morning meeting of the Cabinet and gained its approval to submit the formal declaration of war to Congress. In recognizing the independence of Cuba, he had also disclaimed any American interest in the territory other than providing a stewardship to establish its new government. Secretary of State John Sherman did not agree and resigned. He was replaced by Assistant Secretary William Day, a close friend of both McKinleys from Canton.[14]

Undoubtedly, Ida detected exhaustion in his voice and his somber mood. He was the sort of person who would carry a sense of responsibility for the inevitable deaths of others, regardless of their citizenship. The First Lady promptly cancelled her dinner that night with the mayor and, in fact, the rest of her stay. She announced that she would take the midnight train to Washington, so she could "breakfast with the President" and be with him during the trying first days of war.

Five days later, Ida was hosting a Sunday gathering of the Cabinet family, army generals, and Dr. Wood and his wife. She had asked the singer Geraldine Farrar to entertain guests that night, an especially hot May 1. Isabelle McKenna, the daughter of McKinley's first attorney general, then appointed to the Supreme Court, entered the White House as the upset president rushed down the stairs, headed for the Red Room, "his face . . . tense and serious," waving telegrams. "There has been a big fight in the Bay of Manila. We've had a cable from Dewey. The Spanish fleet has been annihilated. Seven men injured. Poor boys!" He came down to share the news with Ida but handed her the telegrams. "Take these, Isabelle, and read them to my wife." Isabelle entered the Red Room, broke the news to the First Lady while she sat on a sofa, surrounded by some guests. Ida read the cable, struggling with her poor pronunciation of the Spanish names of the ships that had been destroyed by Dewey.

That McKinley would have someone else tell Ida the news indicated to her just how busy he was. She also knew how distraught he became whenever he learned that people had been killed. Before the concert began in the Blue Room, Ida whispered to Geraldine Farrar. After a few songs had been performed, Ida sent a message to the president in the Cabinet Room, insisting that he come down. When the harried man finally appeared in the door, Farrar broke into a stirring *Star Spangled Banner,* and McKinley broke into a smile. Ida orchestrated the little surprise to lift his spirits. As more telegrams arrived with more news, Ida stayed up well past midnight as the military leaders discussed the news of Dewey's victory and predicted its effect. The mood never turned celebratory, however, as the president was haunted by the death of hundreds of Spanish sailors. "Poor devils! Poor devils!" he kept repeating.[15]

Ida's active efforts and concern over her husband's safety and the war's toll on him contradict an enduring story about her from this time, which was later recorded by Herman Kohlsaat. Based on his misperception that she was "frail and ill" at a Blue Room concert in early spring, he presumed that worry for her health was taking a toll on the president. McKinley was physically and emotionally worn from anxiety and lack of sleep at the time, not because of concern for Ida, however, but because of the lack of armament and troop supplies. In a previously unpublished excerpt from Cortelyou's diary at the time, he recorded a conversation he had with the First Lady: "I spent over an hour with Mrs. McKinley today . . . appeared quite well for her. . . . [S]he talked much about the President, his need of rest, that he had lain down on the couch in her little room last night and fallen asleep there, sleeping until 11 o'clock; that he then came into their room but did not sleep well the balance of the night. We thought he had not appeared well today and needed to get away."[16]

Two other reports from the period make clear that it was McKinley who insisted on interrupting his work to check on Ida, rather than she demanding that he do so. Sometime between June 14, when U.S. forces left Tampa for Cuba, and June 24, when the first land battle there began, a friend of Secretary Porter stopped by the executive offices to see him, unaware that the president was working in the Cabinet Room. McKinley, who was meeting with Hanna (who had been elected to the U.S. Senate from Ohio months earlier) on how to compensate for the supply shortage once troops landed in Cuba, asked to be alerted when Ida was ready to turn in for the night. When her maid tapped the door of the adjoining Oval Library, McKinley left Hanna and headed down to the bedroom for about twenty minutes and read to her briefly to help her fall asleep. Porter explained the ritual: "No matter how busy he may be, nor how deeply engaged in any subject, he invariably drops everything on the instant and goes into their own apartments." He returned and worked well past midnight. Hanna recalled that McKinley was immersed in "a conference of war counselors" when he suddenly "buried his head in his hands" and gasped, "I must return to Mrs. McKinley at once. She is among strangers." He quickly went down to the Blue Room. Ida was entirely engaged in conversation, having neither requested nor expected his presence.

In this same period, McKinley followed a similar pattern on occasions whenever Ida returned to the mansion. When he worked late on March 24 in the Cabinet Room, he sent word to the ushers that he wanted to be rung as soon as Ida's carriage returned from the theater, so he could run down to welcome her back. A week later, he decided to break from work, had a one-horse cab hailed for him, and took off for the depot, where the presidential coach was waiting for Ida, who was returning from Baltimore. He arrived in time to surprise her, and they returned to the White House together in their carriage. Taking small breaks to see Ida also served a more practical purpose. No Cabinet members, senators, or generals would take issue with the president if he left a meeting under the guise of devotion to his wife. These quick exits, however, also gave him an opportunity to think through the momentous decisions he was about to make without feeling pressured by questions or scrutiny from those waiting for an answer.[17]

In her telegram from New York, the First Lady's warning to the president, "Do not expose yourself," was not in reference to being out in the rain. The war had provoked a greater number of threats against him. A week after the *Maine* tragedy, Ida received a letter from Louisville signed by "A Vet" with threats against the Major. Two weeks after Dewey's victory, she received a report about two Spanish-speaking men in Lafayette Park, across from the White House, "threatening to shoot the President whenever he is seen in the streets." Threats came signed even by Republicans and Ohioans. There were Cubans who promised to kill him if he didn't retaliate for the *Maine*—or if he did. Other threats specified that he would be poisoned or strangled. Five threats were received on March 28, for example, and sixteen the next day.[18]

Even if she hadn't insisted on opening much of her own public mail, Ida McKinley knew a president always faced danger. Both she and Cortelyou urged him early on to be accompanied by a member of the White House police force or Treasury Department detective in the Secret Service unit, which focused on counterfeiting and other plots subversive to the government. In late March, McKinley authorized a White House night watchman to secure the hallway of the family quarters. According to journalist Winfield Scott Larner, there were times when the president furtively slipped from the house to stroll downtown streets late at night, once he was certain that Ida was asleep and unable to prevent him from taking such a risk.[19]

Wartime was the only period, recalled electrician Ike Hoover, "that anyone ever saw him in the least indifferent towards Mrs. McKinley. . . . He would be literally dragged away from her by the clamorous demands of one person or another for a confidential talk." There is neither any recollection nor suggestion that the First Lady intruded on him in the middle of a war meeting. On those nights when she was certain that he was working alone, however, she would often come to check on him, using her cane to walk down the hall from the family quarters to the executive offices, where she would sit beside his desk and knit. If he wasn't coping with a time-sensitive crisis, her presence also gently suggested that they return to their room for a full night's sleep. On other occasions, the First Lady protected the president's health more assertively. When Abner, who lived at the Windsor Hotel, dropped by the McKinley suite to see his brother, Ida smiled at him, but said, "I shall not let you see him for an hour. He is resting."

Even close observers of the couple were unable to determine which spouse's worry prompted that of the other. "Sorrows and success seem both to have so tempered their lives as to have completely blended them into an inseparable one," said *Repository* editor George Frease. During the war this mutuality rarely benefited either. "The President and his wife could not be as much together in those anxious days and evenings, as they had usually been," Crook wrote, adding an astute note about their dynamic: "Mrs. McKinley was greatly distressed because her husband was worried, and of course this added to his anxiety." The Major often worked as late as two in the morning, but when he got to their bedroom, Ida was wide awake with worry, waiting to see if he was all right. McKinley was worried as he knew that lack of sleep could provoke her seizures, so he sat beside her on the bed, wrapped his arm around her, and she fell asleep.[20]

Although appreciative that the Major "never forgets me, no matter how busy," Ida was acutely aware that his few moments with her were "all the time he can [spare]." After a rare joint interview with them, a *San Francisco Evening Call* reporter concluded that the First Lady "does not permit herself to make demands upon his time; she knows that he would respond to those demands even though he had to remain at his desk twenty-four hours at a stretch to make up for it." After McKinley left the White House in 1888 to catch a series of trains and come to her side in Canton, she claimed, she knew she had to "guard her own health like a dragon, knowing how much it means to his success that there shall be no anxiety."[21]

As the war got underway, Ida McKinley continued to be public and active. In the third week of May, she hosted a formal dinner and large reception, attended three dinners in private homes, and entertained several hundred members of the Mother's Congress during their annual convention. After the president's call for volunteers, over 1 million signed up and, at the end of May, the First Lady joined him in his first visit to Camp Alger in Virginia, which was one of the eight national training centers. After a review of some 12,000 troops, she ignored the risk to her weak immune system to meet with soldiers, tent by tent, alongside McKinley, for two hours in the heat. Ida and the Major both had a personal interest in the conditions at Camp Alger as it was the base for Ohio's 8th Regiment of volunteers from Stark County. It included the First Lady's nephew John Barber and the president's nephew James McKinley (George Morse, the husband of McKinley's niece, entered the 9th Infantry with the rank of second lieutenant). Weeks later, after spying an unusually young man in uniform touring the White House, she invited this Garfield Finlayson of Michigan, the army's youngest drummer boy, to join her for lunch and tell her about training at Camp Alger. Ida then gave him a bag of fruit to take back there. Later that summer, Ida joined the Major in making a similar visit to Pennsylvania's Camp Meade.[22]

During wartime, the First Lady received endless requests from relatives, friends, teachers, and employers seeking to help, in one way or another, their loved ones in the volunteer army. Ida even received such requests from close friends and relatives, like her old teacher Harriet Gault, who asked that two highly qualified brothers of the Farnum family be granted higher rank than private, and her Aunt Maria, who pleaded that her cousin Sam not be sent to the Philippines. Even her nieces made such requests. Ida Barber wanted Charles Bissell discharged so he could resume college, Mary Barber pleaded for E. H. Ferguson's release before he was sent to Cuba.

Lt. Col. Roosevelt, waiting in San Antonio for permission to move his cavalry to Tampa, where transports would carry U.S. troops to Cuba, was "restless beyond control," according to a contemporary report. His torrent of telegrams pleading for help from the powerful men in the Cabinet, War, and Navy departments got him nowhere. Desperate, Roosevelt finally "sought an [telephone] interview with Mrs. McKinley and begged her intercession with the President that an order be issued to have his regiment join the army of invasion."

Within ten days, Ida convinced the president to grant the request, which let the Rough Riders go to Tampa, bully their way onto a transport, and

"Teddy" set foot on Cuban soil before anyone else. "Pray present my warm
regards to Mrs. McKinley," he wrote McKinley on May 25, "and tell her
that she will never have cause to fear being ashamed of the First Volunteer
Cavalry which is, in a peculiar fashion, her regiment." However unwittingly, Ida McKinley changed the course of history by helping to put
Roosevelt on his fateful path.[23]

Except for sponsoring the two efforts to honor those killed in the *Maine*
explosion and their widows and children, the First Lady's "established rule
not to allow the use of her name as patroness" applied to wartime efforts
as well. She turned down a newspaper request to make a flag presentation
to the "most valorous ship that engages with the Spanish Navy," just as she
limited her support of a fund-raiser for those orphaned by the Galveston
flood to a goodwill letter.

Of less press interest was how Mrs. McKinley maintained her long-
standing support of the local Metropolitan Methodist church's Ladies' Aid
Society by sending them private donations and Garfield Hospital by delivering flowers, books, magazines, and other small gifts for distribution
among patients. The two national organizations she continued to help
both focused on aiding individuals in the most dire need, who had often
been abandoned by their families: the Crittenton Mission, which housed
and educated indigent women, and the Salvation Army, whose American
president Evangeline Booth, a close friend, recalled, "Mrs. McKinley was
a liberal donor." She also continued her "unobtrusive philanthropy" of
sending money or food directly to individuals, usually strangers, whom
she learned of through friends without concern of "pauperizing" them.
As the *Seattle Post-Intelligencer* put it, "she likes to give where she knows
the gift is needed and will be welcome." Ida McKinley viewed her support, however, as that of a private citizen, not a First Lady. She was wary
of organizations seeking to honor her. She accepted the Mary Washington
Association's first award to help establish the new organization, but seemed
impatient with the ceremonial praise for her. Waving away the ornate presentation box of the star-shaped medal, she told the group leader to just
"pin it on me" and then left.[24]

In preparing for the Spanish-American War, voluntary women's organizations also failed to get the First Lady named to their board of directors,
even by honorary title. Circumstantial evidence does suggest that she successfully encouraged the president to let the War Department accept the
services of a professional women's nurse corps, organized by the Daughters
of the American Revolution. The plan was brought to fruition by four

members, all within the First Lady's circle: Charlotte Hanna, Annette Alger, Mary Manning (the Cleveland treasury secretary's wife), and Martha Sternberg, the wife of Ida's new doctor, who was appointed on May 7.[25]

George M. Sternberg, a sixty-year-old army surgeon general with expertise in yellow fever, was a pioneer bacteriologist, a specialty that was especially suited to the First Lady with her compromised immune system. "In years of intimate association we learned to love and esteem President McKinley and his wife very highly," Martha Sternberg recalled. The First Lady's regular checkups proved to have broader consequences, however. Sternberg, according to the *New York Times,* "urged on the President the advisability of avoiding what he considered would be a useless and wholesale sacrifice of life in that the thousands of deaths which he predicts will occur among our troops as a result of the fever and kindred diseases."[26]

Not long into summer, however, Sternberg was overwhelmed by the larger controversy of poor planning and care of soldiers that quickly beset the U.S. Army. Problems included the mismanaged transportation of troops by rail to training camps and by vessel to Cuba, Puerto Rico, and the Philippines; rancid beef in canned food rations; and the lack of sanitary conditions in camps. Then Sternberg's worst fear materialized. By July 18, Ida learned that yellow fever had broken out in an American camp in Cuba, affecting three hundred soldiers. The First Lady wanted to determine the well-being of two nephews based there with the 8th Regiment. After some effort by army brass, Ida wired Pina three days later: "From advices received, health of Eighth Ohio is good. No fever." It was likely that the First Lady pulled rank to get John Barber and James McKinley away from potential yellow fever in Cuba and safely reassigned to General Miles's staff in Puerto Rico; the undemocratic move was contrary to the Major's character.[27]

Any public resentment over the First Lady exercising such privilege paled in comparison to the anger at War Secretary Alger's refusal to accept responsibility for the lack of medical care and coordinated removal of sick soldiers in Cuba, which increased the death toll. There were demands for McKinley to fire him. While the Major continued to endure extreme stress as Washington's oppressive summer set in, Ida declined offers to escape to estates in cooler locations and remained with her husband. She convinced niece Ida Barber to spend part of July and August with them and sparked a romance between her and Secretary Day's son. She also coaxed the president to take a few lengthy breaks and cruise down the Potomac. During a Navy Yard stop, the First Lady paused unexpectedly in the gunnery shop as she was "especially interested" in watching the process of casting cannons.[28]

At summer's end, after brief rests with Abner in Pennsylvania, the Herricks in Cleveland, and the Barbers in Canton, the McKinleys headed to New York, where they planned to visit returned troops at Camp Wickoff at Montauk Point, on the tip of Long Island. Along the way Ida contracted a cold, and a reporter thought she looked "*almost* ill" upon arriving in New York. To avoid exposure to any lingering yellow fever among soldiers, Ida remained in the city while the Major went to the camp. Weeks later, during McKinley's White House lawn reception for returning troops, she took a similar precaution and, from the shelter of the portico, greeted them with the assurance that "Mrs. McKinley takes the deepest interest in the welfare of the soldiers."[29]

By balancing her activity with caution, the First Lady went through a stressful time with no need for medical care. On June 4, Cortelyou had written that Ida "continues to improve, she looks vastly better than when she entered this historic old place. Now she can almost walk alone." Four days later, when he thought she "looked ill," she explained that she was just "suffering a very hard headache." She had turned fifty-one that day. At the end of July, the Major wrote that even in "trying weather," she was "very fortunate in the matter of health." A month later, Charlie Bawsel reported on "How well she looks." After another visit at the end of September, he found that "She was cordiality itself. Mrs. McKinley was so gracious. . . . [M]ore like her old self. . . ."[30]

Apart from the unpredictable seizures, Ida's most chronic problem remained the immobility of her leg and its secondary effect on her general health. A *New York Journal* article offered the most candid account about it: "So much has been already said about Mrs. McKinley's health that it seems best to plainly state the facts. She now suffers from partial paralysis of one leg, which makes it difficult, though not painful, for her to rise and walk up and too, from lack of strength which her inability to take healthful exercise naturally brings. Although not one of the so-called 'shut-in' Mrs. McKinley's occupations have necessarily been sedentary."

With her condition stabilized for over a year, the president was eager to attempt a new technique to cure her immobility and contacted osteopath Albert Fisher about "taking charge of Mrs. McKinley's leg's case." The McKinleys' hope for a potential resolution through osteopathy, which was then considered unconventional, was influenced by their close friend Julia Foraker. On her frequent visits to Ida, Julia usually brought her young son

Arthur, whose renewed ability to walk his mother attributed to osteopathy. "This new practice is not a fad, but a science," she declared. If the First Lady was "willing to talk to me of the matter," Fisher wrote McKinley on September 16, he felt "assured of the benefit Mrs. McKinley would receive." Due to the shocking tragedy about to hit her family in Canton several weeks later, however, she would never receive Fisher's treatment.[31]

Just prior to their return to the White House, the McKinleys stopped at an Ocean Grove, New Jersey, camp meeting of 20,000 Methodists, where a presiding bishop unapologetically linked Christianity to patriotism. "We march under the flag, but we also march under the banner of the cross," he said, "we regard the advancement of the one to be the advancement of the other." He furthered the association to include U.S. imperialism, turning to the President and remarking, "you also delight in marching with the army of the Lord under the banner of the cross . . . which will carry victory to the ends of the world." In his remarks, McKinley upheld the concept: "Piety and patriotism go well together. Love of the flag, love of country is not inconsistent with our religious faith." Powerful Protestant organizations with vast memberships had overwhelmingly supported McKinley for president, finding him an ideal representative of their faith, and often invoking his relationship with Ida as being illustrative of their values. Many had also fervently encouraged him to declare war on Spain, anticipating in victory the chance to carry out their missionary conversion work in its Catholic colonies. "You have no idea," his brother Abner wrote privately to their friend Walter McCabe during the campaign, "of the pressure on William from religious people. . . ." They were not a constituency to be ignored during re-elections.[32]

The United States had decimated Spain's defenses in Cuba in a series of summer battles, the most famous being Roosevelt's capture of San Juan Hill. Spain capitulated, and a cease-fire was called on August 12, 1898. McKinley sent Secretary of State Day to head his Paris peace commission and negotiate the terms with Spain. He named Leonard Wood as military governor of Cuba, fully intending to establish its autonomy as quickly as possible. Puerto Rico would become a protectorate. The president hadn't yet decided what to do with the Philippine Islands.

At the end of September, Ida heard the firsthand account of Cuba and Puerto Rico from her nephews, who had returned from Santiago. James McKinley was recovering from the dysentery that hit thousands of American troops, but John Barber had typhoid and was sent directly to Washington's Garfield Hospital at his Aunt Ida's direction and expense.

Pina came from Canton and, with Ida, doted on him until he fully re-covered. A year later he was back in the service, based in Hong Kong as paymaster on a Spanish ship that was damaged by Dewey but repaired by the United States.

The Saxton sisters, relieved by John's recovery, enjoyed themselves at a reception for the General Convention of the Episcopal Church. The First Lady, in white satin and diamonds, wittily engaged bishops from around the country. At one point, an aide whispered to the president about a tele-gram that had arrived for him. He grew somber. More telegrams came in.

After the guests left and the Major was upstairs in the family quarters with Ida and Pina, he gently shared with them the horrible news he had received from Canton. Earlier that evening, someone back home had been shot and killed. It was their brother George. Police were holding Anna George on suspicion that she had fired the gun.[33]

⊰ 11 ⊱

Thwarted Redemption

WHAT THE SAXTON SISTERS really thought about the sad end of their brother's life can only be surmised. Neither discussed it outside of the family. Pina, who had lived with George during his escapades and managed all of the investments that the three Saxton siblings jointly owned, seemed less surprised and got on with the business of the funeral arrangements and the reappropriation of his assets. Ida immediately asserted that she must attend his funeral, and the Major seized the moment to give her a more sordid briefing: her brother's sexual affair with Anna George had resulted in her being divorced for adultery, and George then abandoned his promise to marry her. McKinley's most recent secretary of state, William Day, an old friend of the Saxton family, revealed to newspaper editor Whitelaw Reid that for years the Major made sure that such a socially embarrassing scandal "had been concealed from Mrs. McKinley until now, and must therefore prove a great shock." Reid had just arrived in Paris as one of the five peace commissioners appointed by the Major to begin negotiations with Spain. With "a good deal of candor," Day shrugged and said that George's murder was "exactly what everybody expected."

Nobody dared articulate it, but as much as the circumstances of his brother-in-law's murder might tarnish the president's image by association, it did end the stress that George had caused the Major. Despite George's wealth and lack of living or family expenses, he still had to borrow $500 from the Major just twenty-five days before being shot. "You can send me a note payable on your own time," the president wrote him, "a year or two years—or whatever you think right." If George had used the loan to pay yet another demand for money from Anna George, the Major did not want to know.

The Saxton murder riveted the nation, newspapers printed illustrated inserts, and street-corner preachers railed about how George personified modern sin. An anonymously authored pulp book about the murder was a hit. Decisions were made quickly. The president would attend the strictly private Saxton House funeral and burial at Westlawn Cemetery but would leave immediately from there for a scheduled two-week speaking tour of the upper-Midwest. When the presidential entourage arrived at the Canton depot, they were met by the curious stares of strangers until Marsh whisked them away. When the Major and Pina strolled for some fresh air, locals nodded and whispered their sympathies. New reports said Ida "showed evidences of the sufferings from the shock" but "bore herself remarkably well and was able to be about the house." The sisters viewed George's body in his coffin and were relieved that no gunshots had damaged his face. Despite Ida's seclusion, there was no escaping the telegrams, letters, and floral tributes that poured in from even the diplomatic corps, Paris peace commission, and nearly every U.S. embassy around the world.

At the funeral, the family sat in the south parlor, apart from the casket, and a few of George's bike club chums stood in the north parlor. Two ministers recited prayers, and a quartet sang a hymn in the hall. When Ida emerged from Saxton House to enter the carriage and follow the hearse for the burial, staring crowds surged around her, and it was obvious that she "keenly felt the unfortunate notoriety of the occasion." The press reported everything from the lack of a eulogy to Anna George's plea of "not guilty" to murder charges.[1]

Ida fled Canton, heading to her cousin Mary in Chicago, where she would stay until the Major returned from his speaking tour. A reporter's remark that she was "well and cheerful" proved deceptive. Her public reaction to the scandal was to ignore it. She followed no mourning rituals. To a sympathy letter from Rosalie Bates, Ida dictated a response to say simply that she hoped they could visit when she was next in Philadelphia. Nor did she address speculation about why George chose to abruptly cut her out of a new will he made after the president first publicly hinted at going to war with Spain. George had never committed himself to a woman, let alone pacifism, but the timing of his rewritten will eclipsed a claim that he excluded Ida as a beneficiary because McKinley's insurance would support her in potential widowhood. Her disengagement was so convincing that it provoked a false but persistent rumor in Canton: "Do you mean to say that Mrs. McK does not know that George was shot?

What care and grief she is spared by the ignorance," Charlie Bawsel asked his wife. "Mrs. McK's is truly a bed of roses."[2]

The thought of George's wasted and immoral life faded rapidly from the Major's mind as he began his speaking tour, but themes of fate resonated through nearly sixty speeches he gave in six states. Alluding to the United States' potential accession of the Philippines, he asked his fellow citizens to ponder the need to take responsibility for what fate had put before them. At the Omaha Exposition, he again linked church and state: "The faith of a Christian nation recognizes the hand of Almighty God in the ordeal through which we have passed. Divine favor seemed manifest everywhere. In fighting for humanity's sake we have been signally blessed."

Two weeks after George's death, the Major returned to Chicago to rejoin Ida. As he watched the Peace Jubilee Parade from a grandstand, she was nowhere to be seen. During his Columbus speech, she stayed on the train. In Philadelphia shortly thereafter, she sat out of public view behind the stand where he reviewed yet another parade. She was well, but whether it was a symptom of sorrow or shame, she was overcome with a self-consciousness that begged for privacy. As the *New York Tribune* learned from some friends, there were times Ida suddenly became "averse to meeting strangers whose curious gaze affects unpleasantly her nervous temperament and sensitive nature. . . ." Halstead later revealed that Ida had insisted on remaining unseen not because she was in mourning but because of genuine grief. Further, she insisted that the Major's duty was to fulfill every public commitment and leave her be.

During a brief return to Canton several weeks later, Ida did not visit George's grave, even though it meant forgoing her customary visit to the nearby graves of Katie and Little Ida. At Saxton House, where she had once joined in spoiling the bad boy who grew into a sinful bachelor, there was no escaping his memory. A terminal illness, fatal fall, or vehicular accident were natural causes for grief, but a violent murder by gunshot, a loss inflicted in a second, added a shock that could haunt a survivor. For Ida, who was sensitive yet moral, George's death would have raised questions about earthly punishment and eternal forgiveness. The death of any loved one would usually provoke ruminations about where his or her spirit was now, and whether a survivor might someday be reunited with them. To someone like the Major, whose faith in Jesus and Heaven was the core of his being, there would be no conflict with such issues. To Ida who, as an adult, never suggested she found comfort in conventional religion, it could be troubling and a reason to seek some way of making up for George's sins, some magnificent gesture that would save the lives of others and serve as redemption from the shame that he had brought to her and their family. She may have those lives in the Philippines.[3]

During the four-month Spanish-American War, McKinley had deftly avoided committing U.S. support of Filipino independence to its leader Emilio Aguinaldo. After the August ceasefire agreement with Spain, McKinley began to publicly articulate his options. At the minimum, he would hold the commercial center and fortified capital city of Manila as a strategic base, which was already in U.S. control. A further option was to take Luzon, the largest and most populous island, where Manila was located. Recognizing that there would inevitably be problems in separating Manila from Luzon, he conveyed his decision to retain the whole island on September 16 to the peace commissioners before they left.

For the next six weeks, McKinley focused on his third and most controversial option of having Spain cede the entire archipelago of the Philippine Islands as a U.S. possession without granting it the right of self-rule. An August poll showed popular support for this, and he had been encouraged by the cheering endorsement of crowds on his tour. He also had tremendous support for "expansionism" from industrial capitalists, eager to open the vast markets of Asia to American products, ramping production, increasing employment, and enriching the nation. To forge a U.S. global power, political militarists urged him to make the islands its colonial foothold in Asia. Theodore Roosevelt, who was campaigning for governor of New York, pledged unapologetic fidelity to an American empire expanding into the Caribbean and Pacific. Naive military reports claimed that the Filipino majority would welcome U.S. sovereignty.

Some economic and political expansionists found it so implausible for McKinley to hesitate in seizing such opportunities that he was later accused of staging his tortured hesitancy just to preserve his image. He would not, however, be negotiating only for mineral lands, timber forests, or shipping ports. No matter how pragmatically McKinley used presidential power or disguised his intentions, he would not assume responsibility for a nation of 8 million people lightly. He needed to address this human element.

Even before the ceasefire, many Protestant organizations called for taking the islands, eager to expand their missionary work there after being long banned by Catholic Spain. "The United States possesses at the present hour stepping stones for its commercial and moral pathway across the Pacific," John Henry Barrows lectured in his "Christian Conquest of Asia" series at Union Theological Seminary, "Wherever on pagan shores

the voice of the American missionary and teacher is heard, there is fulfilled the manifest destiny of the Christian Republic. . . ." As Julius W.
Pratt observed in *The Expansionists of 1898,* McKinley was "neither unaware of this sentiment nor indifferent." He didn't need to hear a sermon
in church. He got one at home.

Among questions raised by McKinley's decision-making process is
whether Ida McKinley influenced it. In the fall of 1898, she became so
preoccupied with "saving" two segments of the Filipino population—the
youngest of its children and the Igorrote tribe—that it was noted by a
Senate wife, a Presbyterian missionary, the White House telegraph chief,
and the personal aide of J. P. Morgan. With scant corroborative sources
to verify it, decoding such a potentially consequential example of a First
Lady's role in presidential policy necessitates scrutiny of its complex and at
time conflicting context.[4]

On October 23, the day after Ida returned to the White House with
the Major, following two weeks of the president publicly suggesting the
idea of taking the Philippines, she welcomed a familiar face. Since Bill
Beer's work with the McKinley campaign, he had become a personal
aide to J. P. Morgan, who was scheduled to dine with the McKinleys and
several bishops the next night. Like his wily friend Abner McKinley, Beer
looked around corners for business opportunities. That autumn day, as he
sat across from Ida McKinley, he was eager to talk about the Philippines.
If he hoped that mentioning his plans for a Manila Navigation Company
to transport cargo among the islands would prompt Ida to confirm the
president's likely decision, he got no word in edgewise.

That night Bill Beer wrote his family: "Mrs. McK talked ten to the
minute about converting the Igorrotes. I hope you know how to spell the
name of this tribe because your fond father does not. Anyhow she wants
you and Alice to pray for the Igorrotes or Iggorotes. Tell your mother that
Mrs. McK asked for her. She was wearing a pink dress with green spots."

It was just two weeks and two days since the "savage" murder of "wild"
George, but Ida may have chanced upon an opportunity for her redemption
from the scandal while reading about the drumming and chanting of the
mysterious Igorrote tribe echoing through the remote mountain jungles
of northern Luzon. Many Americans that fall read the riveting description
of these "ferocious head-hunters, drinking the blood of their victims and
celebrating the return of successful raiders with frightful orgies."

Although this was already an outdated caricature when it first appeared
in the 1870 *Ethnographie der Philippinen,* Englishman John Foreman drew

on its vivid impression in his book, *The Philippine Islands,* the only one available in English on the people of the islands prior to the war. All summer, Foreman was so widely quoted in American newspapers about the need for Igorrote resistance to be "civilized" specifically and the Filipino inability for self-rule generally that the two distortions smoothly melded into a generalized fallacy. After reading his article in the August 1 issue of the British *Contemporary Review,* McKinley even asked Foreman, as an expert on the Philippines, to brief the peace commission. In that same month's *The Century* magazine, which the McKinleys read, Wallace Cumming claimed that not only the Igorrote of Luzon but other island tribes "live an utterly savage life, and have never been even nominally subdued," a result perhaps not unrelated to the fact that "no Protestant church can be built, no service held" in the Philippines. The *Washington Post* even offered a solution: some tribes would simply have to be "captured or exterminated." Could saving an unrestrained Igorrote atone for not saving an unrestrained George Saxton?

If Ida questioned the truth of what she read, photographs would soon seem to "officially" confirm it. They were issued as part of a government report on the Filipino people by someone the Major personally entrusted to conduct the study, zoology professor Dean C. Worchester.

With all the expertise gained from classifying the mammals and reptiles of the Philippines, Worchester set out to take photographs of its humans to illustrate his government study, focusing his pictorial chronicle on the bare-breasted females and bare-buttock males of the Igorrote. Popular stories about the Philippines, "illustrated by photographs through the courtesy of the Bureau of Insular Affairs," soon had Americans gasping at what they assumed represented the whole population. By the time Igorrotes were "imported" for the Seattle Exposition, the Women's Christian Temperance Union protested the immorality not of putting them on public display like zoo animals but because they were seen in loincloths. As James H. Blount, a Luzon judge and then the Philippines interior secretary appointed by McKinley, grumbled, Worchester succeeded in "preparing for salvation, the various non-Christian tribes." With her particular interest, however, Ida may have ultimately found some hope in Worchester's misguided wisdom. Worchester's article in the October 1898 issue of *Century Magazine* concluded: "Taken as a whole, then, the pagan tribes may be said to present no serious problem except the one involved in their ultimate civilization. The results of the few half-hearted attempts that have been made in this direction have been such as to convince me that they might make rapid progress, as soon as the condition of the civilized natives could be sufficiently improved to afford a practical illustration of the benefits of civilization."[5]

On October 26, three days after the first documented instance of the First Lady's expressed interest in the Philippines, the president conveyed his decision to the peace commissioners: "leaving the rest of the islands subject to Spanish rule, or to be the subject of future contention, cannot be justified on political, commercial, or humanitarian grounds. The cession must be of the whole archipelago or none. The latter is wholly inadmissible, and the former must therefore be required."

The cable of this message, like all those conveyed in war and peace, was pecked out by Col. Benjamin Franklin Montgomery, whose technological expertise led McKinley to name him chief of the White House Telegraph and Cipher Bureau. The rigorous Virginian with the handlebar mustache was extremely cautious in transmitting McKinley's exact, nuanced words, and utterly discreet about his access to top-secret intelligence. His promotion from captain to major to lieutenant colonel of the Signal Corps was evidence of McKinley's trust. Other than the president's Secretary Porter, Assistant Secretary Cortelyou, and the First Lady, no one else had such unparalleled access to McKinley in wartime. In later discussion with Bill Beer about Ida McKinley, it was none other than Colonel Montgomery who stated that "her incessant talk on the conversion of the islanders influenced the President to retain the Philippines." In light of his usual discretion and the enormity of what he implied, Beer's son's description of it as being "boldly declared" was an understatement.

Montgomery's observation might have applied to any one of several moments. Never known to urge specific policy, Ida likely voiced her own feeling repeatedly and it may have resonated with the Major's own convictions, resulting in his uncompromising decision. Her focus on the Igorrote, for example, was less likely the reason why the Major decided to retain the Luzon; Ida's interest in the tribe may have prompted him to act on his own inclination to do so. Peace commissioners and Cabinet members pointed out the military, economic, and political factors behind his decision. None argued for what a chronicler called "the moral grounds for requiring possession of the archipelago."[6]

Two days after his decision was transmitted, something prompted McKinley to send a second, clarifying message to the commissioners, setting his decision in a more humane context: "It is imperative upon us as victors that we should be governed only by motives which will exalt our nation. Territorial expansion should be our least concern, that we shall not shirk the moral obligations of our victory is our greatest. . . . The President can see but one plain path of duty—the acceptance of the archipelago. . . . To leave any part in her [Spain's] feeble control now would . . . be opposed to the interests of humanity. . . . [T]he people of the Philippines, whatever else is done, must be liberated. . . ."

Even in McKinley's first acquiescence to a settlement for what would prove to be $20 million for Spain's "distressed financial condition," he advised his commissioners that "whatever consideration the United States may show must come from its sense of generosity and benevolence, rather than from any real or technical obligation."

The only explanation McKinley stated about what prompted him to write this second message was that he felt "influenced by the single consideration of duty and humanity." Like all the official communiqués with the commission, this cable was sent out under the signature of John Hay, the former U.S. ambassador to England who had replaced Day as secretary of state. Hay, however, did not write the second "humane" cable, nor did McKinley dictate it to an aide. Not until 1982 did a biographer discover that it was handwritten by the president. The one place outside his office where he preferred to compose his correspondence was the library, where he was often alone with Ida.[7]

McKinley dictated statistical data to a stenographer in his office to "express his own opinion or ideas." The *New York Times* reported that he went to "Mrs. McKinley's sitting room. . . . All his writing is done there." Aides knew that when he "goes to his wife's sitting room it is a sure indication that he is going to drop the official reports." Another indication that Ida McKinley may have discussed this second message is suggested by the fact that in this same period, she was alone with him while he wrote his forthcoming congressional message, anticipating his December 21 "benevolent assimilation" plan to implement control of the Philippines.[8]

Ida McKinley may well have influenced the president's "single consideration of duty and humanity." She was among the few who would presume to suggest that the compulsively thorough president had failed to emphasize a salient point. Author Charles Olcott credited her with being "wide awake to the issues of the day." Olcott, who had the first unparalleled access to McKinley's papers and most intimate friends and political associates, further confirmed that "Often she would express an opinion on public affair so sound and sensible." On several occasions, the president was heard to respond to her views, saying, "Ida, I think you are right."

Assessing whether she influenced his crucial decision to retain the Philippines or the more political one of justifying it—*or both*—required a sense of the couple's interactions on public issues. Which policy, personnel, or public statements they discussed was kept strictly between them. There is reference to the fact that some of the First Lady's ideas reflected her "clever grasp of finance" and her ability to look at economic issues from different "points of view," a result of "business training" in banking and familiarity with exchange rates during her six months in Europe. At best, this might suggest that they discussed currency rates as he considered expansion of American industry into the world market. Kohlsaat claimed that McKinley "never crossed her wishes," and Ike Hoover wrote that "[N]othing was ever suggested by her but what he made an effort to see done," but neither offered any examples.[9]

It was clear that the First Lady was completely enmeshed in the president's political world. When Assistant Secretary Cortelyou entered the Cabinet Room one night, he saw the president reading his mail to her, which "commended his firm policy and his determination to wait until convinced that he was right before going ahead [with] declaring war." *Atlanta Constitution* editor Clark Howell was startled at how seamlessly the president blended politics and domesticity, reviewing the text of his Georgia General Assembly speech while simultaneously adjusting Ida's shawl.

The Library or West Sitting Hall was where the McKinleys freely conversed with one another. After dinner, the president continued his work in one of those rooms. If he needed silence, Ida would read periodicals. Asserting that the First Lady was "well-versed in politics and state affairs, and intensely interested in every phase of Mr. McKinley's work," her friend and biographer, journalist Josiah Hartzell, credited it to her voracious appetite for current events. "A great reader, she kept informed on all public matters by a careful reading of the newspapers," he stated. Without a schedule of daytime appearances, the *New York Tribune* reported, "she has kept more fully informed on current events than she would have been had her life been more active." Ida, who was alone most afternoons, was "usually busy with reading and study."

While pondering the best way to express policy he was formulating, the president frequently read to her, reviewing drafts of public speeches and statements or important correspondence. It was why she didn't mind if she was unable to hear him deliver his speeches. During one presidential trip where she avoided the auditoriums in which he addressed crowds, the First Lady told a reporter she already knew the content. "I read his speeches this morning," Ida McKinley admitted, "I read all his speeches."[10]

Particularly during crises, senators, Cabinet members, and others came unexpectedly at night to meet with McKinley while he was with Ida, their arrival announced by an aide. Before assenting to see them, the president always asked, "Ida, shall we see them?" As 1907 McKinley biographer Amos Corning learned, if officials came in, the First Lady did not leave: "Mrs. McKinley was never excluded from these talks, no matter how much they might deal with momentous questions, for the President made a confidant of her from the very beginning. She talked little and rarely entered into the conversation, but was a good listener."

Julian Hawthorne believed that the acute sensitivity she had developed to anticipate her seizures also made Ida an unusually astute observer of nonverbal "impressions and emotions" conveyed by those conferring with the president, which she likely shared with him. With humor and calculation, she also conveyed her opinion of unwitting subjects by giving them slippers in the "color of [their] personality," as Julia Foraker put it: white for the pure, grey for the wise, blue for the loyal, black for the pessimistic, and yellow—the color she most hated—presumably for those she scorned. While this likely was a wry tactic known only to the Major, he never discouraged her subtle critiques. "Her knowledge of men and measures was superior," his Canton minister Edward Buxton attested, "and often the President deferred to her judgment."[11]

"I only wish that I could help him as I should," the First Lady told a reporter, frustrated by her inability to make independent appearances as the president's ceremonial substitute in order to spare him such obligations. "I always wanted to be able to go out and work for you, as some wives have done for their husbands," she told him one night in the presence of his niece Ida Morse, "but the next best thing is to encourage you. Isn't it?" The president acknowledged that at times, he needed her more than she needed him: "I don't want you out stump-speaking or canvassing. Here is the place where you are needed; right here, near at hand, where I can run to you with my troubles."

It was often Ida who asked, as the Major put it, "to hear about the day's trials." On the same night Ida Morse was with them, when he entered the library later than expected, Ida suspected a brewing crisis. "Have there been all kinds of troublesome matters to attend to this evening?" Ida asked. "I never can remember troublesome affairs when I am with you," he politely demurred. Based on the date of his niece's visit, he was coping with some aspect of the Chinese Boxer Rebellion. Reporter Gilson Willets pointed out a possible reason for his reluctance to discuss it: "When affairs of state were urgent, the President invariably shielded his wife from the unfavorable side, always presenting to her the most cheerful and bright-est view of any question at issue." From the newspaper's evening edition or from speaking with his aides, the First Lady often suspected what he was facing and pressed him to discuss it. On some occasions, he cut her off with, "It's all right, Ida; everything's all right." By morning, however, McKinley invariably relented. As the *San Francisco Sunday Call* reported, over breakfast, he "gives her a sketch of the past twenty-four hours in his official world and she listens eagerly."[12]

Suffrage leader Mary Livermore described Ida McKinley as the presi-dent's "most faithful constituent and adviser," but the furthest he went was to call her his "all-round companion." Beyond his insistence on main-taining the illusion that she was entirely submissive to him, however, he considered any discussions between them, regardless of the subject, to be strictly private. While McKinley freely shared personal details about Ida with William Day, for example, in his context as their attorney, he never disclosed her interest in the issues that Day was grappling with as peace commissioner. Day would learn of this from someone else only long after the treaty was settled.[13]

On October 31, three days after McKinley's second message was con-veyed to him, Day presented the United States' terms to Spanish nego-tiators. While polls showed U.S. support for taking the islands, opponents organized into the Anti-Imperialist League charged McKinley with moral hypocrisy and threatened the loss of the Republican House and Senate in the election just days away. In Paris, among "questions arising that embarrass the Americans" were hundreds of letters from Protestant clergy intent on "evangelizing the islands." It gave pause to the Spanish, who suspected that McKinley supported the Protestant conversion of the Catholic majority.[14]

Trumping his denomination's success rate of conversion in other Catho-lic nations, Robert Speer, head of the Presbyterian Foreign Mission Board, announced their plan to aggressively pursue the Catholic conversion of Filipinos. There were small signs that Ida had lingering suspicions about Catholicism, which she first expressed in her 1869 letters. An 1897 letter from a fellow Presbyterian whom Ida had enlisted to help her find the "proper person" as a White House maid revealed that "what she required" was "a Protestant." Even after her refusal to respond to a Catholic charity's request for a donated item made the news, all it prompted was a vague and belated promise from the staff that she "would send her contribution." It was not the first time McKinley buffered Ida when it came to Catholics. In 1897, Ida declined to meet with Catholic summer school students in

Plattsburgh, sending the Major instead. Two years later, when she again declined to join him in greeting them, he suggested that the students bring her a rose bouquet at their hotel, knowing her weakness for the flower. Once the students arrived, the Major slipped into the reception and stood behind her, watching as she handed a carnation—his signature flower—to each of them. Suspicions among the Protestant majority of Americans at the time reflected a fear that the Vatican sought to control the U.S. government as it had in nations like the Philippines. Any hope Ida may have had that Catholics might turn Protestant, however, paled in comparison to her concern for providing tribal Filipinos with education, medical care, sanitation, and shelter. All four sparse testimonies of this concern reflected an especial sense of urgency.[15]

Ida McKinley's lack of interest in strict adherence to conventional Christianity never mitigated the influence of her grandfather's charity to the needy or her identity as a Presbyterian. Ida was inculcated in the belief that God predetermined destiny, so the idea that he had willed Katie's death was so devastating and traumatic that it ended her regular church attendance. She had also been influenced by the Major's deep faith, and many nights he read to her from the Scripture-based *Daily Strength for Daily Need*. While she did not join him for Metropolitan Methodist Church Sunday services, her support of the church's Ladies Aid Society showed her belief in the valuable role that organized religion could play in addressing societal problems. Friend and fellow member Mary Logan recalled that during McKinley's congressional years, Ida had "commanded the respect" of fellow members for her "advancement of religious work," meaning the provision of shelter, food, and other necessities to the indigent. Whether this meant efforts confined to Washington or support of foreign missionary work is undocumented.[16]

Many women were among the faith's 175,000-member Methodist Woman's Foreign Missionary Society (MWFMS), an organization that likely drew Ida McKinley's attention when former First Lady Lucy Hayes became its president in 1881. Its early efforts to reduce illiteracy among former slaves, as well as its "Little Light Bearers" program for orphans and "Mother's Jewels" for children under age one, spoke more to Ida's concerns, even if its ultimate aim was religious conversion. During her first social season as First Lady, the first reception she hosted was for the MWFMS; the *New York Tribune* learned that "She is greatly interested in their mission work." Since it lobbied Congress against polygamy and liquor sale to soldiers, she avoided political conflict and never joined the MWFMS, but as

it was among the first missionary groups in the Philippines to establish a
kindergarten and a school for girls, her support of their intentions was sincere. What the Methodist General Missionary Committee, with which she
met later, might have found startling, however, was that her concern was less
about which denomination led in conversions than it was about "saving"
the young and female of non-Christian tribes.[17]

By early December, the Spanish seemed ready to accept the American
peace treaty terms. While waiting for news of its finalization, the First
Lady took off on her own again, for the third time that year, to go Christmas shopping in New York with James McKinley and old friends Sue
Rand and Kitty Endsley. "I never felt better in my life," she bragged to a
reporter as she entered the familiar Windsor Hotel suite, which was always
reserved for the McKinleys as their home in New York. Abner, Annie,
and Mabel McKinley lived there in a ground-floor suite, and the manager
Warren Leland treated Ida like royalty, always escorting her from the curb
to her suite upstairs, which his wife Elizabeth furnished in Ida's favorite
blue and filled with flowers and fruit when the suite was occupied.

Ida felt so well that she was about to go out to do her own shopping
in city stores until the Major called to warn her to avoid the thirty-degree
temperature. Instead, she asked that stores send samples of clothes, jewelry,
and other items, and a line of delivery boys soon arrived at her Windsor
Hotel suite. After a lunch that included a new "carnation ice cream" made
with the edible petals of the Major's signature flower, a group of the residential hotel's children came to visit, and Ida came to life. She sat them on
her lap, told them stories, and pointed out the Major's framed picture on a
table, "smothered in roses." Christmastime brought thoughts of Katie, and
as the children left her suite, Ida blurted to them, "I wish I could call you
my own."

"I'm feeling perfectly well and cheerful this morning," she assured the
Major by phone on her second day in New York. "I'm very glad," he
abruptly interrupted. "Don't you think you had better come home today?"
Ida fell silent, surprised. Abruptly, he "asked her to leave for Washington
as soon as possible." She then "made all haste" into the drawing room to
quickly choose what gifts she could from those laid out for her consideration, and caught the afternoon train. Ida's prompt return to Washington
had nothing to do with her health. McKinley, assured that Spain would sign
the treaty on December 10, wanted to share the moment with her, even
though it still faced Senate confirmation in early 1899.[18]

Three days after the treaty was signed, Ida left with the Major for their second southern tour, to Georgia and Alabama. The most inspiring stop was at Tuskegee Normal and Industrial Institute, which was the realized vision of the internationally recognized African American educator Booker T. Washington. A two-hour parade passed McKinley and Washington, who reviewed all of the school's students. Whenever the Major reviewed parades, Ida typically remained in their hotel suite. This time, however, Mrs. McKinley wanted to see the parade and be seen by the crowds. An open carriage carrying the First Lady joined the parade in progress and then pulled aside to let her review lines of African American women students, bowing to them as they passed her. She did likewise during the Atlanta parade. When an African American woman saw Ida shiver in her open carriage, she ran up with a heated stone to warm her feet, adjusted it in place for her, and dashed away. Ida made inquiries to locate the woman, identified only as "Martha" in the press, invited her to the presidential hotel suite to thank her, and even offered her a position on the White House staff, an honor the woman kindly turned down. When the First Lady gave the president's engraved card to one Moses Green, he effusively declared her a "peerless lady" as "good as you are great, or you would never have deigned to notice an obscure colored man, such as I am."

Although symbolic, Ida's gestures indicated a respect not often extended by upper-class white women to working-class minorities. Her attitude is further evidenced in the responsibilities she entrusted to three African Americans. In 1896, she turned over complete control of the campaign house to Harry "Fred" Floyd for him to run simultaneously as a private residence and public staging arena. White House steward William T. Sinclair performed a similar task but also managed the McKinleys' personal expenditures. She had known her White House footman Charles Reeder since her Ebbitt House residency and trusted him to lift her in and out of carriages, if necessary. When he married Frances Lee, the First Lady gave them a set of fine china, an exquisite wedding gift usually reserved for her nieces.

Ida McKinley did not permit White House guests to be filtered by race. She welcomed Women's Christian Temperance Union leader and child welfare reform and education advocate Frances Joseph, an African American, as cordially as her white peer at a reception for the organization's officials. The White House concerts on the south lawn, which she always came to hear on the portico, were attended by a racially integrated public audience. The influence of her father, grandfather, and mentor was

reflected in the First Lady's financial contribution to the preservation of
poet John Greenleaf Whittier's home as a legacy of his antislavery activ-
ism. Not until the end of her life did Ida McKinley disclose her most tangible contribution to helping African Americans improve their lives—she
had paid for the higher education of several young adult African Americans whose widowed mother had supported them as a laundrywoman.[19]

Ida McKinley's belief that education, not race, ensured success was reflected in the president's faith in Manila's class of lawyers, doctors, educa-
tors, and bankers as the leaders of not only eventual self-government but
as sources of influence for the mass population. After this small circle of
Filipinos assured American military leaders that most Filipinos of all classes
would not resist and would even welcome U.S. control of the island nation,
McKinley assumed there was compliance among the Filipino population
majority. Like the First Lady, most Americans who supported taking the
islands did so largely on the popular misperception that the majority existed in "disadvantaged" circumstances similar to the Igorrote. It showed a
naively arrogant bias based on the presumption that the American lifestyle
was superior for all, yet its intent was not to degrade another nationality
into subjugation but to raise its standard of "respectable" living. In contrast
to the racist argument used by many Anti-Imperialist Leaguers who opposed assuming "responsibility" for the Filipinos, Ida McKinley's misguided
perspective revealed implicit belief that all those who comprised the population were as capable of "improving" as her own race. It was an attitude
suggested by the president's promise to respect Filipino culture while taking
control of their government outlined in his December 21 "benevolent assimilation" proclamation.

Blount, McKinley's own appointee as a judge and then interior secretary of the U.S.-run government in the Philippines, however, was the one
who pointed out that the "association of ideas between the Igorrotes and
Filipino" is what helped in "depreciating American conceptions concerning Filipino capacity for self-government." Using this popular misconcep-
tion to justify McKinley's decision to retain the Philippines, Blount
concluded, would be a "distinct political value" to McKinley in the 1900
presidential election. This conclusion called into question whether Ida
McKinley's obsessive concern for the "Igorrote" was merely part of the
calculating president's political agenda. His claim that his policy was based
on concern for the Filipinos and "her faith in the integrity of his character," as his minister put it, suggest the most plausible answer. Although
McKinley shrewdly withheld information from his wife if he felt it was

in her best interest to be kept ignorant, it was out of character for him to mislead her about the fate of 8 million people, the most important decision of his presidency. Nor was she given to deceit; if she didn't believe his given reason for the policy, she would have been silent, not encouraging.[20]

The First Lady left no doubt as to her view of the president's treaty during a January dinner for the peace commissioners, who had returned. As Whitlaw Reid admitted during the negotiations, his "opinions had not always agreed with those of President McKinley." Ida curtly interrupted, "Ah, then you were in the wrong." After quickly adding that he supported the terms, she teased him, "I see there is some hope for you, after all." That winter Ida was unusually spirited, hosting a Christmas dance for a houseful of nephews and nieces, and breaking her rule to shake hands with some of the 3,000 citizens who filed by her at the 1899 New Year's Day Reception. Days later, she dragged the Major out to see *The Little Corporal*.[21]

The White House guest lists in January were heavy on senators and their wives. Despite the Republican majority, Senate ratification of the peace treaty terms remained uncertain on the issue of retaining the Philippines. Among Senate wives, Julia Foraker left a startling recollection of the First Lady during this period that corroborated those of Bill Beer and Benjamin Montgomery from the months just before. "The benightedness of the Igorrotes greatly excited Mrs. McKinley's sympathies," recalled Julia Foraker. "I went to call on her one day during the Philippine agitation and found her full of plans for saving the Igorrotes, particularly the children." A fourth account of Ida McKinley's interest in the Filipinos offers the most emotionally compelling reason for it.

It had been seven years since Ida McKinley had attended the Columbus lecture by the Presbyterian missionary Mrs. T. L. Saxton, who shared her maiden name, but she never forgot it. The lecture had first exposed Ida to the belief in reincarnation, and Mrs. Saxton later told Bill Beer that it had given her a vague sense that the spirits of Katie and Little Ida, dead some fifteen years at that point, might have been reborn. "The women and children of the Orient lured McKinley's wife," Beer observed. "Out there, perhaps, had been a paradise of colors and warm flowers, with Katie and baby Ida born again, brown and naked for her kisses, waiting to be brought up as Christian ladies. . . ." While it would be overreaching to declare that Ida's potential belief in the reincarnation of her daughters was her motivation to, allegedly, implore the president to retain the islands, it was intriguingly suggested by Mrs. Saxton's recollections of her visit to the president's wife. "When we met afterwards in Washington, in

1899," she recalled about the First Lady, "she fairly implored me to see what could be done by the Presbyterian board of foreign missions for the children in the Philippines. . . ."

Examining the testimony of Montgomery, Saxton, Beer, and Foraker also suggests less literal possibilities on the premise that Ida believed simultaneously in Hindu reincarnation and Christian redemption. In the faith in which Ida McKinley was raised, the act of baptism was "saving" a soul, but to be "born again" could also mean a recommitment to Christianity. No records indicate whether either daughter had been baptized. If they were, then Ida's alleged desire to see Filipinos "saved" might mean to see them rescued from poverty. If they were not, then her hope to have them "saved" would indicate a wish to see them baptized. Beer's phrase "Christian ladies" could either be a reference to religion or just the era's euphemism for Western civilization, which was often used with regard to the Philippines.

In her further reference to the McKinley daughters as "ghosts in the long-ago moonlight," Julia Foraker suggested it was the presence of their ethereal, supernatural spirits, not their reincarnated souls, that motivated the First Lady. Finally, she provocatively concluded that the girls were "yet playing a strangely real part in the national career of the man who became our twenty-fifth President." It is unclear if Foraker meant to suggest that Ida McKinley believed that the ghosts of Katie and Little Ida were communicating with her and telling her she must influence the president's decision on the Philippines. No other sources of any kind, however, imply that Ida ever believed in the literal existence of ghosts.[22]

McKinley was a man of rational pragmatism when it came to devising his policy. His intensely held religious beliefs, however, also enabled him to make a leap of faith on theories that could never be proven true or seen. As the press widely reported, for example, the president told a Presbyterian General Assembly leader, "I hope you won't revise out the doctrine of predestination" because he believed in its truth. Foraker's statement that the long-gone Katie and Little Ida were "playing a strangely real part" in McKinley's decision-making process falls short of inferring that he believed in reincarnation, but it does suggest that he was considerably receptive to ideas Ida may have implored him to consider. While all the factors that he thought through to arrive at his decision to retain the Philippines can never be known, President McKinley's emotional reasoning had unquestionably been influenced by Ida, shaping the core values of his belief system. "Without her," McKinley fully confessed to a *Canton Repository* reporter, "I should not have been such as I am."[23]

Ida McKinley's personal influence developed elements of William McKinley's personality and pervaded his presidency. In analyzing War Secretary Elihu Root's remark that McKinley was "always considerate of the rights and feelings of others," Reverend J. J. Carson believed that "This habitual thoughtfulness was no doubt due, in large measure, to McKinley's lifelong habit of caring for his wife. . . . The sufferings of Mrs. McKinley and her dependence upon her husband brought lessons of patience and forbearance, which were reflected in his tactful consideration for others." His remarks to a *Campbell's Illustrated Journal* reporter, which was the only instance in which McKinley publicly shared insight about himself, credited Ida for a virtue he developed that proved vital as he toiled during the war and gave an idea of his heavy burden of responsibility for her and the public persona he had to create for himself as president:

> Yes, I have learned self-control. It has been a matter of discipline. Mrs. McKinley has been an invalid for many years. Her life has at time hung by a thread, and her physician believed I could strengthen or weaken that hold on life. I schooled myself, and never went into her presence without a smile on my face and the assurance in my manner that the universe was moving as I had ordered. It mattered not how the world treated me, or what were my trials; I had to go to my wife as though the world were mine, and everything run as I would have it. It was not easy at all times to follow the directions of the doctor, but there was my wife's life at stake. It was the highest stake a man ever played for, and I played to win.[24]

By the time he became president, McKinley's perception of Ida's dependence on his care and guardianship had shaped his thinking and how he viewed life for over two decades: for reasons predestined by God, Ida was left in a condition that limited her freedom, necessitating that she relinquish control of determining much about her life, so his moral duty was to regulate it with the promise of recovery. Even if he did not believe this was a moral imperative for a true Christian, it was civilized society's expectation of a husband. This self-imposed obligation to Ida echoed his public expression of commitment to a God-given duty to retain the Philippines.

"We accepted the Philippines from high duty in the interest of their inhabitants and humanity and civilization. Our sacrifices were with this high motive," McKinley declared, "We want to improve the condition of the inhabitants." While the reasons were "shrouded for the time being in impenetrable mystery," he was certain that "providence had made us guardians." The Filipinos were "people whose interest and destiny, without us willing it, had been put into our hands. . . ." It required him to "respond in a manly fashion to manly duty . . ." and "accept all the obligations which the war in duty and honor imposed on us. . . . Duty determines destiny." He did so "not to subjugate . . . not to rule in the power of might" but provide a "freedom" they did not have.[25]

On February 6, the Senate ratified the McKinley Administration's treaty with Spain. Five days later, in the Oval Library, which was as much the First Lady's space as his own, the president opened a crimson velvet folder and signed the enclosed document. Official witnesses to the president's signature were the vice president, Secretary of State Hay, and the First Lady.

Any hope Ida may have had that the treaty would signal a return to their cozy evenings of cribbage that once eased the Major's anxiety vanished within hours. His worry while preparing for war and anxiety in managing it now gave way to the horror of a bloody resistance to his imposing control on a foreign land. By the time the sun had set on the day of the treaty-signing, the president became "much troubled" and begged off, without explanation, on celebrating with Ida at the theater. At the president's urging, General Corbin took his empty theater seat. He went, it seems, less to see the show and more to break some news. The day before, Corbin told the First Lady and her theater party, two Filipinos had defied an order to halt as they approached an encampment of troops at Santa Mesa, an outpost of Manila. An American fired, another Filipino gave a signal, and then native forces launched a simultaneous attack at three points. Twenty-five Americans were killed and 120 were wounded. In the next morning's *Washington Post,* she read it for herself: "The Igorrotes, armed with bows and arrows, made a very determined stand in the face of a hot artillery fire, and left many men on the field." Some seven hundred of the "naked savages" she had hoped to save were recruited from the mountains to join the fight.

In his December 21 "benevolent assimilation" proclamation, McKinley had also warned Filipinos that thousands of arriving troop reinforcements in their country would "overcome all obstacles to the bestowal of blessings of good and stable government." Before the terms of the treaty had been finalized, the peace commissioners refused to hear Aguinaldo's independent Filipino government (established once the Spanish were expelled) make the case for self-government. When McKinley signed the ratified treaty, U.S. occupation of the Philippines was official. Native outrage resisting the mighty U.S. military presence was manifested in guerrilla warfare, aided by previously indifferent Filipinos. Even the First Lady was the brunt of Filipino resentment. When an American asked a Manila dressmaker to use her "very best weaves" to craft a native *jusi* dress "as it would go to the White House to Mrs. McKinley," it caused an uproar. "With a great deal of scorn in her voice and manner she declared she would not make it."[26]

When American soldiers reported the Filipinos' unimaginably bloody and horrific attacks on them, they often used racial insults. To crush the resistance, the Americans used bayonets, burned villages, water-boarded, killed the wounded, and tortured complicit citizens. Even critics of the U.S. occupation resorted to racism. In *Outlook,* George Kennan was upset that "soldiers of civilized nations, in dealing with an inferior race," did not use "honorable warfare" as they would against "their equals and fighting fellow-Christians." Going on for four years, some 5,000 American lives were lost in what McKinley called an insurrection. The surviving Filipinos, with 200,000 of their population decimated, called it the Filipino-American War.

William Howard Taft, after becoming the first civil governor-general there, said the fighting had caused McKinley "great grief." Judge Blount concurred, adding that because McKinley's "motives were benevolent," it caused the president "tremendous struggle with his own conscience." Blount, however, faulted McKinley for refusing to even acknowledge that it also meant eventual industrial profit for the United States, concluding, "Philanthropy for pecuniary profit is a paradox. Duplicity ever follows deviation from principle." Taking the Philippines had also quadrupled the War and Navy department budgets from the prewar figure to $200 million.[27]

The situation in Cuba, by comparison, was calm, its self-government more imminent. When the First Lady hosted a dinner and dance on January 12, her attention was quickly claimed by Leonard Wood, who arose to escort her from the dining room. Wood, who was appointed Cuba's military general of Santiago when fighting ceased, was called to Washington on official business, but while there, the First Lady's former doctor made sure he spoke with her about more than her health. He was just then aggressively seeking support from Commodore Dewey to his Rough Rider comrade Roosevelt, the new governor of New York, in his quest to be named military governor of Cuba, a promotion overriding other established military officials. Louise Wood had been especially aggressive in lobbying the First Lady on behalf of her husband. She "called directly" to get her on the phone, and when that failed, began "turning up uninvited" at Ida McKinley's receptions. After Wood had time with the First Lady, however, McKinley finally told Louise that her husband had "the political influence of the President." Wood was promoted.[28]

If Ida McKinley had any bearing on Wood's promotion, it was the most important but not the first instance of her patronage regarding federal appointments for those she knew. She was believed to have also succeeded in having George W. Wallace, a distant cousin who had helped settle her father's estate, named as secretary of New Mexico Territory. As the *Washington Evening Star* cheekily noted, Ida was not "devoid of influence with the administration." Documented instances of her patronage included helping friends Harriet Gault and Charles Bawsel, the former was named the Media, Pennsylvania, postmistress, and the latter was made assistant auditor of the Treasury Department. When relatives Sam Saxton and Marsh Barber sent recommendations on behalf of others who needed the stability of a federal job, she apparently at least reviewed the solicitations. The First Lady refrained from taking action when citizens like J. W. Samson sent her his qualifications for a Treasury Department job requesting that she "read these papers to the President," or when a new bride asked Ida to intervene in embezzlement charges against her groom. When prohibitionist Elizabeth Van Lew urged her to ensure that the postmaster of Richmond job was given to her friend's husband instead of to a "drunkard," for example, the drunkard got it.[29]

If Cuba's General Wood had the First Lady's trust, War Secretary Alger did not. McKinley, joined by Alger, braved a snowstorm to give a February 16 speech to veterans in Boston. Mrs. McKinley avoided the cold and Alger. Once they headed out, she went to see John Drew and Ethel Barrymore at the Lafayette in a new farce called *The Liars.*

When he paraded with McKinley in Boston, Alger was taunted by war veterans jeering "Beef! Beef!" in reference to the tainted canned beef his War Department had supplied and which sickened thousands of soldiers during the war. Their anger encompassed more than that, however, after having endured fevers, watched comrades die from diseases contracted in unsanitary camps, and suffered on overcrowded transports to fight in the tropics wearing wool uniforms. Alger wasn't directly responsible for all the mismanagement, but his disgraceful refusal to address it responsibly became the Administration's first scandal, exacerbated by McKinley's refusal to confront or fire him. Privately, McKinley called Alger "cunning" for concealing an alliance with a McKinley foe to further his ambition for a Senate seat and "a little 'shifty' now and then."

Ida McKinley's Canton, Ohio, family home and likely birthplace, which she shared with her husband as their longest place of residence. It served as the "Canton White House" during his visits home from 1897 to mid-1900 and was inherited through four generations of women. It is now part of the First Ladies' National Historic Site, which is managed by the National First Ladies' Library. (National First Ladies' Library collection)

Ida McKinley's grandfather John Saxton began the local newspaper, *The Canton Repository,* and helped establish the Presbyterian church, where Ida taught Sunday school. Her grandmother Christiana Dewalt lived until her death with Ida. (National First Ladies' Library collection)

Ida McKinley was close to both of her parents. James Saxton owned a bank, was a civic leader, and owned large real estate holdings. Her mother, Catharine "Kate" Dewalt Saxton, was active in supporting the Union Army. (National First Ladies' Library collection)

Eldest of three, Ida (center) counted her sister Mary (left), nicknamed "Pina," as her lifelong confidante, while her spoiled brother George lacked her drive. (National First Ladies' Library collection)

Ida Saxton's mentor and teacher was the political activist Betsy Mix Cowles. Brooke Hall, a college-level women's school in Media, Pennsylvania, offered Ida a broad education, and she indulged her love of hiking on the property there. (National First Ladies' Library collection)

Ida Saxton at eighteen years old; when she returned home, the sharp-witted young woman's financial training led to her father hiring her as a clerk in his bank. Eventually she rose to manage the bank during his absences. (National First Ladies' Library collection)

William McKinley, an ambitious attorney from a working-class background, first met Ida Saxton at a picnic. She always addressed him as "Major," using his Civil War military rank. Her picture was taken during their 1871 honeymoon. (National First Ladies' Library collection)

The McKinleys leased this house from her father; their two children were born and one died here. They leased it again in 1896 for his presidential campaign and bought it in 1899. McKinley lived here less than five years and Ida another six as a widow. (Library of Congress)

Katie McKinley, the eldest of their children and the last to die, lived only to three and a half years old, but her mother kept her memory alive for over thirty years. (Author's collection)

On their 1881 tenth wedding anniversary trip to California, Ida McKinley was well enough to hike the Sierras, relying only on a walking stick as did her husband, now a U.S. congressman. (National First Ladies' Library collection)

Physicians S. Weir Mitchell (top) and John N. Bishop, in seeking to treat her epilepsy, unwittingly harmed Ida McKinley; Mitchell's famous "rest cure" was the likely cause of her developing chronic phlebitis, and Bishop recklessly prescribed bromides without medical supervision, leading McKinley to overdose her. (Author's collection)

As a congressional wife in either their Washington or Canton home, Ida McKinley spent her days in a sitting room, which connected directly to her husband's office, with a picture of Katie always in sight. The door was always open as he held political meetings. Ida listened and offered her advice. (National First Ladies' Library collection)

As governor (1891–95), McKinley waved from the state capitol plaza, where his statue now stands, to Ida at the window of their residential hotel suite across the street. She waved back to assure him of her well-being. (Library of Congress)

Governor and Mrs. McKinley dine as guests of his presidential campaign manager Mark Hanna and his wife Charlotte, who face one another at the head of the table. Facing Ida and the Major are Annette and Russell Alger, later McKinley's controversial war secretary. Mary and Ida Barber (seated next to McKinley), Ida's eldest nieces, often seemed like substitutes for her own lost daughters. (Ohio Historical Society)

Ida McKinley (far right) was a familiar presence during her husband's 1896 presidential campaign on the front porch of their home. McKinley's attentive care of her was central to defining the candidate's character; voters were told he would apply the same intensity of commitment to presidential duties. (Author's collection)

Ida's image, used on items like this button badge, was exploited by the campaign. (National First Ladies' Library collection)

Besides leaving Cabinet meetings to check on Ida down the hall, President McKinley spent evenings reading with her, sometimes while composing speeches. "Ida, I think you are right," he often responded to her advice. From Gilson Willets's *Rulers of the World at Home: How They Look and How They Live* (1899). (Author's collection)

Before he was consumed with work as president, the Major took daily drives with Ida, usually in a closed carriage, discussing a range of topics that even included the tariff. From Gilson Willets's *Rulers of the World at Home: How They Look and How They Live* (1899). (Author's collection)

Ida McKinley sat in an open carriage (lower right corner) to review a parade of Tuskegee Institute's African American women students in Alabama. She personally financed private educations for the children of a black family she knew. (Author's collection)

Calling her knitting "my work," Ida McKinley produced some 4,500 items, which she donated to charities or presented as gifts. (National First Ladies' Library collection)

Leonard Wood (left) owed his appointment as a Spanish-American War cavalry colonel to his service as the First Lady's physician. His lieutenant, Col. Theodore Roosevelt (right), was forever indebted to her influence in getting his "Rough Rider" cavalry ordered to the transport ship conveying them to Cuba. (Library of Congress)

In May 1899, the First Lady toured the battleship *Raleigh* and met Spanish-American War sailors who served under Admiral Dewey on the *Olympia* when it defeated the Spanish navy in Manila Bay, the first U.S. victory. (Author's collection)

The Westlawn Cemetery graves of Katie and "Little Ida" McKinley, which the First Lady always visited on trips home to Canton and unwittingly helped make a tourist stop. Postcards of the graves were even sold to the public. (Library of Congress)

As illustrated by this advertisement for a plant, the popular but inaccurate public perception of the First Lady was as a bereaved invalid, but it bolstered the president's image as saintly in his patient care of her. (Author's collection)

McKinley often staged public demonstrations of his devotional acts for Ida, like wrapping her in a shawl on a reviewing stand at Lake Champlain in August 1897. Second Lady Jennie Hobart (standing) became a close friend to Ida. (Author's collection)

Although the truth about her seizure disorder was never printed during her White House tenure, Ida McKinley made no secret of her frequent immobility, most obviously by receiving guests at receptions while seated. (Author's collection)

The McKinleys arrive at Camp Meade to review Spanish-American War regiments in August 1898. During the war, Ida was at the peak of health, headlining a fund-raiser for the families of sailors killed on the USS *Maine* explosion in Havana Harbor and encouraging missionary aid to tribal Filipinos. (Author's collection)

Sensationalized news stories about the October 1898 murder of the First Lady's brother George and the sordid trial of his scorned but acquitted mistress Anna George drew unwelcome national focus on Ida's family. Originally published in the *San Francisco Call*. (Author's collection)

The First Lady's annual New York trip to buy Christmas presents and indulge her love of theater gave her some rare days independent of the president. She chose gifts from items brought by department store clerks into her Windsor Hotel suite. The hotel's March 1899 fire shocked her; many children were killed. (Author's collection)

In the summer of 1899, Ida McKinley was put in the care of physician Preston Rixey (far right), who resolved to alleviate her chronic health problems. Though pressured by McKinley to ensure that Ida could join junkets important to his re-election, the doctor also confronted him about her unregulated use of bromide. (Author's collection)

As the new century began, the cumulative stress of President McKinley was apparent. During and after the war, he often went without sleep, smoked heavily, and gave up even minimal exercise. Ida was several times in the position of caring for him. (Library of Congress)

Ida McKinley voiced regret that her disability limited a more active partnership role with the president but was not embarrassed about needing to rely on a wheelchair in 1900 and 1901. A San Francisco illustrator depicted the only known image of her in a wheelchair when she arrived in that city in May 1901. Originally published in the *San Francisco Call*. (Author's collection)

El Paso, Texas, women arrive at the presidential train to escort Ida McKinley (far right) to a May 1901 breakfast honoring her across the border in Juarez, Mexico. The excursion made her the first incumbent First Lady to travel internationally. (Author's collection)

A newspaper depicted the worried president hovering over the First Lady, her death imminent. Though she survived, severe dysentery caused heart damage. (Author's collection)

The McKinleys drive into Buffalo's Pan-American Exposition. Ida's written wish that they had remained in Ohio instead and her fear of his assassination proved premonitory. (Library of Congress)

McKinley at an Exposition reception prior to his September 6 assassination. The president's secretary, the indispensable George B. Cortelyou (right), would play a central role in Ida's widowhood. (Library of Congress)

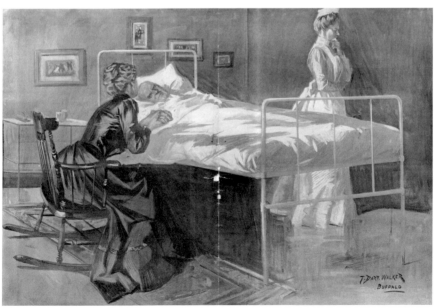

From the moment Ida McKinley learned that Leon Czolgosz shot the Major, she displayed resolute optimism, calm, and physical strength. Despite McKinley's death on September 14, she eased what proved to be his final week of life. Originally published in *Leslie's Weekly*. (Author's collection)

Two days after his funeral, Ida McKinley began a daily ritual of visiting the Major's flag-draped coffin in the cemetery holding vault. She constantly replaced his funeral wreath flowers and kept cut flowers alive as long as possible. (Author's collection)

In reaction to African American waiter Ben Parker's attempt to stop McKinley's assassination, the negligent Secret Service sought to expunge the incident from the record, but the widowed Ida McKinley saw to it that Parker was given permanent federal employment and a home of his own. (Author's collection)

A poignant image of Ida McKinley nine months before her May 1907 death, when a zest for life had returned with the birth of great-nieces Helen (on her lap) and Katie, who was given the honor of sitting in the small rocking chair that once belonged to the same-named McKinley daughter, an object Ida held sacred. (National First Ladies' Library collection)

The First Lady was unlike the president. Even those who called her the "personification of gentleness" conceded that Ida "lacked neither force nor spirit in her defense of him." As she saw signs that Alger's ambitions went beyond a potential Senate seat, she knew he gained credibility the longer he wasn't fired, but it harmed McKinley's reputation in the process. She didn't have the power to force Alger's resignation, but she could provoke his discomfort there. With, as one chronicler put it, "a keener eye for the details of social intercourse than she admitted," the First Lady looked over the Cabinet wives who gathered before a formal event one night. "I know one of you who wants to be in my place," she sniped, "and that's Mrs. Alger." The mortified Annette had no response. Whether intended or perceived as a covert message from the president to the war secretary, Russell and Annette Alger fled soon enough.[30]

Days after McKinley's return from Boston, a *Washington Post* reporter eyed the First Lady, who was vivaciously chatting with women and glowing in her lavender satin dress, looking "unusually well." The paper learned that the president, in contrast, "feels tired and worn out, and in much need of absolute quiet." McKinley accepted Hanna's invitation to rest at his winter home in Thomasville, Georgia, and announced he would make no speeches during the two-week vacation and that he hoped "to be relieved of public attentions as much as possible." Once there, residents were startled at how much "paler and thinner" he now looked. Despite his request that there be no callers, some children came by the house to meet him. Ida McKinley interceded, greeting them as his representative and accepting their gift of violets, which were arranged to spell out "Welcome." All invitations were refused, and all mail received was sent to Washington. After a week, some fellow churchgoers thought he still looked "decidedly pale."

The McKinleys then went to exclusive Jekyll Island off the Georgia coast, which was accessible only by invitation from the bankers, railroad magnates, and publishers who owned property there. As the guest of his first treasury secretary, Cornelius Bliss, the president was spared having to meet the public. An emphatic announcement made it clear that he wouldn't meet with House Speaker Thomas B. Reed, who was also there, to resolve differences. Soon enough, however, they conferred and were joined by the vice president and Senator Hanna, so the vacation was merely a change of scene for conducting business as usual. If he dissipated tension with the speaker, however, he only generated it with the First Lady.

To ensure that their stay was "as informal as possible," the president had also asked that it be announced "no reception will be given" to meet the public. However, he acquiesced to his host's request to hold a welcoming reception. Having striven to give the Major some peace and quiet in Thomasville and to help him recover his strength, Ida was justifiably resentful and eager to keep their appearance at the reception brief. McKinley, however, indulged long-winded guests, effusively shaking hands and trading flatteries. Having to stand rather than sit next to him increased Ida's physical pain, and her displeasure was evident to guests, whom she barely acknowledged. Years later, guest Annie Hegeman recalled this impression to Margaret Leech, who said that Ida was trying to "attract his notice by pulling at his arm and twisting his sleeve." In reality, Ida required the Major's arm to lean on when she stood for a period of time, and tugging on his jacket was far less rude than verbally interrupting him, yet Leech characterized it as a "more serious lapse than any private tantrums."[31]

Something else was also upsetting Ida while they were on Jekyll Island. Four days into their stay at Thomasville, she learned that a fire had engulfed the Windsor Hotel within minutes, including the apartment suite where she and the Major always stayed while in New York. Seventy people were killed, a large number of them children. News stories carried the tale of one mother who jumped from a window with a child in her arms, hoping to save them both. The manager's daughter Helen and his wife Elizabeth Leland, who always arranged the McKinley suite to please Ida, were also killed in the fire. The McKinleys sent a wreath for the family's double funeral. News that Andrew Carnegie's disabled niece had perished while trapped in her room, unable to walk out without help, must have especially chilled Ida. The most haunting accounts were of loved ones who watched from below, unable to save family members who were at windows, desperate to escape. It must have been a trauma not unlike what Ida had experienced when Katie died of scarlet fever. The First Lady did not issue a statement about the fire, but her last memories of being at the Windsor were of telling some visiting little girls how she wished that they were her children.

More painful reminders of another lost loved one came three weeks later. When the Major returned from Georgia, he was consumed by an "immense amount of business" involving the new Hawaiian government and a commission to oversee construction of a Central American canal. The First Lady, meanwhile, steeled herself for humiliating newspaper stories about the trial of Anna George for George Saxton's murder, which began on April 3.[32]

George Saxton was defended by some at the proceedings for his respect toward "upright and virtuous" women, but the more numerous tales
of his salacious exploits with Anna created a "great strain" on Ida. On
April 13, the Major confided to Ida's nephew, John Barber, who was handling his late uncle's estate, that "Your Aunt Ida has not been very well for
the last ten days."

While the Major typically pointed out Ida's condition, he remained quiet
about his own. In mid-April, he was again unwell, this time because of an
attack of neuralgia, so he cancelled all appointments and worked from the
Oval Library. Ida recognized the toll on him. As she had the previous spring
when he was under pressure, she resisted scheduling any musicales or house
guests. Both wished to keep a commitment to join Julia Grant in Philadelphia to unveil a statue of her late husband and then go to New York for
a few days for unknown reasons. There was no escape, however, from bad
news. On April 20, Filipinos captured 140 American troops near Binango-
nan and killed a colonel in a violent battle at Quingua three days later.[33]

Not yet a year since Dewey's victory at Manila Bay, most Americans
were shocked by the numbers of lives being lost and were less optimistic
than the military leaders promising the imminent surrender of the *insurrec-
tos.* In Philadelphia, Ida and the Major toured the battleship *Raleigh,* where
the First Lady gamely managed steep stairs and slippery decks, silently examining its massive iron cannons and meeting sailors who had served on
the *Olympia* during Dewey's famous battle. At almost the same moment,
large crowds cheered Anna George as she exited the Canton courthouse,
acquitted of murder charges.

When, several days later in New York, the McKinleys declined actress
Julia Marlowe's invitation to see her at the Knickerbocker Theater, the
press was told it was because Ida was "somewhat tired" from a Hudson
River cruise earlier that day. Ida, relieved that the Canton trial was over,
energetically went shopping with her sister-in-law Annie, even musing
that she would like to stay longer "as she has much shopping to do this
week" and let the president return to Washington alone. McKinley admitted to a reporter that "I must take all the rest I can get. I came here for a
brief season of quiet and not to see the sights."[34]

The respite, however, failed to rest him. Four days later, the White
House announced that he needed a complete break of perhaps up to
three weeks. He would go to the mineral baths of Hot Springs, Virginia,
not just to overcome "the strain which has been upon him for many

months," but to relieve his rheumatoid arthritis. The McKinleys left on May 8. Ida's only trouble was a brief adjustment to the elevation. She felt so well that she joined the Major on a side excursion to the famed "Natural Bridge" rock formation but wasn't allowed to descend the ravine there due to the rough ride on the mud-washed path.

Reports from Washington of the constant attacks by Aguinaldo's forces led the Major to cut short their vacation and return on May 20. Despite his promise to make only one whistle-stop speech, he couldn't resist stopping the train eleven times to shake hands with waiting crowds, visit cemeteries, and make speeches. His political sensibilities, if not his health, were restored. Ida McKinley withdrew entirely and remained on the train. There were no more reports of her attempts to spare him the stress of public duty so he could rest. What exhausted him also seemed to invigorate him. For two years, the same could be said of the First Lady. Although she had at least one known seizure, she had matched his killing pace, exceeding even his expectations. As the summer of 1899 began, the stress only increased. More fearful about the Major's health than her own, Ida McKinley longed for a slower-paced life for them. After their trip to Hot Springs, she grew noticeably tense. And then good news came from Canton.[35]

Elizabeth Harter, who had leased the McKinleys' first home to them three years earlier during the campaign, had finally decided to sell it. McKinley sprang into action. Harter would not budge from her high price of $14,500, but the value for him was in its association, not the square footage. He surprised Ida by buying it. As he had hoped, she was moved by his vision of how they could transform the first home they would own. Over three days, he not only distracted her attention but prompted her excitement over plans to enlarge and improve it to make it their dream house. The giddy Major told Navy Secretary Long that it was "just as if they were newly married" and going "on their honeymoon." While sitting at one end of the Cabinet table with Assistant Secretary Cortelyou, McKinley changed his voice until it was "soft and low" and began a sentimental monologue, "almost musing to himself." McKinley's eyes filled with tears, declaring that the house held the "tenderest memories of my life."

He drew the changes he wanted on the back of a telegram, "extending the hall, adding to this room, enlarging here and there." If the assistant secretary began to wonder just why two people looking for peaceful privacy needed all this, he soon got his answer. "If I have a place like that," the Major suddenly asserted, "we could transact all the executive business there."

On their arrival in Canton after they bought the house, the Major went alone to look over the construction of the extension, which had already begun. Ida went directly to Saxton House. At some point during the three happy days when she began to envision their future there, she must have realized just why the Major would not postpone the renovations so they could at least stay in the house for the few days they would spend in Canton that summer. He wanted to ensure that the extension was finished before the next summer began, the summer of 1900, exactly four years since they had last occupied the house. Not all of McKinley's fond memories of the old home were of the rooms where he had lived with Ida, Katie, and Little Ida. Some were of Hanna and the front porch. "I could see the extreme satisfaction it gave the President to get back his old place," Cortelyou noted in his diary.[36]

As the months moved closer to that time, Ida McKinley was receiving heavy dosages of disorienting drugs that the Major deemed necessary to avoid any seizures. Despite the effect of the medication, she was sufficiently aware of the conflict into which she was about to be drawn. However physically limited she was, her willful mind would confront the issue, regardless of how others judged her.

If McKinley detected a problematic situation arising with Ida during the summer of 1899, he was distracted by new crises arising in the Philippines. The war's first gunboat battle erupted. Over 10 percent of the U.S. forces there were sickened with tropical fevers. An American general now declared that the threat to holding Manila was "very serious." An injunction was obtained in Singapore to prohibit all further sales of John Foreman's book, *The Philippine Islands,* with its racist depiction of the Filipinos, which was now seen as having inflamed trouble in the region. Former Peace Commissioner Whitelaw Reid publicly denounced McKinley's Filipino policy. U.S. citizens writing home from the Philippines protested the McKinley Administration's censorship of their outgoing letters, calling it a deception of the American people. Desperately needed cavalry horses and some 40,000 more troops could not now be transported to the flooded islands. The rainy season had begun.

In the Filipinos' resistance to being neutralized, they used passive, covert methods. So too would the First Lady, which the Major would detect. When asked to sign a guest book in the home of an admirer, he flipped through to see pictures of different flowers on each page. Recognizing one that Ida liked, he penned an encrypted tribute to her on that page: "*You cannot guess the power, of a simple little flower.*"[37]

⤖ 12 ⤖

Descent from Mount Tom

IN HER FIRST MONTHS as First Lady, Ida McKinley had gone to see the farce *A Contented Woman,* written by Charles Hoyt and advertised with the line, "Why shouldn't we vote!?" It was about a wife who successfully wins an election for mayor against her husband only to discover she can't take office until she surrenders homemaking. The witty satire on how society demeaned women, *The Coming Women*—about women running the government with men powerless at home—which she had also gone to see, appealed to her sense of irony. To point out gender inequities, Ida enjoyed repeating a true story about a laundrywoman she knew. When the woman married, Ida asked if the husband was a "good provider," to which she quipped, "Indeed he is. He got me five new places to wash at this last week."

She was the first incumbent First Lady who supported a woman's right to vote. "Mrs. McKinley was no foe to the emancipation of woman," her husband's Canton minister affirmed after numerous talks with her on the issue, "no foe to the rise of woman." As she began her third year as First Lady, Ida's views became increasingly public. The first sign was her rare agreement to permit her name to be used in support of a fund-raiser bazaar for the National Women's Suffrage Association (NWSA), prompting advance publicity for it across the country. In donating linen doll's clothes that she herself had sewn, she added a bit of feminist wit by christening the doll "Carrie Catt McKinley," combining the Suffrage Association president's name and her own. It would command a high price. Ida's support of suffrage was so appreciated within the movement that she would be invoked in Senate testimony by leader Emmy Evald, who pointed out, "You have not trusted the ballot in the hands of Mrs. McKinley simply because she is a woman, but you do trust it in the hands of anarchists?"

In her fourth year as First Lady, Ida would affirm for the public her affinity with the famous suffrage leader Susan B. Anthony. When Anti-Suffrage League leaders, including Governor Roosevelt's sister Corinne Robinson, came to meet the president in the Blue Room, he neither made mention of the First Lady's absence nor her regret for it, which he typically would. As they left, he received members of the Women's Suffrage Association, who were in Washington for their large national convention. Before they left, he had a message from Ida for its leader: "Miss Anthony, may I take you to see Mrs. McKinley, who does not feel able to meet all the ladies?"

Upstairs, in what Anthony recalled as a "bright sunny room," she and the First Lady had an engaging but brief talk. Neither disclosed what was discussed, but Ida "expressed a wish to send some message to the convention" and removed lilies from a vase to place in Anthony's arms. "I carried the beautiful lilies to the convention that evening and held them up before the vast audience and said, 'Mrs. McKinley shakes hands with you all spiritually,'" Anthony recalled. The lilies remained on the platform during the convention, a sign of the First Lady's support.[1]

McKinley's willingness to have the First Lady meet Susan B. Anthony, scorned by many in his political base, reflected his evolution on the issue. Just after he had won the presidency, the newly formed Brooklyn Woman's Republican Club commissioned an extravagant gold vase for Ida, whose "patience," they told the press, "have touched the heart of American womanhood." Less subtly, they announced the "election" of Mrs. McKinley as their honorary member since women were denied the right to elect Mr. McKinley. He denied their request to personally present the vase, fearing it would imply that he supported suffrage or force him to deny it. He issued a public "appreciation" for the "token," offered to Ida "and myself."[2]

Ida's support of suffrage had been mentored by her father and teacher and was the passion of her friend, fellow Ladies Aid Society member and Ohio U.S. Senate wife Cornelia Fairbanks. Fairbanks, trained in law as Ida had been trained in banking, was a suffrage leader too, believing that women were equal to men in the professional world. Ida spoke often and proudly of her early bank employment, and the Major's niece remarked that the First Lady "always claimed that her business training was the most valuable course in her whole education." Willa Cather was one of the few journalists to emphasize that Ida McKinley's employment "before the advent of the business woman" had proven her skills to be "better and more thoroughly than any man." Despite not earning an income for the clothing she spent hours each day producing, Ida thought of it as a job, knowing too that it had a monetary value as a donation. Proud of her craft, she was highly honored to be asked to send samples of her work for public display in the Women's Exhibit Hall for the Tennessee Centennial Exposition.[3]

She also showed her support for a woman's right to work through her White House hostess role. Among the few organizations that requested to meet with the First Lady, she agreed to see delegations of working and professional women, from the Council of Women Scientists Day to the School Teachers of Washington's Normal Kindergarten Institute. She joined the likes of Susan B. Anthony to nationally recognize Mary Manning for coordinating the Spanish-American War nurse corps and was credited with convincing the president to name Manning to the 1900 Paris Exposition American delegation to represent American women.[4]

Ida McKinley's support of women's rights to vote and to work outside the home defied the societal expectation that women restrict their focus to home and family and live pious, modest lives. Ida had no children or home. She never went to church but attended the theater as often as possible. Her favorite pastime was playing cards, and she occasionally drank wine. While she publicly voiced belief in the value of "woman's observance of her household duties," privately it had been her husband who had been assuming those duties for them for some thirty years. Blurring the line between gender roles was natural to Ida, a point she made by telling a story about a friend who complained about her spouse that "He is so slipshod. His buttons are forever coming off." Ida asked if the buttons were properly secured. "That's just it," her friend replied, "My husband is one of the most careless sewers I ever saw."

Ever since she saw European women engaged in hard manual labor, Ida McKinley knew that many women had no choice but to work outside the home and were often vulnerable to exploitation. It is unclear when she began her financial support of the National Crittenton Missions, founded in 1887. Headquartered in Washington, they provided medical care, shelter, and employment training for women enduring abuse or abandonment, who were unwed and pregnant, or who were attempting to leave prostitution. The nationally renowned physician Kate Waller Barrett, who helped founder Charles Crittenton to open mission homes in large cities, believed that education, not dependency on men, gave women permanent freedom. The First Lady's support may have even influenced the president to sign a special 1898 act of Congress granting the mission a national charter in perpetuity, the first given to a charitable organization.[5]

Ida McKinley also believed in a woman's right to pursue higher education. With fellow members of the Brooke Hall Alumnae Association, she made a "generous contribution" to establish the $2,000 principal for a scholarship fund to ensure that enrolled students at the women's Bryn Mawr College who showed "excellence in college work" completed their education to graduation. She hosted one of the association's annual events at the White House, giving the scholarship national publicity. The First Lady again focused attention on the issue of women's education at events that held personal significance for her and the Major. The first presidential trip during the summer of 1899 was scheduled around the graduation ceremony at the women's Smith College, where Mary Barber was a student and where Ida Barber would begin that fall, followed by a visit to the nearby women's Mount Holyoke College, where Grace McKinley would become the first among the Saxton-McKinley nieces to earn a college degree.[6]

On June 19, the McKinleys drove through the Smith College campus for commencement exercises. William McKinley received an honorary LL.D. degree and became the first president so honored by a women's college. After the ceremony, the First Lady received her own tribute, a silver-trimmed cut-glass loving cup, presented in a private, indoor Social Hall ceremony. The reason for the honor and the text of her "expressing her pleasure and appreciation of the gift" were not recorded. Later, in Hadley, Massachusetts, she joined the Major on a trolley ride to the summit of the local Mount Tom. At the top, Ida walked out to stand at the peak point.

Tourists at Mount Tom cheered her. Earlier that day, Smith College girls had tossed bouquets in her carriage. As her husband made history, Ida gained strength by engaging in various activities, disproving those who said she would distract him. As First Lady, she was a guest at the baronial estates of the nation's wealthiest families, fussed over in the fanciest of hotels, feted at dinners. Guards prevented others from intruding on the McKinleys so that, however briefly, Ida had a moment of peace on Mount Tom. The clear sky and pure mountain air offered a breathtaking, three-hundred-mile view. Such perspective on life below must have given her a sense of triumph.

The Major had to keep to schedule. They turned from the peak, entered their trolley, and began the descent from Mount Tom. Nobody could know then that it was the last fleeting glimpse of an unvanquished First Lady, soon to be subjugated by the force of political ambition.

The next day, at the Mount Holyoke College ceremony, the president handed out diplomas to his niece and her classmates. "I am glad that we are demonstrating in the United States today that the boy shall have no more advantage than the girl," he remarked. The First Lady listened somewhat listlessly while seated with the governor's wife. She seemed to rally when graduates rushed the trolley transporting the presidential party, but at the town hall reception that followed, she was nowhere to be seen. The next day, after parading together through Springfield, the Major stepped out to deliver a speech, but Ida stayed seated and the carriage pulled away. Still, this raised no flags for the press corps, which regularly followed McKinley and were now watching for news outside the Adams, Massachusetts, home of their friends, the Plunketts, where the couple was staying.

A hint that there was something amiss in the Plunkett house was the unexplained arrival of Leonard Wood. He was on leave, visiting family in the area, and came in his capacity as Cuba's governor to report to the president on conditions there. However, the press knew him best as the First Lady's former doctor and speculated that she was ill. To stop the questions, the president's assistant secretary told them that Ida "has not yet recovered from a cold contracted on the journey from Washington." When he claimed, as reported in the June 24 *New York Tribune,* that she hadn't joined the Major on a four o'clock drive due to "the weather," he inadvertently revealed that her absence was due to a more serious matter: according to the article, it had been sunny from noon on.

The mood inside the Plunkett house darkened over the next two days. "The illness of Mrs. McKinley has materially changed the plans of the President," the June 26 evening edition of Washington's *The Times* announced. "Mrs. McKinley was not in good health when she arrived here, and has been growing steadily worse. The President is somewhat anxious about her and thinks a return to Washington will be beneficial." When a crowd of locals gathered at the depot to give the McKinleys a rousing send-off, they were requested to remain silent instead until Ida, looking "quite ill," was carried into the train.[7]

By the time McKinley's train pulled into Washington the next morning, the secretary of war, the secretary of state, and a senator were waiting to meet with him about pressing military issues. Instead of meetings, however, the president "spent the greater part of the day in Mrs. McKinley's company as is his custom when she is indisposed." One gawking reporter recounted how McKinley had "almost carried" her up the marble North Portico steps.

For McKinley, the First Lady's health and the description of it provided to the press and the public were of nearly equal importance. He now had two men expertly managing both matters. If his worst decision had been giving ineffective Addison Porter the title of secretary, his slyest sleight of hand had been to give the job's responsibilities to Assistant Secretary George B. Cortelyou. Shortly after Dewey's victory, McKinley promoted this federal stenographer to his current job, finding in the forty-one-year-old Long Islander the discreet professionalism he needed. By April 1900, when Porter left and Cortelyou was officially titled secretary, he had already handled appointments, correspondence, dictation, press inquiries, and travel, including matters related to the First Lady. As she had with Bawsel, Ida came to personally rely on him, like a son.

If Cortelyou was liaison between the First Lady and the public, any issue related to her health first required consulting a navy physician whose objective was to make her as well as possible. As the navy's Bureau of Medicine and Surgery chief in charge of the naval dispensary, Presley Marion Rixey, a forty-eight-year-old Virginian, had been caring for the navy secretary's wife during a presidential trip eight months earlier when the president called him into his private care, discussed aspects of the First Lady's condition, and was "called upon to prescribe for Mrs. McKinley." In recalling this, Rixey neither disclosed which drugs he gave her, nor whether he felt she required them or if he was told to do so by the president.

Days later, McKinley asked Rixey to "take medical charge" of Ida, with checkups at ten in the morning, some evenings, and on lengthy trips. This led the official presidential physician George Sternberg to accuse Rixey of "insinuation" with the First Lady, which prompted Rixey to become "resentful of the implication that he had designedly and by unfair means gained the succession." McKinley let them work out their conflict, purposely avoiding designating one doctor over the other to be in charge. In fact, both doctors were stymied by the fact that McKinley continued to control Ida's bromide dosages. Whatever either knew of this, the record shows that McKinley had most recently purchased a stash of it himself at a time when both doctors were looking after Ida, in March 1899. Bishop had even come to check on her in the White House, hoping he would "find her as well as could be expected," he wrote the Major, adding, "I hear indirectly good reports. . . ." McKinley did not ask Sternberg or Rixey to consult with Bishop.[8]

Rixey, like Cortelyou, showed a lifelong protective support for Ida that went well beyond any measure of serving his ambition. Both also had rigorous integrity about keeping truthful accounts of the McKinleys. Perhaps the most important fact Rixey put on the record after her death was unequivocal confirmation of Ida McKinley's great secret: "Mrs. McKinley, as was generally known, suffered with a mild form of epilepsy and other ailments since the birth of her last child. . . ." Rixey created a protocol for keeping the public informed about her health when the "serious illness of his wife . . . obviously interferes materially with the President's service to his country." He and any other consulting physicians would sign bulletins cleared by Cortelyou. For his part, Cortelyou kept a diary recording McKinley's conversations and even preserved his checks. The president expected both men to be honest yet also adhere to his artful obfuscation.

Their first challenge was explaining to the public what made the First Lady so ill that the president had to rush back to Washington and refuse to meet with Cabinet members on pending business. Rixey's commentary that it was "fatigue of the journey, aggravated by a slight cold," which "need occasion no alarm," offered clues to the truth. With her weak immune system, a "slight cold" was understandable. His reference to "fatigue of the journey," however, contradicted his later declaration that long-distance travel benefited her. The First Lady herself insisted that the "change of scene" of traveling invigorated rather than tired her, suggesting the benefit of mental stimulation for her health. Mention of "fatigue," however, was telling.   Eating and sleeping patterns, emotional stress, and exhaustion all had the potential to induce seizures in those with epilepsy. The lack of detail about what happened to Ida in the Plunkett house limits any conclusion to conjecture. Given the furtive way in which Cortelyou dealt with it and the Major's rather radical response of returning to Washington on the night train and cancelling any meetings, a later opinion that she had a "severe epileptic attack" was likely correct. Still, even during her preceding two years of good health, Ida had not been free of seizures. The first recorded one while she was First Lady occurred in the Choate home in September 1897, and the most recent was during a White House lunch with the Major and a visiting engineer in the fall of 1898. A sudden increase in the frequency and severity of seizures, however, was cause for alarm, especially if her system was weakened with a viral infection, to which she was prone. Her anxiety inevitably led to sleeplessness, which, in turn, further spurred her recurring seizures.[9]

Trying to separate the vicious cycle of physical disabilities and health problems from emotional upsets and psychological issues in the case of Ida McKinley often proved impossible. In addition to the bromides and sedatives the Major gave in his desperate hope to at least stem the episodes of recurring seizures, he usually also had to remove her from stressful disturbances. Enforced inactivity and strict isolation, however, only heightened Ida's sense of powerlessness and futility. During her life before the White House, this regimen had inevitably led to a downward spiral of severe depression. In addition to crying jags and silent weeping, Ida's depression also led her to petulantly lash out at others and demonstrate a selfish possessiveness over the Major. In the summer of 1899, Charles Dawes definitively confirmed in his diary that the First Lady had "sank into a depression such as she had not known for ten years or more."

When Katie died in 1876, and when Ida nearly lost her own life in 1888, the Major's attentive love had been the first step for her gradual recovery from severe depression. During the summer of 1899, however, the Major seemed to be the problem and not the solution. Ida's anxiety about her health had worsened into a depression about her husband. As it became increasingly obvious to her that his plans for a re-election campaign for a second term were already underway, his political ambition proved to be more insidious to her well-being than were her colds and seizures. To Ida, a second term meant it would be six more years before they could go home to Canton and live in peace—and six more years of his exposure to danger.

Days after returning from Massachusetts, Cortelyou recorded that Ida was improving. He told the press on July 1 that she was strong enough to sit unassisted. Her emotional state was a different matter. Later that evening, Cortelyou wrote that McKinley left the office, "afraid Mrs. McKinley might be waiting for him, that this afternoon, when he went out he, by some miscalculation of time was gone longer than he expected to be and found her 'sobbing like a child, fearing that something might have happened to him.' He ascribed it to temporary weakness."

Her "fearing something might have happened," however, was entirely understandable. A news story reporting a potential threat to the president had already suggested that he avoid a second term. Ida would have been interested in the syndicated article analyzing McKinley as husband and predicting his future. Written by clairvoyant Dr. Muehlenbuch, who flattered the Major as an "admirer of intelligent women" and thus Ida's "desirable life-companion," intuited that he was opportunistic, for by his "choice of a wife, he has considered his station in life as much as his happiness, never stepping blindfolded in a mere marriage of love alone." What made Cortelyou clip out the story was Muehlenbuch's vision of a "man of the age of 24 to 26 years, with a foreign type of nationality, with dark and large eyes, of a dark complexion, with black, bushy hair," who carried "a deadly weapon." McKinley could "ward off any attack" if he didn't "undertake a trip" and avoided "all public gatherings." Thus, as he addressed McKinley directly, "the experiences you have gathered in your public life will satisfy your ambition for your remaining years."

More amused than scared by hocus-pocus, Ida was entirely rational in her concern about global anarchists who killed Guatemala's president in 1898, Austria's empress recently, and their threat to go after more world leaders. The First Lady even shared a previously unvoiced worry, telling a reporter, "I dread all his speeches." Despite the Major's calm assurance to her that nobody had reason to attack him, Ida McKinley "never really knew peace of mind when he was out of her sight," according to one friend, for "she had a premonition of his fate."[10]

Assassination, however, was not all that threatened McKinley. Work was killing. On the night of July 13, for example, he met with military leaders and tackled paperwork until midnight since the executive offices were now "daily thronged" by those seeking commissions with rank in response to his call for more volunteer regiments to fight in the Philippines. Despite the same unrelenting workload, wartime had been easier as Ida was healthy and independent then. In the summer of 1899, however, McKinley's presidential duties were at odds with his marital duties, his work and his wife competing for his time. *Christian Herald* reporter Gilson Willets recalled the day Ida was "not feeling very well," forcing the Major to excuse himself from a conference *twelve* times to check on her. Olcott learned of another occasion, when she had him "called from an important meeting" to ask his "preference between two shades of ribbon." As McKinley realized that she was unlikely to know the importance of his meeting, he came as she wished and "never expressed the slightest annoyance," finally returning to business after asking, "Is that all, Ida?"

That summer, his patience finally cracked as he coped with an emerging crisis in the treaty negotiations over foreign construction of what would be the Pan-American Canal. Ida was undergoing dental work down the hall, with her friend Julia Foraker there as company. Suddenly, the First Lady demanded the president's presence. Foraker recalled: "The President sat with her while the work progressed. Finally, he arose; he would have to go; a person of importance was waiting to see him. There was an outburst. Go, of course, if he cared more for some mysterious 'person' than for her! The President sat down again; stayed on some time; then, '[Secretary of State] John Hay is waiting to see me,' he said at last, 'I cannot keep him any longer.' He walked out in complete silence."

The conflict between work and wife affected their regular evening ritual as well, as the Major was unable to read to Ida with his eyes strained by overwork. When he was told to renew plans for two West Coast trips and one to the Midwest, as Cortelyou plotted the tedious arrangements for such extensive travel, he realized that even his toil could be proven worthless because of Ida, writing on July 13 that "all plans for the summer are dependent on her health."[11]

It was uncharacteristic of Ida not to confront the Major about his true intentions for their future, but if he resisted discussing his pursuit of re-election, Theodore Roosevelt did not. Two days after the McKinleys returned from Massachusetts, just before sitting down to dinner with General Wood, the New York governor "most emphatically" told reporters he supported a second McKinley term and felt it "the duty of every man" to do likewise. "We must smash out this insurrection there [Philippines] by force of arms and then we can consider terms of peace."

Ida McKinley would argue her reason for opposing a second term: "I will be glad when he is out of public life. I did not want him to run a second time. I thought he had done enough for the country, and now I know that he has done enough, and when his term expires he will come home and we will settle down quietly and he will belong to me." Perhaps to avoid open conflict with her, McKinley remained mute on the matter. His intention was clear to William Howard Taft, however, who recalled how, after someone warned McKinley that his Philippines policy "would lose him his nomination for a second term," his legendary good temper turned sour.[12]

McKinley refused to choose between wife and work. For Ida, the lack of resolution only created further stress, which weakened her vulnerable immunity. While some suggested that her illnesses were feigned or even unconscious psychosomatic methods to get her husband's attention, there was no way to psychologically induce the fever that Rixey told the press she contracted on July 19, nor was it a fib. That same day, Charlie Bawsel was not allowed to see her, reporting that "she is not well, and is receiving practically no one." Five days later, Dawes wrote in his diary that Ida was "very weak and ill."[13]

Ida's condition finally compelled McKinley to cancel any West Coast trip and postpone the Midwestern tour until fall. When newspapers announced that "Mrs. McKinley's health, unless there is great improvement, would not permit her to make an extended trip" and the fact that "he does not desire to go without her," the president feared that this left the impression he was putting his wife before his work. He had Cortelyou issue an artful arrangement of words in the local *Washington Evening Star* to state that any such implication was "conjecture," since he had "only desired" to take a West Coast tour. To then imply a commitment to regional tours—without actually committing—it was asserted that the First Lady's health "will soon be restored and that she will be able to make such a trip," and that the president vowed not to abandon "his desires."[14]

Even though past experience indicated that enforced inactivity and isolation would only initially worsen her depression, the Major imposed this regimen on Ida, quickly deciding to return her to the Hotel Champlain for a month, on July 27. Immediately, political and military officials' requests for appointments and social invitations "deluged" him, but "on account of Mrs. McKinley's illness, he has been obliged to decline all of them," Cortelyou told the press, making clear that "he will accept no invitations that will take him away from Mrs. McKinley even for a day." The president, however, ensured himself an escape clause, the seemingly final edict qualified by the little phrase, "for the present, at least."

If McKinley realized that he was unlikely to focus all his time on Ida as he once did, Dr. Rixey was there. With no illusions about "curing" her epilepsy, Rixey began a regimen of alternating rest and activity, removing excessive external sensory overload but stimulating internal mental engagement to improve her physical health and decrease her depression. He "urged" rather than ordered her to "walk and ride as much as possible," to take open-air yacht cruises but closed-carriage coach rides, and to appear on their balcony to take in band concerts. He succeeded in not only coaxing Ida to report her daily activities but to compose letters to her nieces Mary and Ida in her own hand. There were soon hopeful signs. Unlike 1897, when she was pushed into participating in a flag presentation ceremony with the 26th Regiment and sat simmering in defiant silence, this time she stood and, with help, walked to present them with a flag they would take with them when they were shipped out to fight in the Filipino War.

At the ceremony, the president declared to the regiment that "Rebellion may delay, but it can never defeat, the American flag's blessed mission of liberty and humanity." Necessarily consumed by work, when it rained one Sunday the Major decided to stay indoors with Ida and skip church. He held meetings with the secretary of state, the ailing vice president, and Governor Roosevelt, who, sensitive to Ida's need for companionship, brought along his wife Edith. It seemed the trip had helped at least Ida's physical health, with Cortelyou reporting to Carolyn Herrick that "Mrs. McKinley's health has very much improved" and Rixey telling reporters that "she is much stronger than when she left Washington." That the First Lady walked several hundred feet on her own, from her upstairs suite down to the carriage, was seen as an accomplishment.[15]

A few restful days at the Jersey shore during which the Major made only one speech practically restored Ida, but she reacted with such dramatic reversal to the twenty-one gun salute greeting their train in Pittsburgh on August 27 that the president felt forced to cancel a public reception planned to honor him "owing to desire for absolute rest." Scheduling a stop of a few days in Canton the following week, the president knew that time at home with her family and visits from friends invariably excited her. Ida, however, considered avoiding the trip to Canton and letting the Major go alone. "If I could stop in home next week with Uncle," she said in her handwritten letter to Mary from Lake Champlain, "I certainly would do it. I have not fully decided what to do. I wish you could be here while Uncle is in Ohio."[16]

Ida did join the Major but went out only to visit the graves of Katie and Little Ida at Westlake Cemetery. Her peculiarly uncharacteristic ambivalence about returning to Canton was perhaps revealed by a press article explaining that McKinley had arrived in Canton, along with Cortelyou, not to make her happy, but "for the purpose of giving his Washington friends a view of the home and to inspect the property with reference to possible improvements. . . ." The president had still not yet publicly announced his plan to run for re-election and use the house as campaign headquarters. "I know how happy you must feel to realize," an unaware old Canton friend wrote her, "when your husband has laid down the cares and responsibilities of public life, that you have a home to which you are so attached ready to return to." Such comments reflecting what she had hoped for in the immediate future made the reality of the Major's plan all the more ironic.[17]

The conflict between the president's work and wife continued. When it was time to leave Canton, Ida suddenly said she uncharacteristically felt motion sickness, which slowed their return to Washington as the train had to proceed at a snail's pace of no faster than thirty miles an hour. The First Lady's best interests may have slowed the president, but it could not stop him. Three weeks later, after stating an "intense desire to retire to private life," he made clear to Charles Dawes that "sense of duty will lead him to stay in office another four years." Two days later, without mentioning campaign plans, the Major reported to Hanna that "Mrs. McKinley is not at all well," but it was Dawes who made clear that the problem was not a fever or cold, severe immobility or an episode of seizures, but rather "extreme mental depression."

A solution, even temporary, was needed. Several days after their return to the White House, however, the president's arrival in Philadelphia

without the First Lady for a naval review, speeches, and other events generated more news than her routine presence on such trips usually did.
The chairman of a veterans gathering that McKinley attended sent the
First Lady a telegram declaring that the 2 million residents and visitors
in Philadelphia that day "regret exceedingly Mrs. McKinley's absence."
As Ida relied on the Major, the public had expected the couple to appear
together, and when Ida was not there, something seemed amiss about the
president. Several weeks later, as Commodore Dewey walked into the
White House library and saw McKinley there alone, his first worried
words were to inquire about "the health of Mrs. McKinley." Led into the
West Sitting Hall, where the First Lady offered Dewey her "most hearty
welcome home," the president indicated that she was physically fine.[18]

No consistent explanation was given for Mrs. McKinley's absence in
Philadelphia. She may have chosen not to go simply to escape the public's
expectations. If she refused to go as a small revenge or as a defiant test of
the Major's loyalty to her, his decision not to cancel or postpone but rather
take the trip without her would have likely worsened her severe depression, which was a risk McKinley would never take. Thus, it seems most
likely that it was Dr. Rixey who urged her not to go. He had continued
the work begun at Lake Champlain to make Ida's life more active. With no
social callers or houseguests while the Major was in Philadelphia, Ida was
put through her paces. Instead of languishing in an armchair in the greenhouse, the papers reported that she "takes a walk daily." No physician had
ever shown such commitment to improving Ida's condition as did Rixey.

Rixey immeasurably helped the president, freeing him from his anxiety
about Ida's well-being whenever they were apart, so that he could now
work without distraction yet maintain his public image of devoted husband. With his own identity built upon his devotion to Ida, McKinley
could never entirely relinquish his need to display it. One night when she
felt too weak to walk, aides fetched a wheelchair for her. "I think I can
wheel you, Ida," he snapped, "if some of you will point out any of the
rough places in the sidewalk." [19]

When he returned from Philadelphia, McKinley questioned Rixey
about Ida's ability to make the formidable Midwestern trip, which had
been postponed in July due to her particularly severe depression at that
time. For two weeks, starting October 4, they would stop first in Akron,
then make two stops in Indiana, and six stops in Illinois with a longer stay
in Chicago. Then their train would go north with two stops in Minnesota
and one stop each in Wisconsin, North Dakota, and South Dakota. Then

it was Iowa with four stops, back to Illinois for one stop, to Wisconsin for three stops, and on to Michigan for four stops. The last of their train's four stops in Ohio would be in Youngstown for a nephew's wedding.

In addressing concerns about the First Lady, the doctor recalled, McKinley said he didn't want to "run any risk to her health, but I knew the President considered this long tour important. . . . [H]e thought it desirable to speak personally to the larger body of the American people on the eve of his nomination and election." Rixey conceded that he felt the persuasive Major pressured him to declare Ida fit, saying, "The responsibility was correspondingly heavy on me."

Ida, however, was quite willing to be held culpable for her own insistence on, as Kohlsaat put it, "going everywhere with her husband." Mrs. McKinley was unconvinced that even running the nation was reason enough for spouses to endure separation, be it for a husband's business meeting or a wife's social event. "I do not understand these wives who put their husbands to bed, and then go out to dinners," she once rebuked Clara Hay. McKinley shared this view. When he assigned Dr. Sternberg to head army medical care in the Philippines, the president implored his wife Martha to go with him. Both McKinleys expected officials who joined the presidential entourage on regional tours to be accompanied by their wives.[20]

Unfortunately, the First Lady's appearances during the Midwestern tour did not go well. When she failed to appear at events with the president where her presence had been announced, the press noted how visibly disappointed her absence left crowds, a large number of which were women and children who turned out to see her. The most immediately obvious sign that her depression still beset her was her uncharacteristic indifference to children. As she accepted a rose bouquet in LaSalle, Illinois, presented by little girls who chanted a welcome rhyme for her, she offered none of her typically effusive gestures of affection. A news wire story about the president's appearance at a unique interdenominational gathering where he was wildly cheered by some 6,000 children, closed on the tart note, "Mrs. McKinley did not attend the services."

Her presence, however, sometimes led to more disappointment than had she not appeared. She wreaked havoc with a scheduled luncheon in her honor and swimming demonstration by the Chicago Women's Athletic Club luncheon by suddenly refusing to attend it unless the president was with her. He had to leave early from the luncheon he was headlining to dash across town and join her, but the altered schedule only left time for Ida's "brief visit" with the athletes. One incident proved especially embarrassing. McKinley had invited three volunteer committee members to share the honor of riding in his carriage with him in appreciation for their organizing his events. As the *New York Times* reported, "At the last moment Mrs. McKinley announced her desire to have the company of her husband during the ride," and the volunteers didn't even get to meet the president. Ida so insistently stuck to the Major during a day of continuously scheduled Sioux City appearances that she even endured what became her last known appearance in a church.

One paper even reported that "it was agreed by the members of the party that she had improved in health on the journey." Days after their return to the White House, however, Ida's depression deepened with news of the vice president's death. She "sobbed convulsively." If she had held out any hope that the Major might still consider not running, however, it ended when he decided not to name a replacement vice president. The convention that would surely renominate him was months away; he would choose a vice-presidential running mate then.[21]

The change in Ida following her descent from Mount Tom in June had not only abruptly ended her active first two years and three months as First Lady but, within six months, it impaired her to a point where it was feared she would never improve. Her behavior on the Midwestern tour showed a pettiness toward strangers that seemed to go beyond any repressed anger she felt about the Major's public duties. The president, striving to accommodate both work and wife, even with Rixey's help, would be hampered by Ida's unpredictable mood swings.

Despite his phobia for confrontation, especially with Ida, he brought himself to do the unthinkable at some point in late 1899. The president suggested that the First Lady should retire.

Details of the incident, like so much involving the McKinleys, remain opaque. It would be two years after the fact when the public learned about it in a *New York Times* story. The basic facts are clear. McKinley was "advised" by Rixey to "let it be known" in a press statement from Cortelyou that Mrs. McKinley "could not discharge the duties of 'first lady of the land'" any longer. While the Major believed this decision might benefit Ida, it was entirely out of character for him to simply announce it without first consulting her. The article further revealed that "It is said that the President favored the idea, and suggested it to Mrs. McKinley, but that she refused to entertain it for a moment, and that she has since rigidly performed the duties of mistress of the White House at considerable personal sacrifice and injury to her health."

Reporters never discovered what prompted McKinley to make the ultimatum to the First Lady but, in doing so, he would have confirmed that he was seeking another term, signaling his intention not to resume the private life he now suggested for her. Knowing Ida as well as he did, he may have intended the ultimatum to be either a bluff to encourage her to make a concerted effort to recover from depression or to make it seem as if he were conceding to her wish to live a private life. Further, it may have been a way to make her realize that he was committed to fulfilling his duties even without her and perhaps prompt her to decide to continue her duties beside him rather than let her nieces substitute for her. Over the decades, as he learned to overcome the obstacles that Ida's myriad issues presented to challenge his ambition, McKinley had become an astute negotiator of human psychology. As Taft put it, he "understood perfectly every slightest motive . . . McKinley was a man strong of will . . . [who] accomplished his purpose over men and over things, but largely through their voluntary acquiescence to his will. The quality that overcame those who dealt with McKinley was his sweetness."[22]

Taft first met Ida McKinley in early November at the home of the Days in Canton, where the McKinleys were so the president could vote on Election Day. A year later, they met again in Canton, this time in the McKinley home, when the Major offered him the job of civil governor-general of the Philippines during dinner with Ida. Taft's record of an incident that night became the most specific recollection of "how tenderly the President protected his wife from possible embarrassment on account of her malady, seeming to conceal and even to ignore it." When he needed a pencil to make notes, Taft asked McKinley for one: "[J]ust at that moment we heard a peculiar hissing sound. Instantly McKinley threw a napkin over his wife's face, and simultaneously, without a trace of excitement, handed me his pencil. In two or three minutes the napkin was removed and Mrs. McKinley was asking about the election as though nothing had happened. Not a word was said about the incident by anybody in the room."

Others saw this same ritual. Mabel Choate's account from September 1897 marked the earliest from the White House years. President Garfield's grandson, when the First Lady received him as a young man, never forgot seeing a woman relative use a kerchief on the First Lady. Estella Joliet of Canton saw Ida have a seizure once during a White House visit. "We were at table at Washington one time when Mrs. McKinley got one of her spasms," she remembered. "Major McKinley threw a napkin over her face." Jennie Hobart believed that Ida may not have always realized when she was having a brief seizure. As they played cards, Jennie noticed "the faint convulsive gesture which preceded these attacks. Instantly the President dropped his handkerchief over her face and played the card from her hand." In a moment Ida was again "her natural self," reviewed her hand, and asked "Who played that card for me?" Hobart's description of the "momentary seizures of unconsciousness which lasted only a second, but which might occur any time" corresponded with the First Lady's epilepsy symptoms recorded by reporter Arthur Dunn ("attacks in which she frequently lapsed into unconsciousness") and Kohlsaat ("[S]he fainted. She did not fall out of her chair, but became rigid").[23]

The president cut off even polite inquiries if guests witnessed Ida experiencing a seizure and discouraged even vague descriptions of it. Ida's friend Mary Logan, who frequently wrote articles about her, obscured it as "the affliction that has held her captive for more than twenty years." Colonel Crook left it at "nervous disorder."[24]

Remarkably, McKinley's sheer determination that the word "epilepsy" never be printed in connection with the First Lady during her lifetime succeeded, but the truth did leak out. John S. McCook inadvertently exposed his knowledge of it by suggesting to McKinley a vacation spot "free from embarrassments or complications of any kind." Charles Willis Thompson, reporting in the *New York Times* that her problems were "not of the body alone," hinted at the truth by using an oblique reference to the ancient belief of epilepsy as spiritual possession, concluding that "The terrible illness which ruined her health permanently impaired her spirit. . . ." In the absence of any honest disclosure about Mrs. McKinley's epilepsy, myth inevitably arose, for example, that McKinley's authorization of the East Ohio Asylum for the Insane near Canton while he was governor led to the tale that he "kept" Ida in its superintendent's residence. This fallacy thrived unchallenged into the twenty-first century and even resulted in the building being called the McKinley Home.[25]

No matter how valiantly the Major tried to protect Ida both physically and emotionally, he realized that her situation now required some drastic measure. On November 10, the day he returned to the White House from Canton, President McKinley opened his personal banking ledger and wrote out a $100 check to the director of the New York State Commission on Lunacy.

McKinley's payment was not for new medications but rather a professional consultation with the commission director, Frederick Peterson, a leading neurologist. The native Minnesotan had expertise in a number of fields. With his understanding of how all human functions were the result of activity in the brain, he had conducted experiments on various external substances that adversely affected it. In addition to medical toxicology, Peterson was emerging as a pioneer in a new field seeking to study, diagnose, and treat those afflicted with a host of mental illnesses not merely as nervous system disorders but as emotional problems. It was called "psychiatry." As a former professor at the Women's Medical College of the New York Infirmary, he specialized in women's psychiatric cases.

Among these related fields, Peterson was most concerned with societal ignorance about epilepsy. In 1898, he cofounded the National Association for the Study of Epilepsy and the Care and Treatment of Epileptics. At the association's first conference, a stark reality was announced: some 140,000 Americans endured seizure disorder either in shameful silence or were rejected, unable to find work, and condemned to institutions. "Avoided by man, seemingly forgotten by God, the epileptic, of all humanity, is the most pitiable and the most pitied," Dr. Edgar J. Spratling explained. "Socially, he is ostracized, morally he is practically irresponsible."[26]

Peterson's frequent articles in the *Journal of Nervous and Medical Diseases* likely drew Dr. Rixey's attention. Rixey had become frustrated that the First Lady's "health fluttered constantly and rarely for a few hours remained stationary." Despite the "irremedial condition" of seizures, he was convinced that her general condition could be so vastly improved that "the periodic attacks from which she suffered would become less frequent and severe." He began what he called a "special study" of her baffling array of ailments and then consulted with Peterson on it. With his expertise in epilepsy and women's psychiatry, Peterson seemed the ideal medical consultant. Ironically, as Peterson studied the First Lady's case for a month, it would be his understanding of medical toxicology that led him to make a shocking discovery about Ida McKinley.[27]

⤙ 13 ⤚

The Resolution

DUE TO THE SENSITIVE NATURE of the case, Peterson came to Washington, Cortelyou's diary noting that "Dr. Rixey called in another physician for consultation this morning" on December 15. In discussing his findings, Peterson must have stunned Rixey with the news that the First Lady was suffering from a condition known as "bromism." A more daunting realization was that, however unwittingly, President McKinley was largely responsible for it.

For about thirty years, the Major had routinely dosed Ida with a formula that typically consisted of the anticonvulsive potassium bromide, sodium bromide, and sometimes ammonium bromide salts, mixed into a small amount of water. Consumed after meals, it was absorbed quickly into the blood through the stomach and affected the central nervous system. Bromides lowered brain activity, which controlled sensory and motor skills, and rendered the person insensitive to outside stimuli. In 25 percent of mild seizure cases like those of Ida McKinley, a short course of bromides proved effective in temporarily halting seizures. For 50 percent of patients who took repeated doses over time, however, bromides became less effective. This led many patients to increase bromide frequency and dosage, which not only failed to eliminate seizures but led to the more damaging central nervous system disorder of "bromism."

With symptoms easily attributable to her other health issues and medications, however, those of bromism were less readily discerned in Ida McKinley. Her severe headaches may have been related to her seizures or were caused by the cerebral edema of bromism. In one of his 1896 letters, Dr. Bishop had indicated concern that some other unspecified sedative he prescribed for her was causing Ida digestive disturbances, which may have also been a sign of bromism. The nausea she suddenly experienced in September 1899, when the presidential train had to be slowed, was also a sign of bromism. On the other hand, not until she was off bromides could it be determined that her heart palpitations were unrelated to bromism.[1]

Bromism, however, was more definitively indicated by memory lapses, confused speech and thought, and aggressive psychoses. These symptoms were already apparent in Ida McKinley as she faced her third full social season. Secretary of State Hay, who was often seated beside her at formal dinners, found "duty of attendance on poor Mrs. McKinley" had become "terrible" over time, her ability to articulate having deteriorated. Reporter Arthur Wallace Dunn was shocked by how Ida now stared "blankly at the procession passing in front of her," unable to comprehend what was, in fact, a lively reception. Historian Henry Adams feared that her severe memory lapses were the First Lady's "grand climacteric," an ancient Greek term for physical change foretelling imminent death. In such context, congressional wife Ellen Slayden's famous account of Ida from 1897 may be evidence of the first signs of bromism:

> She sat propped with pillows in a high armchair with her back to the light. Her color was ghastly, and it was wicked to have dressed her in bright blue velvet with a front of hard white satin spangled with gold. Her poor relaxed hands, holding some pitiful knitting, rested on her lap as if too weak to lift their weight of diamond rings, and her pretty gray hair is cut short as if she had had typhoid fever. She shook hands with us lightly, but didn't speak until the words "Mrs. Maxey of Texas" seemed to strike her and she then said in a faraway tone, as if talking to herself, "That's a long way off." Mrs. Maxey murmured some commonplace about her kindness in receiving us, and she went on, saying "I've had a great deal of experience." I expressed the hope she felt no ill effects from the cold. . . ."No, I've had a great deal of experience, my husband was in Congress a long time, and then he was governor of the state." She was rambling on in the same strange tone when we saw other visitors coming . . . a poor, suffering woman who ought to have been hidden from the gaze of the curious.

Ida showed bromism's symptoms of memory lapse and aggression. She had held a reception for a Missouri women's delegation. "We remember what a pleasure it was to meet you when you were in Kansas City," the group leader began. Ida cut her off: "I was never there." Assuming the First

Lady had simply forgotten the event, the leader continued, "Oh, don't you remember? It was the time the city gave a big banquet. . . ." Ida snapped angrily, "I tell you we were never there. If my husband went, I went with him. But he never went!" One witness found it "quite painful." Ida practically attacked Julia Foraker for simply observing autumn's beauty: "Beautiful? I don't see anything beautiful about it. We've had nothing but rain, rain, rain."

Cabinet members now avoided all but brief interaction with the First Lady, and others pitied her behind her back, but the perceptive Henry Adams sensed that Mrs. McKinley's skill in assessing political figures was intact. "The poor woman is not so imbecile," he recorded, "but that she sees some things intensely."[2]

Rixey had become especially alarmed by the First Lady's worsening mobility. Despite the work he had done with her and the progress she made at Lake Champlain in August and at the White House in October, by winter she was becoming paralyzed. The nerve damage to her leg and frequent vein inflammation that followed may have been the start of her mobility problem in 1873, but it could not explain her sudden inability to stand on both legs. In reviewing Peterson's findings, a little more than a week before Christmas, Rixey would have recognized it as paresis, the gravest of bromism's symptoms, typified by partial loss of limb movement.

Given the urgency of the situation, Rixey was unlikely to have waited long before confronting the president with it. It is impossible to pinpoint a precise time line about the crisis. An important clue, however, may be suggested by the fact that depression is also a sign of bromism. Cortelyou's diary documents her ongoing depression for at least twelve days after Peterson's meeting with Rixey. If her depression was a result not only of her fear for the president's safety and opposition to his second term but also of bromism, this could possibly indicate that Rixey waited until after the holiday season to address the problem with McKinley.

As it was now impossible for Ida to do her annual New York Christmas shopping, and there was little ahead to offer hope, her depression remained entrenched, as Cortelyou's diary chronicled. Only the Major's gift of a blue picture frame seemed to distract her, not for the diamonds studded in the wood but because of Katie's picture in it. "He said she was a Christmas present," Cortelyou wrote of the president's memory of Katie, "born on that day."

Despite wistful New Year's Eve reflections about the end of the nineteenth century, McKinley had already looked ahead, taking steps to lead his nation into the new twentieth century. He approved a $500,000

Smithsonian appropriation to organize an exhibition of new technologies, like an X-ray machine, which generated images from inside a human body and an incubator to keep sickly infants alive until they were strong to survive without it. It would be eighteen months before the public could marvel over these and other wonders, but there was already excitement about Buffalo's Pan-American Exposition.

On the first day of the new century, with her nieces, doctor, and maid hovering behind her high-back chair in the Blue Room and the Major standing beside her, Ida McKinley steeled herself to smile, nod, and murmur to several thousand New Year's Day reception callers. The First Lady's depression seemed to have broken. She was in her element, her favorite room just recently refurbished in her favorite shades of blue and a wallpaper patterned with roses, her signature flower. "You will be glad to know Mrs. McKinley stood the reception well," the Major wrote Jennie Hobart after the event. Ida wanted the first White House letter of 1900 sent to her old friend.

The new century began with new hope for the First Lady. By January 30, her depression had lifted to the point where the Major could report to a friend, "I do not know when Mrs. McKinley has been made more cheerful." Either just before or after New Year's Day, Dr. Rixey politely but firmly confronted the president with the fact that Dr. Bishop's bromide formulations had harmed the First Lady, while also implying that the Major was naively complicit in it. Bishop had refused Rixey's initial request for the composition of his bromide formula. As his colleague and friend William Braisted recalled, Rixey asked McKinley to insist that Bishop provide the formula: "[T]he first requisite to his purpose was information as to the ingredients of a compound which Mrs. McKinley was in the habit of taking. This formula was not easily ascertained, however, for the medicine in question was compounded personally by a New York practitioner who was disposed to hold the prescription a secret. . . . Rixey told the President that he could not be expected to work thus in the dark nor take the responsibility of a case which was being treated by administrations unknown to him, and the desire[d] information was, therefore, obtained."

Rixey immediately returned Ida to the system he had first tried at Lake Champlain, the strictly regimented routine used before the introduction of bromides in 1857. He regulated her sleep, food and beverage intake, physical activity, and exposure to various stimuli, a regimen often found effective in preventing the type of mild seizures the First Lady experienced. "Rixey believed that her general health was susceptible of [had the potential for] great improvement," Braisted wrote, "with progress in this direction based on this assumption, his efforts were attended with the most gratifying success. . . ." It would take a year before the "beneficial results" were seen, but within months Rixey "had her case well in hand." Cortelyou saw improvement by February 4.

McKinley wanted Rixey to be accessible at all times. Rixey checked on Ida twice daily and helped her rise and go to bed. A direct phone line linked his home to the White House family quarters. He always traveled with her, staying in the next room. He escorted her everywhere, chose what she ate, and forced her to nap on schedule. "Other doctors had been on duty at the White House before," observed Braisted, "but none entered so completely into the lives of his patients. . . ."

Ida was not initially pleased. Whatever addiction and damage may have been involved in her overuse of Bishop's bromides, Rixey insisted on substituting other types of drugs that proved to be effective anticonvulsives. During an evening call early on, he recalled, "Mrs. McKinley complained to her husband that the medicine I was giving her was abominable, and she would not take any more of it." The Major informed her that Rixey was due for sea duty, "and if you don't want him we will let him go." After a dead silence, she finally piped up, "We will not let him go until I say so." After that, recalled Rixey, "she was a much better patient."[3]

The most powerful cure that helped Ida recover through the first half of 1900, however, was having more time with the Major than she had had in two years. With a modified social season and the helpful presence of nieces Mabel McKinley and Sarah Duncan, fewer crises in the Philippines, and the aid provided by Cortelyou, both Ida and the Major were able to focus again on each other. This turning point had shifted their marital dynamic into another phase the summer before, when Ida was at her most needy and vulnerable, but in 1900 before the campaign, the Major was able to indulge her with his time. The distorted tales of romantic pathos told by those who knew the couple are largely from this period and solidify the image of Ida McKinley as a lifelong invalid. It not only best served McKinley politically, but had greater mass appeal than the truth that she was an independent First Lady during the first half of her tenure.

McKinley's devotional tableaux with Ida in front of crowds were stagey, but not staged. He did likewise in private, as members of the staff attested. "When she is not well enough a great solemnity hangs over Presidential shoulders and extends over the whole household," his niece Ida Morse observed during her late spring visit. "When she wanted a pen, or a needle, or a book to read, all she did was to say so and the President would start at once, hurrying after it as quickly as possible," Colonel Crook wrote. He continued, "This devotion to his invalid wife was beautiful; but it was also pathetic when we knew the weight of affairs he was carrying." Usher Ike Hoover concurred: "It was either work and worry or a continual endeavor to make the existence of Mrs. McKinley liveable. To this latter cause he was a martyr. Many, many times when he could have found other diversion he would tie himself to her presence and abandon the world. Her peculiar kind of trouble kept her in a constant state of wanting. . . . [T]he satisfaction of her every whim and desire was his very existence."[4]

In earlier years, the long months of congressional and gubernatorial recesses had given McKinley a necessary physical rest from work. In his first fifteen months as president, he managed to drive his own buggy, sitting upright in a way that strengthened his body's core muscles, or stride vigorously along the city streets or the White House grounds. The Spanish-American War, however, proved so consuming that he gave up even these limited breaks of necessary physical exercise. When this was compounded by months of waking at all hours and with little or no sleep, he rapidly became corpulent, and black shadows grew beneath his eyes. He was often in a state of exhaustion. By the summer of 1899, Rixey had become concerned about the president's overweight condition. His life had become entirely sedentary, devoid even of participating in the era's "gentleman sports" of hunting, fishing, or golf. At Lake Champlain, while Ida rested, Rixey started the Major on a routine. "These short walks were usually cut short by his anxiety to get back before his wife woke up and dressed for a drive in the immediate vicinity of the hotel," the doctor recalled.[5]

It wasn't just President McKinley's physical health that suffered as a result of his vow to be on call to Ida when they were confined to the White House. During her period of acute vulnerability, Ida was sensitive to any word or gesture, so he was cautious about everything he said and did to avoid upsetting her. Photographer Frances Benjamin Johnston found McKinley "always a little self-conscious," and Colonel Crook said he consistently "guarded his words," but now even a musical request to the Marine Band, a guest noticed, prompted McKinley to give "a narrow glance at his wife for fear the song might make her sad. Apprehension checked the spontaneity." Once when he told a guest how her mother had been his childhood sweetheart, he suddenly panicked that Ida would become jealous. He took Ida's hand, emphasizing that *this* "lovely girl had won his heart." Such vigilance was stressful.[6]

With nothing but genuine love compelling the Major's efforts to either protect or cure Ida, however, he failed to see how his excessive solicitude might contribute to her problems. By 1900, the ravages of stress and medication were obvious in the face of the somewhat vain First Lady's unretouched photos. The president, however, persistently maintained the charade that she had not aged whatsoever in the decades since the onset of her disabilities in 1873. Regardless of what she wore, for example, he repeatedly voiced his preference for her "white dress," an outfit she hadn't worn since 1870. Over breakfast one day, he referred to the event when she had appeared in it, telling her, "[Y]ou are looking a trifle younger this morning than you did at the ice cream festival, but otherwise I see no difference." He seemed to believe that by romanticizing Ida as if she were the same as she was before they married, rather than accept the reality of which she was now, he could convince her that she was still young and healthy. Even while speaking to others, he bragged of a *past* Ida, "Oh, if you could have seen what a beauty Ida was as a girl!"[7]

With her "absolute dependence and childlike trust" in him, some felt that the Major, by encouraging Ida to believe this fantasy of herself, had only long impeded her full emotional recovery from the trauma of Katie's death. The *New York World*'s White House correspondent observed that in striving to fulfill his vision of her, Ida's "mind, as if arrested on the threshold of that deepest experience of her womanhood was still held in the thrall of youth," and that her "ingenuousness of manner, the modulated voice, all gave President McKinley the sweetheart of his boyhood. . . ." Indeed, as one Canton friend noticed, when her husband was nearby, Ida took on "all the fervor of a maiden in her teens." The emotional harm of this was that it could convince a person to believe that a spouse would always be there to protect them from unpleasant realities.

Crook found it peculiar how the Major "looked after her as if she were a child," and even her good friend Isabelle McKenna admitted that she found it "almost appalling to be the object of such affection." The First Lady's loyal but nevertheless honest friend Julia Foraker gave the frankest assessment of how the president's treatment affected his wife's behavior: "The fact that her husband had been a shield between her and reality, had made of her a pathetically spoiled and difficult woman. . . . Mrs. McKinley knew what she liked and she got it royally. . . . [T]he indulgence she had received made her look upon herself as different from all other women."[8]

Mary Logan, as genuine a friend to Ida as was Julia Foraker, noted how "to her he is far more than a perfect man; he is divine." In fact, Mrs.

McKinley did her part to quite literally turn her husband into an icon, checking the proofs of his posed photographs and releasing only those she considered flawless. She chose the photo from which his official Bureau of Engraving portrait was adapted, and even that was not released until it had passed her approval. Further, she used a chronological series of his paper-framed studio images to tell visitors a heroic version of his life, each period a parable in piety and industriousness.[9]

At times this led the First Lady to suggest that the *president* was the *state,* that McKinley embodied the United States as Louis XVI had for France. She voiced an irrational indignation to at least two foreign citizens visiting the United States for returning home instead of settling in the nation "ruled over by my husband." She was equally harsh about "dirty Democrats," simply because their partisan loyalty was in opposition to the Major's. She considered that a flattering comparison made of him to Daniel Webster demeaned McKinley and even claimed that he was "the only honest man" to serve as U.S. president. There was a hint of her old Presbyterian inculcation of predestination in her emphatic mantra that "He ought to succeed, and therefore will succeed."

Expressing herself with, as the *Washington Post* put it, "a force and breadth of character almost masculine" hinted at a trace of competitiveness, as if Ida McKinley was determined to prove she could surpass the Major's devotion to her. Formidably defending him with a natural passion he lacked more than compensated for her physical limitations and proved she was a full partner. When he was once late in greeting unexpected visitors in the West Sitting Hall and found Ida already in a monologue glorifying him, he had no chance to sing her praises and assumed "a piteous expression." In displaying such strength in her convictions, she usurped his prerogative to a husband's traditional protectiveness of his wife. "When she praises him there is a deprecating look," journalist Murat Halstead commented of the Major's obvious discomfort, "embarrassment that she should show such admiration."[10]

There is further evidence that, in truth, Ida McKinley managed her own identity. In her rare interaction with the press, the First Lady became more conscientious about balancing praise of him as "so kind, so good, and so patient" by presenting herself as weaker. "If any one could know what it is to have a wife sick, complaining always, an invalid for twenty-five years, seldom a day well, and yet never a word of unkindness has ever passed his lips," she told a reporter. By repeating this familiar campaign narrative in 1901, however, Ida unwittingly cracked her facade. By then, the public record disproved her claim that she was "seldom a day well."

Ida's further boast that "He never forgets me, no matter how busy he is" was disproven by a visit of soprano Blanche Marchesi, who recalled that Ida "sent several messages" to the president in his office, "wishing him to come and meet me." He never appeared. Nor was he always so thoughtful of her. Although he knew how smoke sickened her, the Major nevertheless puffed on a cigar as his former Canton minister Dr. Johnston visited. When the minister declined his offer of a cigar, McKinley praised his morality, prompting Ida to point out his hypocrisy. "William, that is not very consistent for you to be smoking yourself, and telling Dr. Johnston you are glad he does not smoke." In private, neither entirely adhered to his scripted persona as stuffy and hers as fragile. Hidden from view on the portico as they heard the distant music of an approaching parade, McKinley began "waving his arms in time to the music . . . [and] to pirouette around the room," a guard recalled. Again using his formal name to tease him in a "semi-humorous, semi-shocked tone," Ida quipped, "Well, well, well, William!"

No anecdote better revealed just how wise Ida was to his modus operandi than her sudden confession to Corinne Robinson that, during their card games, she was fully aware that "he sometimes *lets* me win." It suggested Ida's willingness to maintain his illusion of her.

Ida McKinley's resistance to a second term wasn't a desire to spitefully disrupt his presidency but rather, given her uncertain condition and the risk posed to him by repeated public exposure, a poignant sense of time lost by tempting fate. During a Blue Room musicale in the late winter of 1900, she sat alone in the front row, listening to a contralto sing *The Lerig,* about love enduring even as one partner weakens, drawing away from the one who was the source of strength. Sensing that she was weeping, McKinley slid into the chair beside her and held her hand.[11]

To resign herself to a second term, it was necessary for Ida to separate the politician whose ambition she resented from this "tender, thoughtful, kind gentleman," a point she made clear to a reporter with startling frankness: "I am not speaking now of Major McKinley as the President." She also displaced her lingering anger from him to those she felt had encouraged a second term for their own benefit. She told Gertje Hamlin that "the American people did not deserve such a President as her husband—they did not deserve such a man." When a pompous Republican senator complained to her that the necessity of returning to his home state interrupted his legislative work, Ida snapped back, "Well, I'm glad to hear that. I think it's about time you men did something. My husband has carried the Republican Party for twenty years. Now I'd like to see somebody else do something."[12]

When Ida McKinley was ready to return to the arena, she proved herself still a formidable symbol. Throughout the endless speeches of the March 3 Ohio Society dinner in New York's Waldorf-Astoria Hotel, both an elaborately decorated mezzanine box overlooking the massive banquet hall and the seat of honor next to President McKinley on the dais remained empty. It was nearly ten before Governor Roosevelt finally made a dramatically late entrance and took the seat beside the Major. He so immediately engaged McKinley in "close conversation" that he seemed to ignore the applause. That is, until the five hundred dinner guests began looking toward the mezzanine and burst into a standing ovation.

There the First Lady of the United States stood and bowed to them all. Somehow Ida had made her way into the mezzanine box, partially obscured to diners. "Springing to their feet," one chronicle noted, "the diners cheered her for several minutes."

Ida McKinley had stolen Theodore Roosevelt's thunder. He did not so much as steal it back as share it. From the dais, Roosevelt asked the audience to give "three cheers for Mrs. McKinley." Ida again rose and bowed. Within weeks, rumor had it that McKinley very much liked Roosevelt and planned to name him as his vice-presidential running mate.[13]

The campaign had begun, and Ida McKinley knew it. A month later, having barely recovered from a ten-day bout of influenza, she was back in New York with the president, who would again join Roosevelt as they both addressed a mass gathering of Protestant leaders. It was lucky that McKinley had thought to contact the widowed Jennie Hobart to come along. When she came on the train with Ida's favorite roses, Jennie gently suggested that the First Lady might want to get off the train and rest at her nearby home. On the train trip from Washington, Ida had become "somewhat overcome," and the *New York Times* learned that "tonics were administered to her." Whether or not the Major had quietly set up Jennie's invitation earlier, Ida said no to her and "insisted on making the trip with her husband."

Outside the train station were four carriages waiting for the presidential party. Ida was to ride in the first one, but it would leave without the Major. He took the second one, with the chairman of the Republican National Committee seated beside him. Ida was not entirely ignored, however. A little golden-curled girl ran up and stretched her hand out to Ida, unable to reach her. Finally, the child was lifted up and Ida held her face closely in both hands, took a long look in her eyes, and then kissed her.

When the train first arrived at the depot, the Major walked off without Ida on his arm. Instead, he linked arms with millionaire philanthropist

Morris K. Jesup, a potentially big contributor to his re-election campaign. Rail passengers on the platform who stared in surprise as the president walked by them were even more shocked at the first public glimpse of the First Lady being lifted into an "invalid chair."

Ida was pushed in the wheelchair behind the president.[14]

⊰ 14 ⊱

Turn of the Century

By EARLY SUMMER OF 1900, the newspapers were churning out poetic rhapsody about the McKinleys returning to their "old home," the very place where the sun first rose and would someday set on them. No article speculated on the First Lady's feelings about going back there. During their brief visit to Canton at the end of April, she stayed at Saxton House while the Major went alone to check the progress of the home enlargements.[1]

For the fifty-seven-year-old president, born into the working class, owning his first home was an important benchmark, but for the First Lady, real estate had long been the primary source of her family's wealth. Not only did McKinley House represent that time when she lost her mother, second child, and her own health but also, during the 1896 campaign held there, her claim to her husband's exclusive attention. Nor would the rooms provide a comfort of familiarity; what little furniture the McKinleys owned was being used in the White House or their living space at Saxton House. The furnishings that would be brought to the house from storage in the Saxton Block Building were all associated with the 1896 campaign, when the items were first purchased.

Although still "quaint in design and modest in construction," one paper noted that McKinley House was now "a bit more pretentious" but "more adequate" to accompany the forthcoming campaign's inevitable "flow of personal and official friends." The porch was now extended around the large addition built onto the north side of the house, with a grand double-door entrance, paved oval driveway, and formal porte-cochere. Stables had been constructed in the back, and a tall iron fence enclosed the entire property. The entrance hall and main stairs were widened, the dining room expanded to seat more guests, its walls papered in a rich, crimson fabric. There were now six full guest suites with private bathrooms. What had been the Major's small office during the 1896 campaign was now a reception-waiting room, with double doors that led to his connecting library and office. Unlike the hodgepodge here four years before, the room was now wired for the latest communications technology. "It is no longer the modest cottage," the *Philadelphia Press* reported, "but a modern mansion."

The McKinleys moved into the house on June 30, as did Dr. Rixey, Secretary Cortelyou, maid Clara Tharin, her husband Charles (who worked as groomsman), and the White House's African American steward William Sinclair, who would manage all the campaign events held there. On her daily carriage rides, Ida was usually joined by Rixey instead of the Major, who was constantly meeting with the state party chairman or preparing speeches for visiting delegations. Cabinet members came from Washington for scheduled meetings on new crises and routine business and remained as houseguests. It was Mark Hanna, serving as National Republican Committee chairman, and Charles Dick, the committee secretary, whom Ida most often encountered in the hallways and who worked so late with the Major that they usually slept over. "All the [campaign] managers," one paper reported, "will be housed and fed in the McKinley mansion." Ida would have the company of family members and old Canton friends for four months until they returned to Washington just after Election Day, but she realized that for the next four years, she would enjoy this home life that she longed for only during the summertime. McKinley's defeat for re-election offered Ida the only chance of returning permanently to Canton, but even if she ever secretly entertained this hope, she never suggested it.[2]

The McKinleys got word of the president's nomination by the Republican National Convention in Philadelphia while they were still in the White House, a week before they arrived in Canton. The Major promptly sent a congratulatory telegram to Governor Roosevelt, who was nominated as the vice-presidential candidate. The famous Rough Rider, "Teddy" as the popular press and soon the public would nickname him, would visit the McKinleys both in Canton and the White House during their brief August return there. After a White House dinner where he was their guest of honor, Roosevelt was invited up to the Oval Library to confer with the Major until midnight, and Ida stayed up with them. Her affection for Roosevelt and appreciation for the way he respected McKinley were made clear by the simple gift presented to him, a framed triptych of her oval photograph and those of the Major and Katie. Not all of McKinley's team felt the same way about Roosevelt. Hanna famously declared that only a madman would now separate "that damned cowboy" from the presidency and wrote McKinley, "your *duty* to the Country is to *live* for four years from next March."[3]

Upon arrival in Canton, the Major went directly to his new house, where he hosted a reception for the local committee who would again facilitate crowds coming to Canton. Ida went to stay at Saxton House and the Major joined her there at night. She made her first public appearance at McKinley House on July 12, seated on the front porch as the Major delivered his nomination acceptance speech. Listening to McKinley's speeches and gauging the crowd's reaction to his words had always been an aspect of public life she enjoyed, and the deadly heat in the summer of 1900 never deterred her. During one speech there by the president, a reporter seated next to the First Lady noticed how "her eyes never left him during the entire speech." She turned to tell him, "He always does well and I always love to hear him."[4]

That the parades and visiting delegations in 1900 were fewer than they had been in 1896 was a blessing, for presidential work largely occupied McKinley. In constant touch by phone and wire with Secretary Hay, he was able to devise and manage a neutral foreign policy on Africa's Boer War and continue to monitor the American-Philippines War. Only the Boxer Rebellion in China required his brief return to Washington to meet with the Cabinet, when he decided to send American troops to help protect foreign citizens from further attack by nationalist Chinese who felt threatened by their influence. There is no hint of what Ida McKinley thought about the horrific reports coming out of China about the nationalists' violence, but letters from her nephew James Barber gave her eyewitness reports of life there. As a naval lieutenant stationed in Hong Kong on the seized Spanish vessel, *Don Juan de Austria,* he visited several Asian nations, and portions of his letters home were published in the *Canton Repository,* including the grisly details of a man who was convicted by mob rule and cut up into twenty-four pieces.[5]

Competing with news from China were lengthy profiles about Roosevelt. Tales of his vigorous exercise routines were in marked contrast to the previous year when the late Vice President Hobart's deteriorating health left those who knew of McKinley's exhaustion feeling uneasy. It may have also helped allay any public concern over rumors that the president's heavy cigar smoking had given him "tobacco heart." An editorial denying McKinley had heart disease claimed he was "smoking less at present than he did as governor of Ohio but that is not because of any fear that his heart was becoming infected."[6]

In the second campaign there were far fewer of the lengthy informational profiles that had appeared in 1896 about Ida McKinley and only brief mention of her as a wife in articles about McKinley. After four years of news reports about the president wrapping shawls around Ida or carrying her parasol, the public had developed a voyeuristic sense of intimacy about the First Lady as a wife. The marriage, "given more publicity," observed the *Boston Weekly Magazine,* "has seemed in a way to belong more to the people at large. . . ."

Even as he encouraged Dr. Rixey's plan to have Ida gain enough strength to be rid of her wheelchair and walk again with some independence, McKinley was no less mindful, by 1900, of the political capital he still gained from the myth that she had been confined to a fainting couch for a quarter of a century. Julia Foraker insisted that the president's "slavish protectiveness" of Ida was the proportionate result of his rising level of power onward from his 1888 congressional campaign when he first realized that "the public was weaving a halo" for his devotion. As busy as he was as president, the story of his devotion to Ida had become no less important. Even Speaker of the House Reed was struck by McKinley's need to assert for the record that "in all the thirty years of his married life he never uttered one impatient word to his wife." In fact, unknown to all but Cortelyou, the president put considerable effort into tweaking details for new stories that cumulatively flattered him. Only columnist Frank Carpenter dared to suggest that McKinley manipulated the press while feigning personal modesty.[7]

The value of his love story was certainly borne out in popular magazines and among respected opinion-makers. *McClure's Magazine* declared that "nothing which the public sees of the President does more to awaken respect for him" than his "chivalrous tenderness" for his "fragile, sweet-faced invalid wife," and essayist Julian Hawthorne concluded simply that "the nation's faith in McKinley was founded on his deep love for his wife." Others found that he embodied what Simon Wolf called "the highest traits of chivalrous manhood." Secretary Long declared that McKinley's devotion symbolized "one of the sanctities of the American home." Following this script once again required demeaning Ida, a point reflected in publisher Thomas Nelson Hall's poem, which suggested that the Major had "pity" for his wife.[8]

A sole female voice among the journalists hit a different note. Marian West, in *Munsey's Magazine,* pondered, "[D]oes the making of a President

cost more than the silent partner of struggle can pay?" Without mentioning Mrs. McKinley by name, she concluded, "Some have resented the
sacrifice of a quiet home life."

In the 1896 campaign, Harriet Hallmark's widely syndicated profile of a
Mrs. McKinley with opinions of her own and Willa Cather's *Home Monthly*
article revealing that Ida had been "an enthusiastic musician" whose time in
Europe as a single woman was "one of the happy experiences of her life"
departed slightly from the smooth version McKinley wanted to publicize
about his marriage. Depicting Mrs. McKinley as slightly independent had
done no damage, however, and appealed to women in the four states who
were able to vote and those hoping to do so by 1900.[9]

In the four years since then, however, much had changed. Organized
opposition to women's suffrage had stalled further progress, and a stabilizing economy made moot the push for the silver standard by the 1900
Democratic presidential candidate William Jennings Bryan, who was again
running against McKinley. Instead, Bryan focused on "the President's war,"
characterizing it as an act of cruel imperialism that victimized the most
vulnerable and innocent. Just as the campaign heated up in September,
voters were stunned by the most gruesome reports yet to emerge from the
Philippines, a massive and bloody ambush on American troops at Samar.

By 1900, after two years of insisting that imperialism was benevolence—through speeches he wrote himself, soaring with abstract ideals
and unburdened by statistical data—McKinley had further honed his genius for maneuvering public opinion. There was small chance of being
defeated by Bryan's charge of imperialism. Subtle suggestion of McKinley's unflinching sense of duty and compassionate commitment to those
in dire circumstances, however, would subliminally generate credibility
to his claim of benevolence in the Philippines. An abstract idealization,
unburdened by biographical data, of a now more desperately disabled Ida
(and the presumption that the president had not abandoned his legendary
devotion to her) in the August 11 issue of *Harper's Bazaar* certainly helped
accomplish that.

The unsigned piece was written by Elizabeth Jordan, only recently
named the popular magazine's editor after her colorful career as a *New
York World* reporter. The summer before, in her role as personal representative of its publisher Joseph Pulitzer, Jordan first met privately with
McKinley, who so quickly trusted her that he led her down the hall to
meet with Ida. Jordan had earned her national reputation by getting the
only interview with President Harrison's wife, which, she later admitted,

was pleasingly written to serve the First Lady's purposes. It was unlikely
McKinley would suggest that Jordan write a campaign article about Ida.
Whether he had identified her as the ideal journalist to pen the sort of
piece that would help his campaign is not known. That he would bring
an unannounced stranger, let alone a journalist, to meet Ida when she was
at her most incapacitated as First Lady in the summer of 1899 was unusually suspicious.

Jordan wrote the dual profiles of Ida McKinley and Mary Bryan on the
premise of an "election" between them, heralding a tradition of coun-
terpointing presidential candidates' wives, declaring Bryan a "stimulant"
for inactive women and McKinley a "sedative" for overactive ones. Ida's
depiction reeked with melodrama, but the concluding statement about
McKinley's "concern for the weak ones of earth" supported his claim of
benevolence in the Philippines:

> An invalid for very many years past, Mrs. McKinley's faithful presence . . .
> her frail form . . . describes a gentle martyrdom, the indescribable pathos
> of which is written in the expression of her sweet pale face. Her meager
> physical ability may accomplish no marvelous intellectual or social feats.
> When she has but appeared as First Lady of the Land . . . she has done her
> utmost. . . . Mrs. McKinley's want of strength is the obverse of her hus-
> band's highest power. It is the occasion of supreme devotion, the chief
> source of the great moral force emanating from self-forgetful concern for
> the weak ones of earth.

As long as it made the Major shine brighter, Ida was not concerned
about what the public believed about her, even though the widely circulated *Harper's* piece expunged all reference to her first two active years as
First Lady. Jordan's description reflected Ida's condition when they met
and at the time it was published. The suggestion that she was a permanent
invalid, however, was as misleading as a June *Cincinnati Commercial Tribune*'s
claim that the "bloom of beauty and happiness . . . adorns her cheeks."[10]

The public knew little of how rigorously Ida worked each day with
Dr. Rixey to regain her independence. After their morning drive, they
began training sessions to counteract the nerve damage to her legs and
maintain circulation. Ida would try to stand alone and walk unaided as
long as she could. To ward off depression, Rixey drew on her love of
flowers to encourage her personal supervision of new landscaping on
the property. The garden, already well shaded by apple and maple trees,

was soon blossoming with transplanted shoots of flowers, shrubs, and her other favorite plants from the White House conservatory. "Mrs. McKinley has been occupied in the pleasant pastime of flower-gardening for the most part," according to one paper.

By August 29, however, Cortelyou recorded that "Mrs. McKinley is not so well and the strain upon the President must be very great, his mind being occupied in addition to her illness with these most pressing matters of international concern; added to . . . the campaign. . . ." Given Rixey's involvement in all aspects of her care, it seems odd that the Major would ask his Canton physician Dr. Phillips to investigate the credentials of a Dr. Charles E. Jackson. After consulting a colleague "without telling him why I desired the information," Phillips reported to McKinley that Jackson was "in the drug trade and selling drugs on the road." No further action was indicated. It may be that the Major and Rixey were considering experimental medication to treat depression, which Ida suggested had returned, in her telegram to McKinley during his brief September return to Washington. "Am comfortable," she wired, "but dark morning."[11]

Yet again, Ida would have good reason to feel powerless against impending danger. While she was in Canton, the papers exploded with news that the king of Italy had been assassinated. Soon after, the State Department contacted Cortelyou about an anarchist en route to the United States "for the purpose of attempting the President's life," and Cortelyou swiftly informed authorities. In the process of investigating and deporting the convicted criminal, an international network was uncovered, including another man "chosen by his fellow anarchists to assassinate the President." The First Lady learned about it with the rest of the nation when the story was leaked to the press, and Cortelyou felt compelled to allay concern in an October 4 *New York Times* story about the McKinleys, headlined "Rumors of a Plot to Assassinate Him Discredited in Washington." Such threats, however, seemed to have become progressively more credible since the cryptic note Cortelyou received earlier in the year that was signed by "Jack the Ripper."[12]

In Canton, the president insisted on walking the streets unguarded. Except for visits to the graves of Katie and Little Ida, one long, open-air drive out to New Berlin, and three weddings, Ida kept close to home. She presided over all the luncheons and dinners with familiar friends like Hanna, Herrick, and Dawes, as well as with new faces like War Secretary Elihu Root, who had replaced Alger. Welcome relief from political guests came on Halloween night, when local children yelling on the lawn drew the McKinleys out of the house. The Major stood looking at the children with gracious formality. Ida took a few steps onto the porch and beckoned at eight-year-old Dorothy Kuhns so she could scrutinize the familiar furrowed brow and unsmiling face carved on the girl's pumpkin. Ida looked up at the Major, again at the pumpkin and, with poker face and dramatic pause, cracked, "Do you think that looks like my husband, Dorothy?" She made them all burst into laughter.[13]

Ida McKinley hosted her first large party in the house on Election Day, inviting some forty guests to await the returns and have dinner, mixing the Major's political advisers with many of her long-time Canton women friends. By less than a million popular votes, McKinley again defeated Bryan. A parade, band serenade, and fireworks marked the victory, but unlike four years earlier, the Major offered only a weary, brief greeting to supporters gathered outside.[14]

The McKinleys were back in the White House for Thanksgiving. Escorted by Rixey, Ida went Christmas shopping in New York the next day, bringing an extra list from the president with names of officials and political associates for whom he wanted her to buy gifts. She was joined there by Controller Charles Dawes and his wife Caro. Sharing her passion for theater, the couple took Ida to the hit musical comedy *San Toy*. The press refrained from any sarcasm about the wife of McKinley enjoying the interracial love story of a "civilized" Englishman and a Chinese woman, set in contemporary China and gently satirizing imperialism. The *New York World* did, however, suggest that Ida was making progress with Rixey. Although reporting that she was "wheeled in an invalid's chair to her carriage," it also revealed that upon emerging from the train, "Her step was brisk and she greeted her friends on the platform with animation." Asked how she would hold up for another four years as First Lady, Rixey offered some political spin: "The President's re-election has proved the best tonic yet tried," he claimed.[15]

If Ida hoped that her five days in New York away from the Major forecasted a return of her independence, he had lived for too long with apprehension about her well-being to feel optimistic and perhaps was even dependent on her dependency. During this trip, as always, they talked by phone twice daily and wired each other at least once each day. Hours after one call, he even wrote her: "My talk with you tonight was very satisfactory. I will sleep better having heard from you and hope you will have an unbroken rest and be refreshed for tomorrow and at 10 o'clock I am to talk again with you. Good night. God bless and keep you is my constant prayer."

As she read the brief note, Ida could never have imagined that, within one week, it would be one of the few letters the Major wrote her that she would be able to cherish in the years ahead. It was nearly midnight on December 8 when the First Lady's sister heard fire trucks clanging past Saxton House and joined neighbors on Market Avenue in time to see a rapid and explosive fire engulf the Saxton Block Building, the commercial and residential property inherited by the Barber children upon George Saxton's murder. Nobody was killed, but the loss was total. Among the property destroyed was a third-floor storage room trunk, packed by Ida, with her letters from the Major. Especially prized were those written during their separation in 1877, when he began in Congress and she was under Dr. Weir's care in Philadelphia. "They were a comfort to her," Murat Halstead observed when she told him about the loss. "Her most precious possession—her husband's love letters—perished in the thousands in the fire."[16]

The news came on the heels of a more personal loss. A month earlier, the acting chief of the Naval Navigation Bureau had informed the First Lady that her nephew James Barber, on naval duty in Hong Kong, had contracted typhoid fever. While "nothing was left undone to save his life," he succumbed. Ida gave the news to Pina, expecting that his remains would be sent quickly. Secretary of State Hay ordered the next transport to the United States from the Philippines to stop first in Hong Kong to retrieve the remains. Gen. Arthur MacArthur in Manila refused to do so until the war secretary authorized it. The three-week delay postponed the Canton funeral, which was scheduled at the same time as an East Room ceremony that McKinley had promised to attend.[17]

The conflict between Ida's more meaningful private life and McKinley's public duty perhaps explained the First Lady's mood on December 11 as she sat with the president while silently listening to speakers talk about the past and future of Washington, D.C., ostensibly to mark the city's centennial. The East Room event was driven by the agenda of pompous Colonel Bingham, commissioner of Public Buildings, to enlarge the White House. He made his case to journalist Walter Wellman, who penned a *Collier's Weekly* editorial under the embarrassing headline "The White House a Disgrace to the Nation."

Joined by U.S. senators and the nation's governors who comprised the centennial committee, Ida's glare was fixed on the middle of the room. There, a model of a strangely familiar white plaster building sat on a platform, raised by sawhorses. It was Bingham's futuristic vision of a White House with steep wings and colonnaded domes like merry-go-rounds. The

Washington Bulletin called it "an absurd concoction." Prominent members of the American Institute of Architects said the proposed changes were an "act of vandalism." Neither local press nor professional aesthetes had the power to prevent Bingham's monstrosity from manifesting. Ida McKinley, however, had already formed an opinion.

As the event concluded, the First Lady made her way to Senate Appropriations Committee chairman William Allison of Iowa, who had the power to refuse federal funds for the expansion. "Mrs. McKinley has served notice on me," the senator explained to those "uneasy" about this new presidential mansion, "that she will have no hammering in the White House as long as she is there!" With that, Ida McKinley saved the mansion's historic integrity, unwittingly or not.[18]

Christmas guests included Rixey and Cortelyou and several friends and nieces, including Ida Barber, who would be Ida's social aide for not only the New Year's Day reception but the Inauguration eight weeks later. In the diary the Major gave her for Christmas, the First Lady twice noted that she had greeted 5,350 people at the 1901 New Year's Day reception, while "My Dearest was tired out." It was Ida who did bedside duty through his brief bout of influenza.[19]

For her premier of the second presidential term, Ida McKinley was uncharacteristically determined to make a grand public gesture, telling a friend in February that she would appear at the Inaugural Ball in "the handsomest gown money could buy." Days before the event, details hit the paper. She would wear an understated grey suit and hat, tipped with a spray of blue forget-me-not flowers and blue-tipped aigrette feathers to the swearing-in ceremony. When she realized that the lace dress she wanted required crafting by Belgian lace-workers, Ida had New York designers Bock & Thorpey create an American-made Inaugural ball gown of cream satin, threaded with silver, encrusted with pearls and rhinestones, trimmed with rose-point lace, and that featured a ruffled chiffon train. Her hair, fingers, wrists, and neck glistened with diamonds, including a diamond star she wore to the first Inaugural Ball. The rich splendor of the First Lady's gown would embody the new century's new empire, a gown that would be among the most expensive in presidential history, estimated at a 1901 value of $8,000 to $10,000.[20]

As the Senate chamber filled to capacity on March 4, the morning of the Inaugural, it was the five young children of the new vice president who drew attention. As he repeated his oath of office, everyone noted with amusement that his unimpressed eldest son, Theodore Roosevelt Jr., sat drawing pictures. Alice, his eldest daughter from a first marriage, was declared "charming" and sure to be "accorded all the honors of belle-ship" in Washington. Press interest had already focused on the Roosevelt family at the expense of the McKinleys, who would only "insure the continuation of the quiet, conventional social life of the past three years." However, thunderous applause upon Ida's well-timed entrance, which was delayed until all the Roosevelts had settled down, proved she was still a figure of interest.[21]

As her husband repeated his presidential oath and delivered his Inaugural Address, Ida's focus remained on him. For the first time, he acknowledged that "We are waging war against the inhabitants of the Philippines." Before he finished his speech, a cold rain began, and Rixey hustled the First Lady away into a closed carriage.

Despite the rain and an informal White House luncheon she was hosting for one hundred, including Julia Grant and Lucretia Garfield, Ida eagerly joined the Major to review the parade from an open-air grandstand, after which they held a reception for Cabinet members and their families. At that night's Inaugural Ball, she took her place with the president in the box high above the vast Pension Building, its marble columns soaring to the ceiling and wrapped in tri-colored bunting. The orchestra played *America* and *The Fortune Teller* by Victor Herbert, one of Mrs. McKinley's favorite contemporary composers, but when it struck up the grand march from Wagner's *Tannhäuser,* the couple stayed seated. Unlike at the first McKinley Inaugural Ball, Ida knew she would be unable to walk across the entire length of the main floor, even aided. When Alice Roosevelt, the vice president's daughter, was told to stop leaning on Ida's chair, she stared with contempt at "poor frail little Mrs. McKinley," echoing the comment made days before by her mentor and aunt, the vice president's sister, who thought Ida was a "pathetic little creature."[22]

The McKinleys hosted a concert in the greenhouse for the large contingent of their visiting Canton friends the next day, before they had to leave. Despite Ida's exuberant mood, she grew wistful as they began to leave for the train station and travel home to Canton, wishing she could return there with them. The Major had even begun to come around to her view about what he was making them sacrifice by serving a second term. Hometown friend John J. Kennedy recalled how McKinley had tried to arrange "a few days" in Canton before the Inaugural. "Both were like children in their eagerness to get away." The president said they had even jokingly conspired to "stay in Canton—and not come back to Washington" for the Inauguration. Ida piped up that it had been her "dearest wish."[23]

Before they could rest again beneath the shade of Canton's trees, however, Ida and the Major would see more of the United States than any
previous president and First Lady. Eight weeks after Inauguration Day, they
began a seven-week national journey by train, from the Atlantic to the
Pacific, the Gulf Coast to the Great Lakes. Cabinet members and special
guests would join at some junctures, with the indispensable Cortelyou and
Rixey there throughout. It would be a fully functional, traveling presidency
with three stenographers to maintain ongoing presidential correspondence,
a telegraph technician and cable technician to ensure timely contact with
Washington, and two railroad officials to handle any transportation problems. The press corps joining them consisted of a wire-service reporter,
two newspaper-syndicate reporters, three weekly magazine reporters, three
reporters representing Washington papers, and a photographer.

Events were tightly scheduled on the promise of a presidential appearance: a Confederate parade in Memphis, a New Orleans riverboat excursion, an address to the Texas legislature in Austin, the flower festival in
Los Angeles, the launch of the battleship *Ohio* in Oakland, a cruise from
Tacoma to Seattle, a stagecoach drive at Yellowstone National Park, an as-
cent of Pike's Peak in Colorado, a college address in Kansas City, an arsenal
inspection at Rock Island, Illinois, and a gargantuan banquet in Chicago.
Before returning to the White House, Ida and the Major would make one
last stop. Officials had already declared June 13 as "President's Day" to lure
tens of thousands of citizens to glimpse the president and First Lady and
take in the wonders of the modern age at the new Pan-American Exposition in Buffalo, New York.[24]

One factor remained uncertain. Although no one dared to raise the
issue with the president, even some Cabinet members committed to the
journey felt "considerable apprehension" about the First Lady's presence.
Only Dr. Rixey confronted the Major. "I expressed my deep concern
as to Mrs. McKinley being able to stand such a strenuous journey," he
recalled. With Rixey, the Major gently approached Ida, and "efforts were
made to dissuade her from going." She could begin their planned summer
in Canton early, even stay with Pina at Saxton House for the seven weeks.
The alternative was to cancel the trip; with the election won, there would
be no appreciable political repercussion.

In considering the situation, Ida spoke with a friend, who later recalled,
"She insisted that she liked to travel, that the change of scene would benefit her health and that she could not think either of being left behind
or allowing the President to give up his visit to the Pacific Coast." As Dr.

Rixey put it, Mrs. McKinley "prevailed" once again. "I reluctantly gave my consent." He nevertheless took the precaution of prescribing a sedative to ensure that any potential overstimulation she might be exposed to as the journey began would not provoke any seizures. A single press reference disclosed that "she was nerved up to making the start by the application of powerful tonics."[25]

No similar level of precaution was taken for the president. The public was told where McKinley would make whistle-stops or attend events, and hundreds of thousands of citizens anticipated their first glimpse of a president. Only a few would have the random luck to speak with or even see him close up, but they still turned out in the thousands. The Major looked forward to direct contact with the people. Ida did not. Increasingly, neither did Cortelyou.

Cortelyou saw letters that McKinley never did, keeping them in an "Assassination Plots" file. He sent the chief of the Secret Service at the Treasury Department the more ominous ones as well as those that made predictions, like one from a Colorado woman, who detailed her vision of McKinley being marked by "an assassin . . . in workman's garb, overalls and a cap . . . slight, of medium height, dark hair inclined to curl. . . ." Even though he clipped it, Cortelyou could easily dismiss astrologer Julius Erickson's prediction in the *St. Louis Star* that McKinley was in "grave danger . . . while on a long journey." It was similar to the First Lady's fear. According to her cousin, Ida's premonitions of harm to the Major were always nonspecific.

Still, Cortelyou had Secret Service agent George Foster join the West Coast tour since he had casually trailed McKinley in Canton the previous summer and could call agency field offices along the way if he needed support. Washington's police chief alerted colleagues in locations where McKinley would stop so they could control parade crowds and patrol the depots. The biggest security problem, as *Leslie's Weekly* stated, was that "no previous President has so exposed himself to possible harm." He did away with a sentry box that Cleveland had installed on the White House grounds and recklessly insisted that he not be trailed when he was out as he found guards to be a pretension of monarchy, a waste of public funds, and an impediment to the people. "Who will attack me?" he chuckled at a friend's plea that he have a guard. "I haven't an enemy in the world."[26]

For a man who rarely trusted others long enough to drop his public mask, something was amiss about his innocent trust in human goodwill. He had been in battle and conducted a war. He knew that irrational, dark impulses could run through people's minds and provoke acts of violence.

His friend Garfield was president for just six months before he became the second one to be assassinated. McKinley knew that assassination turned both men into martyrs. Throughout his career, McKinley methodically considered everything, even his seemingly spontaneous words, which were perfected to nurture his public image. The Major's tidy mind had even thought about his own ideal demise. Once when his mask slipped, he spoke of it. "If it were not for Ida," William McKinley confessed, "I would prefer to go as Lincoln went."[27]

⊰ 15 ⊱

San Francisco to Buffalo

AT TEN-THIRTY ON THE MORNING of April 29, the engine wheels of the presidential train began turning on schedule. At one end of the platform stood the Major, a picture-perfect president, doffing his silk top hat to a cheering crowd, his red carnation boutonniere visible even to those at the back. Suddenly, from the other end of the platform, there were cheers from a smaller crowd standing near a private coach car window. In the car's formal drawing room, the First Lady had settled into a high seat to look out and be seen, her bonnet feather fluttering as she gave the crowd a modest bob of her head and wave of her kerchief.

For the next month and a half, for the rest of the transcontinental journey, Ida McKinley would be the focus of at least as much scrutiny and attention as her husband—at some points, in fact, even more. Their home on the rails was as sumptuous as those of Europe's crowned heads of state: there was a drawing room refreshed regularly with Ida's roses, its windows widened to afford a clear view of the diverse regional landscapes of the nation; a large bedroom with private marble-tiled bath; a dining room outfitted with embroidered linens, fine silver, china, and stemware. A parlor car provided the finest cigars and wines. A chef prepared exquisite meals accompanied by printed menu cards drawn in fine calligraphy. A telegraph car kept the president in contact with the White House or guests with their families. Many on board for just part of the time, like Mark and Charlotte Hanna, were personal friends. The entire $75,000 cost was absorbed by the railroad syndicates on whose rails the eight-car train traveled.[1]

Despite her invalidism, the First Lady had every intention of witnessing and participating in as many events as she could. Dr. Rixey, however, would insist that even when she felt well, she had to conform to her scheduled rest periods and at times would confine her to the train's suite. In scheduling the itinerary, Cortelyou vetted events where her presence was requested and kept her uncommitted to anything unless the president wanted her to join him. Often McKinley would be joined by young Mary Barber acting as her aunt's substitute and the Cabinet wives coterie. Parade organizers and welcoming committees were instructed to either refrain from firing any cannon salutes or keep them distant when the train pulled into their towns and cities. Typically, as in Vicksburg, Mississippi, Ida was seen only at the arrival parade with the president in an open carriage. By the time they were scheduled to leave, as McKinley waved from the back platform, Ida had already been sequestered, and Rixey told reporters that she "could not respond to calls" asking her to wave goodbye. When Ida McKinley wanted to attend an event, however, she could be insistent.

As Col. Josiah Patterson finalized arrangements with Cortelyou for an April 30 stag dinner for McKinley in Memphis, he passed on a request by city women who wished to honor the First Lady at a banquet. Cortelyou said it would "be too fatiguing" for her. When the train pulled into Memphis, the women's group leader pushed along with other officials to the train and made her way to the First Lady, pleading that she attend the event, assuring her "precautions had been taken to guard . . . from undue fatigue," which was the reason Cortelyou had given when he rejected the invitation on Ida's behalf. Ida knew nothing of the invitation or its rejection, and "promptly said she wanted to go," the *Memphis Commercial-Appeal* reported. "And she went." She didn't remain the center of attention for long.

After Cortelyou told him of the incident, the president made his way over unannounced, tickling the Southern ladies with his courtly mannerisms until they rose in applause. Their welcome, he went on, was "most pleasing of all that had been done for him." The group leader shifted focus back to Ida by toasting him because "he always has time to be good to his wife." Her glory restored, Ida McKinley stood to offer some rare public remarks: "Yes—and his wife always appreciates his goodness." Then it was back to the train for Ida. In reporting the story, the *New York Times* editorialized that while Cortelyou had "acted from the best of motives," he had learned of the "invincible will of woman." He also discovered that keeping the First Lady away from the action didn't necessarily mean that she wouldn't still make the news.

Upon the party's May 1 arrival in New Orleans, the largest city thus far on the itinerary, Ida's exposure to the colorful local culture was limited to a glimpse of the French and Spanish quarters as she was driven to the presidential suite at the St. Charles Hotel.[2] As the president and others went out to enjoy various public ceremonies and activities, Ida was confined to the hotel.

The next day, while the presidential entourage cruised along on a Mississippi River steamboat, a reporter managed to make his way into the unprotected and otherwise empty presidential suite. He casually engaged the First Lady in her first lengthy interview since the 1896 campaign, when the distracted Major had let down his guard, unaware of the subjects under discussion. Left alone briefly by Dr. Rixey, Ida nevertheless felt well and wanted to air her feelings, and Rixey would have been overstepping bounds had he tried to stop her when he returned to her side. While she praised her husband to high heaven and regretted her inability to participate more fully as a public partner, she also made clear that she opposed the second term and felt uneasy about the crowds around him. It wasn't the sort of upbeat chatter the nation expected of a First Lady or the sort of interview the president preferred. Before it generated wide commentary, however, a crisis arose to engulf both of them and forever make clear that, in a moment of truth, the Major put his wife before work.[3]

Texas was the next major stop, with tours of multiple cities. In Houston on May 3, Ida received a welcoming committee in her Rice Hotel suite, apologizing that her health prevented her fuller participation, and let the local Daughters of the Confederacy president onto the train to say hello, just before it left for Austin. In the state capital city, she ventured out to a dinner in the governor's mansion and, led by Rixey, accepted a medal from the Daughters of the Republic of Texas at the state legislature rostrum in the Capitol Building. In San Antonio, she again made appearances, touring the Alamo fortress, reviewing troops, and listening to McKinley address students. When they headed south to arrive late at night in El Paso, their train was serenaded by mariachi string instruments, but no brass after they had been warned of Ida's sensitivity to loud sounds.[4]

The next morning, the Major went to give a long speech in the public plaza, joined by a personal representative of the Mexican president and the governor of the state of Chihuahua, but he steadfastly honored the tradition of incumbent presidents by remaining on American soil. It was announced that Ida McKinley would remain alone on the train, not far from where the Major was speaking. However, she suddenly changed her mind and decided to attend a breakfast reception being jointly hosted by the women of Texas and Mexico. It was held across the border, in Juarez, on May 6, 1901, and marked the first time an incumbent First Lady entered a foreign country.

As an *El Paso Herald* reporter who attended the breakfast recorded, it had been carefully planned with "the pleasure of the invalid . . . [being] the foremost thought of the committee." The delegation of ten El Paso women arrived at the train with a series of carriages that conveyed the First Lady and her niece and Cabinet wives Helen Hay, Ella Smith, and Mary Hitchcock to Juarez, where they followed a path that took them past historical points of interest to the thick-walled hacienda of the wealthy Don Innocente Ochoa.

A delegation of five Mexican women waited in the vestibule to meet the First Lady and her entourage. With no obligation other than relaxation, Ida walked through an archway and broke into a beaming smile at the sight of the central patio. Knowing her interest in flowers, the committee had sought varieties she would never have seen, sent from Vera Cruz, Mexico City, and the northern Mexican prairies. Helped to her seat by Dr. Rixey, she looked up at birds chirping in hanging cages and quipped that it was "the only music worth hearing." Five tables were covered in intricate lace cloths crossed with ribbons in the Mexican tricolors of red, white, and green. The menu cards were fans with pictures of the American and Mexican presidents and an inscription in Spanish. When it was translated for her, Ida's eyes widened in further delight, if perhaps feigned, and she blurted, "Oh, the breakfast is given for me?" A lavish, fifteen-course traditional Mexican breakfast was served, approved by Rixey for her digestion, and she ate heartily, declaring it the "best meal" she had had on the trip thus far. The meal was followed with exotic Mexican fruits sent from Vera Cruz and some *pulque,* the national drink, sent from the Mexican consulate. Ida was given an antique Mexican drawing and a bottle of tequila as gifts.

Juarez was the Pacific tour's high point for the First Lady. Unlike her Memphis event, Ida shone alone. When Helen Hay remarked that the breakfast "is the most novel thing we have had on our trip," however, Ida quipped with perhaps some remorse for not having stayed in Texas to hear the Major's speech. "Yes," she said, "It will partly repay you for missing Mr. McKinley's speech." Before leaving El Paso at noon, Mary dashed off a letter to her mother in Canton, reporting on Aunt Ida's Mexican moment. "She had never felt better," was the news.[5]

As the train went through New Mexico and Arizona territories, Ida felt uncomfortably hot. Rixey, so it was reported, thought it was a natural reaction she had to the arid air, which was thick with fine sand. When news of it broke, the public as usual had various theories; one citizen feared that the First Lady had been "intoxicated" by the *pulque* in Juarez or that it was tainted with "the same kind of poison" intended to kill Mexico's former Empress Carlota. A news story, headlined "Worries of Handshaking," came close to the truth in suggesting exhaustion, saying that her "constantly shaking hands with enthusiastic people en route" had bruised her hands. She did have some pain from a tiny cut on her left thumb. Rixey lanced and cleaned the swollen finger during a stop in the desert while the Major stepped out to catch a glimpse of the unique vegetation.[6]

Directly from Phoenix, where the Major attended an Adams Hotel banquet, on May 8 the party crossed into the Golden State, with a welcome ceremony at Redlands. Recalling how much she had loved California in 1881, Ida insisted on leaving the train to join the Major on a long drive beneath fragrant orange groves, framed by the snow-peaked Santa Ana Mountains, while the crowd showered them with confetti. Westerners were especially enthusiastic about the rare honor of having a visiting president and First Lady in their midst. A proprietor of a Maricopa, Arizona, ostrich farm was so thrilled after seeing them that he honored the couple by naming two of the birds "Mr. and Mrs. McKinley." As they left the train, a reporter detailed the crowd's awe in watching the Major perform one of his devotional gestures to Ida: "He appeared at the door of the car, arm in arm with Mrs. McKinley and a cheer went up from the waiting crowd, but only one, and then in breathless interest the people watched while Mr. McKinley tenderly led the frail, delicate, sweet-faced lady on his arm from the steps of the car to the carriage waiting not ten feet away. For a moment the President was lost in McKinley the man. . . ."

After brief stops in Ontario and Alhambra, the train entered Los Angeles through its Chinatown, as suspended strings of continuously popping firecrackers were set off. A typical routine followed—parade, reception, women's reception, formal dinner, evening fireworks. The president was gleeful over Ida's enthusiasm; that morning, he had even wired Abner, Pina, his sister Helen, Ida's cousin Mary, and Jennie Hobart, assuring them that she was "much better." While dining with publisher Harrison Gray Otis, the First Lady suddenly had dysentery, but focused excitedly on the astonishing floral displays that were promised the next morning at the city's annual *La Fiesta de la flora*. The McKinleys led the festival parade in a carriage festooned with over 10,000 white carnations. Ida's finger remained swollen, and she attributed her intense perspiration to the sunlight. After the parade, when she met an old Canton friend, Homer Laughlin, who was now an Angeleno, she was filled with enthusiasm, her travel to the Pacific coast prompting plans for future trips.

Only two months into the second term, the couple was already making secret plans for a post-presidency world tour, similar to one the Grants took. They began to consult maps and travel guides, with Ida good-naturedly teasing McKinley about his conventional worldview, which contrasted with the perspective she had from her time abroad. "Mrs. McKinley joked with her husband," Laughlin recalled, "because he had never been abroad, and told him of the experiences she had had across the water. They appeared so very happy and had made so many plans for their future. . . ."[7]

On May 10, they headed north along the Pacific coastline for an overnight stay in Monterey County, and the Major addressed crowds in Ventura, Santa Barbara, and San Luis Obispo. Ida neither appeared outside on the rear platform nor took in the view of the sea cliffs and rocky beaches from inside the train. Her infected finger had swollen larger, and her dysentery became acute, causing an overall weakness. The train was halted at Surf, a small rail service station outside Santa Cruz so that Rixey could again lance her wound. No anesthetic was used, and a Cabinet wife said that Ida withstood the pain "like a heroine." Once settled in the Hotel Del Monte, however, Rixey realized that her temperature had spiked dangerously, and the infection had aggressively spread throughout her system. He and McKinley had vigilantly helped prevent her seizures and carefully accommodated her neurological leg problem. However, neither had given much thought to her compromised immune system.

The president remained at her bedside; he had seen her through many sudden and dramatic illnesses and reminded her that she always recovered. Part of her anxiety had to do with how she was affecting the trip, fearing that the public would resent cancellation of their anticipated visits. "Mrs. McKinley specially requested that the plans of the party should not be disarranged by her departure," one paper reported. McKinley, knowing that she felt calmer in his presence, decided to send Cabinet members as surrogates to his scheduled appearances nearby. When she slept for three hours, he dashed off to fulfill just one commitment, in Monterey.

Before the president left for Monterey, however, Dr. Rixey "admonished" him that despite Ida's history of recoveries, the starts and stops from the train, the carriage, and hotels were seriously weakening her, and she must have "absolute and complete rest." At this, McKinley became "genuinely alarmed." Appearing "haggard and drawn" in Monterey, he spoke "in a disconnected fashion as if his mind was not upon either his words or the scene before him."

The sudden onset of her severe dysentery, the *New York World* reported, had a "serious effect on Mrs. McKinley's nerves." As Rixey tried in vain to stabilize her digestive tract, she remained "extremely nervous all night," and the onset of panic kept her awake. Lack of sleep further weakened her. Sedatives could not be used due to the risk of intestinal irritation.

Rixey decided to make the isolated Hotel Del Monte a temporary hospital ward and wanted expert medical consultation from specialists in nearby San Francisco, but early Sunday morning, a guest on the presidential train, Henry T. Scott, introduced himself. As the president of the ironworks firm that built the battleship *Ohio,* which McKinley was scheduled to dedicate, Scott urged that they make the short trip to San Francisco and use his commodious mansion on the corner of Clay and Laguna streets as headquarters. He would call his doctor to arrange for trained nurses, professional medical testing, and "the best physicians." Despite his dislike of traveling on the Sabbath, the Major agreed and consulted Ida. She "reluctantly agreed" as long as he didn't cancel his public appearances scheduled during their planned week in San Francisco.

The train sped past other intended stops where the public had hoped to welcome the First Lady. With her well-known love of roses in mind, San Jose citizens had even created a mammoth bouquet from thousands of the freshly cut flowers, using a telephone pole as its stem. When the train pulled into San Francisco on Sunday night, crowds cheered McKinley until he signaled them for quiet. There was silence as Ida was briefly glimpsed, carried by Rixey and two porters, from train to platform to closed carriage. According to accounts, she was "wrapped in furs," and had "an unusual pallor, heavy dark circles under her eyes and it seemed to be an effort for her to hold up her head." She was rushed to Scott's Lafayette Park house on the corner of Clay and Laguna.[8]

In light of the cancelled schedule, there was no way to keep the story from the public. From Scott's house, Cortelyou issued a brief statement, going on record only with the facts that she was suffering from indigestion and a finger infection. It proved to be so vague that reporters felt compelled to speculate on other details, some of their stories attributing her problems to everything from Ida grasping a bar too tightly when the train rounded a sharp curve in Texas to fainting on a New Orleans riverboat, which she was never on to begin with. On Monday, Rixey attempted to derail any alarm with a breezy and false report that "Her condition is not serious. She will stay here at least a week and have perfect rest. I think by that time she will be able to continue the journey. She has been gaining strength all afternoon." Unnamed sources in the presidential party, however, leaked the truth that "she is very ill." Cortelyou responded with a more obfuscated statement than Rixey's: "There is no secret about it. Mrs. McKinley is ill, but she is no worse than when she first started on the trip. You must know that she bruised her right hand in some way and that caused her great pain. How she injured it we do not know but we surmise she did it by constantly shaking hands. She wore a number of rings, and the pressure evidently bruised her hand. The doctor has lanced the hand, and that is a painful operation to even a strong person. She will, I know, be much better soon."[9]

On Monday, a feverish Ida was unable to eat solid foods, subsisting on beef broth and brandy. After examining her, the consulting physician, Joseph Hirshfelder, led McKinley from the sickroom, and was "brutally frank" in expressing his concern that Ida was not responding to any treatments. She was too weak to speak, but her state of constant deep sleep was at least an improvement over her restlessness. Hired nurses Evelyn Hunt and Grace McKenzie attended her. Ida was first placed in a large bed and then moved to a narrow, single-size one, which allowed them to clean her more easily. Through Tuesday, the dysentery and fever remained; her general condition did not improve.

It was "at the request of the President," a reporter learned, that there should be "the most rigid reticence" in the level of detail released to the public to avoid any reference to her epilepsy. When it was published that her true condition over the weekend had been "concealed" from the public, Cortelyou retorted that they had simply presumed she would have recovered as quickly as she usually did. In Wednesday's first morning bulletin, he continued to be cryptic: "She has gained in several respects and lost in others."

Feeling that "nothing that science can do should be left undone," McKinley asked that a digestive disease specialist be found on Wednesday morning to fight the dysentery. Henry Gibbons, dean of Cooper Medical College, was located and rushed to the house. He examined Ida and met with Rixey and Hirschfelder by noon. When the third physician arrived, McKinley felt oddly overconfident again and sent word to a committee that he would attend an afternoon ceremony to unveil a statue, as previously scheduled. When they heard this, all three doctors urged him not to leave the house. They couldn't forecast her potential recovery, even for the next hour. Outside, the buggy to take him to the ceremony was already waiting.

It proved to be McKinley's most dramatic moment of choice between his wife and his work. A friend recalled that McKinley, when faced with the fact that Ida might die while he was out unveiling a statue, was "completely unnerved." Her death, the friend continued, "would have been a crushing blow from which he could scarcely have rallied." He stayed. As dramatized in the poem "In Sickness and in Health," his decision "endeared him more to the people than almost any other act of his life."

San Francisco residents became consumed with following the bulletin updates on the First Lady, waiting outside newsrooms for postings or spreading the news by word of mouth. Lafayette Park, which was across from the house, became a gathering place for public vigils. A delegation of children from Chinatown came to leave flowers for her. Both Clay and Laguna streets were closed entirely to pedestrian and carriage traffic. Reporters who had been gathering outside the ground-level entrance were now pushed back across the street into the park.[10]

The First Lady's fever rose to 104 degrees on Wednesday. She was often unconscious, and heart stimulants were used to keep her breathing. In her waking moments, she whispered for the Major if he wasn't there, and he finally decided to cancel all his planned local appearances. Rixey grew concerned about the president's health as he was no longer sleeping and barely eating. He took one thirty-minute drive and, before sunset, walked the perimeter of Lafayette Park.[11]

Otherwise, he sat for hours holding Ida's hand and stroking her forehead. At night, he took a brief break to focus on some work. Despite his guilt over the wasted efforts made by hundreds of planning committees and the disappointment of thousands of citizens, he wrote a statement for public release: "Mrs. McKinley's serious illness compels the President to abandon his proposed visit to other states which he had looked forward [to] with much pleasure."[12]

As fog hung low over the city into the wee hours, the silhouettes of the nurses could be seen moving in the one upstairs room at the Scott house where the lights never went off. At five o'clock in the morning, Ida had "a sinking spell," a severe drop in her pulse, and lapsed into longer unconsciousness, unresponsive to the Major's voice. *New York World* reporter Maurice Lowe learned that her "life hangs on a thread and only a miracle can save her." The infection had taken full hold of Ida McKinley's frail body and left her "hovering between life and death."

Under the headline "At Death's Door," the Thursday, May 16, 1901, edition of the *Washington Star* reported that "Mrs. McKinley is slowly dying unless all human knowledge is at fault. There is not one chance in a hundred that she will recover and be taken back to Washington alive." That morning, Mary Barber and the Major's niece Ida Morse, a local resident, were led in to see their aunt, but she was unresponsive to their voices. The Major began his second day with no sleep.

That the First Lady of the United States was on the brink of death, seemingly with no warning, left reporters feeling that Cortelyou and Rixey had lied or misled them and the American people; neither appeared outside the house to answer questions. Reporters, kept at bay in Lafayette Park, began to rely on more cooperative Cabinet members for news. The *New York Times* criticized the "vague character" of the bulletins, and one paper charged that "the public has been largely in the dark as to the character of the trouble." Although her condition had nothing to do with epilepsy, new articles that included histories of her health began to hint at her "nervous prostration" and "depression" as aspects of her mental state. Thursday's *New York Times* nearly revealed her secret disability, even referring to the "aura" she experienced before seizures:

> It has been known here [Washington] by almost everybody, although the subject has not been discussed in the newspapers for reasons of consideration for the President, and his household, that Mrs. McKinley was an invalid of the most delicate sort, subject at all times to paroxysms that were distressing and the approach of which always has made necessary the watchful attendance of a kind and experienced person to give the invalid prompt and intelligent assistance. Those who have had intimate knowledge of the peculiarities of Mrs. McKinley's affliction have entertained grave doubts of her ability to make the trip. . . . [13]

Whether to appease reporters or discourage their speculation about other health problems contributing to Ida's current condition, on Thursday, May 16, McKinley did an about-face and ordered that the press be given highly specific detail about Ida's current state and the treatments being tried. At ten that morning, the first Associated Press report informed the public that the president was "without hope that she will ever recover." Reports soon spread by word of mouth from those keeping vigil in Lafayette Park that the First Lady of the United States had died, prompting the lowering of flags to half-mast for mourning.

The reports were false, but there were increasing questions about Rixey's treatments. A *Washington Star* reporter on the scene suggested that Rixey's refusal, from the very start, to use powerful antidiuretics had only led to the weakened immunity he had tried to avoid. Rixey later admitted that, sometime after midnight early Thursday morning, he reached the point when he "considered our patient hopeless" and tried the antidiuretics. As the hours went by, according to one report, "The digestive trouble, which had caused great uneasiness, had in a measure succumbed to treatment. . . ." The nourishing fluids she was continuously fed were now given a chance to be beneficial, and her continuing deep sleep prevented any undue waste of body strength. Unspecified "artificial stimulants" kept her heart from nearly failing, and a local paper learned that she was "under the influence of medicines intended to give freedom from pain."

Her high fever and alarmingly low pulse, however, remained problematic. At nine on Thursday morning, Dr. Clinton Cushing was called in for a consultation. Whether or not it was on his advice, a simple saline solution was injected and, as a result, according to Friday's *Washington Star*, "Her pulse shows quick improvement and she continued to improve all day. . . ."[14]

The crisis caused McKinley to open emotionally in a way he rarely did, and he asked his "official family" to join him in a front parlor at ten in the morning. Secretary of State John Hay and his wife Helen, Interior Secretary Ethan Hitchcock and his wife Mary, Agriculture Secretary Wilson and his daughter Flora, and Postmaster Charles Smith and his wife Ella were there as the president unloaded his "anxiety and heartache," thankful for "the comfort of their presence," and admitted that he needed "as many as possible of his nearest friends close at call." While he returned to Ida's side for two hours, they waited. He came back to them, and they lunched together, after which he spent another hour with Ida. She had lain still for twelve hours. Suddenly, she opened her eyes and quipped, "I am tired of the food the doctors have been giving me!" She insisted on having "a piece of chicken and a cup of coffee." He went down to report the news to the Cabinet.[15]

Both inside and outside the Scott house, the morose atmosphere finally stirred. While Ida Morse visited, her aunt was able to "recognize and feebly greet her." At three, the president asked three Cabinet members to join him for fifteen minutes of fresh air and a walk around Lafayette Park. As he passed the group of reporters, he smiled and told them, "Mrs. McKinley is holding her own. We believe she is a shade better than she was at noon."[16]

On Friday morning, Ida McKinley remained weak, but her dysentery was gone and her pulse strong. She held steady through the day and night. The best news yet was evidenced on the bright and clear Saturday morning. The president and Mary Barber emerged from the Scott house and entered a carriage, which sped them to a docked tugboat that crossed the bay for the launch of the *Ohio* battleship in Oakland.[17]

In the president's absence, Rixey remained with Ida, cautiously optimistic about her slow recovery. Cortelyou issued a statement that the president would remain in San Francisco for at least another week and would fulfill his previously postponed appearances in the city. A scheduled San Francisco Botanical Garden presentation to the First Lady of a new hybrid carnation named for her, the largest of its type, went ahead without her. For the first time in a week, Cortelyou and the clerical staff had a chance to read and answer the letters and telegrams that had poured in for the McKinleys from around the world. Cortelyou's smile surely vanished when he read an un-signed note, which he turned over to the Secret Service. "My Dear Sir," it said simply, "I will murder you this week."[18]

Thankful for Ida's return from the brink of death, President McKinley no longer took his wife's recovery as a foregone conclusion. When Rixey told him on Friday, May 24, that it was "reasonably safe" for her to make the transcontinental train trip, the Major snapped in irritation, "That will not do, you must decide that it *is* safe." After consulting the other doctors on the case, all agreed it was safe. The presidential party left San Francisco the next day on the most direct route possible, and the train would run "slow or fast or be sidetracked as the patient's condition demanded," Rixey recalled. Crossing the Sierra Mountains into Nevada and continuing on through Utah, they stopped once to refill water tanks while McKinley got off only to shake hands with members of the local Digger tribe. Ida rejected the idea of stopping in Canton so she could convalesce there under Rixey's care because she did not want to be separated from the president.[19]

After five days, the train arrived in Washington on May 30. That same day, Ida's former physician, George Sternberg, conferred with Rixey and two other doctors, then took blood samples from the First Lady, which were sent to a pathology laboratory for various tests. All through his meet-ings that afternoon, the president kept returning down the hall to the fam-ily quarters to check on the First Lady. Observers thought that "the effects of the trying ordeal through which he has passed have left perceptible marks on the President."[20]

Cortelyou, at McKinley's direction, returned to limiting news about her condition, which only provoked wild speculation. For example, while Rev. Loring Batten was at the pulpit delivering his Sunday sermon at New York's St. Mark's church, someone whispered to him that the First Lady had just died, and he announced it to the congregation, prompting sobs and prayers. Even more unwelcome than such a morbid inaccuracy, however, was another covert reference to the First Lady's epilepsy in a June 6 *Pittsburgh Press* new story, which made it clear that "other attacks are liable to happen at any time."

However disturbing this breach would have been if McKinley had learned of it, news of her lab results three days later, released to the press, would have mitigated it. Mrs. McKinley was "not suffering from blood poisoning, as was feared. It showed, however, that her blood is very much impoverished and is greatly in need of something to strengthen it before there can be any material improvement in her condition." Sternberg ordered a routine of oxygen intake and a diet designed to provide specific minerals and vitamins that her system lacked.

In gratitude for Sternberg's expert analysis and treatment plan for the First Lady, the president approved the doctor's recommendation for an inspection study of the health and living conditions of U.S. occupational forces in the Philippines, and promoted him as the War Department's medical division representative.[21]

Ida's return to the White House coincided with her birthday, and she was inundated with both congratulatory and get-well telegrams and letters, ranging from a message from the Japanese emperor that he was "pleased to know the progress of her recovery" to one from Vice President Roosevelt, who thought "of you both (and who does not?) all the time." McKinley, however, worried about her potential relapse. Even though his office was down the hall from their room, he decided to move Ida to the small corner "red bedroom" facing the south lawn, where she would either take restful sleep or sit in her wheelchair within his sight. One Saturday afternoon, Ida felt well enough to invite friends to join them and listen to the Marine Band concert from the window. She also resumed her interest in politics, recalled her nurse, and the president appeared, "armed with a load of daily papers, most of them marked copies," and then "read through column after column . . . humoring her wish, that he read all the articles about himself."[22]

While working in the room with Ida, a new frustration was mounting for the president. Just a year earlier, she had persistently registered her opposition to him seeking a second term. His pursuit of that ambition had nearly cost Ida her life and had exhausted him. Now there was rising talk of enlisting his promise to run for an unprecedented third term. On June 10, the Major wrote out a statement, called in Cortelyou, and silently handed it to him; it was "an emphatic statement that under no circumstances would he accept a nomination for a third term." He also announced that his first trip away from the White House would be to take Ida to Canton, and only when she was well. All other trips were cancelled or postponed. Once they were settled in for the summer, the *Washington Post* learned that "the President may visit the Pan-American Exposition. . . ." Canton was relatively close to Buffalo.

After a month of regaining her strength in the White House, the McKinleys left for Canton. Their arrival on July 5, 1901, marked the start of a time when they could truly relax in the familiar house as their home. Ida McKinley would now enjoy the life she had longed for, at least for two months. After having breakfast with Ida, Rixey, and Cortelyou, the Major, in his white Panama hat, strolled undisturbed down Market Street. She began making daily open-air carriage drives with the Major and shorter ones in a new surrey. As she gained weight and strength, Rixey resumed her walking exercises, and she never let up. Marsh, Pina, and those nieces and nephews still living at Saxton House, as well as an increasing number of old friends, often came for dinner. Eva Hunt, the nurse who had served Ida in San Francisco, had been retained and recalled how avidly the couple played cribbage and listened to popular music on their new player piano. As always, the most important ritual of Ida's day was her afternoon visit to West Lawn Cemetery to lay flowers on the graves of Katie and Little Ida.[23]

The Major enjoyed taking Ida to Meyer's Lake, where three decades earlier, he had first laid eyes on her. Park employee William Arntz recalled how they "sat on the grass on the hillside in the picnic area and watched the crowd." More disturbing was the arrogant man whom Arntz recalled walking where the McKinleys usually sat, with "two guns strapped on" his person. Arntz reminded him that firearms were not permitted in the park. "I don't pay attention to things like that," he told the groundskeeper. Arntz called the police, but the man ran and vanished. A month later, Arntz was certain it was the same man who "got to Buffalo."[24]

Ida had become wary of strangers. Occasionally tourists appeared on the porch, asking to meet the president, but when they pulled out their small Kodak cameras, the First Lady turned away or blocked her face with a parasol or flowers. "She seemed superstitious in a measure, and would never allow, if she knew it, any one to take a snap shot of her," Eva Hunt recalled.

For the first time in years, Ida and the Major attended a formal event together in a private home, a musicale hosted by a neighbor. By August, they began hosting overnight guests, Myron and Carolyn Herrick being Ida's favorite. Herrick continued to manage the Major's finances, ensuring their secure retirement. Ida continued to share with Pina the properties inherited from their father and, despite the national publicity, did not hesitate to sue a Nevada ore mining company for illegally plundering the minerals from the adjoining Saxton land. Two years earlier, the Saxton sisters prevented the owner of property in nearby Scioto from oil drilling, reminding him that while their father had sold him the land, he had wisely retained the under-surface rights. The man could sink test an oil well, but if any oil was found, the sisters would get the royalties.[25]

The unanticipated news from Canton that summer was how miraculously Ida McKinley had recovered both her fuller, healthy figure and ability to walk on her own. Whatever neurological damage bromism had caused, she was the most independently mobile, Rixey said, "since I knew her." Her condition promised a full resumption of her public activities as First Lady. "It is hoped that society will see more of Mrs. McKinley than usual in the White House festivities this winter," wrote reporter Francis Gessner. "Her health improved wonderfully during the stay in Canton, and she gained ten pounds, which, in view of her long invalidism, was little short of marvelous."[26]

This vision of Mrs. McKinley stirred memories of old-timers in Canton, who remembered her working in the bank and walking all over town. When the cemetery supervisor saw Ida visiting the graves of Katie and Little Ida, he couldn't help expressing his surprise at her appearance. The First Lady's eyes twinkled. "Yes," she said, "I begin to feel like Ida Saxton once again."[27]

During another drive through the cemetery with their friend William Hawk, she remarked how beautiful it seemed, prompting the Major to say that he planned to improve his family plot there, "but I dislike to discuss the subject with Mrs. McKinley." Hawk gave her a nod, then remarked, "Mr. President, your wife is too sensible not to consider the matter, which ought to be decided while both of you can select a monument." Ida concurred and said, "I do not know why the Major should feel so about it. He knows I always agree with him upon every subject." Other old friends felt free to touch on the sensitive topic, though Andrew Munson wrote the Major apprehensively: "You are the idol of the great mass of the people and immensely popular; but do not think because of this that there are not devils in human shape who would take your life. . . . throw around your person every safeguard known. . . . You owe all this to yourself, to your dear wife and to the nation. . . ."[28]

While appreciating such concerns, McKinley was now aggravated by them. In reviewing his schedule for the fair, Cortelyou pointed out events where he would be exposed to crowds and implored him to forgo handshaking. "Why should I?" McKinley argued, "No one would wish to hurt me." When another friend also expressed worry, the president finally just shrugged and said, "If anything happens to me, I want you to know that I am prepared to meet my God."[29]

"You couldn't pay me to go to Buffalo and mix in that crowd," Charlie Bawsel wrote his wife about the hundreds of thousands of people packing the city. "No expositions for me." He was not the only one wary of the electric utopia. That summer, Ida had resumed jotting notes in the diary the Major gave her at the beginning of the year. Three days before leaving for Buffalo, she wrote simply, "I wish we were not going away from home." Her nurse found it, "strange to say," just how strongly Ida objected to going, yet "gave no reason for not wishing to go."

What Rixey most recalled from that summer was something the president had said before they left Canton: "Mrs. McKinley's health was the best it had been for twenty-seven years."[30]

☆ 16 ☆

Exposition

THE PRESIDENTIAL TRAIN, with a view of Lake Erie through the windows, pulled slowly into Buffalo's Terrace Station at five o'clock on September 4. The party began preparing to get off the train near the entrance to the Pan-American Exposition. Without warning, a deafening twenty-one-cannon blast began and shook the train so violently that windows in the forward car shattered and Ida fainted from the shock. Cortelyou's specific request that the presidential salute be held at a distance had been ignored.

Ida was led through the depot by her husband and doctor, but at the sight of them, crowds roared, the train's whistle shrieked, a band struck up, and bells tolled. The sensory overload left Ida disoriented and uncertain. McKinley wrapped a shawl around her, boosted her into the carriage, and tucked a blanket over her legs. Their open carriage made a quick tour of the fairgrounds. Back at the main station, thousands had also been startled by the cannons, and a foreign-looking man standing near a cannon was harassed with screaming taunts of "anarchist."

The next morning, the McKinleys paraded along the Triumphal Causeway into the Exposition grounds with its president, local businessman John Milburn, whose commodious home the presidential party would use for their few days scheduled at the fair. The change in the First Lady was noticeable to all. As the only moving picture film clip of her showed, Ida was led onto the stand by the Major, and she walked steadily, acknowledging a familiar face with a quick lift of her head and a laugh. Ida McKinley took her seat and listened, with rapt attention, to what many would consider the president's most prescient speech.[1]

Calling the fair a "timekeeper[s] of progress," he welcomed representatives of Western hemisphere nations or those with colonies in it to the "triumphs of art, science, education, and manufacture, which the old has bequeathed to the new century." In his speech he referred to modern communications technology and a vision of it forging an inevitable global community:

> [H]ow near one to the other is every part of the world. Modern inventions have brought into close relation widely separated peoples and made them better acquainted. Geographic and political divisions will continue to exist, but distances have been effaced. . . . We travel great distances in a shorter space of time, and with more ease than was ever dreamed of by the fathers. Isolation is no longer possible or desirable. . . . The telegraph keeps us advised of what is occurring everywhere and the press foreshadows with more or less accuracy the plans and purposes of the nations. . . . No nation can longer be indifferent to any other. . . . May all who are represented here be moved to higher and nobler effort for their own and the world's good . . . to all the peoples and powers of earth.

After his speech, McKinley went to ceremonies in the stadium, a luncheon, and had coffee in the Puerto Rican pavilion. A Women's Committee had hoped that the First Lady would attend the one o'clock reception and luncheon being held in her honor. Mary Barber and Louise Wood were already there, but Ida did not appear at the reception. After a half-hour wait, a lobster Newburg lunch was finally served. Rumor spread that Ida had come early to see the women's exhibits and was lunching in an upper room. It proved to be a fib told to placate the women. Rixey had taken Ida to rest at Milburn House to ensure her strength.

After an early dinner with the Major, Ida was eager to return for the fair's great spectacle, a massive electricity display as the evening sky darkened. As the bulbs' wattage increased, what first looked like pink dots formed the outline of all the fair's buildings, rectangular and domed. After the electric display, the presidential party stepped into a Venetian gondola, which was conveyed through man-made canals to give them a glimpse of the buildings at close range as they passed. After watching a water ballet, they gasped at the extraordinarily detailed firework displays, which were of various motifs, including Spanish-American War battleships and Niagara Falls. The highlight for the First Lady was undoubtedly a bursting rainbow of colors in the heavens, which formed the ephemeral image she knew best. Her Major's profile momentarily dominated the entire night sky.

Just after seven in the morning of September 6, President McKinley, dressed in formal black coat and tall silk hat, eluded the few Secret Service men who surrounded Milburn House and took a solitary walk down Delaware Avenue. After breakfast, he and Ida began a cumbersome excursion to nearby Niagara Falls. They drove to the Exposition grounds, boarded a special train car, then transferred to trolley cars, which brought them into the town where the falls were located, at which point they climbed out of the trolley and into an open carriage. They eventually transferred to a specially built railroad car, which descended the steep decline into the gorge, in order to view Niagara Falls from below. During the steep descent, the Major kept glancing at Ida. "When assured that instead of being frightened she was greatly enjoying it, his eyes lighted with satisfaction, and then for the first time did he permit himself to gaze uninterruptedly at the beauties of nature all about him," Walter Wellman reported. Back at the Exposition, with barely an hour to spare before a scheduled public reception in the Temple of Music, Rixey took Ida to Milburn House to rest again. "Good afternoon, Mrs. McKinley," the Major called out, "I hope you will enjoy your ride; good-bye." Rixey would return, leaving Mary to watch her sleeping aunt.[2]

McKinley arrived at the Temple of Music Building on time, at four. He was eager to shake hands with the general public, who were often awed into silence when they found themselves before a president. Cortelyou had tried to talk McKinley out of the event by saying that he would disappoint more people than he could satisfy, since there was time for him to meet only a small number of the crowds. "At least they'll know I tried," he retorted, ending further discussion. The music of Bach was played on the massive pipe organ.

McKinley stood in a corner of two converging aisles around the hall's empty seating. In his immaculate snow-white vest, he was flanked by potted fern plants, with the American flag draped behind him. He nodded for the doors to be opened. Hundreds of people rushed in, fell into line, and began quickly passing by, nodding, shaking hands, or offering a few words to McKinley. Cortelyou kept glancing nervously at his pocket watch and arbitrarily decided to cut off the flow of humanity, ordering the doors to be shut. Only those now in the hall would see the president: laborers in overalls, bankers in suits, housewives, school tots, elderly men with canes, fancy ladies in big hats, from Anglo, German, Spanish, Irish, Italian, Polish, African, and other ancestries. Facing McKinley, not the crowd, were Secret Service agents Foster, Al Gallagher, and Sam Ireland. Scattered out in the fair were some seventy-five local policemen, a special force of Exposition guards, private detectives, and Coast Guard artillerymen.[3]

Two men and a little girl were ahead of six-foot-six "Big Ben" James Benjamin Parker, so he looked over them with his eye on the president. Parker, an African American from Atlanta, had come to work as one of the fair's Plaza Restaurant waiters but was either on break or had been let go due to slow business—reports conflict. Parker recalled the little girl with blonde curls greeting the smiling Major. Next an Italian immigrant shook McKinley's hand and moved on. It left President McKinley looking directly into the eyes of a young Polish American steel-mill worker with dark, curly hair and a bandaged right hand. He put out his left hand to McKinley, who reached for it.

Two shots rang out. McKinley rolled back on his feet in a second of dead silence as smoke rose from the man's bandaged hand. In a flash, everyone realized that the president had been shot. Parker jumped on the man with the bandaged hand, pinning him down before he could shoot a third and likely fatal shot. Police guards rushed in to seize one Leon Czolgosz.[4]

His life potentially over in a matter of seconds, McKinley blurted his first instinctive reaction to his trusted aide: "Cortelyou, be careful. Tell Mrs. McKinley gently."[5]

One of the fair's directors, Gen. W. I. Buchanan, arrived breathlessly at Milburn House to fetch Rixey. Rixey quickly slipped out, leaving the First Lady's nieces Mary and Ida to watch over her when she awoke. Taking McKinley's words to Cortelyou literally, Buchanan relayed the news to Mary. She decided that if Rixey hadn't returned within a reasonable time, Buchanan should somehow tell her aunt the news. The phone began ringing. Mary had it taken off the hook to avoid any chance of it awakening Ida or raising any suspicions.

Back in the Temple of Music, McKinley was led to a chair, his white vest now stained red. He saw the assassin being roughed up and cried out, "Don't let them hurt him!" Despite the pandemonium of terrified people pushing their way out of the building, an Exposition hospital ambulance managed to pull up and clear a path. When he was carried out by stretcher, McKinley again mentioned his primary concern: "Please see that no exaggerated report reaches Mrs. McKinley." In the dimly lit first-aid station, he tried to get out of his own clothes, but interns did the job. One of the two bullets dropped, having hit his coat button. Calls went out to leading physicians. Among the first to arrive was Matthew D. Mann, a University of Buffalo Medical Department professor of obstetrics and gynecology, who took charge of the surgery.

As ether took effect, McKinley silently repeated the Lord's Prayer. Rixey had arrived and found himself holding up a mirror to reflect the last glints of sunlight to provide better light as the surgery to remove the one bullet began. Nobody thought about retrieving the new X-ray machine on display at the fair to locate the bullet that had pierced his stomach and lodged in his back. The bullet remained in him, the wound was sutured, and some disinfectant was applied.

Ida McKinley awoke refreshed at five-thirty, and began knitting slippers. With no clock in the room she was unaware of the time—or of the policemen who now surrounded Milburn House and roped off access to it. Only when the sky began dimming did she call for Mary. "I wonder why he does not come?" Mary feigned ignorance. Ida asked her nurse, "Eva, is it not time for the Major to return? I had better dress for dinner."

Her doctor approached Ida's room and when Rixey entered, Ida grew alarmed. "Where is Mr. McKinley?" she asked. "I have some bad news for you, Mrs. McKinley," he simply said without explanation. Fearing the shock might induce fainting or hysterics, he brought what were only described as "drugs" to handle both. She fainted briefly, and "stimulants had to be administered." She revived, however, with a latent power that the *New York Times* called "wonderful fortitude." Rixey told her more details. "The President has met with an accident—he has been hurt," he continued. "Tell me all," Ida snapped, "keep nothing from me! I will be brave—yes, I will be brave for his sake!"[6]

The press, making the most of its familiar caricature of Ida the invalid, stretched the drama, with some papers claiming that Rixey told her the Major was shot, but it was a minor wound, while others claimed that he said McKinley had "fallen and had suffered some injury." Even Charlie Bawsel believed that Ida "does not know of the attempt on his life—thinks it is a mere accident." For once, Ida McKinley was able to speak to history for herself. The scribble in her September 6 diary entry made clear that she knew everything except the correct spelling of the word "anarchist," which was being used to describe Czolgosz: "Went to visit Niagra [sic] Falls this morning. My Dearest was received in a public hall on our return, when he was shot by a . . ."[7]

Confronted with the fact that someone had harmed the person she counted on to protect her, however, seemed to transform Ida McKinley into an assertive, emboldened person, reviving qualities she hadn't shown since her European trip thirty years before. At first she declared she "must go to him." Rixey told her that wasn't necessary. Without asking if he was alive or dead, she said if the Major could be brought to her immediately, she "wanted it done." Her assertiveness must have surprised Rixey, but he "assured her that the President could be brought with safety." McKinley was already being transported there, but in allowing her to believe this would be done on her orders, he seemed to encourage her empowerment. He warned her that the president must not be upset by excessive emotionalism. "His life may depend on your courage," he told her, "and you must be brave."[8]

As word of the president's surviving an assassination attempt began to spread, most people across the country expressed concern over how the First Lady was "bearing the strain." When Mark Hanna heard the news in Cleveland, he bolted to his carriage and took the next train to Buffalo without so much as a change of clothes. Emerging from Milburn House, he smiled to reporters and said that "Mrs. McKinley has disappointed me—happily disappointed me. She has borne up wonderfully and looks at her husband's condition philosophically, instead of becoming hysterical." He too had warned McKinley about a need for personal security. Vice President Roosevelt was contacted at his remote vacation spot on the Finger Lakes. All but two Cabinet members were there by the next day.[9]

A large, back corner room of Milburn House was cleared for the patient's hospital bed, with an adjoining room for medical personnel on one side and Ida's room on the other. When he was first brought in, a bit unconscious, Ida was allowed to see the Major for just a few minutes before Rixey administered a sedative to ensure that she would have a full night's sleep. Ida's nurse Eva said that "from the first," William McKinley sensed that his wife "would soon be alone." Knowing that his recovery required him to avoid any upset, the Major assumed a degree of impassiveness, even toward Ida, routinely remarking to the nurse about her, "Poor little woman, what will she do?"

The next day, his temperature rose. Fearing that blood poisoning and peritonitis had taken hold, the doctors considered surgery to remove the bullet, but McKinley cared only about seeing Ida. From the moment she arose, with "good control of her nerves," Ida repeatedly said she wanted to see him as soon as possible. Rixey permitted them fifteen minutes together, but warned them to avoid much talking. As Ida sat by his bed, grasping his hand, the Major told her, "We must bear up. It will be best for both of us." Ida nodded in silent assent. There was no crying. Afterwards, Rixey described the potential medical problems that might arise and was left in "wonder" at how she was "sustaining herself so well as she is." As one reporter put it, "grief seemed to lend her strength." As the world learned that the First Lady had predicted some such incident would occur, there was appreciation for her wisdom. "She never spoke of it," her cousin told reporters. "I have never seen any act of hers that would indicate a feeling of timidity for her husband."

Along with McKinley's sisters and nieces, Roosevelt arrived in Buffalo the day after the shooting. He "objected strenuously" to any protection for himself, declaring that he had no "use for them." Doctors refused to let even him see the president, and he left after a half hour and headed for the home of Ansley Wilcox, where he would stay. The press was stationed in a tent across the street while Cortelyou and some clerical staff worked in the house next to Milburn's. After consulting a Cabinet member, Cortelyou and Rixey decided to keep medical bulletins vague to prevent overreaction in the press. After being given nothing but water, McKinley's vital signs began to stabilize by the time Rixey and Dr. Herman Mynter began the night shift. Besides Mann, who had performed the surgery, the other consulting physicians were Charles McBurney, Roswell Park, and Eugene Wasdin.[10]

On Sunday morning, after McBurney told Ida her husband would survive, the doctor announced to reporters that he couldn't "find a single unfavorable symptom." Nothing quite convinced the skeptical press corps of this, however, than the sight of the First Lady, confident about leaving the house, walking slowly but steadily out of Milburn House and into a carriage for an hour's drive with her cousin. Rixey stepped outside but felt Ida was strong enough to go without him. Her small act of independence vied for the good news that day. As one shocked reporter wrote, "it could scarcely be believed. . . . It was true though." As the bright day drew to an end, newsboys shouted the evening headline, "The President will live!"[11]

On Monday, September 9, Ida was again permitted to see the Major, who had managed to lift and turn himself in bed with no ill effect. She again went out for another one-hour drive into the city. Afterwards, she even received visitors in the downstairs parlor of Milburn House. Her strength had benefited the president's condition since "all reasons for worry for the President about Mrs. McKinley's condition has also passed." Nothing, however, quite so exceeded any expectations of the First Lady's new fortitude than the moment she stopped briefly on her way back to Milburn House after her day's drive to speak to a gaggle of reporters in her one and only brief press conference to answer some questions and make her first known public reference to the Almighty: "We trust in God and believe Mr. McKinley is going to recover speedily." When asked about the president's physicians, she replied unhesitatingly, "I know he has the best medical attendance that can be obtained and I am perfectly satisfied that these doctors are handling the case splendidly." She also expressed her appreciation at the wider support: "It is a great pleasure to know the deep interest and sympathy felt by the American people. The case is progressing so favorably that we are all very happy."[12]

By Wednesday morning, after his best night's sleep since the shooting, McKinley began to believe he might improve. Ida was allowed to spend time with him and was now receiving "many callers" in the parlor. Cortelyou was also admitted. A Cabinet meeting around his bedside was scheduled for Friday, and plans were made to return him to convalesce in Canton or Washington, depending on the heat. Dr. Mann was praised for his surgery in saving the president's life, and Dr. McBurney announced he was going to Niagara Falls. Hanna returned to Cleveland, feeling relieved. When he was about to leave Buffalo to return to his vacation, Roosevelt clapped his hands, declaring that "God wouldn't let such a noble man die by an assassin's bullet!" Then he chided a Secret Service agent behind him, "I do not want you to follow me. I don't need any one, and I'm not afraid."

With all of her husband's Cabinet gathered in Milburn House, Ida McKinley found herself in the unprecedented role of receiving them as personal callers—she was able to stand and walk without need of a chair or the Major's arm. After their "informal discussion of public business," they dispersed, and the First Lady walked out for her daily drive. She returned, however, within a half hour. The afternoon air had changed from bracing and cool to "heavy and oppressive." The papers noted how the "sky became overcast." From the southwest, "a storm threatened."[13]

September 11 dawned with hope. Ida McKinley was "bright and cheerful" as she again headed out for her carriage ride. While she was gone, the doctors addressed reporters about an incident from the previous evening when the president complained about an irritation at the wound, which was subsequently opened and cleaned. McBurney admitted that a small piece of McKinley's coat, where the bullet had entered, was found less than an inch internally, along with slight contamination. Dr. Mann added that, although it had punctured McKinley's repaired digestive tract, there was "no need of extracting the bullet," nor locating it with the X-ray machine, which had been brought to the house. McBurney explained that the bullet had simply "slipped on through the fat" of McKinley's gut. The digestive tract surgery was successful, and the doctors would give him food that night. The reporters offhandedly noted that Mrs. McKinley was seen "returning after the doctors had concluded their consultation." They did not provide her with the medical details they gave the reporters.

The first reports out of Milburn House on Thursday offered one of the best bits of news—McKinley awoke and felt "better this morning than at any time." Having digested some broth the night before, he was given a "little solid food" of toast. He "relished it" and jokingly asked for a cigar. So confident was McBurney that he left for New York.[14]

By three in the afternoon, although complaining of "fatigue," McKinley continued to "take a sufficient amount of food." Ida, delighted by the good news, spent time with him and then went for her daily ride. Her appearance outside Milburn House had by now become a sure sign to the press and the public that McKinley's progress was continuing. She would not leave him if he was unwell.

By eight-thirty that night, it was clear that he could not yet process solid food. Calomel and oil were used to expel the food from his system. Lack of nutrition, however, was weakening him. Outside, the gas street lamp cast dancing shadows on the one hundred reporters and some two hundred onlookers who were shivering in a soft wind, standing in front of the white cloth tents, the silence punctuated only by clicking telegraph machines. Emerging from a light fog, a weary Cortelyou walked into the glow of the street lamp to hand out slips of paper with news that McKinley was "resting nicely now and the feeling is better." James McKinley, who just arrived from California to see his uncle, smiled hopefully as he left Milburn House that night.[15]

Just after two in the morning, the lights in Milburn House went on. The president was having heart failure. He was plied with digitalis, strychnine, and other stimulants. The press was given a bulletin admitting that the doctors had the "gravest apprehension." An hour later, the bulletin stated flatly, "His death might occur any time from heart exhaustion." Messengers fled from the house to fetch all members of the Cabinet and medical team. Despite this activity in the wee hours, the First Lady remained in deep slumber, unaware that there was a "change for the worse." Rixey somberly told the reporters, "The worst has not yet come and there is no necessity for disturbing her."

It proved a wise decision. McKinley stabilized by sunrise on Friday, but Ida did not appear outside all day. Rixey discouraged her drive this day, nor did she ask to go. Outside, an elderly woman insisted to a Secret Service agent that she be allowed to speak with Mrs. McKinley—she had a remedy of certain herbs and prayers that she was sure would save his life. The agent promised to pass on the message. Ida immediately sensed the change in McKinley, despite Rixey's attempt to keep her ignorant. Her fear of the worst was confirmed; when she asked what time she could see the Major, Rixey said, "it would be better . . . not to see him this morning." Ida "assented without protest, but she seemed to realize the full import of the request, though she said nothing." Through lunchtime and afterward, McKinley's condition remained the same. She was now unrelenting in demanding to see him. He now needed oxygen, and his heart was struggling. Finally, by early evening, as one report put it, "she came to the room strong in her weakness compared with the weakness of the strong man whose life was so fast ebbing." All others withdrew, except for one of the doctors, who hovered at the door. Some reports suggested they were together for more than an hour. The Reuter News Service claimed that Ida sat there while the Major was given oxygen from a tank, which helped to revive him briefly. Fading into delirium, he began to repeat the words of his favorite hymn, *Nearer My God to Thee,* but he also whispered in her ear, "God's will, not ours, be done." Ida whispered, "I want to go with you," to which he gently murmured, "We are all going, my dear."[16]

Dr. Mynter finally emerged to speak to the press in language less clinical than the daily bulletins: "He is growing cold. The death chill has settled upon him and is spreading. All efforts to save him have been abandoned. They are waiting for the end. It may come soon, it may come in two hours." Above the treetops high over Milburn House, the sky had an unusual glow to it: the electric lights of the Exposition were on display for another night.

Inside, by ten at night, the president was in and out of a comatose state; when he spoke, he often seemed delirious, mixing the words of his favorite hymns with memories of his "boyhood days and home." After ten-thirty, he had a brief moment of lucidity and asked to see Ida again, likely knowing it would be their last glimpse of each alive.[17]

Rixey had the power to tell Ida about the Major's request or keep it from her, but he knew McKinley would soon slip into unconsciousness.

Rixey went to her room, but hesitated to speak. Ida rose, walked out firmly, and began to wander the hall outside the closed door of the Major's room and the doctor's conference room, where she was met with blank looks, but no words. She went downstairs, searching for someone to confirm what was happening. At the instruction of the doctors, however, no one told her. When she heard sobbing and saw Pina, Abner, her nieces and nephews crying, Ida got her answer. Rixey attempted to retrieve Ida and return her to her room.

Ida confronted Rixey point-blank in what a witness called a "calm, unnatural" voice, while continuing to contain her emotions as the Major had asked her to do since the shooting. "The President is dying," she snapped at her doctor. "You can't deceive me. I must see him." He neither responded nor took her to the president. Fearful of the potential physical shock to Ida if he told her the truth, Rixey had Mary Barber take her aunt to her room and keep her there, then joined the eleven o'clock medical conference and raised the issue. All concurred that Ida had to be gently prepared for the imminent reality. Rixey returned to her. The First Lady addressed him calmly: "I understand the President is sleeping." Confirming this, he paused and continued, "He is sleeping that sleep that knows no awakening."

Without flinching, but full of repressed grief, Ida commanded Rixey to do the impossible: "You will save him. I cannot let him go. The nation cannot spare him." Tearlessly, she rose and walked into the hall, passing others who quickly turned their heads to avoid letting her see them sob. Ida went directly into the Major's room and to his bedside.[18]

She took both of his hands in hers, stared directly into his face, and smoothed his hair from his forehead. He was still breathing, but there was no response. Leaning over and raising him slightly, she put her arms around his body and held her face close to his, embracing him for a few silent moments. She then stood up, turned around, and looked at Rixey, who had stood back watching. "Her gaze was fixed, her grief evident," he apparently later told one reporter, "but still there were no tears."

Rixey escorted Ida to her room, where Mary waited. Finally, Mrs. McKinley began to sob and wail in "heartbreaking lamentations." Her niece and doctor tried to calm her, but she was "wrapped in her grief and had ears for none." Rixey gave her a heavy sedative and by midnight, she had fallen into a "disturbed" sleep.

As the minutes after midnight grew into an hour, and then one more hour, McKinley's breathing became labored. Rixey "deemed [it] desirable not to awaken her for the last moments of anguish." The president died just after two on Saturday morning, September 14. His brother Abner; sisters Sarah and Helen; his and Ida's nieces and nephews Sarah Duncan, Mary Barber, James McKinley, William Duncan, and John Barber; his cousin Will Osborne; Ida's sister Pina; and Cortelyou, Rixey, Webb Hayes, and Dawes were all there when he died. Abner's business partner, a Colonel Brown, was allowed to encroach on such an intimate moment, but Ida McKinley had been denied the chance, was medicated, and put to sleep.[19]

As soon as Mrs. McKinley woke the next morning, she sensed "in some intuitive manner" that the Major was dead. She again "wandered from room to room, uttering no word, broken, stricken, dazed" as she looked into the faces of her various relatives, the Cabinet, and friends who were coming in and out. Nobody would confirm the fact for her, but the atmosphere became so "oppressive" that most callers left quickly. Mercifully, Pina finally broke the news to her sister. Ida took it calmly, without immediate reaction. She acquiesced to Pina's suggestion to let Cortelyou arrange all the funeral details while she kept to her room throughout the day.

"Mrs. McKinley does not seem to fully realize the awful blow," Brown told the press. "She is in sort of a dazed condition and acts mechanically. We expect her to collapse during the day, but we do not anticipate any fatal results." Milburn's remark seemed contradictory. "Mrs. McKinley is deeply bereaved, utterly grief-stricken, and very, very much broken down," he said, but added, "when her none too robust health and delicate nervous system are taken into consideration it must be said she has shown marvelous fortitude in the hour of her great misfortune." The Central News Service reported that Ida whispered to Abner, "God help me."[20]

Why she would have to be not merely carefully watched but also kept in isolation seemed unusual. Charles Locke, the son of McKinley's Canton pastor, provided a clue to the primary concern now of the medical team when he remarked that, "She is keeping up wonderfully well, although there may be a double tragedy." There was serious concern that the stress might kill her.

Vice President Roosevelt arrived in Buffalo at 1:35 in the afternoon. "He insisted first of all on visiting Mrs. McKinley and offering condolences to her," Everett Marshall reported. Only then was he willing to be sworn in as the twenty-sixth president, in the Wilcox home.[21]

Ida was kept upstairs in ignorance. Cortelyou made decisions about the funeral events in talks with several Cabinet members but did not even consult with the widow. McKinley's status as president was the sole focus; consideration of Ida was based on concern for the risks to her health in involving her—not on her feelings about such an intensely personal process. There would be a private service in Milburn House in the morning, Sunday. Urged by local business and political leaders, Hanna, War Secretary Root, and Judge Day committed to having the president's open casket lie in state in Buffalo City Hall, which meant removing him from Milburn House immediately after the private service there. When Ida learned this just before the morning service began, her "feelings were put to a severe test." She apparently expressed her anger to Cortelyou. He admitted to the *Washington Post* that "She is much depressed today on account of the [planned] removal of the President's body to the city hall. She seemed to want to be as near as possible to him." After some pressure, she "waived her personal wishes." The fact that just hours after the death, a check for $15,000 was rushed to the house for her—the proceeds of a life insurance policy the Major had purchased—was utterly meaningless to Ida.[22]

She slept without drugs on her first night as a widow. She awoke and remained calm and spent the morning hours "alone with the body," Cortelyou told the press, when she "did not seem to realize that he was dead." Staring into his face and gently touching it in the black coffin, Ida soon changed. Cortelyou continued: "From then on it was difficult to restrain her. . . . She remained there alone for an hour or more, and gave herself over to more violent weeping and grief than at any time since the death of the President." Although two coffins had been sent for her to choose from, she was not part of the decision making, nor did she have the satisfaction of choosing the roses, violets, and chrysanthemums that were to rest on the casket. She had always considered the red or white carnation, his trademark boutonniere, to be his flower. Rixey led her out before the coffin was carried down for the private service for one hundred guests. Ida was not permitted to attend, so she sat at the head of the stairs to hear it, surrounded by Rixey, Jennie Hobart, Mary McWilliams, Pina, and Mary. "He is gone," she told them, "and life to me is dark now."[23]

The service began at eleven, with the new president attending as McKinley's two favorite hymns—*Lead Kindly Light* and *Nearer, My God, to Thee*—were heard for the first of many times over the next few days. The Reverend Locke began with a reading from the first chapter of Corinthians I, and in his prayer made reference to Mrs. McKinley.[24]

Ida, however, heard little of this herself. The moment she began to give way to her emotions, she was taken back to her room. There, as a reporter learned from a family member, "her paroxysms of grief were pitiful, and her lamentations almost unceasing. For almost the first time since the death of Mr. McKinley she was subject to violent and continued weeping." Since guests were not told that she was prevented from appearing at the solemn service because her doctor wanted to control her grief, misinterpretations hit the papers with reports that Ida was in "a state of mental collapse" and had been made "mentally irresponsible through the administration of drugs and opiates." Any suggestion that her grief was so extreme that she had to be drugged, Cortelyou belatedly retorted, was "an infamous lie."

Rixey did not want to risk having Ida endure the funeral procession from Buffalo to Washington to Canton and decided that Pina or Mary would take her directly to Canton so she could reserve her strength for the funeral and burial there. Ida refused to be separated from the Major's presence for any period of time, so she disagreed with Rixey, and perhaps even Pina, on this decision. Ultimately, however, Ida had no power, particularly since the distracted Cortelyou simply agreed with Rixey.

As if she mistrusted even Rixey and Pina, and after having been forced to accept the decision to display the coffin in Buffalo City Hall, Ida knew she had one ally with power over everyone. She bided some time and waited until Roosevelt returned. "Her desire is to go to Washington," the *New York Times* reported, "She has signified this to President Roosevelt. It is stated that she asked to go with the funeral train to Washington, to remain in the White House while the body is lying in state, and then to go with the funeral train to Canton. It is understood that President Roosevelt has said that her request will be granted." Even the anticipation of her return to the White House prompted the staff to refuse her use of the bedroom she had shared there with the Major for fear of her emotional reaction. When Ida learned of this, she "expressed a wish to have her old rooms ready for her . . . her request is, of course, being complied with," the *Washington Post* reported.[25]

The mayor of Philadelphia now lobbied to have the train stop in his city and have the coffin rest there for public viewing, as did the mayor of New York, who at least made the request of Mrs. McKinley and not just the secretary of state. Mrs. McKinley refused both requests. As she prepared for the next day's journey through western New York, Pennsylvania, and Maryland, Ida learned that the coffin would lie in state at the U.S. Capitol Building all day Tuesday and overnight into Wednesday, when a formal morning service would be held. She stood her ground against this, even though it was already announced. She won. A new statement was issued that the Capitol services would end on Tuesday "In compliance with the earnest wishes of Mrs. McKinley that the body of her husband shall rest in her home in Canton Wednesday night. . . ."[26]

As McKinley lay in state in Buffalo City Hall on Sunday, churches around the nation praised the late Major's Christian faith, prayed for Ida, and scorned the assassin.[27]

Czolgosz, convicted in a two-day trial and sentenced on October 26 to death, admitted being a disciple of the famous anarchist leader Emma Goldman but made it clear that "No one else told me to do it, and no one paid me to do it. . . . I never thought anything about murder until a couple of days before I committed the crime." When he was brought to Auburn prison, where he was electrocuted two days later, he suddenly offered a poignant reflection about Ida: "If I had an extra life of my own to give which could benefit Mrs. McKinley, I would cheerfully give it for her." Emma Goldman was held at Chicago's Harrison Street Police Station on suspicion of inciting the assassin. When she read the bulletin announcing the president's death, she observed, "I feel very bad for the sake of Mrs. McKinley; outside of that I have no sympathy." Self-identified anarchist members at a Central Federated Union meeting voted to send Ida McKinley a resolution of sympathy. Only once would she refer to Czolgosz. "How could that man kill my husband?" she asked. "Why did he, how could he? . . . [M]y husband was no man's enemy."[28]

Ida McKinley was on everyone's mind it seemed. A Daughters of the American Revolution magazine editorial observed that there was "a peculiar and poignant grief felt by women" for Ida. Along with a high volume of sympathy notes from Southern African American women and an especially "tender" one from Booker T. Washington's wife Margaret, the queen of Italy expressed particular concern for her. "I cannot get her out of my mind," Margherita told reporters, "at least poor Mrs. McKinley should, in her state of health, have been spared." The Women's Christian Temperance Union's hatchet-bearing Carrie Nation, however, was unsympathetic to Ida, who refused to ban alcohol in the White House, adding, "McKinley would have recovered but his blood was bad from nicotine."[29]

While Roosevelt was taking the oath of office, doctors drew up a report on the death, agreeing that it was a result of inevitable gangrene along the bullet's path through the stomach and surrounding tissue but suggested that "under favorable conditions," he might have been saved. The "conditions" they referred to were "the body of a man of youthful vigor and of such strenuous vitality that nature may enter at once upon the work of reconstruction and healing." Dr. Rixey conceded for the record that Ida McKinley had unintentionally factored into McKinley's "lowered vitality and little resistance to disease or injury." He explained further:

The man was not the cause of this, but an invalid wife whose whole life without children was tied up in her husband, and in his absence she was never really happy. He, recognizing this, reduced his absence from her side to a minimum and even then she was constantly on his mind. His outdoor exercise was a short walk or ride beside his wife, usually in a closed carriage. Mrs. McKinley did not wish any change, and would have soon dispensed with my services if she thought I was urging any. However, I tried to have him drive himself in an open trap with a good pair of horses, his wife beside him and a footman in the rumble. After a short while Mrs. McKinley put it aside. Then I tried short horseback rides. This took him too much from her presence. When the emergency came, his enfeebled constitution could not stand the shock, and gangrene around the wounds caused death.[30]

The public also learned that the president's widow did not want a thorough autopsy to be conducted, even though in a murder case her consent was unnecessary. During their postmortem investigation, the doctors tried to retrieve the lodged bullet, but failed to because of "Mrs. McKinley objecting—though *without* legal right so to do—to the search being longer continued." It was "only with the greatest difficulty that permission was obtained" from her that a microscopic tissue study was done, concluding that Czolgosz hadn't poisoned the bullet.[31]

None of that mattered to the widow. Waking at seven on Monday morning for a light breakfast alone, she began to politely but persistently ask, "When can I see the Major?" She wanted to be near him and be able to look into his face as often as she needed.[32]

The public got its first fleeting glimpse of Mrs. McKinley as she stepped into the windy but sunny morning, and immediately any impression of her as weak was dispelled. To "the surprise of all," Ida, in a long black veil drawn so that her face could not be seen, "walked briskly, with her head quite erect" from Milburn House into a waiting carriage, with Rixey, Abner, and Mary. As the carriage went through Buffalo to the depot, Ida "sat erect," with no need for support, as she turned to look at the streets hung with mourning bunting. Remarkably, no one snapped her picture during the few times she appeared in public over the next several days. No photo of her in mourning exists.

It was ironic that in light of her "surprising fortitude" and "control of herself" as she boarded the same *Olympia* car used on the Pacific tour, a hospital bed for her anticipated need was nevertheless loaded into the baggage car. The train left Buffalo at about eight-thirty and made occasional stops in depots where tens of thousands of citizens waited for a glimpse of the flag-draped coffin in the observation car at the end of the train. Still, Ida McKinley implored Rixey, "When can I see the Major?" Fearing that the sight might shock her, he put her off, but during a long stretch between stops, he and Pina brought her to the coffin. The flag was removed and the upper portion opened. Reports concurred that the once-portly man's remains were radically desiccated, but it didn't trouble Ida. For nearly an hour, she stood and knelt in prayer and then, seated, looked into his face and began talking. A member of the honor guard found it disturbing: "She does not seem to realize the president is dead and talks almost constantly to him. . . . She had an abstracted, far away look upon her face, as though her thoughts were elsewhere. I think the strain must have affected her mind." Finally, Rixey coaxed her into the parlor car to rest.[33]

During the trip, Ida alternated between resting and staring out the window at the passing scene and remained perfectly silent, "as if the meaning of this awful blow could not be comprehended," noted Everett Marshall, a chronicler of the trip. When they pulled into Harrisburg, the crowds stared intently at her and, suddenly conscious of them, she moved away. A choral group sang *Nearer, My God, to Thee* and as it echoed through the large station, she "bowed her head and wept."

Arriving in Washington before nine that night, Abner and Rixey escorted Ida into a waiting carriage, kept her out of view, and whisked her to the White House. She stumbled slightly on the North Portico steps and was brought up to her room. After the coffin's mournful procession from the station, it was placed in the East Room to lie in state, surrounded by an honor guard, and left undisturbed through the night, with McKinley's head facing north as had Lincoln's. White shades covered the windows, and a printed card with the word "Closed" was tacked on the North Portico door. Ida came down before she went to sleep. "Mrs. McKinley came in on the arm of Dr. Rixey to take a long look at her dear husband. It was very sad," the doorkeeper Tom Pendel recalled.

Pendel also noted that again on Tuesday morning, "she took her final farewell of the remains before they were removed to the Capitol." Although she sobbed heavily when she first returned to her room, she was sufficiently in command of herself to receive Jennie Hobart, Mary Logan, and Edith Roosevelt. She took great comfort in knowing that on Wednesday night, she would have the Major to herself, in the complete privacy of their Canton home.[34]

"The reasons were not known," the *New York Times* reported, for the now-former First Lady's absence at McKinley's U.S. Capitol rotunda funeral service, but she was alluded to by the eulogy's reference to "that domestic love which has so often been commented upon." The public streamed past the coffin for several hours before it was brought to the funeral train.

Oddly, there was no arrangement made to meet the carriage carrying Mrs. McKinley from the White House to the station. While driving it through the streets in a heavy rainstorm, the coachman became disoriented, which

delayed their arrival at the station and the train's departure. When it arrived
at the correct train platform and Ida McKinley stepped out, she performed a
small act that seemed an apt metaphor of how she, as a disabled person, had
adapted the First Lady's role to her life. Whether it was a conscious decision
or not, Ida McKinley left Washington in September 1901 as she had arrived
in March 1897. There was a wheelchair waiting there to spare her the "tir-
ing effort of the long walk" along the lengthy train platform, just as one
had been provided for her when she arrived for the Inauguration. She now
did what she had done then. When offered the wheelchair, Ida McKinley
"declined this," and "walked with surprising firmness to her place."[35]

Some who knew her well resented that there was no mention of Ida
McKinley's strength of character during the ordeal. While President
McKinley was "held up to the world by his eulogists as a Model Husband, a
Knight of Today, whose devotion never wavered," novelist Marion Harland
noted, "few of the admiring multitude guessed at his debt of gratitude and
at his chivalrous remembrance of the same [to Ida]." Julia Foraker was es-
pecially proud of Ida's resolve throughout the two weeks after the shooting.
"The world's sympathy went out to Mrs. McKinley. It thought her crushed.
Yet how marvelous she was! How erect in grief! Suddenly deprived of the
prop of life, she seemed to draw strength and self-control. . . ."[36]

The train left Washington just before ten in the evening, carrying the
McKinley and Saxton family members, the Cabinet, and the new president. A leaden morning sky broke as the train neared Pittsburgh, and
along the more remote pastoral regions of northeastern Ohio, hundreds of
farmers and workers stood silently, hats in hand. The sun appeared briefly
at Lewisville, and six miles later, they arrived in Canton at nearly noon.
In Ida's view, the Major would not really be home until he arrived at the
house they had left just two weeks earlier. She shook and sobbed as Rixey
carried her from the train and took her home in a closed carriage. The
trauma of loss was now more obvious.

Meanwhile, the coffin was conveyed by horse-drawn hearse to the
Court House, where thousands waited for the chance to glance one last
time on their favorite son. The president and Cabinet were the first to pass
through, some barely glancing in the open coffin under the bright electric chandelier. Besides desiccation, the skin had darkened. Many friends
regretted looking in the coffin rather than remembering McKinley as he
looked when they last saw him alive. Ida had tried to avoid this by ordering the coffin to be kept closed in Canton. Tens of thousands had already
stared at the Major; she felt "there has been enough publicity with the
dead." Her wish had again been ignored.[37]

The papers described many of those who passed in single file through the Court House—a veteran on crutches, a tall man with a red mustache, a mother holding her baby, schoolboys, factory workers carrying their dinner pails. When the doors closed at six in the evening, some 30,000 had paid their last respects. The very first who had filed by the casket were two little girls who seemed to be there without their parents. Having waited the longest to see the president, they left individual red geraniums, simply plucked from the earth. Ida McKinley remained waiting at home, eager for the Major's body to return for one last night there, alone with her. His coffin was carried into the house, covered with the floral wreaths that had been placed on the lower portion during the viewing. Tucked in were the geraniums, which, strangely, had remained fresh.

The coffin was placed in McKinley's study. Ida "pleaded to be allowed" to sit quietly beside it, beneath the dim light that illuminated it, and "consent was reluctantly granted." Her only request was to have him to herself this night, to look at him again. However, seeing the Major one last time was "impossible." The coffin had been permanently sealed. "Her anguish broke out afresh," went one report, "she was led away to her room. . . ."

The next morning, family members and intimate friends arrived for a short, private service, but Rixey, concerned again about Ida's emotional state, insisted that she stay in bed and listen to the service through the open door. It prevented her from seeing the Major when he was taken from her for the last time. In hoping to avoid "a collapse," Rixey did not allow her to attend the funeral at the family's First Methodist church or McKinley's interment in the vault in Westlawn Cemetery. Instead, she "wept piteously, hour after hour." Rixey told the press that "she has been doing as well as any woman could do under similar circumstances." Roosevelt later wrote Ida that he was told that President McKinley promised to make Rixey the next surgeon general, and "I shall faithfully observe Mr. McKinley's wishes." The appointment was made "in recognition of devoted services" to her.[38]

After five days of having had her wishes ignored unless she was insistent, Ida McKinley had a few words of her own when she "rebelled" upon being told the coffin was sealed. "I have given everything of him to you, even his life," she said to no one in particular, "and his body belongs to me."[39]

Based on what Rixey told the press, it was widely reported that the final words McKinley spoke were, "His will be done!" The physician, however, had decided to withhold from the public what the dying president's actual last remark was—a simple, stark question: "What will become of her?"[40]

⤞ 17 ⤝

The Holding Vault

"Mrs. McKinley's grief is intense," Rixey told the press the day after the funeral, while also offering hope with news of her strength: "Mrs. McKinley was one of the first at the house in North Market Avenue to arise today. She said she had enjoyed a good sleep, and that she felt better than any time since the fateful night in Buffalo when her husband was shot." She had fallen asleep naturally, he pointed out, without opiates or any other drugs. He was cautious to withhold the more alarming fact that, when she did arise, Ida was determined that she "must die and join her husband."

Before the new president left for Washington, he told Rixey to remain in Canton as long as necessary to stabilize the widow's health. As he had done in lessening the degree and frequency of her seizures, Rixey knew he must now focus on her mental state. That Ida was motivated enough to rise for the first day alone in the house where she had intended to retire with the Major and was able to slumber deeply were good signs. While Rixey did not expect Ida, in these traumatic circumstances, to emotionally recover rapidly, he "calculated to take her mind from the depressing incidents." He decided that visual stimulation and behavioral change could at least mitigate the severity of her grief. "Something was needed to get her on her feet and in her carriage" to return her to a normal routine. Rixey, who was all too familiar with her contrary willfulness, however, appealed to rather than challenged her intention to "be with the Major," not by willing her own death but by visiting him in his final resting place. She had been prevented from witnessing any of Canton's tributes to her husband the day before, and she did not even know where he was now. The idea "aroused her at once and arrangements could not be made too soon." She would rejoin the Major at the holding vault.

Rixey quickly rang Pina and then ordered the carriage before Ida's mood shifted. Moments after her sister's speedy dash up Market Avenue to arrive at the McKinley house, the party of three headed out. The carriage got through the crowds still in Canton for the funeral, picked up a fast pace and passed through the gates of Westlawn Cemetery, then headed toward the small stone building that resembled a church. Several hundred curious visitors milled about the adjoining green slopes, which were dotted with floral wreaths for the president. They surged around the enclosed black carriage. Soldiers on guard duty at the vault cleared a path to let the carriage roll over the grass and up to the entrance.

Alighting, Ida was awed by the size and vivid artistry of the wreaths and arrangements against the wall of the holding vault, which added so much color to the slate path and stone structure. She was worried that crowds in the days and months ahead might disturb the remains but was assured that the vault would always be locked, and there would be guards on duty. Ida relaxed and entered. Inside, a chair was brought for her so she could sit beside the coffin, which was still draped with the flag and flowers, and placed atop a raised platform. At first, the experience was traumatic as she sobbed uncontrollably, but she soon ebbed into silent contemplation with such a growing sense of comfort that it then became "a struggle at first to get her to leave the abiding place of her dearest." She finally patted the casket, adjusted flowers atop it, and left. Rixey told the coachman to drive her around the cemetery and outlying area until she began to tire out. On the ride out, she began to pepper Rixey with questions about the day of the funeral, and he prompted her "interest in affairs going on in Canton." Tired but satisfied, Ida heartily ate dinner and fell into a deep sleep. The ritual was repeated daily, and the carriage rides increased in length. *The Oregonian* reported on September 28 that each day when she returned from the vault, there was a "slight but steady increase in the strength of the sorely afflicted woman. It is not improbable that she will regain the full measure of strength that has been her portion for some years and perhaps pass through serene, gentle invalidism down to old age."

Although he would come to check in on her over the months and continue to consult on her condition with her primary Canton physician, Thomas Portman, Rixey returned to Washington on October 1, stating that he had "no further apprehension for the future and the general health of Mrs. McKinley. . . ." By then, the last houseguests, in-laws Abner and Annie, and her cousin Mary, were gone. One morning before Rixey left, Ida noticed that the streets around her house were quiet and free of gawkers.

She peered out, stunned to see armed men on her lawn staring down her passing neighbors. "I do not need them," she snapped to Rixey. "They are unnecessary." Within minutes, there was only a gardener raking leaves from the lawn. Ida was fearless about her safety. She threw worrisome letters sent by paranoid-schizophrenic Francis W. Benque in the trash. When one George Fisher came to Canton to tell her about the secret plotters behind the Major's murder, the door was simply shut in his face.[1]

As Rixey worked to establish Ida's physical and emotional stability in Canton, her maid Clara Tharin was back at the White House, sorting through the McKinley household furnishings and personal items, and packing them off to Canton. Ida would choose to display, as a permanent exhibit, about two dozen of these objects "dearly prized by Mrs. McKinley as mementos of her husband's great career."

While Clara Tharin worked in the west end of the second floor, Cortelyou worked on the east side, organizing the president's papers in his office, which he eventually deposited at the Library of Congress. Cortelyou, retained briefly as the president's secretary before Roosevelt named him the first commerce secretary, nevertheless rushed back to Canton to arrange the practical realities of Ida's new life. Although the Major had named Ida his estate executor, she relinquished the role to Cortelyou and Justice Day, with the latter's Canton law partner Austin Lynch handling matters related to legal claims, income, billing invoices, home maintenance, investments, and staff. Although Ida began "looking after such business matters as it is necessary," she always sought advice, first from Cortelyou.[2]

His first task was to read to her the terms of the president's will, and the "ordeal was difficult." Signed seven months into his presidency, the Major had declared, "My chief concern is that my wife from my estate shall have all she requires for her comfort and pleasure. . . ." The Major left an estate worth over $250,000, including substantial life insurance. This was hardly her only income. The Saxton sisters earned a great profit when the first carloads of zinc ore were mined from Illinois property inherited from their father. Besides the federal government covering the Major's funeral expenses and his last medical bills, Congress would approve an appropriation of nearly $40,000 to Ida, representing the salary that would have been due to the Major by July 1902. With so much "independent income," Congressman Bell of Colorado balked that it was "wrong and indefensible" to grant her the annual $5,000 presidential widow's pension, arguing that hundreds of servicemen's widows denied pensions could be supported on the amount. By April 1902, however, she got the pension.[3]

Cortelyou assiduously looked after every one of the widow's needs. He got "very satisfactory terms" in selling two of her diamond necklaces, saw that her financially distressed friend Sue Rand was immediately wired money, had a pipe organ removed from her house, interviewed and hired her entire household staff, got her steam pipes covered, helped her draw up a will, obtained a reference book of history she wanted on hand, and determined which McKinley horses to retain for her use and which to sell.

Although she thought of herself as now being alone, there were never fewer than about five people within call. Rixey assembled a team of reliable nurses, including the San Franciscan Anna Moses, who had cared for her there during her illness; British native Nellie Williams, a graduate of nearby Aultman Hospital nursing school; and Irish-American sisters Maud and Gertrude Healy, the latter having worked for Jennie Hobart. Among the household staff were coachman John Bederman, maid Rosa White, cook Amelia Weisman, butler Warren Shaw, and a handyman identified only as Frank.[4]

With her clear penmanship and experience at dictation, Maud Healy quickly became the former First Lady's secretary. The few letters that Ida McKinley had dictated to her husband throughout their marriage had filtered her genuine thoughts through his political lens. Now that she was on her own again, Ida's opinions would be expressed uncensored for the first time since she regularly wrote her family while single and traveling through Europe. A few were formal responses to decline invitations or to acknowledge gifts; the vast majority of them were private letters to her close friends Carolyn Herrick and Caro Dawes. Congress granted her the presidential widow's franking privilege four months after the assassination, permitting her a lifetime of free outgoing postage. In response to public sympathy letters, Cortelyou composed a formal acknowledgment card with a personally signed statement on her behalf, printed in handwriting on the verso. He had several thousand printed.[5]

In the weeks after the funeral, Ida was inundated with some 5,000 sympathy letters, including elaborate testimonials from foreign organizations like the Municipal Board in Manila and an American women's group in South Africa. Letters from children comforted her greatly, many saying that they wished they lived nearby so they could visit her, while others worried about her spending Christmas alone. She especially appreciated receiving random snapshots taken of the Major during his regional tours. While most wrote to her about the Major, some focused with sensitivity on Ida as an individual. Kansan Thomas Higgins, "an invalid for many years," expressed the hope she could "bear up" on her own. A heavy percentage of letters came from African American women who felt an affinity with her. "There is no one who can sympathize with Mrs. McKinley as the Negro can," black minister W. L. Hunter of New York's Bridge Street Church explained. "Thousands of colored women are widows and mourners today. Their husbands have been butchered, murdered and burned without judge or jury."[6]

Public interest in Ida McKinley remained great. Elizabeth Jordan penned a moving *Harper's Bazaar* piece, hoping Ida would cease to regret that her invalidism had prevented her from being a more active First Lady, in light of how "unselfishly she supported her dying husband in the last great scene of his life." Jordan predicted that "light will come" back to her life. Never passing a chance to capitalize on the McKinleys, Alice Danner Jones published her poem "Little Kate" in *Roller Monthly* magazine and then reprinted it on souvenir cards to be sold in Canton. The poem imagined Katie McKinley as a winged angel hovering over the Major, who saw "his darling's sainted face" and flew off with her. It ended with Katie and the Major as "angelic forms," hovering over Ida weeping at home.

For the grieving nation, the widow became more a representational figure than a real person. A St. Louis Methodist Women's Missionary Society meeting credited her with making "domestic life everywhere . . . more beautiful and sacred." Declaring her "symbolic of . . . uplifting thought," a New York public school principal hung her picture in classrooms to "unconsciously exert . . . inspiration." In Philadelphia, a German cook of the Scharff family used Ida to point out how the lowest of men could ruin the loftiest of woman, and wailed repeatedly "Das poor Mrs. McKinley!" In his congressional eulogy of McKinley, Secretary of State Hay immortalized her as a patient saint, the "sufferer who counts the long hours in their shattered home."[7]

Ida thanked Hay for sending her a copy of his eulogy but otherwise took no interest in the numerous public tributes intended to honor the Major. When Congress appropriated $2,500 for his White House portrait, she turned the privilege of choosing an artist over to Cortelyou. Although he briefly considered a publisher's offer to write McKinley's official biography based on his papers, she wouldn't authorize one. She would not attend the unveiling of his Columbus statue, erected on the spot where he had waved his handkerchief to her at the window of their suite across the street. Protecting his image from being exploited did rouse her. When she saw his image being used on rye whiskey bottle labels, the distributor responded to an angry Cortelyou to "assure Mrs. McKinley that we exceedingly regret if we incurred her displeasure in making use of this label" and agreed to destroy the remaining stock. Despite threats of legal action, however, Ida failed to stop a new Canton hotel from being named "The McKinley."[8]

In forming the McKinley National Memorial Association, Cortelyou and Justice Day asked her whom she wished to serve as its trustees. She voiced no opinion, requesting instead that President Roosevelt decide. He named men who were well known to Ida, including Ohio's senators Hanna and Fairbanks, John Milburn of Buffalo, Josiah Hartzell (author of her campaign biography), Myron Herrick, and Charles Dawes, the latter two being husbands of her closest friends. Fund-raising for the intended burial monument began in January 1902.

After the funeral, some trustees scouted possible sites, including the hill McKinley had thought the ideal place for a monument to Stark County's soldiers and sailors. Knowing that she would eventually lie beside the Major, Ida was displeased by the location, finding it "a little too far removed and isolated." Her attitude changed when they presented a further incentive. As Dawes recorded of their meeting, "Until this time Mrs. McKinley did not know that the children's bodies were to be placed by the side of the President. When she learned this it seemed to reconcile her more to the location. . . ."[9]

Charles and Caro Dawes were Mrs. McKinley's houseguests for two days in early December. They were welcomed by Mary Barber, who was just then taking her turn, along with her sister Ida and their mother Pina as overnight companions for the widow. Dawes left a revealing account of the visit:

[We] . . . sat for a time talking over things about President McKinley which seemed most to interest Mrs. McKinley. She is in a better condition of health than we expected, though very frail, weak and painracked. Much of the time she is in tears and her mind constantly reverts to her great loss. . . . Nothing could be more pathetic than the daily life of this stricken woman. Her sister, with a noble fidelity to duty, is with her constantly. Judge and Mrs. Day were invited to dinner with us and asked us to visit them but Mrs. McKinley said that while she lived we must come only to her house. As best we could we tried to cheer her and succeeded best when we spoke of the many kind and generous acts of the President.

Ida realized how depressing it was to be with her, even using some wit at her own expense to express this. When looking out the window at a rainstorm in the black winter sky, she mused how it was "dark both out-side and inside the house."

The previous week, Cortelyou and his wife Lilly had spent Thanksgiv-ing with her. Once the Dawes left, her sisters-in-law Helen and Sarah came to stay. They departed on the same day that her Chicago cousin Mary McWilliams arrived. Just after the funeral, a consortium of relatives and friends coordinated their schedules and dutifully took their turn at attempting to minimize Ida's intense loneliness. It was not easy. Some, like Jennie Hobart and William Hawk, had to travel a distance. Others, like Cortelyou, Rixey, Hanna, Dawes, and Herrick, had official responsibili-ties in Washington or Columbus. Pina, the most devoted of all, endured the greatest challenge. Patiently, gently, she tried to fully integrate Ida into her own family, but the widow resisted entering Saxton House. Even at Christmas, she refused to join the Barbers there and be "forcibly reminded of the Christmas days of the past. . . ."[10]

From winter to spring to summer of 1902, whether at breakfast, lunch, or dinner, Ida's guests were encouraged to tell and retell examples of the Major's greatness. If repeating stories of the past about someone now dead seemed macabre to them, they saw it was the one way to abate her tears and depression. The technique had been used by the Major with Ida as a way to keep Katie's memory alive. Ida's life had been busier and fuller at that time. Without much else to engage her now, recounting memories of the Major had the effect of delaying the natural stages of grief, one of which was ac-ceptance. "I miss my 'precious' more and more," Ida admitted in a July letter to Carolyn Herrick, "I think of 'my precious' all the time. I take no interest in anything or anybody." At times, she recognized it could become alienat-ing. "I do not feel I am company for anyone," she often wrote.[11]

Inevitably, guests began to realize that no matter how many visits they made or however long they stayed, her state of mind never seemed to lighten. "It seems to be either a feast or famine at our house with visitors but I am so lonely and unhappy all the time," she confessed, "I miss my pre-cious more and more every day I live."

The house's memories only magnified her depression, yet she refused to leave it except to visit the holding vault, even while acknowledging that remaining there exacerbated her isolation. "Mrs. Hobart was very in-sistent that I should return with her to Patterson but I have no heart to go any place," she wrote Carolyn Herrick. "General and Mrs. Hastings came the same day and remained overnight. From here they went to Fremont to visit Webb Hayes. They wished me to go with them but I cannot make up my mind to leave my lonely home."[12]

After resisting all invitations to the private homes of friends and family, in or outside of Canton, some like Jennie Hobart suggested they bring her to the shore or mountains, simply for "a change." Not wanting to disappoint Pina and niece Ida, the widow agreed to join them for a stay at Atlantic City in March, and it was even publicly announced. Just before they left, Ida withdrew her promise. She took enough interest in the Cleveland wedding of the Major's niece Sarah to send pieces of her antique lace collection to incorporate in her wedding gown but refused to attend the ceremony, fearing it would remind her of past weddings she had attended with her husband.

Not wishing to leave home for months was understandable, but her self-imposed imprisonment in the house lasted more than a year. It is difficult to understand the reason. In one letter, she claimed that it was not leaving the house that was the problem, but returning to it. As she explained, "I have not the heart to leave home only to come back again—alone."[13]

Another potential explanation was Ida's fear that something stressful might provoke a seizure while she was away from her Canton doctor, whom Rixey would certainly have instructed on her treatments. After the death of her husband, there were no more reports of Ida's epilepsy, but the absence of any mention of seizures in a private medical record or in the letters of others does not mean, as has been assumed, that she never experienced them again. She was never far from at least one of her staff of professionally trained nurses. The paradox of McKinley's murder, however, was that Ida no longer had to fear further danger to him. Despite her compromised immune system, she remained remarkably strong. She also continued to push herself to walk independently. Rixey had little need to visit. As she wrote in June 1902, "I am as well as usual but still very unhappy."[14]

"I have not been in a house in Canton since my return and have no desire to go," Ida felt compelled to repeatedly report to her friends with what seems to almost be a sense of pride in her discipline. Even had the McKinleys not been as close as they were, it would have been understandable for Ida to experience tremendous survivor's guilt after the trauma of the assassination and that may have played an unconcious part in her determination to remain sequestered at home and avoid the appearance of beginning to enjoy life again. By frequently pointing out her self-denial, Mrs. McKinley also affirmed an image of strong character which countered the general impression that she was weak and dependent. Was it perhaps a dramatic excuse that also served as a cover for more mundane reasons? At the same time that she was emphatically refusing to comply with Caro Dawes's insistence that Ida visit her in Indiana, Mrs. McKinley had also contracted with the local Bowen Brothers construction company to undertake the completion of a house extension originally planned by the Major.[15]

Several letters also suggest, however, that a more intensely emotional reason based on her belief in the supernatural world was why she was determined to exist entirely in the house. With trust in the Buddhist tenet of reincarnation, Ida McKinley was already convinced that the souls of her daughters, who both died before being baptized as Christians, had been reborn into new physical bodies. The Major, however, had been baptized and his soul saved as a Christian. To her, the late President continued to live, not as a physical person but as a ghost, within the realm of the spirit world. She emphatically expressed her conviction of this to a freind, who came away affirming that, "Her faith that the loved, unseen, are not lost, is perfect." Relying on the promise of such mysticism, Ida McKinley was waiting for a sign or visit from the Major as a ghost. Explaining to a friend that the North Market Avenue house was "very dear to us," she was certain that his apparition would appear there. As she finally explained to Caro Dawes, "I cannot leave home without my Precious." This was a matter of more than sensing his presence. It was that, "I feel as though he must come back to me," she flatly told Carolyn Herrick.

Whether Ida McKinley ever felt satisfied that the ghost of her late husband had made a return to her is unknown. To perhaps search for more evidence of such phenomena or to find proof that they would be rejoined, Ida McKinley began to consult the Bible, a copy of which a visitor noticed next to her knitting bag and needles. While her earlier sense that God had abandoned her by taking her two daughters may have lingered, she also began beseeching Him to take her soon, so the family of four could finally be together again.[16]

Despite what she stated, there is every indication that Ida longed for human contact. However devoted her friends, by the time a year had passed since the assassination, their inclination to make visits for several days' duration began to wane. It led her to make the invitations all the more insistently. "I hope the next time you come to Canton, you will not have to make such a flying visit," she gently chastised Carolyn Herrick. She mentioned that "Webb Hayes stepped in the other day for a short call, but it was so short that I hardly realized he had been [here]." She even found fault with Jennie Hobart, who went to great lengths to write and visit Ida as regularly as she could. "I have not heard from Mrs. Hobart and am afraid she has had to postpone her visit to me on account of some charitable work she is much interested in. It would be more charitable to come to me in my great loneliness."

Maud Healy may have stepped out of bounds in trying to convince Carolyn Herrick to remain more than a few hours: "[W]e can make you very comfortable if you will stay. The piano is tuned and Mrs. and Miss Harter have been here three times and played beautifully. Mrs. McKinley enjoys it so much. I hope you will come. I believe . . . it is not so depressing now. I try to believe Mrs. McKinley is improving but she has been an invalid for so long, it is a wonder to me she has not lost her grit."[17]

Guests or no guests, Ida's life was limited to her first-floor bedroom, the front parlor, dining room, and the Major's adjoining office-library. She rose early for breakfast, knitted while mail was read to her, and then dictated responses. She had newspaper and magazine articles read to her, especially those about former Administration officials. The staff paid bills for repairs and groceries, decided on menus, and made preparations for houseguests. By late morning, she went out for her drive, nodding to those who waved, and kept an eye on new houses being built, remodeled, rented, or sold, civic landscaping, and "the progress being made in the different buildings in process of construction." On some mornings, she took a lengthy drive to the Saxton farm in Minerva, which was still overseen by Jack Adams. She returned for a simple lunch and nap, followed by the highlight of her daily existence, which was visiting the holding vault.

In the evenings, the nurses read entire books to Ida. The four-volume history of the women's suffrage movement, which especially engaged her, was sent by Susan B. Anthony, who wrote, "You will rejoice over the progress woman has made in the last twenty years." She always had the latest novel by Weir Mitchell (the Philadelphia physician who had treated her with the "rest cure" some thirty years earlier) who flourished as an author. Carolyn Herrick sent her recently published books and magazines, Ida always "much interested" in any new material about the Major. She was served a plain dinner in her room or the parlor, and ate alone in silence. On Sunday evenings, she counted on a visit from her infirm, elderly uncle Joseph. As was the case earlier, Ida never went to church.[18]

The public had a different perception of the former First Lady's life. Embellishing the bare facts, the *Washington Post* described an active Ida: "Private advices from Canton telling of the great improvement in Mrs.

McKinley's health, say that the former mistress is now entirely capable of managing her household affairs and is again taking an active interest in the world's work and life. She drives daily about Canton, and personally supervises the management of her entire establishment. She reads the daily papers, writes her own letters and in every way leads an active life such as she has not known for more than twenty years."[19]

When, however, her friend Murat Halstead visited in May, Ida granted him an unvarnished interview, published in the September *Ladies Home Journal.* "It has been said in zeal without knowledge that Mrs. McKinley has borne up wonderfully well under her frightful trial," the article stated, "It is not true. It is worth while that the world that cares for her should know the truth. She has aged since that sad, dread September, as if many bitter years had passed. There is a . . . haunting, tremulous, wistful expression. . . ."

When approaching McKinley House, Halstead had a sense of a cemetery. Where crowds had noisily cheered the Major's speeches, there was now merely the sound of chirping birds and rustling leaves. Inside, the shut windows made the uncirculated air all the more stifling. The telegraph machines that once noisily clacked in the Major's office lay silent, disabled.

Sitting alone at her parlor window, Ida knitted feverishly in silence, writing a friend, "this work is all that I do." Although the activity was all the more important to her, there were fewer organizations asking for her slippers, and she implored friends to tell her if they knew people "who would care for any." She now made them only in mourning black or gray. "I am waiting, and my hands must have something to do," she explained when Halstead first entered the room. As far as Czolgosz's murderous motivation, she simply "does not understand it," Halstead noted, as she let out a "piercing" cry of "Why, oh, why?"

As she spoke, it dawned on the reporter that from every possible angle, an image of the Major was looking down on his wife. The photographs and engravings and oil paintings hung on the walls in her parlor, but there were also many in his former office and study, where tributes, gifts, and other presidential memorabilia had been placed.

Ida began to tell him about each picture—from what period of his life they were taken, which she liked or disliked. Pointing to an exquisite portrait that showed him as a solemn president, she became agitated. "My husband never wore a scowl like that—it is not a likeness." The reporter tried to soothe and flatter her, remarking that had she been in the room when the painting was being done, the Major would have smiled. "She did not tolerate the suggestion," he noted. Ida ended any further discussion: "He never looked like that." The passion she had in talking about old pictures led Halstead to conclude sadly that she "dwells with them in the past."

Trying to focus the conversation on the present, he remarked on how well she looked. Ida frowned and unapologetically repeated her death wish: "Oh, no, I wait—it is all that I can do—there is nothing for me now in life—I only wait and want to go. I always thought my husband would survive me, but never thought he would stay long without me. I do not know how I came to think he would soon follow me if I should go first, but I did. Why should I care to stay? What can there be for me until I go to him? There is nothing left for me but this."

Only one aspect of life could bring Ida into the present, the "love the little children have," as evidenced by the tokens that many across the country sent her with letters they dictated through their parents. As she read samples to the reporter, he noticed her face above the pages. "Over them her rare smile is seen, bright for a fleeting moment," he astutely observed.

If the rest of the nation now knew Mrs. McKinley's thoughts as her closest friends did, they also got a sense of what her daily pilgrimages to the holding vault were like. Ida, always accompanied by a nurse, asked Halstead to join her in the balmy weather, and wore a fur jacket to ward off the cold she was sensitive to. By now locals knew that what looked like a funereal milk wagon pulled by two black steeds was carrying the presidential widow.

Resting on stone riser supports, the flag-draped casket of President McKinley could be seen at close range by anyone who looked through the grated iron gate. As the heavy, enclosed, plain black carriage turned into Westlawn Cemetery and proceeded to the vault, infantry guards on duty there quickly hustled curious onlookers back "beyond the range of vision to the interior of the vault or close proximity to the carriage." The vault was guarded around the clock by forty 14th Infantry soldiers, who lived in wooden barracks erected on the cemetery grounds.[20]

Guards unlocked and swung open the heavy black gates as coachman Bederman gently guided Ida from the carriage and led her into the holding vault. Even in summer, it was damp inside the stone-floored vault. Besides the arrangements around the room and the flag-draped coffin, Ida requested that visiting delegations also bring their "colors," the flag of their organization, which she had hung on the walls. She had comfortable chairs placed there for herself and guests to sit in contemplation.

Even when accompanied by special guests, Ida went in first, directly to the head of the coffin. "In all the tragedies of the stage there is no scene more sorrowful or dramatic situation more striking and painful than Mrs. McKinley at the coffin of her husband," Halstead continued. "No persuasion can cause the mourner to cease from weeping . . . bitterly, lamentably, without restraint . . . until she summons resolution and totters away, tearful and sobbing, sinks into her carriage. . . ."

As her carriage pulled away, Ida had Bederman drive the same paths each day through the shady grove to fulfill a ritual of pausing at various plots to visit her other beloved dead—her parents, brother, in-laws, nephew, and, of course, her own little Ida and Katie. It was "the cemetery," Halstead went on, "where her heart and her interests are. . . ."

Among those who depicted Ida as being happier as the months went by, reporter George Ernest McMurphy claimed that being in the holding vault "refreshed rather than depressed" her. In reality, as she admitted a month after the one-year anniversary of the Major's death, "I am more and more lonely and unhappy every day I live." Visiting the vault had initially given Ida a reason to leave the house and offered comfort during her initial grief as the place to commune with her dead husband. Now, however, it validated her life of lifelessness. Shuttling between two places where she was never free of the Major's spirit, body, and even picture, Ida had created her own emotional vault, putting her life on permanent hold. As late as May 1904, she reported being "still in my lonely unhappy condition and in which state I expect to be as long as I live."[21]

In both the house and holding vault, Ida forbade the profusely displayed cut flowers to decay. Floral arrangements continued to be sent to remember President McKinley from personal friends and organizations, and Ida would shift them to the place of honor atop the coffin only if the blooms were fresh. At the first sign of deterioration, she had, as McMurphy reported, "fresh ones added to replace those that have faded." She also insisted that the memorial wreaths that were first placed in front of the vault on the day of the funeral remain on display exactly as they first appeared. Before any flowers in those large arrangements withered, they were replaced by identical blooms. Colorful blooms in her house, Halstead thought, "soften the pervading gloom." Every week, Caro Dawes sent greenhouse flowers she grew, and Ida reported her efforts to keep them artificially alive: "I take such care of the flowers, having the stems washed and snipped each day. At night, they are either put in a bath of water and covered or else put in a cold place." Ida liked extending the appearance of what was already dead. "It is quite interesting to me," she admitted, "to keep them as long as possible."[22]

A story about the floral exchanges between the former First Lady and her successor revealed another peculiarity she had about flowers. Frequently, the *Washington Post* discovered, "Mrs. Roosevelt sends flowers to Mrs. McKinley, and in return she gets a pathetic little note, and sometimes flowers, dry and faded, which came from the grave of the late martyred President." While readers might have perceived Ida's habit of sending dead flowers from a coffin as ghoulish, Edith Roosevelt seemed to understand that for Ida, it was comparable to relinquishing a sacred relic and thus a generous honor.

As stories of Mrs. McKinley's new life circulated, a number of remarks in newspaper stories demeaned her White House tenure. While the *Washington Post* overtly declared that Ida had "enveloped the Executive Mansion in a gloom," most papers more subtly contrasted her with the new First Lady. The *New York Press* praised Mrs. Roosevelt for heralding an era of "dash, brilliancy and smartness" at the White House, and London's snobbish *Pall Mall Gazette* declared her to be American aristocracy "by birth and not by act of Congress." Neither woman acknowledged such idiocy. Edith was moved when Ida, after reading that her son Archie was ill, knitted him slippers.[23]

In the weeks following the anniversary of the assassination, Ida found sudden reason to break out the rose-patterned Havilland china set that she and the Major had ordered in 1900, anticipating frequent entertaining in their private home. Various officials began paying her homage, perhaps in reaction to the increasing press coverage suggesting that those who had benefited through her husband had neglected her. She hosted her first large, formal luncheon on September 26 with Mark Hanna, War Secretary Root, and General and Mrs. Hastings as her guests. When she arrived at the vault with Hanna, she was surprised to see that both President Roosevelt and Jennie Hobart had sent wreaths. Hanna returned a month later with Herrick, Cortelyou, John Milburn, and other association trustees following a meeting.

Despite her husband's forthcoming gubernatorial campaign, Carolyn Herrick made a point of staying with Ida for several days at the beginning of the holiday season, knowing what it meant to the widow. "I don't intend to observe Christmas," Ida wrote her shortly after. "It will be a very sad day to me. It is little Katie's birthday."[24]

At the end of 1902, Ida realized she could no longer avoid entering another house other than her own. Mary was getting married in Saxton House. Her groom was Ralph Hartzell, the son of Ida's campaign biographer, and brother of Fred, the McKinley Memorial Association secretary.

On December 30, the presidential widow finally crossed the threshold of Saxton House again. Seated during the event, she watched Mary descend the staircase in her wedding gown, enter the parlor, and pause before the flower-bedecked fireplace where the ceremony was performed. After exchanging vows, the couple came to Ida first, and she joined the other 150 guests for the wedding supper. Her lavish gift to them was a full silver table service, but she did not hide her sadness that they would be living in Denver.[25]

On New Year's Day, Ida delivered flowers to the Major's casket, then to the graves of Katie and little Ida early in the morning. Later that afternoon, she accepted an invitation for afternoon supper at Justice Day's home. Exactly four weeks later came the most exciting moment yet in the widow's solemn house. President Roosevelt was coming to Canton to honor his predecessor at a commemorative birthday banquet sponsored by the local Republican League. The stag event was held at the Grand Opera House, with some five hundred guests, but before the event, the president laid a wreath at the holding vault and came to call on Ida at the house. It was the first time they had seen each other since the assassination. Roosevelt's speech largely reviewed those McKinley policies he was continuing, but he also praised Ida as "the woman who wept." Throughout most of Ohio, carnations were worn to honor McKinley on his birthday, and it was eventually adopted as the state flower. Ida now made certain she was never without a supply of fresh carnations in the house in case visitors came to call.[26]

While the attention stimulated Ida, she held onto her dark perspective, even in light of promising news. "Dr. Rixey did not expect to find me as well as I am," she reported to a friend following her examination by the visiting physician in April. Her physical health, however, only sharply contrasted with her emotional state. "If I only had my husband how happy I should be," she continued in her report, "for I always wanted to get well and live for him."[27]

Despite a new willingness to be more open to the outside world, Ida McKinley's insularity had resulted in a pronounced self-absorption even toward those who were most generous to her. "I was pleased to hear from you for I was wondering what had become of you," she responded to a letter from Carolyn Herrick, then added without irony, "I was very sorry to hear of the death of your brother also your father's illness." Two weeks later she wrote again, and continued as if by rote, "I have not heard from you for quite a long time. . . . I am more and more lonely and unhappy everyday I live. I miss my husband more each day. When are you coming down to see me?"[28]

Carolyn Herrick finally told Ida that, with the imminent spring weather, it was time she visited Cleveland where she had so many friends. Ida agreed. A month passed. "About making my plans to visit you in May," she wrote Carolyn, "You come and see me dear for I am so lonely and unhappy without my husband and I am much better to be home." After a purposeful absence from Canton of three months, which seemed intended to lure Ida out, Carolyn finally relented and scheduled a September visit. Before she even arrived, Ida wrote her, "I wish you could arrange to do so oftener," and even further asked, "Couldn't you arrange to bring your husband and he [son] to make me a visit?" When others stopped responding, Ida recognized why, writing a friend, "I realize that I am not company for anybody."[29]

In truth, no matter how tenaciously Ida McKinley held on to the past, life was moving on for those around her. President Roosevelt, recognizing the greater value of Cortelyou, appointed him as interior secretary. Despite the sudden responsibility of Cortelyou's Cabinet post, Ida implored him as persistently as she did her social friends to visit her. Politely but pointedly, he explained that there were "quite a variety of things to be attended to before I shall feel warranted in leaving the city." One impending change shocked her. "Have you heard the report about Mrs. Hobart's marriage to Senator Frye to take place in the early fall? I cannot believe it is true," she told a friend, less perplexed by Jennie forgoing widowhood than the groom being "so much older."[30]

Jennie Hobart's adaptability prompted Ida's first expression of curiosity about the larger world, especially about traveling in one of the newfangled machines, which began to appear frequently on the roads. "I should be rather timid," Ida admitted, "as there have been so many accidents lately with automobiles." She was stunned that Jennie's itinerary of five hundred miles was "being made in an automobile. . . . I shall be interested to learn of their experiences." Ida McKinley soon discovered that the unexpected could disrupt even her efforts to remain in a horse-drawn existence.[31]

On April 3, while being driven through Canton to the vault, her carriage passed a streetcar. One of the carriage's horses playfully lunged at the streetcar. His neck strap broke and the tongue bar dropped, dragging on the street. The horses were frightened and ran wildly while the carriage careened. Bederman, the coachman, lost control until the horse fell, and Ida was knocked about from side to side. The local *Stark County Democrat* reported that Ida was "pale with fright." It made good drama. Mrs. McKinley sent a reassuring telegram to Cortelyou: "Glad to report no serious result from yesterday's accident. Am as well as usual this morning."[32]

The very real brush with death nevertheless shook her with a more rational reconsideration of longing to join the Major anytime soon. This shift in her perspective was slow and subtle. Two months after the accident, for example, Charles Dawes wrote about a June 13 visit that he and Caro made to Ida. His description of Ida might have been made during the first weeks after the assassination: "Mrs. McKinley greeted us in tears and was depressed in spirits as is always the case with her now. . . . Mrs. McKinley refers to her husband constantly. She will not or cannot keep her mind from him, and hopes she will soon be called to follow him. Caro remained with her all day but in the morning . . . We took lunch and dinner at the McKinley house . . . the saddest into which I have ever entered. I talked of the President as best I could, for Mrs. McKinley is best satisfied when he is the subject of our conversation. . . . The day was a sad one at best."[33]

Unquestionably, Ida's depressive tendencies remained a constant. While it is entirely speculation, a recurrence of her seizures was a possible explanation for her brief but sudden withdrawal from life in June. A week after the Dawes' visit, for example, she decided at the last minute not to attend the Saxton House wedding of her second niece, Ida Barber, to Luther Day. Not only was young Ida marrying the son of her aunt's close friend Mary Elizabeth Day and her lawyer Justice Day, but as First Lady she had arranged the couple's first meeting in 1898. The reason given to the press for her absence seemed to hint at some type of sudden physical issue—that she was not "able to undergo the ordeal of a reception."[34]

Still, as the summer of 1903 continued, Ida's morbid refrain of wishing she would soon die seemed to be more a demonstration that she was now as devoted to the Major in death as he had been to her in life. Ida never remotely expressed suicidal thoughts and she became less emphatic about the release of death, even from physical pain. For example, regarding her uncle's death four months after her own accident, she said, "He suffered so much that it *would seem* [emphasis added] a mercy that he was taken." Her old wit even returned that August for the first time since her widowhood. Reporting that the Aultman mansion had been sold for what she derisively called "the Old Ladies Home," she quipped, "It may be nice for the old ladies but I do not know about their neighbors." She, of course, was a neighbor.[35]

She was also pained by the consequences of having relinquished any direct control over her finances. Abner McKinley, coping with kidney disease while on the brink of bankruptcy, appealed to Ida. She was all too eager to help. "Of course if Mrs. McKinley sees fit to make the loan with an understanding of the situation, that is her affair," Day wrote Cortelyou, "but I wrote [his law partner] Mr. Lynch that I thought we ought to advise her upon business principals." Austin Lynch did not "advise Mrs. McKinley to lend" and confidently reported that even though inclined to "make the loan for personal reasons," she "will not do even that unless advised so to do." Abner thus went bankrupt and died shortly after a painful decline. Since Lynch also controlled the Major's estate, his sisters Helen and Sarah were powerless to substantially aid Abner. The incident sowed a resentment that would affect the McKinley legacy shortly thereafter. It also led Ida, who began to mistrust her old friend Day and Lynch, to regret having followed their advice.[36]

The end of 1903 also brought news of a new family member. In Denver, on November 29, niece Mary Hartzell gave birth to a baby girl, Helen. "My sister is very proud of this first grandchild," Ida noted without a hint of the jealousy that would emerge four months later in a letter to Caro Dawes about Ida Day's first pregnancy. "My sister is having her grandchildren arrive quickly. Maybe if my little girls had lived I should be 'grandmother,' too, instead of the lonely, unhappy woman I am."[37]

On December 30, a year to the day that Mrs. McKinley had broken her vow not to enter a home other than her own, she broke another self-imposed restriction and made her first public appearance. In both instances it was her love for two nieces that overcame her mournfulness. The first had been to attend Mary Barber's wedding, and the second was to attend Mabel McKinley's musical performance in Canton. Held at Canton's Grand Opera House, the show consisted of various musical acts, with ticket sales going to a charity. Ida's decision to watch Mabel sing popular and operatic numbers was, however, more than an effort to stimulate the charity fundraising or even just familial solidarity. Abner's daughter had signed a contract to do a twenty-five-week vaudeville tour. Some two years earlier in the White House, two classical singers who had pursued theatrical careers told Mabel that "she was doing wrong in keeping such a superb operatic soprano voice as hers from the public." With her spinal deformity, however, Mabel remained dependent on her crutches for mobility and would have to appear on stage with them. She was excited at the prospect, but the McKinley family—all except Ida—had long resisted the public exposure of a relative with such an obvious disability. Mabel was still "regarded with special affection" by Ida, the New York Times noted, for refusing to let her "affliction" limit her life.[38]

Mrs. McKinley's appearance at the Grand Opera House seemed to further signal a new sense of appreciation for the city she had loved calling
home all her life. Before spring even arrived, Ida McKinley began to drive
through town in open carriages and even surreys, so she could better
observe the changing city. Without complaining about the cold, she even
wrote about the benefit of winter because it kept the streets clean and
afforded the picturesque scenes of sleighs gliding down Market Avenue.[39]

"Canton is very busy now—the new markethouse and auditorium, the
new Carnegie library, and a new large hotel now nearly completed will be
opened soon," Ida excitedly reported to Caro Dawes three months into the
new year. One particular building project in Canton would not only capture the nation's interest but keep Ida fresh in the minds of its citizens. In
June 1903, while Cortelyou had stayed as her houseguest, he broke the good
news to her that the McKinley Memorial Association had raised nearly the
full amount necessary for construction of a permanent memorial to her
husband. Soil gradation and the pouring of a concrete foundation would
soon begin.[40]

Although she declared yet again that she was "more and more unhappy
every day I live," her letter to Caro Dawes on March 28 suggested a slight
change: "Canton seems to have had an unusually long white winter, but
today is quite spring-like and I was able to drive in the open carriage. The
country roads are still muddy and rough to return on yet, so driving is not
quite so pleasant—as it will soon be. . . . Everyone seems to be preparing to spring-clean." In the coming months, her letters began to reflect a
renewed conscientiousness and finally passion for the living wonders of
the natural world. That previous fall, in a note to Cortelyou, Maud Healy
had inadvertently revealed the reason for this change in attitude: "Mrs.
McKinley does not go to the vault as often now."[41]

"Really all her life is gone," Edith Roosevelt had observed of Ida in
1901, "poor lady."[42]

Her old life was indeed gone. A new one was beginning.

⋇ 18 ⋇

The Comfort of Katie

THE YEAR 1904 MARKED a decided turning point in Ida's widowhood. It was the year she had once longed for, the one that would have been the end of the Major's second presidential term and his political commitments and the beginning of their retirement. As the months went by, she seemed progressively released from the hold of the Major's memory. She began to respond to the political scene of Canton, the natural world outside her home, and the public arena of theater and music. It was all unwittingly prompted by two little girls.

Had he lived, the Major would undoubtedly have supported the Republican presidential nomination of his vice president. Now Roosevelt, as the incumbent president already, was seeking his first full term by election to that office. Perhaps it was easier for Ida to think of Roosevelt as president once he was elected in November 1904 than to remember the reason he assumed the job in 1901. Ida McKinley followed the nomination closely. "All the news of the convention has been read to me," she wrote Carolyn. "Yes—the convention does recall the days that my dear husband was with me and I like to read the tributes to his memory."[1]

During what would have been the Major's second term, Ida had not hesitated to exert influence on President Roosevelt in seeking the appointment of past McKinley supporters or reappointment of those who had received the Major's initial political patronage. In the midst of the campaign, Ida wrote Cortelyou of her appreciation that the president had appointed her friend, a Mrs. Church, to a federal position in San Leandro, California: "and that I trust she may prove very satisfactory." Even after the widely reported 1902 firing of her cousin as supervising immigration inspector on Ellis Island (who owed his job to Ida) she pressed on.

Days before the term of Frank McCord, the federal Internal Revenue collector in the Cleveland district, ended, Ida wrote Roosevelt for his continuance, feeling loyal to the man who some two decades earlier had thrashed someone who demeaned McKinley. Roosevelt not only did as she requested, but four years later, after she asked, he reappointed McCord again and even more generously declared the man "will be permitted to serve indefinitely." She was equally successful in arranging the reappointment of Abner McKinley's mother-in-law as the Somerset, Pennsylvania, postmistress and her doctor's nephew Thomas Flattery as Wooster, Ohio's, postmaster. The Wayne County chairman opposed the latter and came to speak with the president. Ida, however, wrote to both Ohio senators, friends of hers, who were advocating for someone else, and they backed down. As she wrote Roosevelt, the Major had first appointed Flattery. She was certain that "if Mr. McKinley had lived," he would have reappointed the man and "felt confident" Roosevelt "would carry out the wishes." He did. She wasn't always successful. She convinced Roosevelt to renominate her friend Edith Gault as a postmistress, but the woman's Senate confirmation failed when the county's Republican chairman "demanded the place" for his brother with the backing of a powerful political boss no senator dared defy.

On election night, his predecessor's widow sent a "deeply touched" Roosevelt a gracious telegram of congratulations, to which he responded on November 9, "I . . . appreciate it more than any other greeting I have received." Roosevelt remained forever thoughtful of Ida, sending flowers on occasions special to her and wreaths for the Major, including one on every Memorial Day. When, en route to Washington from Chicago, he belatedly learned that the train would pass through Canton, Roosevelt dashed off a note to Ida, apologizing for not stopping to see her.[2]

Ida McKinley also took a renewed interest in the fate of the Filipino people. By mid-1902, as Aguinaldo's independent Filipino government disbanded, violence there sharply decreased. A visiting Bill Beer recorded how the former Presbyterian Sunday schoolteacher in Ida even mused that "if she had any strength left, she would go and teach the babies of the Philippines." A moment later, the idea led to sadness when her thoughts returned to her late husband, recalling how "the Major had planned to take a trip to the Orient." A sense of the changing island nation, however, came to her. That same year, Felipe Buencamino, leader of the Filipino Federal Party and, until recently, part of Aguinaldo's Cabinet, visited Washington to make the case for funding a civil government. He proceeded to visit Mrs. McKinley in Canton, along with a State Department interpreter, in order to present her with a memorial plaque calling McKinley "protector of the Filipinos." The former First Lady, Buencamino told her, could be "assured of the love of six million Filipino Christians."

On the last day of June in 1904, five members of a Philippines Committee then touring the United States also made their way to Canton. They included the editor of the Manila newspaper *La Democracie,* L. Gonzales Liquete; Iloilo mayor Juan de Leon, former Cavite province; the governor Gen. Mariano Tries; lawyer Juan Sumulong; and Cacao, Cebu, mayor Judge Vicente Noel. After visiting Justice Day's offices in the federal building to view an oil portrait of President McKinley, they proceeded with a local reception committee to visit Ida. Led into her reception room, Noel made a short ceremonial speech, which was translated for the former First Lady. After her words were translated for them, she presented each commissioner with a large cabinet-sized photograph of the Major. After a half-hour with Mrs. McKinley, they went to lay a wreath at the holding vault and get a glimpse of the rising monument. At the depot, Liquete spoke in his broken English to express delight with Ida: "Mrs. McKinley is, ah, ah, what you call it, ah, ah. You see, I can not speak your language very well. Ah, yes, ah, distinguished lady. Mrs. McKinley is the very, very distinguished lady, and I like to meet her very much. She was of much kindness to us. She gave us these pictures."[3]

The Philippines committee visit capped the end of Ida McKinley's busiest month since her widowhood. Two weeks earlier, she had houseguests for the sad occasion of Abner McKinley's funeral. Ida had just returned from a drive when she received word that her brother-in-law had been found dead earlier that day, victim of a kidney disease he had sought to combat with all possible treatments. Knowing he was to be buried in the McKinley family plot at Westlawn Cemetery, Ida immediately wired Annie and Mabel. Wanting to attend his funeral, she offered an alternative to a church service, suggesting that it be held in her home, and invited them to stay with her through the ordeal. They accepted both offers. Abner's was the second loss in four months of one of the Major's personal confidantes, Mark Hanna having died in February. Despite Abner's illness, Ida had confidently believed he would recover. Her new optimism about life was no accident, but had begun to blossom when she had the chance to meet a new family member, her first great-niece.[4]

Three weeks before Abner's death, Mary Barber Hartzell had returned to Canton for the summer from her home in Denver, bringing along her first child, a girl she called Helen, who was several months old. Almost immediately, Mary brought baby Helen for an initial introduction to McKinley House. In an instant, Ida was absorbed by her little great-niece, dropping all signs of mourning, real or feigned. Recognizing the strong attachment, either Mary or Pina saw an opportunity to draw Ida more regularly out of her house and back to Saxton House. It worked. "I have been several times to see them," Ida reported to Carolyn Herrick, "the baby is a very dear little thing."

Although her aunt had tried Mary's patience during the White House years by relentlessly imploring her to stay and assist her, the young woman had a natural generosity and began to entrust her baby with the former First Lady. An honor more meaningful than any official award or recognition could ever be, the simple act of holding the child on her lap awakened love and even a certain pride in Ida McKinley. As she happily reported, "Mary brings her up to see me quite often and she is very contented with me." Months later another child entered Ida McKinley's life, a little girl named Katie.[5]

In August, thirty-one years to the month she lost the first of her two daughters, the former First Lady's niece Ida Barber Day gave birth in Canton to a girl. Her great-aunt announced almost with reverence that that baby was "named for my mother," the child's great-grandmother, Catharine. The light of life shone into her dark world, and she seemed to welcome it. The child was nicknamed Katie.

By summer's end, Mary Hartzell had to return home to Denver with baby Helen. Although Ida Day's permanent home was in Washington, D.C., it was only when the Supreme Court was in session as her husband Luther was the assistant to his father, Justice Day. It gave Ida McKinley more time to indulge the new Katie in her life, and she was avidly interested in the baby's every new response to the world. Since Luther, Ida, and Katie Day made their Canton residence at Justice Day's home, the widow now thought nothing of leaving the Major's ghost to spend hours each day there. While always enjoying the company of William and Mary Elizabeth Day, it was their granddaughter, her great-niece, who drew her. "I often call in to see her," she told Caro Dawes. When autumn came, and Katie returned to Washington with her parents, Ida had difficulty parting with her, however briefly and temporarily. "I wish they lived here in Canton," she confessed, "the baby would be such a comfort to me."

The patience and care required of the babies drew out thoughtfulness in Ida that had begun to trump her earlier selfishness. While still scolding Cortelyou that his visit "was so short I could hardly imagine you had

THE COMFORT OF KATIE

been here," for example, she added with understanding and gratitude, "but it was very kind of you to come for I know how full your time is, with important matters."

Instead of indulging in depression as she had done during her three previous holiday seasons as a widow, this year Ida focused on drawing up long lists of friends, neighbors, family, and political associates whom she felt compelled to remember with gifts. As a new aide, Jessica Bailey, promisingly told Caro Dawes, "Mrs. McKinley is giving a little interest to the coming Holidays. . . . The Holidays are always a sad time to her, and her greatest pleasure in them is remembering those who are dear to her."[6]

Having to venture out to Saxton House and the Days household to see Helen and Katie, respectively, Ida McKinley now felt a new freedom to go elsewhere. She began to visit the homes of friends and invited them for her luncheons and card games. "I have been out among my friends more and they often come in and play euchre with me," she proudly announced later that autumn.[7]

By the fall of 1904, she was further delighting in her passion for the performing arts of opera, theatrical comedy, and classical music concerts in all of Canton's public venues. Her enjoyment was not so much in making splashy public appearances but being among the animated buzz of people who crowded into theaters, finding their seats and greeting friends. Ida admitted that she liked to arrive early at the theater and take her box seat so she could watch the rest of the audience arriving.

In September, she invited Pina to join her at a showcase performance at the Grand Theater, a fund-raising benefit for the Aultman Hospital. A month later, she was eager for the opening of the Canton Auditorium. "I expected to attend the dedicatory services but it was such a stormy night," she told Caro Dawes, while anticipating "there will be something nice going on so that we can see it together." There would, in fact, be quite a bit "going on" during the winter evenings ahead for Ida. At the end of November, she attended a performance of *Il Trovatorie* at the Grand Opera. On New Year's Day in 1905, she generously invited an entourage of some twenty people to join her in the central mezzanine boxes of the auditorium for a concert.[8]

Her guests reflected the essential egalitarianism of her character: her sister, her lawyer, her doctor's wife, the Memorial Association secretary, her maid, her nurse, an elderly neighbor, and old childhood friends. That night, the former First Lady's escort was Harold Magonigle, the memorial's chosen architect. The concert orchestra was conducted by a Signore

Creatore and included the work of *La Czarina* by composer Canne. Ida McKinley joined in the boisterous calls for an encore.[9]

All her appearances in Canton's music halls and theaters were a prelude to the massive dinner held on that year's "McKinley Day" or, as it was increasingly becoming known in Ohio, "Carnation Day," two days after the Major's January 29 birthday. It was a visually powerful scene. There were some 3,000 guests, nearly all of them men in formal black tie, in attendance at the dinner, held in the new, massive Canton Auditorium. A larger-than-life, full-length oil portrait of the Major hung high above and behind the stage. Seated at the long dais on stage was Justice Day, who presided with Vice President-Elect Charles Fairbanks, Gov. Myron Herrick, and Lt. Gov. Warren G. Harding, among other Ohioans of national stature. Above the band in an orchestra pit hung a large canopy with the impression of a sky made from a field of blue and white stars hung over the auditorium. Sitting in the upper seats of the surrounding balcony, reporter Joe Chapple took in the event and "thought how closely united was the spirit of the dead with the living. . . ."

Suddenly a murmur rippled through the crowd. "Mrs. McKinley entered the right-hand box and everybody arose," the reporter continued. With the mass of men in formal attire, the floor of the auditorium shimmered in black, and everyone focused on the small figure of Ida in her elaborate gown of black mourning, looking down from the balcony. "There was a moment of impressive silence, of reverence and respect," and then, with perfect timing, "Mrs. McKinley threw back her veil," and the entire hall erupted in applause as she smiled and nodded in acknowledgment. The reporter concluded, "to me, as to many, that was the great event of the whole evening."

It gave her some pride too. When a friend failed to comment on it after she sent a clipping, she asked "Was the paper I sent to you forwarded? It contained an interesting account of the McKinley banquet and I thought you would enjoy reading it."[10]

With Ida's emerging sense of an independent identity, she began considering what she had previously refused to entertain before. Though she turned down another friend's invitation to go to Atlantic City, she indicated that she might do so in the future. "Perhaps later on I may feel differently and can then do as my dear friends wish," she confessed to Carolyn Herrick. Despite her increasing vibrancy, Ida McKinley had not entirely lost her sense of missing the Major, further confessing, "[J]ust now I dread the thought of going about without my Precious." Then, however, she continued with the stunning admission, "I was so dependent upon him for everything—as you know."[11]

While no friend would have wished Ida to suffer the irreparable loss she did, several who had known the McKinleys for many years did venture to observe that without the Major's control of her every waking moment, Ida developed into a more rounded person. "No one would have said that she could have lived with so much courage through the lonely years that followed," Julia Foraker said of Ida after a visit. "She who had been shielded from every sort of responsibility and weariness now recognized reality. . . ." Gretchen Groetzinger, a young Canton woman who had been calling on Ida for many years, was unsentimentally blunt about it, remarking that "McKinley babied Mrs. McKinley too much. She was better after he went."[12]

Despite bitter cold and heavy snow that winter, Ida refused to curtail her engagement in the larger world. Although her nurses prevented her wish to experience a rare Canton blizzard by venturing out in the 14 degrees below zero temperature, she nevertheless announced, "if it gets warmer this evening I may attend a concert in the new Auditorium." A stronger motivation kept Ida in Canton that winter, however, beyond waiting for the Major's ghost to appear.

Even though she much preferred warm weather, she resisted the lure of balmy Florida as reported in letters from friends or tropical Puerto Rico, described by Josiah Hartzell as "the choicest of the possessions that came to our country as the result of the Spanish war." Nothing was more important to Ida McKinley now than the imminent return from Washington of six-month-old Katie. During their lengthy winter stay in Canton, Ida Day brought the child for frequent visits with great-aunt Ida. "I wish you could see what a dear bright little child this baby is," Ida bragged to Caro Dawes about Katie. She added, with favoritism, "she is more lively than her cousin Helen in Denver."[13]

As the spring came, and the soil warmed, excavation for the McKinley memorial soon began and continued throughout the summer months. Curious about its progress, Ida, joined by frequent houseguests like Edith Gault, often made trips to the site. The long visit of her former teacher brought out many of Ida's fellow Brooke Hall classmates, and Ida found herself busily entertaining "quite a reunion" for the "old scholars" as she wryly called them.

In October, she grew excited by the confirmation that both Vice President Fairbanks and Governor Herrick were coming to Canton for the annual meeting of the memorial's executive committee. They would be joined by their wives, her friends Cornelia Fairbanks and Carolyn Herrick. Along with Caro Dawes, who was also joining her husband for the meeting,

Ida announced she would host her first full-fledged reception in the house. As each guest came to her in the receiving line, she presented them with a carnation. As the Major's favorite flower, the carnation went from being a symbol of his memory to Ohio's state flower. A month later, seated and veiled, Ida attended the ceremony of laying the memorial cornerstone.[14]

Two weeks later she sailed into the Canton Auditorium to hear a Madame Cabro in concert. The onset of the holiday season, however, still had its depressing effect on her spirits. "Christmas is a very sad day to me. Little Katie was born on Christmas day and if she had lived would be thirty-four. What a comfort she would have been to me now," she admitted to Caro Dawes. "I have not the heart to do anything during this season."[15]

If the end of each year still left Ida McKinley vulnerable to depression, the coming of spring now gave her hope. In her later years of widow-hood, the former First Lady took her knitting and reading and worked on the front porch, amused by the "continual stream of sightseers passing and re-passing the house" who stole a peek at her. The more she was outdoors, the less she wished to be in the house. While the physical stamina of her early years could never be restored, she found herself happier in the fresh air and sunshine, and there were no reports of the light-prompting seizures. "I have been obliged to forego my usual drives and afternoon walks on the veranda," she complained during a week of heavy rain. "It is very depress-ing to have so much dull weather and be obliged to stay indoors. . . ." The remark indicated a great change from the few years earlier when she could not feel comfortable anywhere except inside the house.[16]

Ida took pride in her garden. Although the private property was sur-rounded by an iron gate, she noted, "Strangers went right in to admire the hyacinth beds—they have never been so perfect." In the two massive raised urns that flanked the entry gate, Ida wanted red geraniums planted. The flowers became something of a trademark over time. The spring of 1906 seemed especially to stir her senses and love of the outdoors. "Can-ton is looking beautiful—the fruit trees are in blossom. I do not remem-ber when the trees and grass looked so fresh and pretty."

Carriage rides continued to be her primary daily excursion outdoors. Through the spring and summer of 1906, they now always included her inspection of the rising memorial. "It is so surprising how quickly it is being erected," she remarked, "Each time I go its appearance has changed." Although she resumed some visits to the holding vault, her outlet for honoring the Major's memory had shifted to the monument. After the Memorial Association's October 14 meeting, the trustees called on Ida with the final landscaping plans and a dedication date set for the end of September 1907. She declared that she would live to witness the event.[17]

Although she agreed to fund the installation of four stained-glass windows to honor the Major in his Methodist church, Ida McKinley remained true to form and never entered the church to see them. Yet nothing now prevented the president's widow from attending public concerts and opera, from *La Bohème* in April to the Canton Musical Festival in May, and from Rossini and Mozart arias in November to a Pittsburgh Orchestra concert in December. "Going to the theater occasionally takes my mind off my troubles for a little while," she wrote an old friend on March 12, 1906.[18]

That year, Christmas proved to be somewhat extraordinary. The festivities were modest at best, but the spirit of the season may have been the greatest Ida McKinley had experienced since the three consecutive ones she shared with the Major and Katie in the early 1870s. She presented over thirty gifts to all the individual members of the McKinley and Barber clans, numerous neighbors, friends, and her entire household staff. She sent most of her nieces and nephews gifts of modest sums of money, but sensitive to the fact that the Major's niece Ida in San Francisco was struggling financially, she sent her the large amount of $150.

The joy that the now two-and-half-year-old Katie brought her great-aunt increased twofold with the seasonal arrival of Mary and her three-year-old Helen from Denver. It prompted Ida McKinley to hold the first party in the house since her own daughter Katie had celebrated her third and final birthday on the holiday, thirty-three years earlier. "We had a small Christmas tree for the little folk on Christmas morning, which was a source of pleasure to them and to Mrs. McKinley as well," her nurse Jessie Bailey reported to Caro Dawes. "Another source of pleasure is a phonograph sent by Mrs. Hobart, a very fine one. One little girl, looking into the horn, wanted to know of the singer, 'if they didn't come out.'" The holiday passed, Bailey further noted, "as pleasantly as could be expected with her beloved husband absent."[19]

Despite her first enjoyable Christmas among children in many years, Ida was privately troubled. In December, she wanted to inspect some of her jewelry, which had been placed in the Canton Central Savings Bank years earlier and asked her Canton attorney and estate trustee Austin Lynch to retrieve it. She, however, "in various ways has been dissuaded," nurse Jessie Bailey wrote confidentially to Cortelyou. After several days, Ida "demanded them of Mr. Lynch." He refused on the premise that "keeping things of so great value in her home, explaining that a night watchman would be necessary, and it would be at her own expense." Behind Mrs. McKinley's back, Lynch then asked Cortelyou to use his "influence against their removal." In the midst of getting out her Christmas presents, Ida momentarily put the issue aside.[20]

Ida McKinley was more publicly engaged in early 1907 with activities that had nothing to do with her late husband or even her family members than at any other point in her widowhood. She invited young vaudeville performer Antonio Auremma to visit her at home after seeing one of his performances. When a relatively new friend, Salvation Army leader Evangeline Booth, was in Canton for the April 9 dedication of the Salvation Army's local headquarters, Ida had her stay as a houseguest. "One evening last week I attended the Rosenthal piano recital," she reported in early February, "Next Wednesday evening [for] the Ben Great Company play 'The Merchant of Venice' I am engaging a box . . . I go out as much as I can. . . ."

Such activities were noteworthy, however, in relation to the annual celebration of the Major's birthday. That year, a fund-raising performance for the memorial had included local schoolchildren in a tableau of a human flag, the sort of event that traditionally appealed to Ida. "The papers stated that I attended the McKinley Birthday concert in the Auditorium," Ida confided to Cortelyou, "but I remained quietly at home with Miss Helen and a few friends." Time with her three-year-old Denver great-niece had become more important for Ida McKinley than remembering the Major.

Despite her belated embracing of life, an instinctive impulse drove Ida McKinley to have her "business affairs" in order, even after she recovered quickly from an influenza bout. She bluntly wrote Cortelyou in a February letter: "I am anxious to have the things up from the bank and to have you assist me in making my will. The illness that I had some weeks ago has made me think it is high time for me to provide for my friends." A week earlier she had written him that she felt "far from well." She made no suggestion, however, of what was wrong. "Dr. Portman comes in to see me almost everyday. Each day, I walk a little and today I started off alone again so you may know I am stronger. I feel that you know my affairs better than anyone and I am most anxious to consult with you." She asserted that during her twice-daily drives, even in winter, she would always "use the open carriage." Whatever it was that drove her to execute her will, it was certainly not her mood. In the same time period she reported that she found that winter's bitter cold and heavy snow to be "bright and cheerful." There was no indication of seizures at all or the stress that traditionally had provoked them. In the same letter, she admitted, "I can walk more easily." She made reference for the first time, however, to a serious stiffness in her hands, suggesting that she had recently experienced difficulty getting a firm grasp on her knitting needles: "I am trying to crochet but I am not making progress. I miss my work so much. It helped to pass the time and take my mind from my sorrow."[21]

Unfortunately, just then, Cortelyou was preparing to transition on March 4 from his Cabinet post of postmaster general into that of treasury secretary and was completely inundated with work. Something else, however, seemed to also be at work. Ida had again implored her lawyer Austin Lynch to bring her safety deposit boxes to her and help draw up her new will. He agreed to do so, but as she wrote Cortelyou on March 2, "I have not seen nor heard from him since." Unbeknownst to her, a month earlier, Cortelyou shared one of her letters with Justice Day (his fellow trustee of her estate) and concluded that "it did not seem to me Mrs. McKinley was in proper condition to make a will. . . ." Whether he meant her state of mind is uncertain. On March 13, Ida dictated another letter to Cortelyou, and while her frustration and anxiety were evident, she was also somewhat cunning in calling on his declared loyalty to the Major's memory:

I thought of sending you a telegram this morning but remembered that you must be very busy getting the business of your new office in order, and that it is more likely than not you could not leave Washington at this time to come to Canton and talk with me about my affairs. I feel that my husband made a confident [sic] of you, and you know better than anyone just what I possess. Mr. Lynch brought up the boxes from the bank but it did not correspond (the contents) with the list I have. There must be another box somewhere and I would like to find it. I have not any confidence in the people about here and I would like you to advise me, as I wish to have my will made. You know what a dear good man my husband was, and that he never refused his wife anything. I have not been well for several days and have been in bed. . . . I have grip but not badly. I feel as though I ought to begin to put my affairs in order and am anxious to know where everything is.

Later that same day, Maud Healy took it upon herself to give Cortelyou "the lay of the land clearly," stating that "the patient is much excited" that Lynch failed to bring her what she knew was a box of valuable jewelry at the bank. Ida had then insisted that all of her bank boxes be "brought up to the house and left here." Healy then revealed that there was a small conspiracy among herself, Lynch, and—by acquiescence—Day and Cortelyou to prevent Mrs. McKinley from having access to her jewels since she did not securely store those she already had at home. She continued, "I believe it would be as safe as the brown bag, only it would be a little more anxiety for the nurses—especially when the contents were being shown to visitors, sometimes strangers."[22]

Indeed, Ida McKinley may have been naive in her trust of neighbors and visitors to whom she casually disclosed what valuables she kept at home. Certainly this concerned those who were charged with protecting her interests. That the jewelry was hers to do with as she pleased may have been less of the problem, however, than that an entirely competent Ida had quietly decided to disperse some of it. There was a hint of this in her letter two days later to Caro Dawes in which she declared that "It would give me great pleasure to know when your birthday comes for I have a few interesting, little gifts for my friends."[23]

Whatever she suspected might be going on behind her back by those she trusted, Ida remained absolutely determined to have her new will drawn up. Lynch continued to forestall her. On March 20, she wired Cortelyou, "Am anxious to hear from you." Just hours later, she sent him a second, more explicit telegram: "Would like to make my will but have nobody I can consult in Canton." He received a third one from the household, this time from Maud Healy, who now asked him, "Please write to her."[24]

Strangely, Cortelyou did not respond. Ida did not relent. Three days later she dictated him a strident letter. Not only did she make another admission that the Major's overprotectiveness had disabled her in its own way, but she also now openly disclosed her intention to give away valuable items: "I have been expecting a letter from you almost daily. I am anxious to have my will made and my affairs in general settled up. I have been quite ill with grip. The doctor says I did not have it badly, but I have never felt more uncomfortable and even now that I am better, the cough remains. . . . I wish you were near so that you could advise me in making a just distribution of my personal belongings among my friends. My husband was so attentive and thoughtful that I find it doubly hard to take care of such matters for myself."[25]

Cortelyou was almost certainly relying on the direction of either Ida's lawyer or even perhaps her sister, with whom he had an independent correspondence. There had never been any rift between the two sisters, nor was there one now. Pina, however, saw situations in practical terms. She had sacrificed hours and days of her life to care for Ida and leaned on her daughters to do likewise. The loss of inheritance that her children sustained when the uninsured Saxton Block building was destroyed was impossible to compensate for no matter how much Pina and Marsh would be able to leave them. Finally, many of the valuable jewelry pieces of Ida McKinley's collection were family heirlooms, more appropriately passed to the Barbers than to Ida's friends. Pina not only knew that she would be the primary inheritor of Ida's estate but also how obstinate her sister could often be when it came to following practicable advice. Thus, it is possible that, after consulting Pina, Cortelyou decided to passively discourage Mrs. McKinley from giving away her valuables. "My sister is having a luncheon tomorrow. I shall not attend," Ida flatly noted to Caro Dawes in a letter that was written just one day before her urgent one to Cortelyou. Her excuse that "so many people are expected and it tires me" seemed less likely given her avid attendance at the crowded Canton theaters.[26]

When it came to keeping a filter between her and the public, however, Cortelyou's support of Ida never failed. Whenever she received correspondence of an official nature or with some connection to the McKinley Administration, Ida sent it to him to handle. "Every day I receive dozens of requests for donations for churches, schools, etc. It is very annoying," she wrote him after sending an especially irritating one. "I had not acknowledged the letter I forwarded to you and shall not do so." Otherwise, she decided how to respond to the many individuals and charities that still sought her support. "The begging letters are not so numerous but it would seem as though the world was made up of struggling churches," she wrote at the end of April 1907. One such letter, however, caught Ida's attention and appealed to her heart:

> Kind Madam. I write you to ask a favor of you. I have been sick in the hospital for some time and am sick yet. I want you to help me. I done all I could for your husband in trying to save his life and if I had of been successful I know he would of place me for my efforts a word from you to Mr. Cortelyou is all I need. Will you for God's sake say that word. You don't know the hearts you will make glad. I don't ask for a clerkship but anything he will give me if he choses from driving a wagon to a place in the U.S. capital if you will do this for me in remembrance of your dear husband I will always pray to our heavenly father to spear [sic] your life and have mercy on you in great distress. I am your humble servant. . . .[27]

In the days immediately after McKinley's shooting, James Benjamin Parker was hailed as a hero in newspapers across the country and was an especial point of pride for African Americans. Despite having recently been laid off as a restaurant worker at the Pan-American Exposition, he steadfastly refused to sell the buttons off his coat as souvenirs for the high prices being offered, believing it would exploit the tragedy. During Czolgosz's trial, Parker was prevented from testifying. His heroic act of preventing a third bullet from hitting McKinley, which would have been fatal, would have only made the Secret Service far more culpable for the president's death in the public's view. At the end of the trial, one agent even stated that no agents had seen Parker do what he claimed he did. What happened to him in the ensuing years was unknown, but by 1906 he had ended up in Washington, D.C., indigent, hospitalized, and lucky to have found a local attorney who urged him to write Ida McKinley.

Ida McKinley did not ignore Parker. She sent along to Cortelyou the letter "from J. B. Parker, the negro who evidently did his best to aid my precious husband when he was in such need and if you advise me as to the best way in helping him, I will be very much obliged." The former First Lady's interest in Parker, in fact, had an enormous effect on his life. Almost certainly through Cortelyou's power and influence, perhaps even President Roosevelt's, Parker was not only given permanent employment at the U.S. Capitol Building as a congressional messenger but also, remarkably, a house in Washington. It was an unknown but perhaps the noblest act of Ida McKinley's years alone.[28]

Whatever may have transpired between Ida and Lynch, whatever influence, if any, that Pina had with Cortelyou in preventing Ida from drawing up a new will, the matter seemed to have been resolved or dropped within the following week. In her April 1 letter to Cortelyou, Ida thanked him for Easter flowers he had sent, and reported that she spent the holiday "with Mrs. Barber at the old home." She made no further mention of a new will to him. Three weeks later, Ida reported to Caro Dawes that "I am amusing myself these dull days, looking through my trunks at things that have been put away for years and which I shall never use again. I did not suppose I had so many things."

Ida was eager for summer. "Very soon I shall have seeds planted and hope to have quite a nice garden. In a week or two the tulips will be up," she wrote at the end of March. "I have three large beds of beautiful colors, which give me much pleasure. I love the flowers and trees."

She had the same level of enthusiasm about the landscaping of the memorial grounds. Work began in February, and some forty maples and elms were transplanted there. Cedars, spruce evergreens, poplars, rhododendrons, privet hedges, and grass sod were still being planted as she regularly drove by to watch the progress. She assured friends and family that she would live to see the September memorial dedication.

At the same time, Ida seemed at peace with what was left undone in her life. Though it was time for a full spring cleaning of the house, she did not want to be bothered with it this year, declaring in an April 27 letter to Caro Dawes that "my part of the house will have to remain as it is for sometime." If anyone wished to have a pair of her famous slippers, she urged them to tell her soon. "My supply has almost run out," she reflected of her cherished handiwork, "and I cannot make them now." Almost in passing, she mentioned that her persistent "cough is very troublesome." Yet, she looked ahead with hope for the near future when Ida Day, with little Katie, now two and a half years old, "would soon be at home in Canton again."[29]

Five days after writing the letter, Ida visited the Major in the holding vault. It proved to be her last time. The next day, her cough became bronchitis, and she again contracted influenza. The condition worsened over the next two and a half weeks. On May 20, she suffered a stroke while out driving. She remained weak, but was able to speak. Three days later she fell into semiconsciousness.

Rixey, Cortelyou, Justice Day, and her niece Ida Day came from Washington, and sister-in-law Sarah Duncan from Cleveland. Pina and Marsh were in constant vigil with the four rotating nurses. Schoolchildren offered prayer vigils for her. While ambivalent toward religion, Ida did believe in a God. Evangeline Booth wired, urging her to rely on that belief: "His face will light your way as the waters rise. His everlasting arms uphold you." Booth added her "deepest appreciation of all that you have been to my work." Occasionally reviving, Ida asked that no effort be made to keep her alive, repeating, "Why should I linger?" The *Washington Post* revealed, however, that, "Mrs. McKinley never knew of the efforts made for days to prolong her life." Toward the end, she experienced hallucinations. "Sometimes she imagines that she sees 'the Major,'" a friend told the *New York Times*, "and stretches out her hands to grasp his. . . ."

Eleven days before her sixtieth birthday, Ida McKinley died on May 26, 1907. The cause of death was listed as "brain tumor," once believed to be a cause of epilepsy, but it is a guess at best as there was no autopsy. Rixey offered a poetic statement about her last moments: "She died as a child going to sleep. . . . as she breathed the last few breaths of this life, the expression on her face changed, the lines of pain and sorrow seemed to leave it, and she looked as she must have appeared in her girlhood, before the physical affliction from which she suffered for thirty years came to her in her early motherhood."[30]

After consulting with Pina, Cortelyou announced that there would be a private funeral three days later, on Wednesday. Consistent with her lifetime avoidance of attending church, it was decided to conduct her funeral not in the Methodist church where the Major's service had been held, but rather in their home. His minister, Reverend Buxton, with whom she had remained on close terms, would conduct the brief service. The four songs *Beautiful Isle of Somewhere, Rest Thy Angel, Nearer My God to Thee,* and *Lead Kindly Light* were sung, exactly as they had been for the Major.

On the day of the funeral, flags were flown at half-mast. Schools and other public buildings were closed. Many businesses ceased activity as well. A single lavender mourning ribbon was hung on the front door of McKinley House. When the public learned there would be only a private farewell, there were immediate expressions of regret that the city she loved most would be denied a chance to pay final tribute to her. Arrangements were changed. For several hours the day before the funeral, some eight thousand people filed into the house through the front porch, past the coffin, which lay in the library on the spot where the Major's had been placed almost six years earlier. A reporter noted a large number of older Canton women who had known her since childhood.

After lunch at the Day residence, President Roosevelt and Vice President Fairbanks led the official delegation to the McKinley home for the short service, while the streets remained jammed with curious onlookers. Sitting there, Roosevelt reflected his thoughts in a letter to his son Kermit: "They have left no children, and her death seemed to me like the final drawing of the curtain." The coffin was placed next to the Major's in the holding vault, followed by final prayers. In Akron before departing the region, Roosevelt recalled Ida by shifting the focus to the Major, remarking, "it was in his own home, perhaps, that in the devotion to the loving woman we have just buried, he gave the best example to us all." An *Outlook Magazine* editorial echoed this: "[T]he people of the country saw in the White House a family life in accord with the highest American ideals of purity and chivalrous devotion."

Five days later, a memorial service was held for Ida at the Methodist church, where her picture was placed near the altar. Buxton eulogized her with a reversal of what Roosevelt had emphasized. "Her faith inspired him, her confidence assured him, her very weakness strengthened him," he pointed out.[31]

Meanwhile, newspapers largely gave Americans the obituary of Ida McKinley's public persona, not a look at her real life. As if the first active half of her tenure as First Lady had never occurred, the *Washington Post*, for example, asserted that "Mrs. McKinley was in very poor health, and did not take a very active part in the social life of the Capital." The harshest assessment came from McKinley biographer Robert Porter, on the front page of the *Repository*, explaining away her existence as inevitably that of women who face tragedy: "When the average woman is bereft of her children and of her strength, is exiled from society, and compelled to deny herself all those little pleasures that sweeten life, she is apt to degenerate into an indolent and selfish invalid, whose existence is as burdensome to others as to herself." The independent spirit of Miss Saxton was largely ignored. Only the obscure publication, *The Phrenological Journal and Science of Health,* editorialized about her diligent work in the bank, pointing out that "This example should be a lesson to every other girl in the country."[32]

Ida McKinley, who never worried about what strangers thought about her or little else for that matter, cared only for the company of the Major, preferably in Canton. Ten days after the McKinley memorial's dedication on September 30, the couple's caskets were brought there from the holding vault, preserved "from the violation of the earth," as a Springfield Metallic Casket advertisement bragged. Placed in a massive dark-green granite sarcophagus raised on a maroon granite base above eye level, they repose beneath the center of the rotunda, Katie and Little Ida soon at rest near them. The grief of separation was over. Her family of four was on the same side of existence until the end of time.

At superficial glance, it appears as if Ida and the Major were placed in one large, carved green sarcophagus. Closer observation, however, reveals that they lie in separate chambers in one resting place. Perpetually together, they remain as distinctly individual as they had been in life.[33]

Notes

Abbreviations

CB, Charles Bawsel

CBPL, Charles Bawsel manuscript, McKinley Presidential Library

CD, Caro Dawes

CH, Carolyn Herrick

CR, Canton Repository

DEHS, Dawes Family Papers, Evanston Historical Society

EHPL, Edward Thornton Heald manuscript, McKinley Presidential Library

GC, George B. Cortelyou

GCLC, George B. Cortelyou Papers, Library of Congress

HWRH, Herrick Family Papers, Western Reserve Historical Society

ISM, Ida Saxton McKinley

LC, Library of Congress

LW, Leonard Wood

LWLC, Leonard Wood Papers, Library of Congress

MALC, William McKinley-Addendum Papers, Library of Congress

NYT, New York Times

RH, Rutherford B. Hayes

RHPC, Rutherford B. Hayes Presidential Center

TR, Theodore Roosevelt

WM, William McKinley

WMPL, William McKinley Presidential Library

WP, Washington Post

WRH, Western Reserve Historical Society

The Red Room, 1899

Quotations are from the letter written by Pauline Robinson to Anna Foster Robinson, May 8, 1899, Series II: Anna Foster Robinson, Robinson Family Papers, MS 520, MS 2309, New York Historical Society.

1. A Daughter Studies

1. John Denny Raridan, "125 Years of Yesterday," *CR*, Mar. 31, 1940. The grandparents of Ida Saxton McKinley (ISM) were John Saxton, married to Margaret Laird, and George Dewalt, married to Christiana Harter. John Saxton was born September 28, 1792, and served on garrison duty at Black Rock, N.Y., during the War of 1812. His first job was in his father's Huntingdon, Pa., nail factory, the first of its kind in that colony. The October 24, 1839, *United States Gazette* announced that Saxton's brother Joseph had become the first American to make a camera and then produce a photograph. His father (ISM's great-grandfather) James Saxton was born in Fredericktown, Md., in 1768, and married Hannah Ashbaugh (ISM's great-grandmother). ISM's great-great-grandfather George Saxton was an English immigrant (about 1748), and his wife Sarah Havelon was an Irish Quaker immigrant (www.harlanfamily.com). ISM's great-great-great grandfather was German immigrant Johanne Heinrich Echbach (born 1706). ISM's paternal grandmother Margaret Laird was of Scottish ancestry. Hart, *A Genealogy*, 159; the Medill family: Perrin, *History of Stark County*, 351; Horace Greeley: Cain, "Ida McKinley," 168; John Saxton's faith: Perrin, *History of Stark County*, 348–49; Morgan, *William McKinley*, 33.

2. James Saxton's background: Danner, *Old Landmarks of Canton and Stark County*, 1464; Wright, *Representative Citizens*, 16–17. James Saxton opened a hardware business on East Tuscarawas Street, which he sold in 1858 to his brother Joe and a partner. Joe Saxton (ISM's uncle) married Harriet Danner and had five children. "Some Reminiscences," *Wyandott Republican*, Sept. 7, 1899, clipping, WMPL.

3. Dewalt family history: Perrin, *History of Stark County*, 308–9, 359; Cain, "Ida McKinley," 167. George Dewalt used his daughter's legal name of "Catharine" in his will; she is so listed in her marriage record; George Dewalt's will, no. 14, dated June 24, 1848, Marriage Record, "B," 268, Stark County Probate Office. However, on her gravestone, Ida McKinley's mother was identified as Kate, the name she was called throughout her adult life. ISM's great-great-grandfather Philip Dewalt Sr. emigrated from Germany with his pregnant wife in 1761; he lived to be 105 years old, and she to 100 years old; both are buried in Canton's first cemetery, on Plum Street. The tavern of Philip Dewalt Jr. and his wife Eva (ISM's great-grandparents) stood at Tuscarawas and Cleveland streets; George Dewalt (ISM's grandfather) was the third of their seven children. Kate Dewalt's brother John (ISM's uncle), born in

1823, had no children; her sister Harriet (ISM's aunt), born in 1831, died unmarried at age twenty. Kate Dewalt's obituary: Mar. 14, 1873, *CR;* family Bible, Belden Box 12, WMPL; Charles D. Kreider, Linden Hall, principal, to ISM: Dec. 4, 1900, Oct. 2007 catalogue of Heritage Auction Galleries sale.

4. *Canton City Directory,* 1859–1860, WMPL. At the time of her death, *CR* claimed that ISM was born in the upper level of a two-story brick building at 226 South Market Avenue, later the headquarters of the Japanese Tea Company. Thirty-six years later, however, it claimed she was born at Saxton House. "Sketch of the Eventful Life of Mrs. McKinley," May 27, 1907, *CR,* and "The Girl of His Choice," Jan. 24, 1943, *CR.* Obituary of ISM's sister Mary Barber (n.d., n.p.) states her birth as being in a house adjacent to Saxton House (identifiable in period photographs), suggesting that ISM was also born there, as affirmed in Hartzell, *Sketch of the Life,* 8, 12. Whiting hosted his friends, suffrage leaders Elizabeth Cady Stanton and Lucretia Mott, in his home, which was also an Underground Railroad way station. Grace Whiting Huntington to Mr. H. T. O. Blue, Mar. 29, 1955: WMPL; "Great Names in Canton History: No. 13—Dr. Lorenzo M. Whiting," n.d., n.p.: WMPL; a family photo identified her as "Ida Dewalt Saxton": WMPL; family closeness: Olcott, *The Life of William McKinley,* 1:71.

5. Canton public school education: Perrin, *History of Stark County,* 356–58; EHPL, 2:10; first Union School: *McKinleyite* yearbook, 1922, 15–16; Cowles was born in Bristol, Conn., in 1810, but moved to Ohio a year later. In 1834, she helped found the Young Ladies Society for Intellectual Improvement in Austinburg, Ohio. Her nephew Edwin helped establish Ohio's Republican Party. In 1838, she enrolled in Oberlin College's "Ladies' Course." Her first teaching job was in Portsmouth, Ohio; by 1848 she was principal of girls at Massillon's public school. While in Massillon, she wrote for the *Anti-Slavery Bugle* and racially integrated her Sunday school classes. She created the Ashtabula County Female Anti-Slavery Society in 1837. By 1851 she had helped found the Ohio Women's Rights Association for the "extension of human freedoms . . . without respect to sex, color, or other conditions." At the 1851 Women's Rights Convention in Akron, Cowles called for gender pay equity. Melder, 393–94; Royster, *Profiles of Ohio Women,* 182; Geary, *Balanced in the Wind,* 84–86.

6. ISM as a student: Hartzell, *Sketch of the Life,* 15; war work: Andrews, *One of the People,* 58; "Life Sketch of the Late Mrs. Ida McKinley," *Stark County Democrat,* May 28, 1907; Kate Dewalt's war work: EHPL, 2: 9; James Saxton to Betsy M. Cowles, Mar. 14, 1862, Correspondence, 1862, no. 256, Cowles Papers, Department of Special Collections and Archives, Kent State Univ. Library; Delhi Academy: Geary, *Balanced in the Wind,* 901; Cleveland Female Seminary: *J. H. Williston & Co.'s Directory of the City of Cleveland,* 259–60; *Baker's Cleveland City Directory,* 103; Harriet Sherman's recollections: undated (circa 1899), Michigan City [Ind.] *News-Dispatch* article, among research compiled by Michigan City historian Edna Kitchell for "Moments to Remember," Indiana Room, Michigan City Public Library, Ind.; *Genealogy: Our Heritage.* See Michigan City, Indiana Public Library online Web site.

7. "Was Famous in Its Day: Brooke Hall Seminary, Where Mrs. McKinley Went to School," *Washington Evening Star,* Jan. 19, 1898; Ashmead, *History of Delaware County,* 601. Brooke Hall was demolished in 1959. Heald's chronological sequence of ISM's attendance at Brooke Hall, Sanford School, and Delhi Academy is disproven by the 1862 Saxton note to Cowles, the 1863 naming of the Cleveland School as "Sanford School," the recollection of ISM at Sanford School during Lincoln's 1865 assassination, ISM's photo with identification as "ca. 1865, Philadelphia," and her presence at a Canton fund-raising event in February 1868. EHPL, 2: 9; ISM's personality at Brooke Hall "left her . . .": Call, "A Love Story," 18.

2. The Well-Employed Belle

1. Photo, WMPL; "Every man . . .": the Hallmark interview comprises an entire chapter in Halstead, *1896,* 324.

2. Saxton on ISM's suitors: Cain, "Ida McKinley," 170; EHPL, 2: 10; information on John Wright is from his Sept. 9, 1869, *CR* obituary; Saxton's business endeavors and bank: Wright, *Representative Citizens,* 16–17; *CR,* June 21, 1854, July 19, 1854.

3. "Did not believe . . .": Cass, "Mrs. William McKinley," 4; "the position of assistant . . . with practical . . .": Russell, *The Lives of William McKinley and Garret A. Hobart,* 138; ISM's employment, quoting her father on single women working: Call, "A Love Story," 18, and B. W. Smith, *The Romances of the Presidents,* 322; "little Latin": Hallmark interview; "never ceased": Russell, *The Lives of William McKinley and Garret A. Hobart,* 138.

4. "New woman," *Journal of Phrenology,* ISM's obituary; ISM meeting WM: Call, "A Love Story," 16; Hartzell, *Sketch of the Life,* 15; EHPL, 2: 15; social events: *CR,* Oct. 7, 14, and 16 1868; WM's background: Olcott, *The Life of William McKinley,* 1: 36; "love at": EHPL, 2: 12–13; Wright's employment, obituary: *CR,* Sept. 9, 1869.

5. Trip overview: EHPL, 2: 11–12; Pina Barber's diary, Aug. 10, 1869, WMPL; McKinley, Belden, and Barber, *Grand Tour of Ida Saxton McKinley and Sister Mary Saxton Barber, 1869?* 1–5, 8, 24, 99, 112, 119, 121, 129, 203, 209–11, 223–25, 233, 319, 363; arrival, June 13, 1869; Pina Saxton to Saxton parents: 3, 11, July 12, 1869, 79; ISM to Saxtons: July 13, 1869, 84, 93, 94; July 26, 1869, 119; ISM to Saxton: July 26, 1869, 127–28; ISM to the Saxtons: July 29, 1869, 137–38; ISM to the Saxtons: July 29, 1869, 134–35; ISM to the Saxtons: July 29, 1869, 136, 139; ISM to Saxton parents: Oct. 3, 1869, 325; ISM to the Saxtons: Aug. 6, 1869, 150D, 150H; ISM to Saxton parents: Oct. 3, 1869, 325, 328.

6. Blarney Castle, Pina Saxton to the Saxtons, Aug. 19, 1869: McKinley, Belden, and Barber, 192, and ISM to the Saxtons, Aug. 21, 1869, 198; rode horse: ISM to Saxton parents, Oct. 3, 1869, 322; Scotland: ISM to the Saxtons, June 22, 1869, 30; crown: ISM to the Saxtons, June 28, 1869, 57; ears pierced: Pina Barber's diary, Aug. 10, 1869; citations on times they drank wine: Pina Saxton to the Saxtons, June 27,

1869, 45; ISM to the Saxtons: July 26, 1869, 129; ISM to the Saxtons: July 29, 1869, 138; Pina Saxton to the Saxtons: Aug. 8, 1869, 157; ISM to the Saxtons: Aug. 10, 1869, 166; ISM to Saxton parents: Sept. 16, 1869, 284; tea, caffeine habit ("I am sure to have the headache if I do not take tea for breakfast"): ISM to Saxton parents, Oct. 22, 1869, 396; opera, gambling, "seems bad . . .": Pina Saxton to the Saxtons, Aug. 19, 1869, 192; and ISM to the Saxtons: Aug. 21, 1869, 198; Pina Saxton to the Saxtons: Aug. 21, 1869, 200; male friends: ISM to the Saxtons, July 13, 1869, 85; Alexander's reaction to ISM: Leech, *In the Days of McKinley,* 14–16; ISM to the Saxtons, Aug. 6, 1869, 150E; ISM to the Saxtons, Aug. 15, 1869, 179; James Webb, ask McKinley: ISM to the Saxtons, Aug. 21, 1869, 200; ISM inquires about Wright: Aug. 15, 1869; ISM to Kate Saxton, 181. ISM also made one reference to Cantonians "Mr. Osborne" and "Mr. Kuhn," who sent her *CR:* ISM to the Saxtons, June 20, 1869, 24 and Aug. 15, 1869, 180; "crucifixes on each side of the harbor," antipathy toward Catholicism, "were out to church this morning": ISM to Saxton, July 26, 1869, 127–28; ISM to the Saxtons, July 29, 1869, 137–38; meeting Pope: ISM to the Saxtons, Oct. 30, 1869, 416; Jewish quarter: ISM to Saxton parents, Sept. 3, 1869, 245–46. In Prague, they explored a thirteenth-century synagogue and Jewish burial ground. Pina Saxton to the Saxtons, 236–37; disabled artist: ISM to the Saxtons, Aug. 12, 1869, 173; poverty in rural Switzerland, Belgian farmlands, young female lace-makers in Brussels, elderly poor Swiss women, Brieg: ISM to Saxton parents, Oct. 3, 1869, 325; ISM to the Saxtons, Aug. 6, 1869, 150D and 150H; ISM to Saxton parents, Oct. 3, 1869, 325, 328; Shakespeare's birthplace, no British royalty, Madame Tussaud's: ISM to the Saxtons, July 12, 1869, 79; ISM to the Saxtons, July 13, 1869, ISM to the Saxtons, 84, 93–94; July 26, 1869, ISM to the Saxtons, 137–38; Wright's death: Pina Saxton to the Saxtons, Sept. 24, 1869, 313; "I know I should not feel so . . . very glad to leave": ISM to the Saxtons, Oct. 3, 1869, 319; Montanvert and Rigi Kuhm: "When I first woke up this morning," ISM to the Saxtons, Sept. 16, 1869, 284–85; donkeys: ISM to the Saxtons, Oct. 3, 1869, 322; "It is hard to tell about": ISM to the Saxtons, Sept. 21, 1869, 291; demise of Wright: ISM to the Saxtons, Oct. 3, 1869, 325; ISM to the Saxtons, Oct. 6, 1869, 331; Lake Como: ISM to the Saxtons, Oct. 10, 1869, 346–47; "beautiful Italian sky," chestnuts, Milan, Venice, Florence, Pisa, and Fiesole: ISM to the Saxtons, Oct. 10, 1869, 348–49; ISM to the Saxtons, Oct. 14, 1869, 372A–372B; ISM to the Saxtons, Oct. 22, 1869, 395; remaining in Europe or returning for longer with family: ISM to the Saxtons, Oct. 27, 1869, 400; ISM to the Saxtons, Nov. 1869, 435–36, 438H and ISM to Saxtons, Nov. 1869, 435–36, 438E, 438H; buying china: ISM to the Saxtons, Nov. 28, 1869, 425; ISM separation and closeness to her mother Kate: ISM to the Saxtons, Aug. 6, 1869, 150E; ISM to the Saxtons, Nov. 1869, 436; "You know": ISM to the Saxtons, Aug. 29, 1869, 214, 217; Kate "woman of cultivation": Russell, *The Lives of William McKinley and Garret A. Hobart,* 137; letters to George: ISM to George Saxton, June 19, 1869, WMPL; "no value": Pina Saxton to the Saxtons, July 18, 1869, 106; "I often wish": ISM to George Saxton, June 19, 1869, WMPL; "I would like to stay": ISM to the Saxtons, Oct. 3, 1869, 331; "I am up . . .": June 22, 1869, 29;

"half so busy": ISM to the Saxtons, July 20, 1869, 111; writing letters, "I was afraid": ISM to the Saxtons, June 20, 1869, 24; "you know my": ISM to the Saxtons, July 13, 1869, 83; "list of," "I hope my letters," and "I do not want": ISM to George Saxton, June 19, 1869, WMPL.

7. "One ambition . . . master," "Hanna Praised Devotion of McKinley to Ill Wife": *Washington Post* (hereafter cited as *WP*), Aug. 21, 1933; "so well" and "running the bank": Olcott, *The Life of William McKinley,* 1: 68; Greeley speech: Alice Danner Jones, 10 [unpaginated]; Raridan, "125 Years of Yesterday," *CR,* Mar. 31, 1940; Saxton wary of WM, "proudest moment": B. W. Smith, 321–22.

8. WM's Canton cousin was William K. Miller, who prospered from helping establish and manage Russell farm reaper and implement factory in Massillon; general background on WM from his biographies by Porter, Russell, and Leech.

9. Hartzell, *Sketch of the Life,* 8, 12; Klein's recollections: EHPL, 2:13.

10. Nancy McKinley information drawn from Porter, Russell, and Leech; new church: Ramsayer, *History of Christ United Presbyterian Church,* 16–22; Frease's recollections, gifts: EHPL, 2: 13, Hartzell, *Sketch of the Life,* 14; "Ma, who": ISM to Saxton parents, Oct. 3, 1869, McKinley, Belden, and Barber, 325; religious training: Halstead et al., *Life and Distinguished Services of Hon. William McKinley,* 341; ISM and WM meet on the way to church: Russell, *The Lives of William McKinley and Garret A. Hobart,* 141.

11. Ice cream: "President McKinley at Home," *The San Francisco Sunday Call,* Nov. 4, 1900; Morgan, *William McKinley,* 36; Olcott, *The Life of William McKinley,* 1: 68–69; cigar, trellis, ISM stops at WM's office, Kuhns recalls love notes: EHPL, 2:15; "Not at all," "After he began . . .": Hallmark interview; uncle's party: Leech, *In the Days of McKinley,* 16; "You are": Porter, 111; "both agreed": Cass, "Mrs. William McKinley," 4.

12. Gold ring: "Glimpse of the White House and the Distinguished Invalid," June 8, 1901, *The Philadelphia Times; WM to Rutherford and Lucy Hayes, December 13, 1870, RHPC.

13. Wedding: Ramsayer, *History of Christ United Presbyterian Church,* 16–22; Hartzell, *Sketch of the Life,* 22; ISM on WM's early years and RH: Hallmark interview; ISM agrees with WM's father, ISM remarks on return from Washington: "Mrs. McKinley Is Fatally Stricken," *Washington Times,* May 27, 1907.

3. Birth and Death

1. "Closely associated": Olcott, *The Life of William McKinley,* 1: 70; John Saxton's death: *CR,* Apr. 18, 1871.

2. "McKinley House" ownership history: *CR,* Mar. 30, 1965; "No young woman does as well as under her own roof," article on WM's home: "Made Famous in '96: McKinley Home at Canton and Its Alterations," *The Washington Post,* July 5, 1900.

3. WM to John Dewalt, Apr. 9, 1872, WMPL.

4. EHPL, 2:6.

5. Kate Saxton's obituary clipping, Mar. 14, 1873, Belden Box 12 (with Bible), WMPL.

6. *CR* lists the death of Little Ida as August 22, 1873, as does the tombstone. October 17, 1873, on her death certificate reflects the recording date of death. Record of Deaths, Probate Court, Stark County, 1873, 132–33; Pina Barber's recollections and Olcott assessment: Olcott, *The Life of William McKinley,* 1: 70–1; Little Ida: EHPL, 2:23.

7. "Something happened," "She slumped," "After the birth of": EHPL, 2:23; "My husband's right arm": Call, "A Love Story," 6. Mention of lame "foot" would corroborate phlebitis as a complication to neurological damage from contemporary accounts: "partial paralysis of one leg made it difficult, although not painful, for her to be upon her feet, and this inability for exercise in turn had a serious effect upon her health." Tyler, *Americans in Eastern Asia,* 137; "actual invalidism": Logan, *Thirty Years in Washington,* 730.

8. "Her nervous system shocked," *CR,* Mar. 31, 1940, 20; "her nervous system was nearly wrecked": Hartzell, *Sketch of the Life,* 25; "Nerve specialists": EHPL, 2:23; background information consulted on seizure disorder: National Epilepsy Foundation Web site; National Library of Medicine and National Institute of Health (www.ncbi.nlm.nih.gov); Epilepsy Canada Web site with history of epilepsy provided by World Health Organization (www.epilepsy.ca); Berrios, "Epilepsy and Insanity," 978–81; Ziff, *Asylum on the Hill;* Gerlach-Spriggs, Kaufman, and Warner Jr., *Restorative Gardens;* Friedlander, *The History of Modern Epilepsy;* Briggs, *Epilepsy, Hysteria, and Neurasthenia.*

9. Some sources suggest that ISM and WM moved from their rented home to Saxton House either before Little Ida's birth or even after the death there of Katie—both are incorrect. "Life Sketch of the Late Mrs. Ida McKinley," *Stark County Democrat,* May 28, 1907; Andrews, *One of the People,* 58; James Saxton's statement from Chicago, September 22, 1873, William McKinley-Addendum Papers, Library of Congress (hereafter cited as MALC), Series 17, Box 1, Folder 10, 1873–79.

10. James Saxton to WM, EHPL, 2:46; "The McKinley Block": *CR,* Dec. 26, 1873; WM to ISM, May 12, 1875, WMPL; "never entirely recovered": "Mrs. McKinley's Sorrow," *The New England Home* Magazine, insert of the *Boston Sunday Journal,* June 2, 1901, 23; Frease party, WM temperance: *CR,* April 24, 1874, May 8, 1874, June 6, 1874; ISM did not support temperance as suggested by Morgan: Morgan, *William McKinley* 38; "It was Ida who . . .": Brogan, *American Presidential* Families, 539.

11. Abner McKinley accounts: Beer, *Hanna,* 102; Record of Deaths, Probate County, Stark County, Ohio, 104–5; new information on Katie and Little Ida McKinley: "Marjorie Morse, Favorite Niece of the President," *San Francisco Call,* May 12, 1901.

12. "Black pall," Everett, *Social Service Magazine,* 295–96; "came near ending": Olcott, *The Life of William McKinley,* 1: 71; "Ida would have died": Cass, "Mrs.

William McKinley," 3; old woman curse: Beer Family Papers, manuscript draft of *Hanna,* Chapter 3, 54, Yale Univ. Library, Manuscripts and Archives. ISM attended church with Dr. Bishop when he visited Washington in November 1897 and a second known time in Iowa while on tour with WM in October 1899. "The President at Church," *The Times* [Washington, D.C.], Nov. 8, 1897; "knew that with their lost ones": "Mrs. McKinley's Sorrow," 23.

13. "Interest in existence," "so patient": Cass, "Mrs. William McKinley," 7; "If you would suffer by the circumstances," "Your ambitions are mine": "Mrs. McKinley's Lover," 31; "mind remained," "There was never," "You know," "Under his pleasant," "concealed them": EHPL, 2: 23–24; "fulfilled his basic": Morgan, *William McKinley,* 39; Massillon meeting, August 18, 1876, RH's diary, RHPC.

14. Charles Morris, doctorate of law and Queen Victoria's biographer, learned that ISM kept Katie alive through memory association of items; "baby clothes and playthings": McClure and Morris, *The Authentic Life of William McKinley,* 113; WM to John Hay, 1901, quoted in Morgan, *William McKinley,* 39n46.

4. The Active Invalid

1. WM alone during initial Washington stay: *CR,* Feb. 2, 1877.

2. ISM's treatment by Dr. S. Weir Mitchell, Halstead: "Mrs. McKinley," *Saturday Evening Post,* Sept. 6, 1902, 6–7. Mitchell was sympathetic to patients like ISM, writing about them in *Injuries of Nerves and Their Consequences* that "few persons who are not physicians can realize the influence which long-continued and unendurable pain may have on both body and mind . . . the temper changes, the most amiable grow irritable . . . the strongest man is scarcely less nervous than the most hysterical girl," 196. He also wrote novels. Weir Mitchell to ISM, Feb. 9, 1898, WMPL; see www.library.ucla.edu/biomed/his/painexhibit/panel4.htm#weirimg; whonamedit.com; Perkins Stetson biography, Answers.com.

3. Camping incident: Kuhns, "My Favorite Character in History," 56; invitation to Saxton House recital: McKinley File, "Calling Cards, Invitations," WMPL; WM and ISM in Washington: *CR,* Oct. 12, 1876.

4. ISM at RH events: Leech, *In the Days of McKinley,* 20; RH's diary entry Mar. 16, 1878, WM and ISM accept invitations for Jan. 6, 1879, Feb. 20, 1879, Jan. 16, 1880, Feb. 19, 1881: WM to RH, Dec. 29, 1877, all RHPC; Heald, *McKinley,* 43; EHPL, 2:17; "conspicuous figure": McClure and Morris, *The Authentic Life of William McKinley,* 113; Geer, *First Ladies,* 189; Platt-Hastings romance and wedding: *New York Daily Graphic,* June 17, 1878 and June 19, 1878; Hartzell, *Sketch of the Life,* 29–30.

5. Independent trip to New York: WM to Abner McKinley, Feb. 24, 1879, WMPL; mention of ISM's Washington activity: EHPL, 2:17; ISM absent from RH tour: *Cleveland Herald,* Sept. 19, 1879; "politically eminent": *WP,* Apr. 19, 1879; Ladies Aid Society: Willets, *White House,* 418; "bad cold": James McKinley to Abner McKinley, Feb. 5, 1880, quoted in EHPL, 2:10.

6. WM to Meredith Clymer, Mar. 12, 1880, WM press copy correspondence, container no. 233, Ohio Historical Society. Meredith Clymer (1817–1902) graduated from the University of Pennsylvania Medical School in 1837; studied in London, Paris, and Dublin under eminent physicians, began New York specialist practice in nervous diseases; served as an Union Army physician; was twice president of the New York Society of Neurology, professor of mental and nervous diseases Albany Medical College; contributed frequently to the *Journal of Nervous and Mental Diseases* (1878–85), wrote medical works: *Notes on the Physiology and Pathology of the Nervous System with References to Clinical Medicine* (1868), *Ecstasy and Other Dramatic Disorders of the Nervous System* (1870). In 1874, he wrote his eighth medical work, *The Legitimate Influence of Epilepsy on Criminal Responsibility.* Three years before the onset of ISM's seizures, Clymer noted in his work, *The Mental State of Epileptics and Its Medico-Legal Relations,* that those with this condition suffered the "sad fate to be condemned . . . to banishment" to asylums. Clymer treated Mary Lincoln: Hirschhorn, "Medicine Posthumous," 44; James Saxton to WM, May 24, 1879, Series 17, General Correspondence, Box 1, 1873–79, Folder 10, MALC.

7. "I suppose from the tone . . . take three doses of Bromide": WM to ISM, Mar. 17, 1880, WMPL; "Have your Father telegraph": WM to ISM, Apr. 6, 1880, WMPL; "temporary trouble": James Saxton to WM, Mar. 23, 1884, James Saxton to WM, Mar. 23, 1884, Box 1, Series 17, General Correspondence, Jan.–May 1884, Folder 15, MALC.

8. WM to ISM, Mar. 8, 1880, WMPL; WM to ISM, Apr. 6, 1880, WMPL.

9. Reunion: *CR,* Sept. 1, 3, and 13, 1880; *Cincinnati Gazette,* Sept. 3, 1880; WM to ISM, Aug. 23, 1880, WMPL; EHPL, 2:25.

10. "Elegant Reception," *WP,* Mar. 6, 1881; enjoying California: WM to Allen Garnes, May 2, 1881, WMPL; Lucretia Garfield: WM to Anson McCook, July 4, 1881, WMPL.

11. "Thought herself neglected," quote of WM, "Please don't . . .," "handsome lady," "wearying," "burden," "The phase ended": Beer, *Hanna,* 102–3; "McKinley could not come": RH to Lucy Hayes, Sept. 22, 1881, RBPC; Jansen statement: EHPL, 3:28; "Ida is growing": WM to Abner McKinley, Jan. 13, 1882, WMPL.

12. WM to RH, Feb. 2, 1882, reprinted in EHPL, 3:20; Ebbitt House life, receipts, and ephemera in "W. McK's Bills, 1882–1884" file, Box 75, George B. Cortelyou Papers, Library of Congress (hereafter cited as GCLC); photo of bedroom: "McKinley-Social Life" file, Prints and Photo Collection, LC; WM's smoking habits: EHPL, 2:18–19; Leech, *In the Days of McKinley,* 20–1. ISM's knitting legacy is consistently mentioned in practically every periodical profile of her; also see Morgan, *William McKinley,* 63–64; ISM's sewing bag is in the WMPL.

13. Niece Ida McKinley (Morse): David W. McKinley to WM and ISM, Dec. 4, 1881, WMPL; Mabel McKinley: WM to Abner McKinley, Feb. 24, 1879 (copy), WMPL; Barber nieces: WM to Marsh Barber, May 25, 1890, WM to Mary Barber, Aug. 16, 1887, WMPL; Saxton and George: Borowitz, "The Canton Tragedy," 624–25; Kauffman recollection: EHPL, 3:27; Beer, *Hanna,* 103.

14. WM to ISM, Aug. 23, [1885], WMPL; WM to Ruddy Hayes, Dec. 30, 1880, RHPC; "your Aunt Ida . . .": WM to Mary Barber, Sept. 17, 1897, WMPL.

15. "So she could hear . . .": "Mrs. McKinley's Sorrow," 23; Ada Miller: James Saxton to ISM, Feb. 29, 1884, Series 17, General Correspondence, Jan.–May 1884, Folder 15, Box 1, MALC; Kitty Endsley: Leech, *In the Days of McKinley*, 439; WM to Kitty Endsley, Aug. 8, 1893, and WM to R. W. Taylor, July 24, 1895, McKinley Family Papers, Container 1, Folder 1, WRH; Mary Kail: *WP,* Jan. 31, 1880.

16. James Saxton's death: clippings, n.p. Mar. 16, 1887, Belden Box 12 (with Bible), WMPL. ISM's widowed stepmother Hester Medill returned to Chicago, where her brother published the *Chicago Tribune.* She died on March 6, 1907. Blue, *History of Stark County,* 1:964.

17. WM to ISM, Mar. 17, 1888; "Received your": WM to ISM, Oct. 18, 1895; "I do not know": WM to ISM, Apr. 4, 1888; "The opposition": WM to ISM, Apr. 10, 1888, all WMPL; "how precise" and "He can say": "Mrs. McKinley's Life Ideal," *WP,* May 27, 1907.

18. "Washington is very": ISM to Major Vignos, May 14, [n.y.], WMPL; "Mrs. McKinley's illness never": McClure and Morris, *The Authentic Life,* 113.

19. Convention, reaction, "no longer to put his money": Leech, *In the Days of McKinley,* 40–42; *CR,* June 29, 1888; "one of those expansive moods," EHPL, 3:92; "Ida, it is," and "I knew you'd": Olcott, *The Life of William McKinley,* 2:362–63; "Mrs. McKinley continues": WM to Charles Bawsel (hereafter cited as CB), Aug. 29, 1888 and "Mrs. McKinley is improving": WM to CB, Sept. 21, 1888, both reprinted in EHPL, 3: 3; WM granted indefinite leave from Congress: *Congressional Record,* 19:8074.

20. "Everybody wants him," and "of course we are hoping," both quoted in EHPL, 3:102; *Home Magazine* article reprinted in *CR,* Mar. 1, 1889.

21. "Nip and tuck": CB to Liddy Lindsay, May 4, 1889, WMPL; "Major cannot meet": ISM's telegram to RH, Sept. 20, 1889. ISM turned down a second invitation: ISM to RC, Sept. 24, 1889, both RHPL; "somewhat unexpectedly": *WP,* Nov. 13, 1889.

22. "An Appeal for McKinley," *CR,* Nov. 3, 1890; "I agree": WM to Hanna is quoted in Leech, *In the Days of McKinley,* 48–49.

23. Canton Flower Mission Guild: Hartzell, *Sketch of the Life,* 34; Minutes of the 1885–86 meetings of the Daughters of Union Veterans of the Civil War: "Mrs. Major McKinley Tent No. 1" on their Web site, www.duvcw.org ; Dueber recollection: EHPL, 3:28; "children of Canton": Beer, *Hanna,* 102.

24. "Arranged with Mrs. McKinley": WM to Mark Hanna, June 2, 1890, 1890 file, (see also WM to Mark Hanna, Sept. 1891, 1891 folder), Box 2, Hanna-McCormack Family Papers, LC; "in the glory of early summer": Mark Hanna to WM, May 2, 1884, Folder 15, General Correspondence, Jan.–May 1884, Box 1, MALC; Mark Hanna to WM, June 2, 1891, EHPL, 4:24, "Ida McKinley Club": EHPL, 4:44; "Won't McKinley": Blaine to Alger, quoted in Morgan, *William McKinley,* 120; "I will live": "Mrs. McKinley Is Fatally Stricken," *Washington Times,* May 27, 1907.

5. "Tremendous Leverage"

1. "Motherless children": "Life Sketch of the Late M   Ida McKinley," *Stark County Democrat,* May 28, 1907; WM to Kitty Endsle   Aug. 8, 1893, McKinley Family Papers, Container 1, Folder 1, WRH; first gu'   natorial residence: "A Big Fire in Columbus," *New York Times* (hereafter cite'   NYT), Nov. 25, 1893.

2. Legion of honor for Ohio girl: Hartzel'   .ch of the Life, 31, C. L. Wood to WM, Apr. 9, 1894, Frank Smith, editor o'   .ia Gazette, to WM, Apr. 9, 1894, Laura E. Stout to WM, Apr. 10, 1894, '   1894 folder, Box 5, McKinley Gubernatorial Papers, OHS; Elsie Janis'   .e biographies, including, www. travsd. wordpress.com, www.library.os'   ojects/elsie-janis; Ensley job, WM to R. W. Taylor, July 24, 1895, M   .amily Papers, Container 1, Folder 1, WRH.

3. Charles Bawsel'   .pt "New Slants on William McKinley": McKinley Presidential Libr>   .iter cited as CBPL), 4–6; CB to Liddy Lindsey, Jan. 22, 1892, CBPL; "'   .cKinley's whole being . . .": CB quoted, EHPL, 4:74.

4. 1891-   WM/ISM's travel chronicled in *NYT* and *WP* indexes; "looking well": F'   , 4:42.

.e greatest exhibition": WM to Kitty Endsley, Aug. 8, 1893, McKinley
.y Papers, Container 1, Folder 1, WRH; George Saxton and Anna George: .>orowitz, "The Canton Tragedy," from "Crimes Gone By," 625–26; "They want many Barbers": CB to Mina Bawsel, July 9, 1894, "No one knew": CB to Mina Bawsel, May 10, 1893; "Mrs. McKinley was highly": CB to Mina Bawsel, July 11, 1894, CBPL.

6. Dr. Albert Fischer Jr. to WM, Sept. 16, 1898, Series 1, Reel 4, WMPL. Fisher was the first to open a medical practice in osteopathy in New York State and moved to Little Falls in May 1896. When a patient died, and he gave "cerebral hemorrhage" as the reason on the death certificate, local physicians claimed he was responsible, and the district attorney made an inquest to secure evidence against him. An autopsy cleared Fisher: www.meridianinstitute.com/eamt/files/booth/ chapter05.htm; background on Dr. Joseph N. Bishop: Mowbray, *Representative Men of New York,* 50–52; "I suppose you have seen": CB to Liddy Lindsay, Feb. 10, 1893, CBPL; "Views of Governor McKinley," *NYT,* Feb. 12, 1893.

7. Walker scandal: Fallows, *Life of William McKinley,* 116; "A Blow to Governor McKinley," *NYT,* Feb. 18, 1893; "Governor McKinley Assigns," *NYT,* Feb. 23, 1893; Kohlsaat, *From McKinley to Harding,* 10–13; Feb. 20–25, 1893 articles, *CR;* CB to Liddy Lindsay, Feb. 28, 1893, 39–41, CBPL; "Do not worry": H. H. Kohlsaat and Myron Herrick to ISM, Feb. 19, 1893, Herrick Family Papers, WRH (hereafter cited as HWRH); "Her friends": "Governor McKinley Assigns," *NYT,* Feb. 23, 1893; "My husband has done": Morgan, *William McKinley,* 130; "What Mrs. McKinley has": Thomas McDougall to Myron Herrick, Feb. 22, 1893, Container 4, Folder 5, HWRH; WM to Myron Herrick, Feb. 25, 1893, quoted in EHPL, 4: 11, see also 105; "Governor McKinley Assigns," *NYT,* Feb. 23, 1893. Whether she knew

McDougall and Kohlsaat were also listed as executors is unclear. See "Deed of Trust Received of Ida S. McKinley," Box 2, Marcus Hanna Correspondence, 1892–95 folder, Hanna-McCormick Family Papers, LC; WM's meeting with Walker: Morgan, *William McKinley*, 130; "Mrs. McKinley": CB to Liddy Lindsay, Feb. 28, 1893, 39–41, CBPL; "to be used if needed": quoted in Heald, *The William McKinley Story*, 67; Thomas McDougall to Myron Herrick, Sept. 12, 1893, Container 4, Folder 5, HWRH; "Everything Swept Away," *NYT*, Feb. 22, 1893; Herrick form letter, Feb. 21, 1893, Container 4, Folder 5, HWRH; WM to Myron Herrick, Feb. 23, 1893, as quoted in THLC, 4:106; C. C. Shayne to WM, Mar. 3, 1893, James MacArthur to WM, n.d., poem, "Tested," Joseph W. Allen to WM, Feb. 22, 1893, W. J. Magee to James H. Hoyt, Feb. 22, 1893, all in Container 4, Folder 5, HWRH; Morgan, *William McKinley*, 130–33; "I am no beggar": quoted in EHPL, 4:102; "Copy of Subscription Agreement," Box 2, Marcus Hanna Correspondence, 1892–95 folder, Hanna-McCormick Family Papers, LC; "Governor McKinley's Affairs," *NYT*, Feb. 25, 1893; Kohlsaat, *From McKinley to Harding*, 10; H. H. Kohlsaat to Myron Herrick, Feb. 25, 1893, Container 4, Folder 4, WM Collection, WRH.

8. Harland (who went by the last name of Terhune as a professional actress), *Autobiography*, 469; Harding's recollection is from Samuel T. Williamson: "Public Recreations of Presidents," *WP*, Oct. 14, 1923; Herbst's recollection is from THLC, 4:132; Chicago World's Fair: "Mrs. McKinley's Sorrow," 23; Union League Club speech: CB to Liddy Lindsay, Oct. 4, 1889, CBPL; 1893 Republican State Convention: EHPL, 4:159.

9. "My wife loved to buy things": from Bentley Mott, *Myron Herrick*, http://net. lib.byu.edu/~rdh7/wwi/memoir/Herrick/MTH01.htm (unpaginated); "crochet a little piece," "buy [a] needle," "crochet a little," "get her a half yard": WM to Carolyn Herrick (hereafter cited as CH), Mar. 10, 1893, HWRH; Clara Therin and finding a replacement: WM to CH, Jan. 11, 1895 and ISM to CH, Jan. 18, 1895, HWRH; "in his big, kind, domineering": Mott, *Herrick*, n.p.; "wishes that you might have": WM to CH, Nov. 9, 1894; "But Mrs. McKinley wants you": WM to CH, Feb. 7, 1895; "we will go to the hotel": WM to CH, Feb. 21, 1895, all HWRH; "the home" and "We were so sorry": WM to Myron Herrick, Feb. 23, 1893: as quoted in EHPL, 4:106; "Instead of inviting," "The cultivation": "Not a Man of the People," *NYT*, July 30, 1893. ISM did not seem to stay at Hanna's home unless she was with WM, though telegrams were sent to her there. WM to Mary Barber, July 20, 1895, EHPL, 4:144; "Charley's Aunt": "No Conference with McKinley," *NYT*, Nov. 18, 1893.

10. Second gubernatorial inauguration: CB to Mina Bawsel, Jan. 10, 1894: quoted from Bawsel, EHPL, 4:21; ISM opposes WM continuing his political career: Halstead et al., *Life and Distinguished Services of Hon. William McKinley*, 98.

11. "Trip around the world": "People Met in Hotel Lobbies," *WP*, Feb. 26, 1908; the recollection of Mrs. Saxton from an account left by Beer, *Hanna*, 102, 303. Most periodical profiles of ISM and contemporary biographical works of WM emphasize ISM's intensity with small children, especially girls, the latter focus shared by WM:

" . . . he was like Mrs. McKinley in the respect that little girls could command him for a courtesy, and he was always pleased to be in their company. . . . Mr. and Mrs. McKinley were glad to see, and gratified to hear, the conversation, and notice the smiles and laughter, and the more serious moods of children who happened to be about the age that their children might have been" (Halstead, *Illustrious Life,* 410).

12. "I fear she will never": CB to Liddy Lindsay, June 5, 1894, CBPL; Minnesota sailing trip in the summer of 1894 was made on the yacht of financier Julius Seymour with his wife and little girl: July 30, 1897 memo, MALC. WM was in New York with ISM, but made no public appearances, likely around the time of Bishop's care: "How Governor McKinley Spent Sunday," *NYT,* Feb. 19, 1894; disguising the purpose of the southern trip: "McKinley Hard at Work," *NYT,* Mar. 20, 1895; Leech, *In the Days of McKinley,* 62–63; "Fixing His Southern Fences," *NYT,* Mar. 12, 1895; Kohlsaat, *From McKinley to Harding,* 23–27; *NYT,* Mar. 29, 1895, front page, column 2, no article headline, Jacksonville, Fla., dateline; WM to A. E. Buck, Feb. 1, 1895, reprinted in EHPL, 4:115–16; "How does it feel": Murdock, *"Folks,"* 126; "she yielded": Halstead et al., *Life and Distinguished Services of Hon. William McKinley,* 98.

13. "The McKinleys": CB to Mina Bawsel, Aug. 4, 1895, quoted in EHPL, 4:145; "We shall go to": EHPL, 4:168.

14. "Chautauqua," *Ohio State Journal,* August 25, 1895; WM's speech at Alliance's Goddard Opera House, ISM's absence: "The Governor's Speech," *CR,* Nov. 3, 1895; further appearances by WM: EHPL, 4:127–28, 136–37; "almost a sacrilege": "McKinley and His Life," *WP,* Nov. 13, 1893; Waite quoted in Harland, *Autobiography,* 469. Leech interviewed three of ISM's Barber nieces about her: Leech, *In the Days of McKinley,* 432, 656; James Boyle to Helen McKinley, Oct. 8, 1895, quoted in EHPL, 4:174–75.

15. Murray, "First Aid to the Injured," 726; Shannon, *Eugenics,* 404–5; Roosevelt: Samuels and Samuels, *Teddy Roosevelt,* 59; Morris, *The Life of a Star,* 213–15.

16. WM went "east with Mrs. McKinley to seek an improvement in her health": James Boyle to Charles Walcutt, Apr. 17, 1893, WM Gubernatorial Papers, OHS; Bishop first publicly identified as ISM doctor: "No Conference with McKinley," *NYT,* Nov. 18, 1893; "You know she is": CB to Liddy Lindsay, June 5, 1894, CBPL; Bishop's bill: Feb. 2, 1896; WM's check to Bishop, Apr. 4, 1896; "I wish you:" WM to Bishop, Dec. 3, 1895, WMPL; "surrounded by many": Frease, EHPL, 7: 74.

6. "At Home"

1. WM to CH, Dec. 5, 12, 21, and 30, 1895, Jan. 1, 2, 6, 14, and 16, 1896, Feb. 15, 1896, Mar. 4, 1896; Heistand to CH, Jan. 15, 1896, HWRH.

2. *Stark County Democrat* quoted in EHPL, 5:31; house blueprint: WMPL; rooms: Halstead et al., *Life and Distinguished Services of Hon. William McKinley,* 231, 423; "Life Sketch of the Late Mrs. Ida McKinley," *Stark County Democrat,* May 28,

1907; "Mrs. McKinley During": EHPL, 7: 74; "She is ever happy . . .": Cain, "Ida McKinley," 172.

3. Staff background: EHPL, 6:18; campaign strategy: Kohlsaat, *From McKinley to Harding,* 30–31. Dawes created an index of thousands of WM supporters, "next to . . .": Kohlsaat, *From McKinley to Harding,* 21–22; ISM with advisers: Dawes, *A Journal,* 67, 74. McKinley's cousin Will Osborne, former Boston police commissioner, also worked at the Chicago headquarters. Present at the February 3 Canton meeting were WM, Dawes, Smith, Osborne, and Abner McKinley, and at the March 29 meeting in Cleveland were WM, Hanna, and Smith. Suggests foreign language speakers for WM and time for WM to complete bust sitting: Virginia Dodge to ISM, Feb. 10, 1896, and Samuel Saxton to WM, Feb. 12, 1896, both WMPL; "always on the alert": "Mrs. McKinley's Life Ideal," *WP,* May 27, 1907; afflicted with influenza," and contact during their separation while WM was in Chicago and ISM in Canton: ISM to WM, Feb. 13, 1896, ISM to WM, Feb. 13, 1896, WMPL; WM to CH, Feb. 20, 1896, HWRH.

4. J. N. Bishop to WM, Apr. 30, 1896, WMPL. A usual routine of bromide use was potassii bromidi 10 grains; sodii bromidi, 10 grains; boracis purificati, 5 grains; Aquæ, 1 fluid ounce. Two tablespoonfuls of the salts were mixed in water and consumed three times a day after meals. ISM had been using bromides at least since 1880. Generally, it was most helpful to those experiencing seizures classified as "mild" and those in the first stages of the disorder. Another general finding was that when bromide use ended, the seemingly "cured" patient again experienced seizures. J. B. Morrow's memo, undated [1905] General Correspondence, Box 3, "1905–1910 and undated" file, Marcus Hanna, Hanna-McCormick Family Papers, LC.

5. Croly, *Marcus Alonzo Hanna,* 363; White, *Autobiography,* 251.

6. June 1896 *New York Independent* editorial quoted in EHPL, 5:82; ISM walking, told by Ida Mae McCoy Orwig and brother Ed J. McCoy, EHPL, 6:311–12; Foraker's reference to ISM in nominating speech: McClure and Morris, *The Authentic Life,* 184.

7. WM hums Scottish air: Butterworth, *The Young McKinley,* 299; detailed description of the day WM won the nomination are left by friend Murat Halstead in his two books: Halstead, *Life and Distinguished Services of William McKinley,* 355–70 and Halstead et al., *Life and Distinguished Services of Hon. William McKinley: And the Great Issues of 1896,* 421, 433; "Ida, Ohio": McClure and Morris, *The Authentic Life,* 185; Canton: EHPL, 5:1–16; destruction of lawn: Kuhns, *Memories of Old Canton,* 60–1; poor house quote: Hopley, *McKinley and His Campaign,* 5 (in later compendiums the quote was mistakenly attributed to Caroline Harrison in reference to the 1888 campaign).

8. The Hallmark interview in its entirety was reproduced in Halstead et al., *Life and Distinguished Services of Hon. William McKinley: And the Great Issues of 1896* as a chapter.

9. Lucy Hayes was away only once for a two-week period, beginning about March 6, 1878. However, not only RH was there but the First Lady's cousin, Lucy

Cook. Neither RH nor Cook mentions ISM assuming any role and joining WM at only one March 15 dinner as a guest. ISM may have visited the Hayes children during the daytime, but RH was in his office just down the hall from them, so the children required no further oversight, especially as RH permitted them to dine at a friend's home without supervision. No correspondence exists between ISM and Lucy Hayes. Nan Card, RHPC, to CSA, May 15, 2007; ISM requests photos: ISM to RH, June 18, 1880, RBHC; Willa Cather's ISM profile and brief interview quoted in Stout, *Willa Cather,* 84.

10. Hanna and WM on taking campaign beyond front porch: EHPL, 6:80; "My own view . . .": Whiting to Bill Beer, July 14, 1896, Box 56, Folder 14, Beer Family Papers, Yale University Library. Whiting further wrote with some sense of hope that McKinley might later consider taking the stump: "I talked with him today about his speaking from the same platform with Bryan. I am able to state positively that nothing of the sort is contemplated or possible. . . . I do not think he will speak at all but I heard it urged today he could reach and convince thousands with his voice who would not read or heed another and I believe in an emergency that he would accede to the wishes of the committee." Heald further wrote that "But it was a no greater reason in 1896 than during the campaign years for Congress and Governor. In fact, Mrs. McKinley's health seemed to be better during the early part of 1896." Heald did not rely on the WM-Bishop correspondence, which show that ISM was unwell from February to April 1896: EHPL, 6: 17; *Seattle Post-Intelligencer,* Sept. 13, 1896.

11. The role of women in the 1896 campaign from primary sources (such as *Woman's Journal,* Oct. 17, 1896): at www.projects.vassar.edu/1896, Vassar College's Web site project, created by Rebecca Edwards and Sarah DeFeo; Canton women's reception: *CR,* June 26, 1896, and June 27, 1897; Russell Chase's recollection of women's reception: EHPL, 6:43; "Women Visit McKinley," *NYT,* June 27, 1896.

12. Harpine, *From the Front Porch to the Front Page,* 48; *Centennial Celebration of the City of Cleveland,* 103–4, 132; Halstead et al., *Life and Distinguished Services of Hon. William McKinley: And the Great Issues of 1896,* 491; EHPL, 6:44; various articles on WM/ISM, ceremony, local activities, etc.: *CR,* June 26, 1896 and June 27, 1896.

13. "She is such a devoted . . .": Russell, *Lives,* 143; "She takes a deep interest . . .": Andrews, *One of the People,* 58, and "Life Sketch of the Late Mrs. Ida McKinley," *Stark County Democrat,* May 28, 1907; Byars, "*An American Commoner,*" 298; "Aunt Emilie" to ISM, August 10, 1896, WMPL.

14. ISM to CH, Jan. 6, 1896, HWRH; [article on William McKinley's gubernatorial campaign] Busbey, *Ohio State Journal,* Oct. 3, 1891.

15. Charles Bockius to the Bonnot Company, Nov. 4, 1896, WMPL; "Making History in Canton," *CR,* Oct. 25, 1896; [no author], *The Canton Favorite Cook Book,* 23, 45, 140; "Because, he's . . .": Baillie, *High Tension,* 29; ISM in newsreel: www.imdb.com.

16. L'Overture Rifles, EHPL, 6:84; "They are made": Hopley, *McKinley and His Campaign,* 6–7; Governor": EHPL, 6:30. "Certain women's groups especially appealed to her. So moved was she by the sentiment expressed on the ribbon of

flowers left for her by a group of women stenographers ('Mrs. McKinley, you are always mistress of our hearts. We want to see you mistress of the White House.'), she invited them into her bedroom to meet"; women stenographers: EHPL, 6:246.

17. "Showered": EHPL, 6:192; Belden later married ISM's niece Kate Barber and lived in Saxton House: Belden, 303, Groetzinger sisters, 304, Seesdorf sisters, 312, relative's son, 313, all in EHPL; "Twin Children," *CR,* Oct. 30, 1896; special badge with image of Katie and WM: Hopley, *McKinley and His Campaign,* 6.

18. "McKinley League" operatives: Beer, *Hanna,* 156; John McHolland to Bill Beer, May 18, 1896, Mark Hanna to Bill Beer, June 9, 1896, A. F. Call to Bill Beer, June 9, 1896 (all Folder 13); "entirely personal": Julius Whiting to Bill Beer, Sept. 7, 1896 (Folder 15); "There is no change": Whiting to Bill Beer, July 14, 1896 (Folder 14), all Box 56, Beer Family Papers, Yale University Library; "we are all of the opinion . . .": Howard Hanna to Cornelius Bliss, Sept. 1, 1896, Beer, *Hanna,* 157.

19. Aug. 3, concert at Mary Reynolds's home; Aug. 9 concert at Elizabeth Harter's home; Aug. 5 and Sept. 4 concerts hosted by ISM: *CR,* Aug. 6 and Sept. 5, 1896. ISM slipped out undetected on October 19 to attend the theatrical comedy, "The Bachelor's Romance": EHPL, 6:230; "constantly at the front . . .": "Life Sketch of the Late Mrs. Ida McKinley," *Stark County Democrat,* May 28, 1907; ISM and Nancy McKinley at speeches: Hopley, *McKinley and His Campaign,* 7. Beer referenced "farm an old friend," but more likely the Saxton family–owned farm in Minerva: Beer, *Hanna,* 51; crowds inside McKinley House, Dannemiller's account of ISM's seizure during the campaign there: EHPL, 6:76, 303.

20. J. N. Bishop to WM, Sept. 22, 1896, WMPL.

21. Halstead et al., *Life and Distinguished Services of Hon. William McKinley: And the Great Issues of 1896,* 234; Halstead was born in Butler County, Ohio (1829), rose from reporter to editor, part owner, then president of the merged *Cincinnati Commercial-Gazette;* he moved to New York, editing the Brooklyn *Standard Union,* writing novellas, and features for the popular women's *Cosmopolitan Monthly.* Massachusetts native Henry B. Russell was a *Springfield Republican* and *Boston Globe* reporter, then *Meridian Recorder* [Vermont] editor-in-chief and part owner. Russell stated that his work had been "authorized" by WM, who "was asked, and kindly consented to examine the proofs." He emphasized ISM's interest in art and theater. "Mrs. McKinley did everything": Russell, *Lives,* 143, "brightness . . . strength . . . sensible," 323; practical . . . knowledge," 137; "From the beginning," 143; "In many ways . . . She is," 323–24; "very seriously," 138; Porter, 114–16. In the publisher's introduction to his biography of WM, Robert Porter (b. 1852) was called a "personal friend." Porter was U.S. tariff commissioner (1882), on Whitelaw Reid's *New York Tribune* editorial staff (1884–87), founder of *New York Press* (1887), and director of the U.S. Census (1890–94). Porter's claimed "co-author," James Boyle, (b. 1853) was *Cincinnati Commercial Gazette's* editorial writer before serving as WM's private secretary.

22. In January 1895, Maria and Herbert Saxton, the widow and son of James Saxton's cousin Tom, the last of the Saxtons to hold majority shares, sold *CR: CR,* Mar.

31, 1940. The new *CR* editor George Belden Frease was a longtime friend of both WM and ISM, wrote the keenly intuitive article "The Man McKinley, as seen by a Personal Friend," in the March 2, 1897 issue of *Our Day Magazine,* and an accurate description of ISM's condition in "Making History in Canton," *CR,* October 25, 1896:"seldom so ill as to be obliged to take to her bed and never so well as to be bustling about the house . . ."; Andrews, *One of the People,* 53–57; *Seattle Post-Intelligencer,* Sept. 13, 1896. Speed, "A Study of Major William McKinley," 570.

    23. Hartzell, *Sketch of the Life,* 10, 13, 15, 25, 27, 28, and 29. A later edition was renamed *The McKinleys.*

    24. "Who Is the Anarchist?" *New York Journal,* editorial, Oct. 24, 1896; "complete control of McKinley's fortunes . . .": *New York Journal,* Apr. 13, 1896.

    25. ISM bedridden: EHPL, 6:299; ISM's condition two weeks before election, absence: "Patriotism in Song," *WP,* Oct. 28, 1896; and "McKinley Is Confident," *NYT,* Nov. 2, 1896; "McKinley's mother": Kohlsaat, *From McKinley to Harding,* 53–54; "never really knew. . . . This little woman . . . , Oh, Major . . .": Colman, *White House Gossip,* 255.

7. Silver Lights

    1. Charles Dawes's record of Nov. 8, 1896, and Herricks's: EHPL, 7:1.

    2. Bishop noted that he would be away from New York from Dec. 5–19: J. N. Bishop to WM, Nov. 27, 1896, WMPL.

    3. Amelia Bockius [Mrs. Morgan] Huntington to ISM, Dec. 17, 1896, WMPL; Harriet Gault to ISM, Nov. 6, 1896, WMPL; Jennie Hobart to ISM, n.d. (answered on July 7, 1896), WMPL.

    4. "I received your message": WM to ISM, Dec. 11, 1896, WMPL; "enjoyed hearing . . . I am sorry": WM to ISM, Dec. 12, 1896, reprinted in EHPL, 7:58; "looking for . . . lonesome": WM to ISM, Dec. 14, 1896, WMPL; ISM in Chicago: EHPL, 7:30–37.

    5. "Your kind": Ida and George Morse to ISM, Dec. 21, 1896, WMPL; ISM's Christmas 1896 activities: *CR,* Dec. 26, 1896; ISM dances: *CR,* Dec. 31, 1896.

    6. Jan. 1897 events adapted from calendar of events: EHPL, 7:43–45; *Chicago Times-Herald,* Feb. 1, 1897.

    7. Vacating house, travel arrangements, "had to close": EHPL, 7:48–50; ISM's Inaugural clothes: EHPL, 7:49; James Barber to WM, Jan. 10, 1897, WMPL; "buoyed up . . . a pathos in it . . . It is no secret . . . has never . . .": all from Frease, "The Man."

    8. Train cars: *CR,* Feb. 8, 1897; "Brilliant Scene: Thousands of Cantonians and Others Escort Major and Mrs. McKinley," *CR,* Mar. 2, 1897.

    9. "Quite evident": EHPL, 7:85c; "Arrival at the Ebbitt House," *Chicago Record,* Mar. 3, 1897.

10. Arrival in capital: "McKinley in Washington," *NYT,* Mar. 2, 1897; Ebbitt House bill to WM, March 10, 1897, WMPL; Ebbitt House suite and Mar. 3 activities: *WP,* Mar. 4, 1897. A reporter noted of the White House dinner, "the table decorations and menu were exceedingly simple and in good taste. Freed from the restraining influence of others the retiring and incoming presidents and Mrs. Cleveland chatted without formality." EHPL, 7:102.

11. "Those who saw . . . Her chalky": Dunn, *From Harrison to Harding,* 208; "ought to consider . . . wanted to fill": WM to Mark Hanna, Hanna-McCormick Family Papers, Box 2, 1896–1897 folder, LC. Hanna outraged congressional and civic leaders by seizing control of Inaugural arrangements. Asked if he had "overstepped your prerogative," he retorted, "I have decided to make appointments as I see fit. I hope to make the event a national affair, and, what is more, I will take a distinct pride in the showing that will be made by Ohio. This is a matter of state pride, and I believe Ohio Republicans will back me up." "Hanna Is Surprised," *Akron Beacon Journal,* Nov. 22, 1896.

12. "Formal," "extremely cordial": EHPL, 7:29, 36–37; "Recollections of Mrs. Cleveland," *NYT,* Mar. 7, 1897; "Mrs. Cleveland however was detained at the White House waiting to greet Mrs. McKinley, until nearly three o'clock and could only drive over and tell us all goodbye": Wilson, *"It Is God's Way,"* 249; another account of Frances Cleveland's arrangements for ISM: Davis, *A Year,* 182; "Mrs. McKinley made . . . ," "That woman kept a . . .": Louise Wood to Leonard Wood [hereafter cited as LW], Oct. 31, 1898, in Hagedorn, *Leonard Wood,* 220; the diary reference is found in Leech, *In the Days of McKinley,* 457.

13. "Incidents of the Day," *NYT,* Mar. 5, 1897; Mrs. Grant: EHPL, 7:24–25; Lucretia Garfield to WM, Jan. 1897, WMPL; "Major!": Crook, *Memories of the White House,* 242.

14. "The Inauguration Ball," *NYT,* Mar. 5, 1897; Morgan, *William McKinley,* 209; Madame Roos to ISM, Jan. 18, 1897, WMPL; Audubon Society: Leech, *In the Days of McKinley,* 120; Davis, *A Year,* 187; "gently hustled": Leech, *In the Days of McKinley,* 120; Tarbell, *All in the Day's Work,* 186–87.

8. American Ida

1. "Gen. Hastings Resting Easy," *WP,* Mar. 12, 1897.

2. "White House Incidents," *NYT,* Mar. 6, 1897. Even if her parents stayed at the nearby Ebbitt House, Mabel McKinley (seventeen years old in 1897), disabled with infantile paralysis and reliant on use of a staff, was always a White House guest when in Washington at ISM's insistence. By early April, all relatives of ISM and WM had left, except for ISM's widowed aunt by marriage, Maria Saxton. "Fair Penitents Ride," *WP,* Mar. 14, 1897; "Mrs. McKinley's reception," *NYT,* Mar. 19, 1897; "Mrs. McKinley at the Theater, *WP,* Apr. 29, 1897; "White House Hostess," *WP,* Mar. 10, 1897; clipping, n.d., n.p. [circa Nov. 1896–Mar. 1897], WMPL.

3. Amelia Aiken to "Clara," Mar. 9, 1899, quoted in [no author], *A Treatise on Bookkeeping,*" *Grammar, Punctuation, and Capitalization,* 61–62; the Oval Library: "Social and Personal," *WP,* May 21, n.y., clipping, WMPL; portraits, eagle: "Here and There," *WP,* June 21,1897; bedroom: Willets, *White House,* 45; "Society at Home and Abroad," *NYT,* Oct. 20, 1901; "President Moves in," *WP,* Oct. 31, 1902.

4. "Mrs. McKinley's Easter Lilies," April, n.d., n.p., clipping, WMPL; "How the McKinleys Have Transformed the White House by the Aid of Flowers," *New York Herald,* Mar. 20, 1898; Archie Butt to his mother, June 10, 1908, quoted in Butt and Abbott, *The Letters of Archie Butt,* 28. In the rest of his letter, the military aide reported on the post-McKinley White House landscaping: "There is a great preponderance of yellow flowers over the grounds, a colour which Mrs. Roosevelt loves. She said the other day that when she came to the White House there was hardly a yellow flower to be seen anywhere. . . ."

5. List of employees in the Executive Mansion, greenhouses, and grounds: May 16, 1900, WMPL; Sinclair had a ground-floor office and government salary of $1,800; Kohlsaat, *From McKinley to Harding,* 63; advertisement, *San Francisco Evening Call,* June n.d., 1901, clipping, WMPL.

6. Condition of house and elevator: Smith, *The Romances of the Presidents,* 42, 45; clothing costs: Colman, *White House Gossip,* 247; bonnets: Pell, Buel, and Boyd, *A Memorial Volume,* 177; "Mrs. McKinley's Bonnets," *Harper's Bazaar,* Nov. 1901; "Mrs. McKinley," *New York Tribune,* Jan. 17, 1897; Harry March on ISM setting new trend for small hats in theaters: EHPL, 7:123; "She is fastidious . . .": Willets, *Rulers,* 44; tiara anecdote from forthcoming McElroy book.

7. Willets, *White House,* 45, 118; "The McKinley Household," *NYT,* Jan. 8, 1899. Among ISM's bedroom items at the time of her death were the three-volume *Complete Works of Robert Burns* and three other poetry books: newspaper clipping with letter reference to ISM with regard to the books, May 27, 1907, n.p., WMPL; daytime drives: Pendel, *Thirty-Six Years,* 154; Hoover, *Forty-Two Years,* 22; Charles Reeder: "Weds White House Footman," *NYT,* Dec. 8, 1899; examples of checks and expenses, including a sample of checks to Rauscher's, were those for $103 and $42.25, for Jan. 2 and 30, 1901, respectively: Box 73, Miscellany File, George B. Cortelyou Papers, Library of Congress (hereafter cited as GCLC); Nordica: Foraker, *I Would Live It Again,* 258.

8. Lynch recollection: EHPL, 6:313; George B. Cortelyou's (hereafter cited as GC) diary entry of Jan. 3, 1899, GCLC.

9. Sunday in the garden: Willets, *Rulers,* 39; hymn books: Osborn, *John Fletcher Hurst,* 347; the doorkeeper recalled the hymn-singing taking place on Saturday evenings in the Blue Room: Pendel, *Thirty-Six Years,* 161.

10. Porter and Bingham: I. R. T. Smith, *"Dear Mr. President,"* 41; Hoover, *Forty-Two Years,* 21.

11. *Century Magazine,* 828; Abby Gunn Baker to GC, Aug. 4, 1898, GCLC; Dawes incident: "Priceless White House Crockery," *WP,* May 16, 1909.

12. "Mrs. Grover Cleveland," *WP,* Oct. 27, 1907; "Dr. Rixey's Great Work," *Philadelphia Times,* June 4, 1901; "White House in Summer Attire," *WP,* June 13, 1897; sale of WH china and antiques: "White House Auction," *WP,* Nov. 17, 1902.

13. Seating charts for private dinner on July 17, 1897 and Diplomatic Corps dinner, Jan. 26, 1898, WMPL; second formal dinner was held on Mar. 24, 1897. Evidence that ISM continued to enjoy strong health a year later, descending stairs and promenading on the arm of the Costa Rican president, for example, at a state dinner in his honor; WM/ISM seated beside each other, ISM seated at receiving line: Hobart, *Memories,* 29–31; receiving guests while standing: Crook and Rood, *Memories of the White House,* 246; first Diplomatic Corps dinner: Crook and Rood, *Memories of the White House,* 238; Cabinet dinner: "White House Dinner," *WP,* Mar. 25, 1897; "Mrs. McKinley was always at her husband's side in any public affair . . . regardless of custom, precedent, or tradition": Crook and Rood, *Memories of the White House,* 239; "Received by Mrs. McKinley," *New York Tribune,* Oct. 7, 1897.

14. ISM's eating habits at state dinners: *The Chautauquan,* Jan. 1902, 465; "No Wine Was Served," *WP,* Mar. 6, 1897; "Letter of Thanks to Mrs. McKinley," *WP,* Mar. 8, 1897; "Why Not?" *WP,* Apr. 18, 1897, editorial reprinted in *WP* from *Springfield Republican.* In her memoirs, Carrie Nation wrote: "I was glad when McKinley was elected for I had heard that he was opposed to the liquor traffic. I did not know then that he rented his wife's property in Canton, Ohio, for saloon purposes. . . ." The alcohol issue rose again in 1899 following WM's attendance at a Chicago banquet, where two editors of the *New Voice,* a Prohibition Party paper, reported his drinking wine there. Vigilant about his virtuous public image, he asked Lafayette Williams (ISM's cousin's husband) to seek written contradictions. In "compliance with your suggestion," Williams got a pro-McKinley minister who had attended to write a denial that WM drank wine, and another to confront one of the editors, who agreed to retract his account. John M. Caldwell to Lafayette Williams, Nov. 25, 1899; Lafayette Williams to WM, Dec. 2, 1899; J. M. Caldwell to Lafayette Williams, Dec. 21, 1899; Rev. N. A. Sunderland to WM, Dec. 11, 1899, all WMPL. In fact, WM served guests and moderately imbibed in wine, his secretary once thanking a friend for a gift of it by adding, "The President says he likes the taste of the wine very much": Morgan, *William McKinley,* 239.

15. "Ella Russell to Sing at the White House," *WP,* Mar. 13, 1897; Mar. 24 Cabinet dinner: "White House Dinner," *WP,* Mar. 25, 1897.

16. Piano, Lent, Douglass performances: Kirk, *Music at the White House,* 158–61. The Elsie Janis information is from an online Ohio State University Libraries Exhibition: "Elsie Janis: Some Sort of Some Body," under "Stage Star" (http://library.osu.edu/projects/elsie-janis/stagestar.html) and entry on her at the Web site Ohioana (http://www.ohioana.org/features/women/ejanis.asp); WM/ISM befriended the Turkish native, "Madame Bey," during their congressional years (www.summitnjhistory.org/Historian_MadamBey.php).

17. "Sang the Yale Songs," *WP,* Apr. 20, 1897; "A Mexican Musical," *WP,* May 17,

1897; "Beautiful Blue Danube," *WP,* Sept. 10, 1899; "Washington Likes Old Tunes," *NYT,* Sept. 13, 1899; WM loved the ragtime hit *Louisiana Lou,* "The President and Music," *NYT,* Dec. 26, 1897; Kirk, *Music at the White House,* 158–61; Kirk, *Musical Highlights from the White House,* 81–83; "Britons in High Favor," *WP,* Mar. 8, 1899.

18. WM to Mary Barber, Sept. 17, 1897, WMPL; ISM to Mary McWilliams, Nov. 23, 1898, WMPL; "In the Public Eye," *NYT,* June 27, 1897; "Not at all": Foraker, *I Would Live It Again,* 262; Mary Barber to Pina Barber, Mar. 9, 1897, WMPL; Marshall Barber to Pina Barber, Mar. 9, 1897, WMPL; Mary Saxton Pendleton to Pina Barber, Mar. 9, 1897; and Mrs. W. W. Catlett to Pina Barber, Mar. 9, 1897, all WMPL.

19. Library reception: "To See the First Lady," *WP,* Mar. 18, 1897; 1899 Engagement/Appointment Book, entries of Feb. 17, Mar. 31, and Nov. 11, 1899: container 54, GCLC. Gault invited ISM to the annual Brooke Hall alumnae reunion on April 23, 1897. ISM regretted she could not attend that year, but proposed hosting the next year's reunion at the White House, which did occur. ISM dictated her response to Harriet Gault, April 15, 1897, WMPL.

20. Carriage rides, walks lobby: "Mrs. McKinley's Life Ideal," *WP,* May 27, 1901; Walker and Queen Liliuokalani: I. R. T. Smith, *"Dear Mr. President,"* 40–1; "Ex-Queen at the White House," *NYT,* June 19, 1897.

21. "Mrs. McKinley Has Made 8,000 Slippers," and "How Mrs. McKinley Knitted 4,000 Pairs of Slippers," n.p., n.d., clippings, WMPL; "She was unable": Crook and Rood, *Memories of the White House,* 248–49; other items: "The One Day a Year When Children Rule the White House," *WP,* Dec. 21, 1919; hospital ward: "President McKinley at Home," *The San Francisco Sunday Call,* Nov. 4, 1900.

22. Public mail: "The McKinley Household," *NYT,* Jan. 8, 1899; Lizzie Ramey to ISM, Cambridge, n.d., 1898, WMPL; Cecilia Sherman for Mrs. Gana, Mar. 20, 1898, and Mary Louise Landa to ISM, June 16, 1897, both WMPL.

23. Ida Barber to ISM, n.d. [1898]; ISM to Mary Barber, Sept. 17, 1897; ISM to Mary Barber, Aug. 24, 1900, all WMPL; "Your Aunt": WM to Mary Barber, Sept. 17, 1897, WMPL.

24. Wiemer, "New Discoveries in McKinley Autographs"; Subcommittee of the Appropriations, United States Senate, *Legislative, Executive, and Judicial Appropriations,* 26–27; J. Smith, "The Philippines as I Saw Them," 33–34.

25. Long and Mayo, *America of Yesterday,* 225; Foraker, *I Would Live It Again,* 192; Crook and Rood, *Memories of the White House,* 245–46.

26. Foraker, *I Would Live It Again,* 257; Hobart, *Memories,* 30.

9. For the Sake of Appearances

1. Transcript of mayor's remarks in Philadelphia Commercial Museum Meetings of the International Advisory Board, 48–49.

2. "The President Did Not Land," *New York Tribune,* Apr. 10, 1897; "The Presi-

dent Returns," *New York Tribune,* Apr. 13, 1897; "Departure of the City's Guests," *New York Tribune,* Apr. 28, 1897; CB to Mina Bawsel, May 1897, 94, CBPL.

3. Newton Bates biography by Capt. Louis H. Roddis, Medical Corps, U.S. Navy memo of Dr. Ludwig Deppish to the WMPL, n.d., WMPL.

4. The press corps with WM/ISM to Tennessee represented the *New York Herald, New York World, New York Times, New York Tribune, New York Mail & Express, New York Sun, New York Illustrated American, Boston Herald, Chicago Times-Herald, Chicago Tribune, Philadelphia Ledger, Baltimore American, Cincinnati Post, Canton Repository, Washington Post, Washington Evening Star, Washington Times, Louisville-Courier Journal, Nashville Banner,* and the *Brooklyn Eagle.* "Camera Erodes Field of Illustration," *NYT,* Nov. 3, 1901.

5. Coiffure: *CR,* n.d., clipping, WMPL; "Woman about Town," *WP,* Mar. 14, 1897; "A Study of Mrs. McKinley," n.d., n.p., clipping; Lucia Evans to ISM, Decoration Day, 1900; ISM also received a box of inlaid Sorrento wood from the Paris Exposition: Eve Gawdes to ISM, Dec. 14, 1900, all WMPL.

6. The dinner of three First Ladies was held on Mar. 30, 1897; "The Schoolmistress in Washington," *New York Tribune,* Apr. 19, 1897. Letitia Semple and ISM met years earlier when the former was teaching in Baltimore, and the latter knew some students from Canton: Willets, *Inside History,* 251–54. Semple gave her mother's portrait to ISM for the White House: "Gift to Mrs. McKinley," *WP,* Nov. 12, 1898.

7. GC to Josiah Hartzell, Jan. 24, 1898, and Josiah Hartzell to William R. Day, July 15, 1897, WMPL.

8. ISM file, Prints and Photographs, LC; Daniel and Smock, *A Talent for Detail,* 66–69; GC's diary entry of Apr. 13, 1898, GCLC; ISM's pictures appeared in *New York World,* Apr. 15 1900; Willets, *Inside History,* 463; color image, Eastman House Web site; Inaugural photo sold out the *Ladies Home Journal* issue: *The Manifesto,* 32, 176.

9. "Mrs. McKinley's Birthday," *NYT,* June 9, 1897; diamond pendant from Bonnet's in Columbus in August 1897, GCLC; CH's gift for ISM, GC to CH, June 11, 1898, HWRH.

10. B. P. Lamberton, commander, U.S. Navy, to LW, n.d. [1897], and copy of Theodore Roosevelt (hereafter cited as TR) to Edith Roosevelt, June 18, 1897, both in "1897" file, Box 26, Leonard Wood Papers, LC (hereafter cited as LWLC).

11. "Naval War College Opened," *NYT,* June 3, 1897; "Mr. Roosevelt Is All Right," *WP,* June 4, 1897; "Our Minister to Spain," *New York Tribune,* June 8, 1897.

12. "Cleverness": Rixey, Braisted, and Bell, *The Life Story of Presley Marion Rixey,* 87; mushrooms: Cass, "Mrs. William McKinley," 7; "McKinney": Pell, Buel, and Boyd, *A Memorial Volume,* 175. So stunned were some of the official set that they insisted ISM's remark was a malapropism. Adams and Levenson, *Letters of Henry Adams,* 4:657; Beer, *Hanna,* 103; WM on ISM's humor: "President McKinley at Home," *San Francisco Sunday Call,* Nov. 4, 1900; "Whether at receptions, dinners, or theater parties she is always the woman who directs the wit and mirth of the occasions," *The Home Monthly,* Sept. 1896, 4–5.

13. Nashville presidential party, June 7, 1897, list signed by Addison Porter, MALC; exposition and "knightly chivalry": Rivas, *Beautiful Jim Key,* 110; "McKinley Leaves Nashville," *NYT,* June 13, 1897; "The President's Sunday," *NYT,* June 14, 1897; "McKinley Visits Biltmore," *NYT,* June 15, 1897; "The President in the South," *NYT,* June 13, 1897, editorial.

14. "Greet Mrs. McKinley: Milwaukee Ladies Meet the President's Wife," n.d., n.p., clipping, WMPL; "Newsboys Great Day," *WP,* June 25, 1897; sees children while driving: Pendel, *Thirty-Six Years,* 160; children in the lobby: "Mrs. McKinley's Life Ideal," *WP,* May 27, 1901; western schoolgirls: Littell, *Living Age,* 345–46; the fibbing girl: Bruce, *Handicaps,* 264; refused flower: Foraker, *I Would Live It Again,* 146; jewels: Opha Moore's recollections, WM Gubernatorial Papers, OHS; Marjorie Morse: "President McKinley at Home," *The San Francisco Sunday Call,* Nov. 4, 1900; "Reminiscences of Lilly Cortelyou," Box 72, GCLC; "pathetic, beautiful": *New York Tribune,* Jan. 17, 1897; tells of her daughters: Dingley, *The Life and Times,* 431.

15. Some newspaper repetitions of the story confused the two girls as two boys: "The White House's Mistress," *WP,* June 5, 1898; ghosts: Foraker, *I Would Live It Again,* 147; Logan: Willets, *White House,* 417; "The President's Children," n.d. [1897–1901] magazine clipping, WMPL; "White House Hostess," *WP,* Mar. 10, 1897; clipping, n.d., n.p. [circa Nov. 1896–Mar. 1897], WMPL. Also sold in Canton was Alice Danner Jones's book-length poem *A McKinley Romance.*

16. Leech, *In the Days of McKinley,* 436–37; Pell, Buel, and Boyd, *A Memorial Volume,* 175; "The President's Children," n.d. [1897–1901], magazine clipping, WMPL; "President off for Canton," *NYT,* July 3, 1897; "President Back from Canton," *NYT,* July 7, 1897.

17. Canton doctors: "A Man Named McKinley," *CR,* Mar. 31, 1940; M. E. T. Smith for J. N. Bishop to WM, July 15, 1897, WMPL.

18. "The President's Vacation," *NYT,* July 29, 1897; "The President's Summer Home," *NYT,* July 30, 1897; "President Sees the Sun," *NYT,* July 31, 1897; "McKinley's Holiday," *New York Tribune,* Aug. 2, 1897; "The President in Vermont," *NYT,* Aug. 5, 1897; "President McKinley's Rest," *NYT,* Aug. 6, 1897; "Mr. Foster Sees the President," *WP,* Aug. 10, 1897; "President at Brown's Tomb," *WP,* Aug. 12, 1897; "President at Brown's Tomb," *WP,* Aug. 12, 1897; "Guests of Senator Proctor," *WP,* Aug. 13, 1897; "Greeting by Vermonters," *WP,* Aug. 13, 1897; "The Troy Programme," *NYT,* Aug. 15, 1897; troop review: "President Reviews Troops," *NYT,* Aug. 19, 1897; "The President's Vacation," *NYT,* Aug. 21, 1897; "President's Vacation Ends," *NYT,* Aug. 24, 1897; "To Visit Camp Jewett," *NYT,* Aug. 26, 1897; "The President at Troy," *NYT,* Aug. 21, 1897; "As Seen by a Woman," *WP,* Aug. 23, 1897.

19. "Her Game Was High," *WP,* Aug. 16, 1897; "GAR at Buffalo," *WP,* Aug. 22, 1897; "Mr. McKinley in Buffalo," *NYT,* Aug. 25, 1897; "President Its Head," *WP,* Aug. 26, 1897; "A Buffalo Episode," *WP,* Aug. 28, 1897; "McKinley to Children," *WP,* Sept. 4, 1897; "For Cuban Hospitals," *WP,* Sept. 1, 1897; "Canton," *NYT,* Sept. 5, 1897; "The President at Canton," *NYT,* Sept. 6, 1897; "Flowers for Two

Little Graves," *WP,* Sept. 7, 1897; William Randolph Hearst telegram to ISM, n.d., WMPL; "The President at Somerset," *NYT,* Sept. 8, 1897. WM declined to visit the people of Johnstown who had recently endured a devastating flood: "McKinley at a Ball Game," *NYT,* Sept. 9, 1897; "Band Serenaded McKinley," *WP,* Sept. 10, 1897; "McKinley Addresses Veterans," *WP,* Sept. 11, 1897; "Judge Wallace Named," *NYT,* Sept. 9, 1897; "Mr. McKinley's Holiday," *WP,* Aug. 18, 1897.

20. "Back to White House," *WP,* Sept. 14, 1897; Pringle, *Roosevelt,* 115; Miller, *Theodore Roosevelt,* 259–60; "A Dinner at the White House," *NYT,* Sept. 18, 1897; "Crowds at the White House," *WP,* Sept. 17, 1897.

21. "Surgeon General Tyron," *NYT,* Sept. 12, 1897.

22. Barnes, *From Then Till Now,* 218–19; memorandum, Will Garrison, historic resources manager, to Naummkeag Guides, May 22, 2002, WMPL.

23. "Mrs. McKinley Better," *NYT,* Oct. 5, 1897. WM and ISM returned on September 30 from Massachusetts and left for Ohio and Pennsylvania on October 21. "Mrs. McKinley Better," *NYT,* Oct. 5, 1897; "President Goes Home," *WP,* Oct. 30, 1897; "President in Cincinnati," *NYT,* Oct. 31, 1897; "The President's Sunday," *NYT,* Oct. 31, 1897; "Mr. McKinley in Pittsburgh," *NYT,* Nov. 4, 1897; "Mr. McKinley in Pittsburgh," *NYT,* Nov. 4, 1897. The Canton stop was long enough to let WM vote. Their fourth trip there during the presidency came weeks later with Nancy McKinley's final illness.

24. Cass, "Mrs. William McKinley," 6; Rixey, Braisted, and Bell, *The Life Story of Presley Marion Rixey,* 294–95; Crook and Rood, *Memories of the White House,* 245; Young, *Sunny Life of an Invalid,* 247; "Mrs. McKinley, Mrs. Bryan: A Comparison," *Harper's Bazaar,* Aug. 11, 1900, 955–56.

25. Pell, Buel, and Boyd, 173; *The Schoolmaster Magazine,* May 1901, WMPL; M. J. C. Krimer to WM, Dec. 28, 1898, WMPL.

26. Harland, *Autobiography,* 469; public stares: "President Home Again," *WP,* Apr. 13, 1897; seeing her limp: Iredale, *An Autumn Tour,* 114; Logan and Logan, *The Part Taken by Women in American History,* 281–82; "Mrs. McKinley," *New York Tribune,* Jan. 17, 1897.

27. "White House Receptions," *NYT,* Nov. 25, 1897; "White House Receptions," *WP,* Dec. 1, 1897; WM's check to Bishop, Nov. 4, 1897, Box 73, Miscellany File, GCLC; John Addison Porter to J. N. Bishop, Nov. 5, 1897, WMPL.

28. Cass, "Mrs. William McKinley," 6; Morris, *Edith Kermit Roosevelt,* 171; "The President's Holidays," *New York Tribune,* Aug. 3, 1897; "Our Minister to Spain," *New York Tribune,* Oct. 7, 1897; TR's views: Samuels and Samuels, *Teddy Roosevelt,* 59.

10. In Time of War

1. "President McKinley at Home," *The San Francisco Sunday Call,* Nov. 4, 1900.

2. Debut: EHPL, 7:12; Jeffersons: "Theatrical Notes," *WP,* Nov. 11, 1897; Cline visit: Edgerly, *Give Her This Day,* 3; Oliver: "White House at Home," *WP,* Dec. 1, 1897.

3. Hagedorn euphemistically described LW as giving ISM "the abundance of life . . . the romance of strength and vitality and physical beauty, the elixir of ambition and assurance," and that as a result, "She grew stronger in mind and body." Hagedorn, *Leonard Wood,* 38; "How Leonard Wood Rose," *NYT,* Aug. 23, 1903; Baker, "General Leonard Wood," and as quoted in Wood, *Leonard Wood,* 53; 1897 and 1898 diaries, container 2, LWLC. WM awarded the Congressional Medal of Honor to Wood for his conduct of service eleven years earlier during the Apache War. Russell Alger to LW, Mar. 29, 1898, Box 26, 1898 file; Louise Wood to LW, Oct. 22, 1899 and Oct. 31, 1899, Box 190, all LWLC.

4. E-mail from Janet Metzger, WMPL archivist, June 30, 2007; "White House Crowded," *WP,* Feb. 3, 1898; "Statesmen Visit Dole," *WP,* Jan. 28, 1898; Hawaiian dinner: Damon, *Sanford Ballard Dole,* 321. WM strongly supported Hawaiian annexation, calling it "manifest destiny." GC's diary, June 8, 1898 entry; ISM at annexation signing: "Signed by President," *WP,* July 8, 1898; *Ruffles and Flourishes:* Kirk, *Music at the White House,* 157–58; song honors ISM: "A Scene of Splendor," *WP,* Jan. 20, 1898.

5. "A Diplomat's Career," *WP,* Feb. 13, 1898; Cisneros came to the White House on Oct. 22, 1897: Crook and Rood, *Memories of the White House,* 252–53.

6. WM resists: Hoover, *Forty-Two Years,* 24; "Thurston's Cuban Speech," *NYT,* Mar. 25, 1898.

7. Fund-raiser for widows: "Social and Personal," *WP,* Mar. 7, 1898; "Maine Fund," *NYT,* Mar. 25, 1898; social events: "Social and Personal," *WP,* Apr. 6 and 7, 1898; "Is not father": Brotherhood of Locomotive Firemen, *Locomotive Firemen's Magazine,* 786; E. V. Ambler to LW, Apr. 3, 1920 quoted in Hagedorn, *Leonard Wood,* 141.

8. Rosenfeld, *Diary of a Dirty Little War,* 22.

9. "White House Conference," *NYT,* Apr. 22, 1898; "Mrs. McKinley Arrives," *NYT,* Apr. 23, 1898; "Women Sanitary Workers," *NYT,* Apr. 22, 1898; "Mrs. McKinley Applauded," *NYT,* Apr. 24, 1898; "Mrs. McKinley Cheered," *NYT,* Apr. 23, 1898; "A Quiet Day for Mrs. McKinley," *New York Tribune,* Apr. 24, 1898; "Mrs. McKinley's Visit," *WP,* Apr. 25, 1898; "Mrs. McKinley Returns Home," *New York Tribune,* Apr. 26, 1898; war: Leech, *In the Days of McKinley,* 190–93.

10. J. N. Bishop to WM, Apr. 25, 1898, Series 1, Reel 3, WMPL.

11. "The McKinley Slippers Sold," *The Philadelphia Press,* Dec. [n.y.], clipping, WMPL.

12. TR's quotes from Apr. 19, 1898: Pringle, *The Life and Times,* 127. Supporters heavily petitioned the governor of Massachusetts to grant LW permission to mobilize a regiment, an unnecessary effort, with his nomination as major general coming three months later. Montran Graham to Governor Roger Wolcott, Apr. 10, 1898, Alger Memorandum, Apr. 28, 1898, War Department appointment of July 12, 1898, Box 26, 1898 file, LWLC; "Cowboy Cavalry," *NYT,* May 8, 1898.

13. GC's diary, Apr. 13, 1898 entry, GCLC; ISM to WM, telegram, Apr. 21, 1898, WMPL.

14. Separate phone line: EHPL, 8:36, WMPL.

15. McKenna's account: Duffield, *Washington in the 90's,* 42–46; Crook and Rood, *Memories of the White House,* 262; Gipson, *The Life of Emma Thursby,* 372–73.

16. If Kohlsaat was referring to the March 31, 1898, Leo Stern concert, the Dawes were then houseguests; if ISM was in poor health at the time, Dawes and GC, both assiduous chroniclers, would likely have noted it, but neither one did. GC's diary, Apr. 9, 1898 entry, GCLC.

17. "Devoted Husband," *WP,* Oct. 13, 1907; "Hanna Praised Devotion of McKinley to Ill Wife," *WP,* Aug. 21, 1933; Mar. 18 and 24, 1898 diary entries, GCLC.

18. All from "Assassination Plots Against McKinley" folder, Jan.–April 1898 and May–Aug. 1898 files, Box 65, GCLC.

19. GC's diary, Mar. 25, 1898 entry, GCLC; "Gathering News on Foot Related by W. S. Larner," *WP,* Dec. 6, 1927.

20. Hoover, *Forty-Two Years,* 25; Abner: Wilder, *The Sunny Side of the Street,* 44; Frease: EHPL, 7:77; "Hanna Praised Devotion of McKinley to Ill Wife," *WP,* Aug. 21, 1933; Foraker, *I Would Live It Again,* 262–63; Crook and Rood, *Memories of the White House,* 259–61.

21. Never forgets: Cass, "Mrs. William McKinley," 7; *San Francisco Evening Call* interview was likely arranged by WM's niece Ida Morse, who lived in that city and cooperated with the piece. "President McKinley at Home," *The San Francisco Sunday Call,* Nov. 4, 1900.

22. Camp Alger: Rosenfeld, *Diary of a Dirty Little War,* 19, 87, EHPL, 8:83; Washington streets: Pendel, *Thirty-Six Years,* 155–56; "Lieut. Morse Falls a Victim," *WP,* Aug. 16, 1899; "Boy Soldiers at White House," *WP,* June 7, 1898.

23. Harriet Gault to ISM, June 25, 1898; Maria Saxton to ISM, Nov. 28, 1898; Ida Barber to ISM, n.d., 1898; Mary Barber to ISM, n.d., 1898, WMPL; "sought an interview . . .": Pell, Buel, and Boyd, *A Memorial Volume,* 318–19; TR to WM, May 25, 1898 quoted in Samuels and Samuels, *Teddy Roosevelt,* 46.

24. Navy ship award: Julia Grant to ISM, Apr. 30, 1898; "established rule": third-person response for ISM to Agnes Long, Feb. 26, 1898, WMPL; Ladies Aid Society: Willets, *White House,* 417; drives to hospitals: *Review of Reviews,* 45; ISM preferred giving aid to individuals: *Seattle Post-Intelligencer,* Sept. 13, 1896; "For Galveston Orphans," *NYT,* Oct. 16, 1900; Ladies Aid Society: Willets, *White House,* 418; Logan, *Thirty Years in Washington,* 732, 735; Evangeline Booth quote: "Keeping Death Vigil," *WP,* May 26, 1907.

25. P. Anderson, *The Daughters,* 6; "Report of National Society of the Daughters of the American Revolution, 1897–1898," *American Monthly Magazine* [NS-DAR publication], June 1898.

26. "President Hears the News," *NYT,* May 8, 1898; "Army Going to Cuba," *NYT,* May 10, 1898; Sternberg, *George Miller Sternberg,* 142.

27. Sternberg, *George Miller Sternberg,* 184; ISM's wire to Pina, transfers: EHPL, 8:204–5.

28. "Let Us Have Light," *NYT,* Aug. 3, 1898; "President Has an Outing," *WP,* July 24, 1898.

29. "The President's Arrival, *NYT,* Sept. 3, 1898; "Laboring Men Cheer McKinley," *NYT,* Sept. 6, 1898; "Ready to Greet Them," *WP,* Sept. 8, 1898.

30. GC's diary, June 8, 1898 entry, GCLC; WM to consul general of the United States, July 29, 1898, WMPL; CB to Mina Bawsel, Aug. 29, 1898, Sept. 24, 1898, 108, 110, CBPL.

31. "Mrs. McKinley," *New York Tribune,* Jan. 17, 1897. Julia Foraker was a public advocate of osteopathy's value after its apparent cure of an illness plaguing her son Arthur, and her testimonial appeared in the foreword of Columbia College of Osteopathy's 1902 textbook; she likely advocated on its behalf with WM and ISM. Albert Fisher to WM, Sept. 16, 1898, WMPL. During the 1896 campaign, WM sought potential treatment for ISM from Fisher.

32. WM equates religious piety with national patriotism: "President Tells Philippine Policy," n.d., n.p. [his transcribed speech at Sept. 1898 Methodist meeting, Ocean Grove, N.J., Auditorium], clipping, WMPL; Abner and Hanna quotes: Beer manuscript, 27, Beer Family Papers, Yale Univ. Library.

33. "President's Nephew in Hospital, *WP,* Sept. 24, 1898; "President's Soldier Nephew," *Philadelphia Press,* Dec. 26, 1899; "Lieutenant Morse Falls a Victim," *WP,* Aug. 16, 1898; EHPL, 8:233.

11. Thwarted Redemption

1. Reid and Morgan, *Making Peace with Spain,* 65; "Shock to Mrs. McKinley," *NYT,* Oct. 8, 1898; "Received by the President," *WP,* Oct. 8, 1898; WM to George Saxton, Sept. 12, 1898, WM letterbook, 1897–1901, Box 75, MALC; "President Goes West," *WP,* Oct. 11, 1898; "The President in Canton," *NYT,* Oct. 10, 1898; "At Their Canton Home," *WP,* Oct. 10, 1898; "George D. Saxton Buried," *NYT,* Oct. 11, 1898; Albaugh, *Canton's Great Tragedy,* 73.

2. "Mrs. McKinley Arrives at Chicago," *NYT,* Oct. 14, 1898; Rosalie Bates to ISM, Oct. 28, 1898, WMPL; George Saxton's will: Albaugh, *Canton's Great Tragedy,* 73. Her brother's death did little to alter ISM's wealth as she still retained a third share of three rental properties, and her Barber nieces and nephews were the beneficiaries of his estate. EHPL, 10:15–16. Canton seemed more sympathetic to Pina, presuming that gory details were kept from ISM. CB to Mina Bawsel, Oct. 8, 11, and 21, 1898, 1110–113, CBPL.

3. "Humanity's Triumph," *WP,* Oct. 13, 1898; "The Jubilee Parade," *NYT,* Oct. 20, 1898; "President in Columbus," *NYT,* Oct. 21, 1898; "Saw His Legions Pass," *WP,* Oct. 28, 1898; "Mrs. McKinley," *New York Tribune,* Jan. 17, 1897.

4. The other commissioners were *New York Tribune* editor Whitelaw Reid; lawyer Joseph Choate; and three U.S. senators, William P. Frye, George Gray, and

Cushman K. Davis. In June, the Rev. Robert S. MacArthur had argued the case with his "Our Patriotic and Religious Duty to the Philippine Islands" sermon at New York's Calvary Baptist Church. "Our Duty in the Orient," *NYT,* June 13, 1898; Barrows, *The Christian Conquest of Asia,* 238, 248; "God's Hand in Recent American History," *The Interior,* Nov. 24, 1898, 1441–42; Pratt, 313.

    5. Beer, *Hanna,* 211; Cumming, "Life in Manila," 563–72; "Sketch of the Philippines," *WP,* Feb. 9, 1899; "An American in Manila," *NYT,* July 30, 1898. To quell threats of war by arriving at an understanding with Filipino leaders and to investigate the viability of self-rule, Worchester had convinced WM to send a commission to the Philippines. WM did this and named Worchester as a member of the commission. Blount charged that Worchester's pictures helped ingrain the myth that all Filipinos were but a variation of the Igorrotes: Blount, *The American Occupation,* 569–73; online Univ. of Washington exhibit on Seattle Exposition: clippings; "Here and There," *WP,* Jan. 27, 1901; Blumentritt: www.encyclopedia123. com/I/Igorrotes. Foreman was a British salesman of tropical agricultural equipment; his book was first published in London and Hong Kong in 1889. Furman's claim that the Igorrotes would not convert was false. By 1892, 30,000 Igorrotes had become Catholic. Sawyer claimed that the Igorrotes' previous rejection of Catholicism "may influence them in favor of some simpler doctrine." He quotes from page 213 of Furman's book: "Like all the races of the Philippines, they are indolent to the greatest degree." As he stated:

> A people who believe in a Supreme Being, Creator of heaven and earth, in the immortality of the soul, in an upper and lower heaven, in punishment after death, if it has been evaded in life, who are strict monogamists, and who have a high belief in the sacredness of the marriage tie; a people who guard the chastity of their daughters as carefully as the British or the Americans; a people physically strong, brave, skilful, and industrious, have nothing in common with the wretches Foreman described under their name. These people live in the fairest and healthiest parts of Luzon, no fevers lurk amongst those pine-clad mountains, no sultry heats sap the vital powers.

Sawyer felt that of its "partly subdued races," the Igorrotes were "well worth a great and patient effort to bring them within the pale of Christianity, and to advance the civilization they have already attained." The name "Igorrote" had already become a generic one used to describe all the northern mountain tribes of the Luzon, which had a diversity of traditions and were spread throughout four provinces. There was one settlement of Christianized Igorrotes and several of the subtribes who lived near Catholic Filipino towns had begun to adopt the more westernized clothes and customs. Still, Sawyer observed, "in general the Igorrotes have steadily refused to embrace Christianity, and evidently do not want to go to the same heaven as the Spaniards. . . . They are far inferior to the Christian natives in the arrangement of their houses. . . . [yet] closer contact with Christians generally, have tended to demoralize the heathen" (Sawyer, *The Inhabitants of the Philippines*, 254–64). "Preparing for salvation . . ." is from James H. Blount's book. An officer of U.S. volunteer troops in the Philippines from 1899 to 1901, Blount was then named by McKinley as a U.S. judge of the First Judicial District, which included several provinces, including north central Luzon, where the majority of Igorrotes lived. McKinley later made Worchester interior secretary of the American government there. Blount concluded that "The non-Christian tribes in the Philippines have been more widely advertised in America than anything else connected with the Islands. That advertisement has done more harm to the cause of Philippine independence by depreciating American conceptions concerning Filipino capacity for self-government, than anything that could be devised even by the cruel ingenuity of studied mendacity" (Blount, *The American Occupation*, 577).

Blount also pointed out that Worchester's images fueled zealous missionaries and clothing manufacturers in pursuit of new markets and souls, respectively (newspaper clipping on Seattle Exposition, from Seattle Digital Collection, Univ. of Washington Libraries). In the fall of 1898, after two navy officials conducted an extensive fact-finding mission throughout the Philippines interviewing the native population, their report to Dewey asserted they were suited for self-government, a distinct message that the admiral made to WM, who seemingly ignored it. In a September 2, 1899, *Outlook* article, one of them, L. R. Sargent, recalled that a man and woman, "captives of a wild tribe of Igorrotes of the hills," had been exhibited in Barcelona, their scant tribal clothes labeling them as being from "the lowest plane of savagery." Cognizant that the vast majority of the Filipino population lived much the same as Europeans and Americans, Sargent said "no deeper wound was ever inflicted upon the pride of the real Filipino people than that caused by this exhibition."

6. WM's first cable on Oct. 26, 1898: Wolff and Kramer, *Little Brown Brother*, 170; Leech, *In the Days of McKinley*, 342; Beer, *Hanna*, 303; Montgomery: GC's diary entry for May 3, 1898, GBLC; "Major Montgomery Relieved," *WP*, June 10, 1905. Even diplomatic historian Thomas Andrew Bailey concluded that ISM "presumably influenced" WM to retain Luzon. Bailey, *A Diplomatic History*, 473; Leech, *In the Days of McKinley*, 342–43.

7. *Papers Relating to the Foreign Relations*, 1898, 937–38; Gould, *The Spanish-American War*, 108.

8. "President's Habit of Work," *NYT*, Nov. 15, 1898.

9. Olcott, *The Life of William McKinley*, 71; Foraker, *I Would Live It Again*, 262; Kohlsaat quoted in Furman, *White House Profile*, 259; Hoover, *Forty-Two Years*, 20; "President McKinley at Home," *The San Francisco Sunday Call*, Nov. 4, 1900, n.p.

10. Reads mail to ISM: GC diary's entry of Mar. 18, 1898, GCLC; Howell: Kohlsaat, *From McKinley to Harding*, 24–25; "Life Sketch of the Late Mrs. Ida McKinley," *Stark County Democrat*, May 28, 1907; "Mrs. McKinley," *New York Tribune*, Jan. 17, 1897; read speeches: Cass, "Mrs. William McKinley," 7.

11. "Ida, shall we . . .": Corning, *William McKinley,* 138; "Mrs. McKinley never excluded . . .": Pell, Buel, and Boyd, *A Memorial Volume,* 177–78; Hawthorne's observation on her sensitivity to others: Pell, Buel, and Boyd, *A Memorial Volume,* 173; slippers: Foraker, *I Would Live It Again,* 261; "Mrs. McKinley's Slippers," n.p., n.d., clipping, WMPL; Buxton, "Eulogy of Mrs. McKinley," *NYT,* June 3, 1907.

12. "I only wish . . .": Cass, "Mrs. William McKinley," 7, also in Pell, Buel, and Boyd, *A Memorial Volume,* 174; "I always wanted . . . I don't want you to . . .": "President McKinley at Home," *The San Francisco Sunday Call,* Nov. 4, 1900; Willets, *White House,* 463; "It's all right . . .": Foraker, *I Would Live It Again,* 263.

13. Willard and Livermore, *American Women,* 487–88; "all-around companion": "President McKinley at Home," *San Francisco Sunday Call,* Nov. 4, 1900; Day: Beer, *Hanna,* 303.

14. Diplomatic historians have long termed WM's decision to retain the Philippines as imperialism. The issue is extensively explored in works, including *Diplomatic History of the American People* by Thomas A. Bailey and *Diplomatic History of the United States* by Samuel Flagg Bemi. Tactical military decisions on retaining the entire archipelago are summarized in MacNair and Lach, *Modern Far Eastern International Relations,* 131–32. Before his final decision, WM made numerous references to the potential profit from doing so: "Incidental to our tenure of the Philippines is the commercial opportunity to which American statesmanship cannot be indifferent. It is just to use every legitimate means for the enlargement of American trade . . ." quoted in Dennett, *Americans in Eastern Asia,* 621. The best summary of the Filipino perspective on the war is *Little Brown Brother* by Leon Wolff and Paul A. Kramer; "questions arising": "Demand Renewed," *WP,* Nov. 10, 1898.

15. See Josiah Ang's essay, "Presbyterians were first to answer the Macedonian Call from the Philippine Islands," at www.panoramapc.org. General Henry had written WM from his command in Puerto Rico: "This is a good time to establish Churches. These people have no respect for the priests of Spain and they would take to other beliefs. . . ." Gen. Guy V. Henry to WM, Aug. 29, 1898, WMPL. The Catholic Church wanted the islands taken over because the people would receive better legal protection and education and, as American territories, would vastly increase the Church's influence in official circles. Dunn, *From Harrison to Harding,* 278–80; Speer: "Religious News and Views," *NYT,* Aug. 1898. Especially proud of their success in other Catholic countries, the Presbyterian organization seemed the most overt in their intention to convert the 400,000 Catholic Filipinos. Months later, national Presbyterian Assembly leaders meeting in Minnesota organized a protest against WM permitting a Catholic chapel at West Point. "Presbyterian Assembly," *NYT,* May 20, 1899; "Work in Foreign Fields," *NYT,* Nov. 14, 1895; William Hawk to WM, Mar. 9, 1897, WMPL; Iversen, *Molly Brown,* 126. WM went to visit the nearby Catholic summer school at Cliff Haven, as he had two years earlier, but ISM again did not join him. Heald noted: "Whatever institutionalized resentment that may have lingered from Catholic Church officials towards the

Administration policy which seemed to encourage Protestant missionary efforts in the Philippines was certainly not reflected. . . ." EHPL, 10:370; *Mosher's Magazine,* May–Sept. 1899, 324. As a widow, ISM made a financial contribution to the Catholic St. Joseph's College in Queens County, N.Y., a strong indication that she outgrew her antipathy toward "Papists," there being no political motivation to respond so kindly to the solicitation.

16. "Daily Strength for Daily Need": Fallows, *Life of William McKinley,* 226; Logan quoted in Willets, *White House,* 417.

17. *Woman's Missionary Friend,* Dec. 1901, 446; *A History of the Metropolitan Memorial UMC in Washington, DC,* www.mmumc-dc.org/history; Maxine West, "Tell Me the Stories: United Methodist Women Past and Present," United Methodist Women's Division, www. gbgm-umc.org/umw; "Received by Mrs. McKinley," *New York Tribune,* Oct. 7, 1897; 1899 Engagement/Appointment Book, entries of Nov. 16, 1899, Container 54, GCLC; first organized Protestant missionary group of WHMS: see Ang, "Presbyterians," at www.panoramapc.org. WM later told the Methodist General Missionary Committee that his final decision was influenced by responsibility to "Christianize" Filipinos. Later attempts to undermine the account's veracity on the premise that he had never been known to use that word failed to consider that WM may have been employing an artful metaphor to disguise a secular motive. While the committee would assume "Christianize" meant religious dogma, WM was facile in the constituency's vernacular. However pejorative his use of the word might be to others, "Christianize" and his other stated intentions to "uplift" and "civilize" were also lofty euphemisms for the practical labor of missionaries: building and operating schools, hospitals, and other facilities in underdeveloped areas. These projects, begun by mid-1899, would pave infrastructure for some of the government's civil initiatives and save initial oversight cost. This fit into WM's long-range plans as disclosed in his following annual message to Congress to start efforts not at Manila's central seat of government, but "by building up from the bottom" in provinces. It was a plan ISM had witnessed take form. Leech, *In the Days of McKinley,* 427. By encouraging religious organizations to do so, WM also ensured their support of his evolving policy, thus mitigating public charges of his immoral policy, a strategy worth enduring the criticism that missionary work was a presumptuous imposition of one nation's predominant faith and culture onto another. "Christianity," he would observe on May 26, 1899, was the "mightiest factor in the world's civilization." All of this was consistent with the fact that, as one his first religious teachers Rev. W. V. Morrison stated in 1897, "He was a Christian first. He placed the cross higher than the flag." WM was definitive in this: "I am a Methodist, nothing but a Methodist, a Christian and nothing but a Christian, and by the blessing of heaven I mean to live and die, please God, in the faith of my mother" quoted in Corning, *William McKinley,* 177–78. While central to WM's persona, he never expressed disdain for other religions or Protestant sects. In an 1892 speech about American presidents, for example, McKinley made reference not to "Christ," but to an abstract "Higher Power" to affirm his belief that

even those who weren't "observers of the outward forms of religion" had legitimate "piety." He arranged for the convocation to the 1896 convention that nominated him to be delivered by a rabbi. In his famous "benevolent assimilation" proclamation, he affirmed that "religious rights" of all Filipinos would be protected, including the Muslim majority on Mindanao. WM's meeting when the important statement was made took place on November 21, 1899. The recollection of it was made by committee member Gen. James F. Rusling, which was published as "Interview with President McKinley," *The Christian Advocate,* Jan. 22, 1903, 137–38. WM's important, full quotation reads:

> The truth is I didn't want the Philippines, and when they came to us as a gift from the gods, I did not know what to do with them. . . . I sought counsel from all sides—Democrats as well as Republicans—but got little help. I thought first we would take only Manila; then Luzon; then other islands, perhaps, also. I walked the floor of the White House night after night until midnight; and I am not ashamed to tell you, gentlemen, that I went down on my knees and prayed to Almighty God for light and guidance more than one night. And one night late it came to me this way—I don't know how it was, but it came: (1) That we could not give them back to Spain—that would be cowardly and dishonorable; (2) that we could not turn them over to France or Germany—our commercial rivals in the Orient—that would be bad business and discreditable; (3) that we could not leave them to themselves—they were unfit for self-government—and they would soon have anarchy and misrule over there worse than Spain's was; and (4) that there was nothing left for us to do but to take them all, and to educate the Filipinos, and uplift and civilize and Christianize them, and by God's grace do the very best we could by them, as our fellow men for whom Christ also died. And then I went to bed and went to sleep and slept soundly.

The published account occurred only four years after it took place, and none who were present at the meeting ever disavowed the remark. Gould, *The Spanish-American War,* 140–42.

18. "Mrs. McKinley Here," *NYT,* Dec. 7, 1898; "Mrs. McKinley's Busy Day," *NYT,* Dec. 9, 1898; "Mrs. McKinley Goes Home," *NYT,* Dec. 10, 1898; "Mrs. McKinley Goes Home," *WP,* Dec. 10, 1898.

19. "Weds White House Footman," *NYT,* Dec. 8, 1899; Frances Joseph: Mattingly, *Well-Tempered Women,* 94; concerts: no title, *NYT,* May 20, 1900, clipping, WMPL; Booker T. Washington to WM, Nov. 21, 25, 27 and Dec. 22, 1898, WMPL; "President Speaks to Negroes," and "Her Thoughtfulness Rewarded: Negro Woman Who Showed Mrs. McKinley a Kindness Given a Place," *WP,* both Dec. 18, 1898; Moses Green to WM and ISM, Dec. 30, 1898, WMPL; GC to Myra Rowell, June 15, 1898, GCLC; ISM pays for education: *The Utica Observer* as reprinted in *Technical*

World Magazine 8, (1908); information on Tuskegee visit and also the Georgia Agricultural and Mechanical College in Savannah: *The Southern Workman,* 67 and Riley, *The Life and Times,* 224–29. McKinley never addressed the rise in African American lynching (2,600 between 1890 and 1910) or new segregation laws in the South. Fulfillment of his campaign promise to name African Americans to prominent positions seemed limited to that of former U.S. senator, Blanche E. Bruce, as treasury register so his name would be seen on currency by other blacks as a sign that "this government will recognize him the same as it does men of a lighter color." Fallows, *Life of William McKinley,* 226.

20. Roosevelt: McCallum, *Leonard Wood,* 166; Blount, *The American Occupation,* 569–73; "Eulogy of Mrs. McKinley," *NYT,* June 3, 1907.

21. Christmas: "Social and Personal," *WP,* Jan. 21, 1899; "The President's Christmas," *NYT,* Dec. 26, 1898; New Year's Day Reception: "At President's Home," *WP,* Jan. 3, 1899; "Mr. and Mrs. McKinley at the Play," *WP,* Jan. 6, 1899; conversation with Whitelaw Reid: Cass, "Mrs. William McKinley," 6.

22. "Benightedness": Foraker, *I Would Live It Again,* 146. Mrs. T. L. Saxton was secretary of the Presbyterian Foreign Mission's Seward, Nebraska, branch, though her name was misspelled as "Sexton" in the listings of the *21st Annual Report of the Woman's Presbyterian Board of Missions of the Northwest Chicago.* A third person named by Thomas Beer, who recalled ISM's Igorrote discussion, was Charles Deshler, a Columbus banker, real estate developer, and 1896 McKinley campaign fund-raiser and official. His niece was a close friend of both Julia Foraker's daughter and Mary Barber. It may be that both Deshler and Foraker had further confirmation of ISM's concern through their niece and daughter, respectively, coming from Mary Barber. Beer, *Hanna,* 303, 305; "ghosts . . .": Foraker, *I Would Live It Again,* 249.

23. "Presbyterian Sympathy," *Colorado Springs Gazette,* May 18, 1901. WM saw his presidency as "a God-entrusted responsibility" and when faced with uncertain policy choices, would "pray to God to guide my steps aright": Barton, "A Christian Gentleman: William McKinley," 134–37; "Without her . . .": Hartzell, *Sketch of the Life,* 63.

24. "This habitual thoughtfulness," Carson quote: Olcott, *The Life of William McKinley,* 2: 360; WM on self-control: quoted in Newman, *McKinley Carnations,* 64.

25. "We accepted . . .": WM letter of Jan. 8, 1899 to General Otis and Admiral Dewey; "It was no responsibility . . ." and "President's Last Speech," *NYT,* Oct. 19, 1899; "providence": Gould, *The Spanish-American War,* 109; "people" from WM's Boston Home Market Club speech, Feb. 1899; "respond in a manly," "accept all the obligations . . . ," "not to subjugate . . . ," San Francisco speech, 1901: Gould, *The Spanish-American War,* 109, 181, 190.

26. Abner McKinley and Benjamin Montgomery were also present among two foreign service officials and their wives. "President Signs the Treaty," *NYT,* Feb. 11, 1899; Crook and Rood, *Memories of the White House,* 262; "Victory Over the Filipinos,' *WP,* Feb. 6, 1899; "Heroism at Manila," *WP,* Feb. 7, 1899. Commissioned as sec-

ond lieutenant, James McKinley volunteered for a second tour of duty, intending to help establish civil order in the Philippines, only to find himself in combat. Corbin broke news at theater: EHPL, 10: 86; *jusi* dress: Conger, *An Ohio Woman,* 124.

27. Cost of war rising and Kennan quoted in Lummis, "In the Lion's Den," 501–2; Taft article: *National Magazine,* 615–24; Blount, *The American Occupation,* 625.

28. WM to Louise Wood: McCallum, *Leonard Wood,* 145–46.

29. Wallace: "Named for Federal Office," *NYT,* June 3, 1897; CB, 6, CBPL. Hanna refused WM's offer of the position of secretary of state and asked instead to be appointed to the U.S. Senate seat from Ohio left vacant by WM's appointment of John Sherman as secretary of state. WM to Mark Hanna, Hanna-McCormick Family Papers, Box 2, 1896–97 folder, LC; Harriet Gault to ISM, Apr. 5, 1897, WMPL; "Was Famous in Its Day: Brooke Hall Seminary, Where Mrs. McKinley Went to School," *Washington Evening Star,* Jan. 19, 1898; ISM asked WM, Gault got it: Cass, "Mrs. William McKinley," 4; ISM likely never read the Samson letter, but Porter had it routed to Treasury Secretary Gage. J. W. Sansom to ISM, Apr. 13, 1897, WMPL; Kate Krider to Joseph Saxton, July 1, 1897, WMPL, C. E. Manchester to WM, Apr. 7, 1897, WMPL; M. C. Barber to WM, Apr. 6, 1897, WMPL; "Mrs. McKinley Her Hope," *WP,* Jan. 16, 1899; Elizabeth Van Lew to Mrs. McKinley, Van Lew Papers, College of William and Mary Library, quoted in Varon, *Southern Lady,* 248.

30. Jeering Alger: "The President in Boston," n.p. n.d. [circa July 1899], clipping, McKinley scrapbook, Pacifica Univ. Archives, Pacifica Univ., Calif.; WM on Alger: GC's diary, Jan. 2, 1900 entry, GCLC; ISM attends theater: "Fashionable Audience Greet John Drew," *WP,* Feb. 16, 1899; "personification": Colman, *White House Gossip,* 266; Morgan, *William McKinley,* 234; Adams and Levenson, *Letters of Henry Adams,* 4: 674.

31. "Ballots of the DAR," *WP,* Feb. 24, 1899; "President Needs a Rest," *WP,* Mar. 5, 1899; Heald, *The William McKinley Story,* 10:136, WMPL; "The President Goes South Today," *NYT,* Mar. 13, 1899; "Gayety Reigns at Lakewood," *NYT,* Mar. 12, 1899; "President's Vacation Ended," *NYT,* Mar. 28, 1899; Leech, *In the Days of McKinley,* 458, 657.

32. "The President's Proposed Vacation," *NYT,* Mar. 5, 1899; "The President Going South," *NYT,* Mar. 8, 1899; "President Getting a Rest, *NYT,* Mar. 15, 1899; "The President's Vacation," *NYT,* Mar. 18, 1899; "Reed at Jekyll Island," *WP,* Mar. 20, 1899; "The President's Vacation," *NYT,* Mar. 20, 1899; "Slow Work on Ruins," *WP,* Mar. 20, 1899; "The President at Jekyll," *NYT,* Mar. 21, 1899; "Meet on Jekyl Island," *WP,* Mar. 21, 1899; "President Leaves Georgia," *WP,* Mar. 28, 1899.

33. "Abuse of Saxton . . .": EHPL, 10:324; WM to John Barber, Apr. 13, 1899, WMPL; "The President Is Better," *NYT,* Apr. 26, 1899; "Social and Personal," *WP,* Apr. 1899.

34. In a preliminary hearing, Saxton's friend Eva Althouse claimed that he had the key to her home to feed her birds but had no answer as to why he brought the champagne found in his pouch. It bolstered the defense's argument that Saxton moved

from woman to woman, thus rejecting some, a potential motive for revenge with which Anna was unfairly charged. Despite wide knowledge of Anna's threats, only one witness positively identified Anna as the murderer but lost credibility when her opium addiction was disclosed. Anna George became a paid, traveling lecturer, with her first booking—at the Akron Opera House—just two weeks after her acquittal. Remaining in the area, she began dating wealthy physician Arthur Ridout, who lived in nearby Salem with his wife and three children. He divorced two years later to marry Anna; they moved to Wheeling, W. Va. Five years later, he hanged himself from a chandelier. "Tragedy Clears Mystery," *WP,* July 23, 1906; "Mrs. George Acquitted," *NYT,* Apr. 29, 1899; Borowitz, "The Canton Tragedy," 624–26; "Tars Cheer President," *WP,* Apr. 29, 1899; "Mr. McKinley in the City," *NYT,* Apr. 29, 1899; "Mr. McKinley's Quiet Day," *NYT,* Apr. 30, 1899; "Mr. McKinley in the City," *NYT,* Apr. 1899; untitled clipping, Apr. 30, 1899, WMPL; "The President at Church," *NYT,* May 1, 1899; "President Speeding Home," *WP,* May 2, 1899.

35. "Going to Hot Springs," *WP,* May 5, 1899; "President Quits Washington," *NYT,* May 9, 1899; "The President in the South," *NYT,* May 13, 1899; "President at Natural Bridge," *NYT,* May 14, 1899; "Date of President's Return, *WP,* May 15, 1899; "President in Washington," *NYT,* May 21, 1899.

36. Long: Leech, *In the Days of McKinley,* 459–60; GC's diary, July 5, 1899 entry, GCLC.

37. Corning, *William McKinley,* 138.

12. Descent from Mount Tom

1. Laundry woman anecdote: *The Utica Observer* as reprinted in *Technical World Magazine* 8: 1908; minister's recollection: *The Advance Magazine,* Aug. 29, 1907, 255; "Mrs. McKinley's Doll Compels Admiration," *The Philadelphia Press,* Dec. 15, 1900; "Mrs. McKinley Gives a Doll," *WP,* Nov. 30, 1900; "Suffrage Bazaar Opens," *NYT,* Dec. 11, 1909; Evald testimony, Hearing Before the Select Committee on Woman Suffrage, United States Senate, 34–35. While Anthony was invited up to see ISM, it was not happenstance that several anti-suffrage leaders were not, since WM welcomed them along with the national president and vice president of the Women's Christian Temperance Union just after he received the suffrage leaders and brought Anthony up to meet ISM. 1900 Engagement/Appointment Book, February 12, 1900 entry, GCLC; Stanton et al., *History of Woman Suffrage,* 12–13; Anthony recollections: Harper and Catt, *The Life and Work of Susan B. Anthony,* 1169, 1272–73.

2. "Vase for Mrs. McKinley," *NYT,* Nov. 18, 1896; "Mrs. McKinley's Golden Vase," *NYT,* Mar. 3, 1897.

3. "Mrs. Charles Fairbanks," *WP,* Aug. 4, 1907; "President McKinley at Home," *San Francisco Sunday Call,* Nov. 4, 1900; Cather story quoted in Stout, *Willa Cather,*

84; Tennessee Centennial Exposition: James Dunn to WM, May 24, 1897, WMPL; "Council of Women Scientists," *WP,* Apr. 7, 1897; "Guests at the White House," *WP,* June 8, 1899; Second National Congress of Mothers, *Kindergarten Magazine, 672.*

4. P. Anderson, *The Daughters,* 6. WM signed the congressional recommendation for the Paris commissioners on February 23, 1900. *Report of the NSDAR* 1898–1900. In one of the few publicity efforts she permitted herself to be used for, ISM was one of three recipients of a special coin sold to raise funds for the erection of George Washington and Marquis de Lafayette statues in Paris, dedicated in July 1900. She met privately with Mrs. Manning for an hour and a half on January 6, 1899, then two hours the next day. 1899 Engagement/Appointment Book, Jan. 6 and 7, 1899 entries, GCLC. WM appointed Bertha Honore Palmer and May Wright Sewall as additional Paris Exposition delegates. Harper and Catt, *The Life and Work of Susan B. Anthony,* 1159–60.

5. Husband anecdote: *The Advance Magazine,* 255; "Work of the Crittenton Mission," *WP,* Sept. 26, 1901; Crittenton Mission Web site.

6. "Social and Personal," *WP,* Apr. 19, 1897; unsigned third-person typed note to Harriet Gault, Apr. 15, 1897, WMPL; Harriet Felton Peters to ISM, Feb. 18, 1901, WMPL; further information on scholarship: "General Notes," *NYT,* Dec. 30, 1900; James Barber's engagement: "Social and Personal," *WP,* June 5, 1899; Rhees, *Laurenus Clark Seelye,* 225; "The President's Sunday," *NYT,* July 19, 1899; "The President's Trip" and "A Cup for Mrs. McKinley," both *NYT,* June 20, 1899; "President for Guest," *WP,* June 20, 1899; "Smith College Honored," *New York Tribune,* June 20, 1899.

7. Rhees, *Laurenus Clark Seelye,* 225; "The President's Sunday," *NYT,* July 19, 1899; "The President's Trip" and "A Cup for Mrs. McKinley," both *NYT,* June 20, 1899; "President for Guest," *WP,* June 20, 1899; "Smith College Honored," *New York Tribune,* June 20, 1899; speculation about LW's visit: Hagedorn, *Leonard Wood,* 239; "The President at Adams," *New York Tribune,* June 24, 1899; "The President's Sunday," *New York Tribune,* June 19, 1899; "Mount Holyoke's Great Day," *New York Tribune,* June 21, 1899; "The President's Journey," *New York Tribune,* June 22, 1899; "Sunday with the President," *WP,* June 26, 1899; report that ISM contracted a cold: "Church at Adams," *The Times* [Washington, D.C.], June 26, 1899; "Mrs. McKinley's Illness," *The Evening Times* [Washington, D.C.], June 26, 1899; "The President Leaves Adams," *NYT,* June 27, 1899; "The President Starts Home," *WP,* June 27, 1899.

8. "Mr. McKinley's Arrival," *The Evening Times* [Washington, D.C.], June 27, 1899; "Return of the President," *WP,* June 28, 1899; Sternberg, *George Miller Sternberg,* 142; WM to Bishop, Box 73, Miscellany File, GCLC; J. N. Bishop to WM, Mar. 1, 1899, WMPL; Rixey account: Rixey, Braisted, and Bell, *The Life Story of Presley Marion Rixey,* 31–33; "called upon to prescribe . . .": Reid, *Munsey's Magazine,* 76.

9. "Mr. McKinley's Arrival," *The Evening Times* [Washington, D.C.], June 27, 1899; "Return of the President," *WP,* June 28, 1899; "fatigue of the journey," "change of scenery": "Mrs. McKinley Rallying," *The Times* [Washington, D.C.],

May 17, 1901; "severe": Leech, *In the Days of McKinley,* 459. The seizure occurred during lunch with the Major and an engineer who had come to discuss prospective dam and reservoir projects in the West. Beer, *Hanna,* 258.

10. Dawes, *A Journal of the McKinley Years,* 195, 197, as quoted by Leech, *In the Days of McKinley,* 459; GBC's diary entry, July 1, 1899, GCLC; *The Philosophical Journal* in July 1898, "Assassination Plots Against President McKinley, September–December 1898 file," GCLC; world leaders and spouses: "Death of the President," *Christian Observer,* Sept. 18, 1901; "I love . . .": Pell, Buel, and Boyd, *A Memorial Volume,* 174; with slight variation, see Cass, "Mrs. William McKinley," 7; "never really knew . . .": Colman, *White House Gossip,* 255.

11. Willets, *White House,* 463; Olcott, *The Life of William McKinley,* 2:364; Foraker, *I Would Live It Again,* 263; GC's diary July 13, 1899 entry, GCLC.

12. "No Bee in Teddy's Bonnet," *WP,* June 30, 1899; Pell, Buel, and Boyd, *A Memorial Volume,* 174; Taft article: *National Magazine.*

13. "Mrs. McKinley's Poor Health," *NYT,* July 20, 1899; CB to Mina Bawsel, July 20, 1899, 113, CBPL; Dawes quoted in EHPL, 10:442.

14. "Mrs. McKinley's Condition Favorable," *NYT,* June 29, 1899; "Mrs. McKinley Continues to Improve," *NYT,* July 4, 1899; "The President's Visit to St. Paul," *NYT,* July 13, 1899; "Mrs. McKinley in Poor Health," *NYT,* July 20, 1899; "President's Western Trip," *Washington Evening Star,* June 18, 1899.

15. "Declined by President," *WP,* July 29, 1899; Rixey, Braisted, and Bell, *The Life Story of Presley Marion Rixey,* 39; EHPL, 10:369–70; topics in ISM's letters to her nieces were routine ("we find it quite warm and dusty here," "When Uncle Will reached home [the White House] his mail drawers were packed, and all the letters are not answered yet . . ."): ISM to Mary or Ida Barber, Sept. 17, 1899 and ISM to Mary Barber, Aug. 24, 1899, WMPL; GC to CH, Aug. 12, 1899, WMPL; Rixey quote: "Mr. McKinley at Plattsburgh," *NYT,* Aug. 11, 1899; "Mr. Hay to Visit President," *WP,* Aug. 15, 1899; "Concert for the President," *NYT,* Aug. 18, 1899; "The President Goes Yachting," *NYT,* Aug. 20, 1899.

16. "President Leaves Canton," *NYT,* Sept. 2, 1899; ISM to Mary Barber, Aug. 24, 1899, WMPL; "Mr. McKinley to Pittsburgh," *WP,* Aug. 1899; "Mr. McKinley at Pittsburgh," *NYT,* Aug. 27, 1899; "The President's Sunday," *NYT,* Aug. 28, 1899.

17. *CR,* Aug. 30 and 31, 1899, and Sept. 1, 1899; "Mr. McKinley Is at Canton," *NYT,* Aug. 31, 1899; William Hawk to ISM, Aug. 19, 1899, WMPL.

18. Departure from Canton: *CR,* Sept. 1, 1899; Dawes, *A Journal of the McKinley Years,* 199; Dawes quoted in EHPL, 10:442. To Hanna, WM guessed that ISM had been unwell since at least May, but it was June. WM to Mark Hanna, Sept. 18, 1899, WMPL; ISM in White House while WM was in Philadelphia,: "To Comrade McKinley," *WP,* Sept. 6, 1899.

19. "All Hail Admiral," *WP,* Oct. 3, 1899; Everett, *Exciting Experiences in Our Wars,* 519–20; "William McKinley as Man and Friend," excerpted from *Leslie's Weekly, NYT,* Nov. 17, 1901.

20. Rixey, Braisted, and Bell, *The Life Story of Presley Marion Rixey*, 455–57; "Mrs. McKinley Is Better," *NYT*, May 14, 1901; Kohlsaat quoted in Furman, *White House Profile*, 259; Clara Hay story: Adams and Levenson, *Letters of Henry Adams*, 4:657; woman going to Europe: Willets, *Rulers*, 44.

21. "President Was Late," *WP*, Oct. 16, 1899; "President McKinley Votes," *NYT*, Nov. 8, 1899; EHPL, 10:499.

22. "It is said . . .": "Anxiety in Washington," *NYT*, May 16, 1901; Taft article: *National Magazine*.

23. Taft in Canton Nov. 1899: "Suggested in Canton," *CR*, Feb. 9, 1900. The seizure that Taft witnessed took place on election day, 1900, at WM's home. Olcott, *The Life of William McKinley*, 2:363; Garfield grandson: Leech, *In the Days of McKinley*, 437; Estella Joliet recollection: EHPL, 3:28; Hobart, *Memories*, 29; Dunn, *From Harrison to Harding*, 208; Kohlsaat, *From McKinley to Harding*, 155.

24. Logan, *Thirty Years in Washington*, 732; Crook and Rood, *Memories of the White House*, 247. Kohlsaat would be the second individual close to ISM to use the medical term that WM had managed to prevent observers from using, at least in the presence of ISM. "After the birth of baby Ida," he wrote, "Mrs. McKinley suffered from epilepsy," Kohlsaat quoted in Furman, *White House Profile*, 259.

25. John S. McCook to WM [summer 1898], quoted in EHPL, 8:341; Thompson, *Presidents I've Known*, 17; Moore, *Canton*, 11, identifies the superintendent's residence of the East Ohio Asylum (later the Massillon Psychiatric Hospital, which closed in 2001) as being called "The McKinley Home," with the inaccurate speculation that it "may have been used as McKinley's summer home after his election to the presidency"; Shannon, *Eugenics*, 404–5.

26. The first meeting of the National Association for the Study of Epilepsy and the Care and Treatment of Epileptics was held on May 14 and 15, 1901, in Washington, D.C. Ironically, on those days the public was following the bulletins of ISM's near-fatal illness in San Francisco, although it had nothing to do with epilepsy. There is still a tendency to attribute all of ISM's health problems to epilepsy and even term them "fits." This is evident in Goldman's recent book on Buffalo. He claims that Ida had a "fit on the spot" when cannons shattered the train windows when it arrived there in September 1901 (p. 6). He also wrote that she had a "fit" after the Sloane "lunch" and fake eagle incident (p. 5); "The Care of Epileptics," *NYT*, Nov. 6, 1902.

27. Rixey, Braisted, and Bell, *The Life Story of Presley Marion Rixey*, 43. On November 10, a check of $100 was sent to Dr. Frederick Peterson at 4 West 50th Street, New York. A month later, on December 20, a Dr. S. Howland, at 64 Bible Street, was sent $10. Both were notable for the fact that WM continued to purchase ISM's medications through his personal secretary rather than the presidential physician, given that Rixey was a proactive physician and willing to assume any burden for WM. The check to Howland came with the discreet note from GC that it was "to be applied to the fund concerning which you have written." Bishop's check of March 1, 1899, for $300 and note: Box 73, Miscellany File; GC

to Frederick Peterson, Nov. 10, 1899; GC to Dr. S. Howland, Dec. 20, 1899, both Letterpress 1897–1901, Box 75, all GCLC. There is no record of whether Peterson provided medication to ISM; a reason why Rixey may not have been the source of some medications may be that WM wanted no official War Department dispensary record detailing it, as had been the case with WM's arrangement with LW in 1897. Rixey, Braisted, and Bell, *The Life Story of Presley Marion Rixey*, 239.

13. The Resolution

1. ISM's initial bromide use was indicated in WM's 1880 letter to her father. "President's Christmas Plans," *NYT*, Dec. 21, 1899; "Quiet Day in Washington," *NYT*, Dec. 26, 1899; GC's diary, Dec. 12, 15, 19, 20, 23, 27, and 31, 1899 entries, GCLC.

2. Dunn, *From Harrison to Harding*, 208; for both Hay and Adams, as well as other accounts of ISM's symptoms: Adams and Levenson, *Letters of Henry Adams*, 4: 660, 658, 673–74, and 5:218; Slayden, *Washington Wife*, 8–9; Kansas City women, rain: Foraker, *I Would Live It Again*, 259–61.

3. WM to Jennie Hobart, Jan. 1, 1900, is reprinted in her memoirs; WM to William O. Day, Jan. 30, 1900, reprinted in EHPL, 11:12; "Blue Room Splendor," *WP*, Oct. 11, 1899; Seale, *The President's House*, 639–40; GC's diary, Jan. 1, 1900 entry, GCLC; also see GC's diary entries from endnote one. Braisted did disclose the composition of Bishop's bromides, claiming it was "unnecessary to the narrative to here set down the various ingredients as learned . . .": Rixey, Braisted, and Bell, *The Life Story of Presley Marion Rixey*, 35–36, 84–85, 239–40; GC's diary, Feb. 4, 1900, entry, GCLC.

4. This dynamic predated the presidential years, as a Canton neighbor recalled: "A thousand times, I have seen him spring from his chair with an almost startling speed of movement to those not accustomed to his watchful care." Olcott, *The Life of William McKinley*, 2:364; "When he wanted a pen . . .": Crook and Rood, *Memories of the White House*, 268–69; "did not deter . . .": Hoover, *Forty-Two Years*, 20.

5. Foraker, *I Would Live It Again*, 258; GC's diary, June 8, 1899 entry, GCLC; "President McKinley at Home," *San Francisco Sunday Call*, Nov. 4, 1900; Crook and Rood, *Memories of the White House*, 247; Rixey, Braisted, and Bell, *The Life Story of Presley Marion Rixey*, 39.

6. Johnston quoted in Johnston, Daniel, and Smock, *A Talent for Detail*, 68; Young quoted in Morgan, *William McKinley and His America*, 241. Olcott noted that "as a rule McKinley did not commit to paper his plans and purposes, nor his inmost thoughts and aspirations. He much preferred a meeting, face to face, and a confidential talk." Olcott, *The Life of William McKinley*, 1:xi–xii; J. B. Morrow's memo, 1905–10 clippings and undated file, Box 3, Hanna-McCormick Family Papers, LC; Hoover, *Forty-Two Years*, 20; Crook and Rood, *Memories of the White*

House, 251–52; song might make her sad: Foraker, *I Would Live It Again,* 258; "lovely girl, had . . .": Leech, *In the Days of McKinley,* 457–58.

7. Hanna: Olcott, *The Life of William McKinley,* 1:64, and "Hanna Praised Devotion of McKinley to Ill Wife," *WP,* Aug. 21, 1933; Crook and Rood, *Memories of the White House,* 268–69; "all the fervor" and "oh, if you could see . . .": Logan, *Thirty Years in Washington,* 735; "you are looking . . .": "President McKinley at Home," *The San Francisco Sunday Call,* Nov. 4, 1900.

8. "Mrs. McKinley's Love," *New York World,* May 26, 1907; Duffield, *Washington in the 90's,* 40; Foraker, *I Would Live It Again,* 258–59; Olcott, *The Life of William McKinley,* 2:360.

9. Logan, "The Gracious Lady of the White House," 735; Pell, Buel, and Boyd, *A Memorial Volume,* 174; engraving: Cass, "Mrs. William McKinley," 7; photos: "White House Hostess," *WP,* Mar. 10, 1897; also a clipping, n.d., n.p. [circa Nov. 1896–Mar. 1897], WMPL.

10. "Dirty Democrats": Louise Wood to LW, Oct. 31, 1898, as quoted in Hagedorn, *Leonard Wood,* 220; Daniel Webster: Foraker, *I Would Live It Again,* 259; two foreign citizens incidents are referencing an English woman (Foraker, *I Would Live It Again,* 259, and "Social and Personal," *WP,* June 25, 1897) and Irish woman (C. O'Connor Eichs to Father Hudson, CHUD X-4–6, Univ. of Notre Dame Archives); "only honest man": Leech, *In the Days of McKinley,* 457; "He ought to . . .": "Eulogy of Mrs. McKinley," *NYT,* June 3, 1907; "Mrs. McKinley," *New York Tribune,* Jan. 17, 1897; "When she praises": Halstead et al., *Life and Distinguished Services of Hon. William McKinley: And the Great Issues of 1896,* 104.

11. Crook and Rood, *Memories of the White House,* 268–69; Pell, Buel, and Boyd, *A Memorial Volume,* 174; Cass, "Mrs. William McKinley," 7; "Mrs. McKinley's Lover," *The New England Home Magazine,* June 2, 1901, 31; "McKinley's Self-Control," *WP,* Nov. 10, 1901; "Well, well, well . . .": "McKinley Forgot Dignity," *WP,* Mar. 31, 1912; Marchesi, *Singer's Pilgrimage,* 185; visit by Dr. Johnston: *Methodist History* 1 (October 1962): 32; Robinson, *My Brother Theodore Roosevelt,* 201; "the homage . . . ," "quite upset . . .": Foraker, *I Would Live It Again,* 259–60; the Lerig: "Mrs. McKinley's Lover," 31.

12. Cass, "Mrs. William McKinley," 7; "the American people": from Gertje Hamlin's diary quoted in Leech, *In the Days of McKinley,* 457; "Well, I'm glad to hear that": Foraker, *I Would Live It Again,* 259.

13. Kennedy and Burnett, *History of the Ohio Society,* 310–11; GC's diary, Mar. 2, 1900, Apr. 5 and 7, 1900, GCLC. The night before the dinner, as WM stayed in a hotel preparing remarks for the next day's dinner, ISM attended a showing of *Brother Officers* at the Empire Theater, but it made little news. "President's Probable Plans," *NYT,* Mar. 3, 1900; "President McKinley Here," *NYT,* Mar. 4, 1900; "No Halt to Expansion," *WP,* Mar. 4, 1900. Roosevelt publicly insisted he would not take it, believing that "I can add strength to the Presidential ticket by remaining as governor, I do not see why the Vice-Presidential nomination should be forced

upon me. I repeat that I do not want to be nominated for the Vice Presidency." After a private dinner with WM and ISM in May, he met with Hanna, now chairman of the National Republican Committee. "Governor Roosevelt Here: Still Averse to the Vice Presidential Nomination," *WP*, May 9, 1900. After his Washington meetings, TR may have reconsidered, alleged by Heald, a cautious source, to be among a handful of intimates who were told a secret that ISM was unlikely to know—that WM had been diagnosed with the fatal kidney ailment, Bright's disease. Heald makes the case that it factored into his consent to run with WM in 1900. Edward T. Heald, Sesquicentennial of McKinley's Birth essay, "Reflections on William McKinley," 10, WMPL.

14. "President McKinley Leaves the City," *NYT*, Mar. 5, 1900; West, "Our Four Year Queens." ISM was ill with the flu from March 23 to April 4, 1900. "President in the City," *NYT*, Apr. 22, 1900.

14. Turn of the Century

1. "President McKinley at Canton," *NYT*, Apr. 25, 1900.

2. "Made Famous in '96," *WP*, July 5, 1901; "This Is the President's New House," *The Philadelphia Press*, June 26, 1900.

3. The triptych was later donated by TR's daughter-in-law Belle Roosevelt. Prints and Photos, LC; "Governor Roosevelt Here," *WP*, Aug. 21, 1900; 1900 Engagement-Appointment Book, Aug. 20, 1900 entry, Container 54, GCLC; Hanna letter: Leech, *In the Days of McKinley*, 542.

4. "The President at Home," *NYT*, July 1, 1900; "Mr. McKinley Is Notified," *NYT*, July 13, 1900; Pearson and Harlor, *Ohio History Sketches*, 330.

5. "Chinese Execution," *WP*, Nov. 4, 1900.

6. EHPL, 11:203.

7. "Given more publicity": *Boston Weekly Magazine*, quoted in Cass, "Mrs. William McKinley," 3; "the public," "slavish": Foraker, *I Would Live It Again*, 257. Reed quoted in the Taft article, *National Magazine;* GC recorded an incident of WM generating his own flattering publicity, showing off a badge given him by a Confederate veteran, saying, "it would be a good idea to have the true story told," and choosing the *Chicago Record* reporter who was the "suitable person to take care of it." The story emphasized WM's benevolence toward the South. A similar incident involved WM quashing the story that he sipped wine at a dinner. GC's diary, Jan. 3, 1899, entry, GCLC. "He does not like to be told that it [his nose] looks like the nose of Napoleon. It is a watchful nose," newspaper columnist Frank Carpenter joked about the Major's feigned modesty, "and it watches out for McKinley." Edmund Morris, *Theodore Rex*, 612.

8. *McClure's Magazine*, June 1898, 215; Hawthorne quoted in Pell, Buel, and Boyd, *A Memorial Volume*, 173; Wolf, *The Presidents I Have Known*, 168; Long and

Mayo, *America of Yesterday,* 148; Thomas Nelson Hall poem, MS 0013, Box 9, Folder 128, Special Collections and Archives of Colorado College, Tutt Library.

9. West, "Our Four Year Queens," 84; Cather and Curtin, *The World and the Parish,* 309–11.

10. *Harper's Bazaar,* Aug. 11, 1900; *Cincinnati Commercial Tribune,* June 4, 1900, clipping, WMPL; Jordan, *Three Rousing Cheers,* 82–86.

11. Gardening: "Social and Personal," *WP,* Sept. 9, 1900; GC's diary, Aug. 29, 1900, entry, GCLC; ISM to WM, Sept. 21, 1900, telegram, WMLC; A. B. Campbell to H. H. Phillips, Oct. 12, 1900, and H. H. Phillips to WM, Oct. 13, 1900, WMLC. Canton doctors Thomas H. Phillips and F. E. O. Portman were both practicing in 1875 and both attending ISM, the former at the 1897 Inauguration and the latter at her death. "A Man Named McKinley," *CR,* Mar. 31, 1940, 22.

12. William S. Devery, chief of police, City of New York, to Secretary of State John Hay, Aug. 14 and 17, 1900; Alvey Adee to GC, Aug. 16, 1900; GC's memo to Acting Secretary of State Alvey Adee, Aug. 17, 1900, all from "Assassination Plots Against McKinley, August 1900" file, Box 65, GCLC; "Jack the Ripper": Assassination Plots Against McKinley, Jan.–June 1900 file, Box 65, GBC Papers, LC.

13. ISM and WM went to Somerset, Pa., for the September 2 wedding of Mabel McKinley to Herman Baer. ISM presented Mabel with items she embroidered and, with WM, gave the couple a silver-mounted oak chest holding a silver set. Three weeks later, there was the Fogle-Clarke wedding in Canton on September 26, and the Wales-McClymonds wedding a month later in Massillon. WM's sister Helen was a houseguest during the campaign. "Miss McKinley's Wedding," *NYT,* Sept. 8, 1900; ISM to Helen McKinley, Sept. 27, 1900, Series 17, Box 1, Folder 7, MALC; Kuhns, *Memories of Old Canton,* 758.

14. Summer and autumn in Canton: EHPL, 11: 203–6, 315–30, derived from *CR* articles, June–Nov. 1900; 1900 weddings, Election Day: EHPL, 11: 383–403.

15. "Mrs. McKinley Sees 'San Toy,'" *NYT,* Dec. 19, 1900; "President's Victory a Tonic for His Wife," *New York World,* Dec. 1, 1900; "Mrs. McKinley in the City," *NYT,* Dec. 1, 1900.

16. WM to ISM, Dec. 1, 1900, WMPL; the Saxton Block Building fire: EHPL, 12:163–69; various stories: *CR,* Dec. 9 and 10, 1900; Halstead, "Mrs. McKinley," 6.

17. Series of telegrams from Thomas V. Cridler, third assistant secretary of state, and from Secretary of State Hay to the American consul in Hong Kong and General MacArthur, from Nov. 16, 1900, through Dec. 5, 1900: EHPL, 12:137–40; "Mrs. McKinley's Nephew Dead," *NYT,* Nov. 16, 1900.

18. "If any further proof were wanted of the overwhelming need of a new White House it has been furnished during the present winter. It may or may not be true that President McKinley's recent illness was due to a cold caught in the draughts which are said to wander through all the apartments of the Executive Mansion. But it is true that when the President and Mrs. McKinley gave their New Year's Day and diplomatic receptions, the famous old building was crowded

to a dangerous extent. Colonel Bingham . . . has done everything in his power to make the old house inhabitable and less unsafe, but he has no authority to make the structure completely over nor to enlarge it. . . . The truth is . . . the United States at the beginning of the twentieth century has outgrown the Executive Mansion. . . ." Walter Wellman, "The White House a Disgrace to the Nation," *Collier's Weekly,* Jan. 26, 1900; "A Local Celebration," *The Washington Bulletin,* Dec. 12, 1900; C. Moore, *The Life and Times of Charles Follen McKim,* 204.

19. Christmas: "President and Mrs. McKinley Well-Remembered," *CR,* Dec. 26, 1900; EHPL, 12:48–49. It also prevented them from attending the Canton funeral of her nephew James Barber whose remains arrived in San Francisco in early January after two months. "Lieutenant Barber's Body at San Francisco," *NYT,* Jan. 4, 1900; wheelchair: Pendel, *Thirty-Six Years,* 162; ISM's diary entry for Jan. 1, 1901, is from Leech, *In the Days of McKinley,* 567.

20. GC's diary, Jan. 31, 1901, entry, GCLC; "Mrs. McKinley Wishes an American Gown," *The New York World,* Feb. 8, 1901, "Mrs. McKinley's Beautiful Inauguration Gown Made Here," *The New York World,* Feb. 26, 1901; also *Indiana State Board of Agriculture Annual Report,* 1900, 1064–65.

21. "Election Result Will Affect Coming, Gay Season," *WP,* Sept. 16, 1901; "Mr. Roosevelt in Office, *NYT,* Mar. 5, 1901. The Roosevelts and their five children arrived in Washington two days before the Inaugural; that night, they were guests of honor at the home of Sen. Chauncey Depew, along with WM and ISM, relatives Abner, Anna, and Mabel McKinley, Pina, Marsh, Mary, and Ida Barber, "Roosevelt Goes to Washington Today," *NYT,* Mar. 2, 1901.

22. "McKinley's Informal Luncheon, March 4, 1901," WMPL; Inaugural Ball: Colman, *White House Gossip,* 266; Longworth, *Crowded Hours,* 36–37; Robinson, *My Brother Theodore Roosevelt,* 201–2.

23. "People Met in Hotel Lobbies," *WP,* Feb. 1908; Canton party: Kuhns, *Memories of Old Canton,* 61.

24. "Full Itinerary of the President's Trip West," *NYT,* Apr. 14, 1901.

25. Rixey, Braisted, and Bell, *The Life Story of Presley Marion Rixey,* 457; ISM snapped: "Mrs. McKinley Rallying," *San Francisco Call,* May 17, 1901; "Anxiety in Washington," *NYT,* May 16, 1901.

26. Erickson quoted in the *St. Louis Star,* Sept. 7, 1901; GC to John E. Wilkie, Feb. 23, 1901; Callie Bonney Marble to WM, Jan. 11, 1901; John E. Wilkie to BGC, Jan. 22, 1901, Assassination Plots Against President McKinley, Jan.–Sept. 1901 file, Box 65, GCLC; Fawcett, "How the President Is Guarded."

27. WM quotes to Butler are from Morgan, *William McKinley and His America,* 396; Dunn, *From Harrison to Harding,* 355.

15. San Francisco to Buffalo

1. "Presidential Travel," *WP,* June 12, 1907; EHPL, 12:55–61.

2. "As the Women Willed," *NYT,* May 12, 1901.

3. "Mississippi's Greeting," *NYT,* May 2, 1901; "New Orleans Hails President McKinley," *NYT,* May 2, 1901; "The President on His Way to Texas," *NYT,* May 3, 1901.

4. Raines, *Year Book for Texas,* 256–57; EHPL, 12:83.

5. The initial report that the other women of the party went to the breakfast, but not the First Lady, was incorrectly reported in "President McKinley Speaks at El Paso," *NYT,* May 7, 1901; "The Ladies Entertained Magnificently in Juarez Yesterday," *El Paso Herald,* May 7, 1901; Barbara Angus, curator of El Paso Museum of History, to Jennifer Sauers, curator of McKinley Museum, Mar. 1, 2001, WMPL; Mary Barber's letter: "Mrs. McKinley Rallying," *San Francisco Call,* May 17, 1901.

6. "Worries of Handshaking" quoted in Iredale, *An Autumn Tour,* 116; anonymous to WM, June 1, 1901, File "Misc," "A-Z," Box 36, GCLC.

7. Arrival in Redlands: *San Francisco Call,* May 9, 1901; "California Greets President McKinley," *NYT,* May 9, 1901; WM's handwritten telegram draft, May 8, 1901, WMPL; "Los Angeles en Fete," *WP,* May 9, 1901; "The President in a Los Angeles Parade," *NYT,* May 10, 1901; "Flower Carnival," *WP,* Mar 24, 1910; Laughlin story: "People Met in Hotel Lobbies," *WP,* Feb. 26, 1908.

8. "Mrs. McKinley Rallying," *San Francisco Call,* May 17, 1901; "Mrs. McKinley Is Doing Well," *New York World,* May 13, 1901; "Mrs. McKinley Ill, President Takes Her to 'Frisco," *New York World,* May 13, 1901.

9. "Rest for the President: Has Quiet Day at Del Monte," *The Sunday Record-Herald,* May 12, 1901; "President's Wife Ill," *WP,* May 13, 1901; "Mrs. McKinley Rallying," *San Francisco Call,* May 17, 1901; "Official Statement of Mrs. McKinley's Condition," *New York World,* May 13, 1901.

10. "History of the Illness," *NYT,* May 17, 1901; details about ISM on the Western trip: EHPL, 12:55–106; Pell, Buel, and Boyd, *A Memorial Volume,* 175; McClure and Morris, *The Authentic Life of William McKinley,* 114; poem: Adams, *Pathways and Other Poems,* 112.

11. "President Vigil at His Wife's Side," *New York World,* May 16, 1901; "Mrs. McKinley Worse," *Chicago Tribune,* May 16, 1901; 104 degree fever: "Mrs. McKinley Rallying," *San Francisco Call,* May 17, 1901.

12. WM's handwritten statement, n.d. [hand-marked as May 15, 1901], WMPL.

13. "Anxiety in Washington," *NYT,* May 16, 1901.

14. "Still on the Mend," *Washington Star,* May 18, 1901. One Louis Albert Banks found biblical inspiration in the fact that salt saved ISM's life, suggesting it as a potential sermon using Scripture related to salt; see Banks, *Windows for Sermons,* 345–46; pain medication, "Mrs. McKinley Rallying," *San Francisco Call,* May 17, 1901.

15. "Mrs. McKinley Rallying," *San Francisco Call,* May 17, 1901.

16. "An Alarm in the Early Morning," *New York World*, May 17, 1901.

17. "Mrs. McKinley Better Though Still Very Ill," *Philadelphia Inquirer*, May 18, 1901.

18. Anonymous note to WM, May 22, 1901, Assassination Plots Against President McKinley, Jan.–Sept. 1901 file, Box 65, GCLC.

19. "Mrs. McKinley at Ogden," *New York Tribune*, May 27, 1901; William Day to ISM, May 28, 1901, WMPL; largest carnation: "A Change for the Worse," *The Times* [Washington, D.C.], May 16, 1901.

20. "Engagements in the Northeast Abandoned," *New York World*, May 31, 1901; "Mrs. McKinley's Condition," *WP*, June 3, 1901. Later, Rixey would boast that "Her condition on arriving at the White House was as good, or better than when she started." His claim, however, was not borne out by the facts, and he may have been recalling her condition later in July. Rixey, Braisted, and Bell, *The Life Story of Presley Marion Rixey*, 457–58.

21. "Prayers for McKinley on Rumors of Wife's Death," *New York World*, June 3, 1901; "Mrs. McKinley No Better," *WP*, June 4, 1901; "Mrs. McKinley No Better," *The Times*, n.p., June 8, 1901, WMPL; "Mrs. McKinley Doing Well," *WP*, June 6, 1901; Sternberg, *George Miller Sternberg*, 228.

22. "Mrs. McKinley Bids Others Be Amused," *New York Journal*, June 17, 1901; GC's diary, June 10, 1901 entry, GCLC; "Mrs. McKinley Doing Well," *WP*, June 6, 1901; Thomas H. Phillips to WM, June 13, 1901; GC to Thomas H. Phillips, June 15, 1901; Mark Hanna to WM, May 28, 1901; GC to Mark Hanna, May 25, 1901; V. E. Buck to WM, July 6, 1901; Myron Herrick to WM, June 7, 1901; H. O. S. Heistand to WM, June 6, 1901; TR to WM, May 30, 1901, all WMPL; GC's diary entry, July 3, 1901, GCLC.

23. "Life Sketch of the Late Mrs. Ida McKinley," *Stark County Democrat*, May 28, 1907; "Mrs. McKinley at Children's Graves," *New York Journal*, July 8, 1901; Mrs. McKinley Gains Strength," *Washington Star*, July 9, 1901; "Mrs. McKinley's Quiet Sunday," *WP*, July 8, 1901; "Summer Life at Canton," *Pittsburgh Press*, Sept. 1, 1901; 1902 advertisement for A. B. Chase Company Piano, Norwalk, OH, featuring an engraving of the McKinley House, as seen on eBay, April 13, 2010.

24. McElroy, *William McKinley and Our America*, 158–59.

25. Hawk recollections: "William McKinley as Man and Friend," excerpted from *Leslie's Weekly*, *NYT*, Nov. 17, 1901; Jack Adams, *The Roller Monthly*, Nov. 1901, 340. WM was joined by Cortelyou, Rixey, and Herrick in his visit to the farm (photo of them, William McKinley Presidential Library); "Suit by Mrs. McKinley," *NYT*, July 23, 1901, "Mrs. McKinley's Oil Lands," *WP*, Apr. 1899.

26. Gessner quoted in Rixey, Braisted, and Bell, *The Life Story of Presley Marion Rixey*, 242.

27. "Grief at Old Home," *WP*, Sept. 1901.

28. Hawk recollections: "William McKinley as Man and Friend," excerpted from *Leslie's Weekly*, *NYT*, Nov. 17, 1901; Andrew Munson to WM, June 19, 1901, Assassination Plots Against President McKinley, Jan.–Sept. 1901 file, Box 65, GCLC.

29. "Why should . . .": WM to Cortelyou on refusing to give up handshaking, quoted in Morgan, *William McKinley*, 396; "happiest . . .": Wellman, "The Last Days of President McKinley," 414; "If anything . . .": Corning, *William McKinley*, 178–79.

30. CB to Mina Bawsel, Sept. 4, 1901, 118, CBPL; ISM's diary entry quoted in Leech, *In the Days of McKinley*, 585; Rixey recalling WM's remark on ISM's health being the best in twenty-seven years: *Southern California Practitioner*, May 1903, 230.

16. Exposition

1. General information about the McKinleys' arrival at the Exposition and the cannoneer: www.buffalohistoryworks.com/panamex/assassination/mcdeath.htm; "Mrs. McKinley's Love," *The New York World*, May 26, 1907; "up and down . . .": Pendel, *Thirty-Six Years*, 162.

2. Women's luncheon: society page, *Buffalo Evening News*, Sept. 1901; Wellman, "The Last Days of President McKinley," 417–19; "Good afternoon . . .": Leech, *In the Days of McKinley*, 590.

3. Johns, *The Man Who Shot McKinley*, 28–29.

4. Parker references: "President McKinley Shot," *Independent*, Sept. 12, 1901, 2139–40.

5. Although the quote invariably attributed to WM was "My wife—be careful, Cortelyou, how you tell her—oh, be careful!" the alternative remark recorded by reporter Walter Wellman strikes a subtle difference of truth in that it was unlikely McKinley would refer to Ida as "my wife," but rather as "Mrs. McKinley" in light of Cortelyou's closeness to her. Wellman, "The Last Days of President McKinley," 419. Another version was: "I trust Mrs. McKinley will not be informed of this. At least try to see that what she must know of it be not exaggerated in the telling." Fallows, *Life of William McKinley*, 14.

6. The account of ISM learning the news is derived from Wellman, "The Last Days of President McKinley," 422 and Lord, *The Good Years*, 54–55.

7. CB to Mina Bawsel, Sept. 1901, 122, CBPL; "President McKinley Shot," *Independent*, Sept. 12, 1901; ISM's diary entry quoted in Leech, *In the Days of McKinley*, 597.

8. Wilson, "It Is God's Way," 9; "Mrs. McKinley Courageous," *NYT*, Sept. 7, 1901.

9. Jordan's tribute to ISM; "Senator Hanna Sees Cause for Hope," *NYT*, Sept. 8, 1901; Morgan, *William McKinley*, 398–99.

10. "Never Feared Attack," *NYT*, Sept. 1901; "Feared by Doctors," *NYT*, Sept. 8, 1901; "Mrs. McKinley at His Side," *NYT*, Sept. 8, 1901; "How the President Is Being Cared for," *NYT*, Sept. 8, 1901; "President McKinley Holding His Own," *NYT*, Sept. 8, 1901.

11. "Universal Rejoicing Over President's Progress," *NYT*, Sept. 9, 1901; "Details of the Vigil," *NYT*, Sept. 9, 1901; "Relatives Returning to Canton," *WP*, Sept. 1901; "Bulletins More Sanguine," *WP*, Sept. 9, 1901.

12. "Confidence and Joy at the Milburn House," *NYT,* Sept. 10, 1901; "Gaining Every Hour," *WP,* Sept. 10, 1901; ISM's brief press conference: Fallows, *Life of William McKinley,* 23.

13. "The Fourth Day at the Milburn House," *NYT,* Sept. 11, 1901.

14. "Not a Trace of Blood Poisoning," *NYT,* Sept. 12, 1901; "The President Complained of Fatigue, but Seemed to Enjoy His Breakfast—He Asked for a Cigar," *NYT,* Sept. 13, 1901.

15. "Mr. McKinley Has Sinking Spell," *NYT,* Sept. 13, 1901; "Solid Food an Injury," *WP,* Sept. 13,1901.

16. Reuter's News Service story under the headline "Mrs. McKinley," *London Sunday Times,* Sept. 15, 1901, clipping, Ohio Historical Society; "Mr. McKinley Has Sinking Spell," *NYT,* Sept. 13, 1901; "Bulletin Story of the President's Case," *NYT,* Sept. 14, 1901; "Mr. McKinley's Last Day of Suffering," *NYT,* Sept. 14, 1901; "Closing Hours at President's Bedside," *NYT,* Sept. 14, 1901; "I want to go with . . .": Fallows, *Life of William McKinley,* 224.

17. "Callers at the Milburn House," *WP,* Sept. 14, 1901.

18. Reuter's News Service story under the headline "Mrs. McKinley," *London Sunday Times,* n.p., Sept. 15, 1901, clipping, Ohio Historical Society; "God's Will Be Done," *CR,* Jan. 24, 1943.

19. "Mr. McKinley Dies after a Brave Fight," *NYT,* Sept. 14, 1901; www.buffalo-historyworks.com/panamex/assassination/mcdeath.htm.

20. "Broke Sad News to Wife," *WP,* Sept. 15, 1901; "Mrs. McKinley's State Arouses Grave Fears," *NYT,* Sept. 15, 1901; "She Bears Her Grief Bravely," *Buffalo Sunday News,* Sept. 15, 1901; Central News Service story under the headline "Mrs. McKinley," *London Sunday Times,* Sept. 15, 1901, clipping, Ohio Historical Society.

21. Everett, *Complete Life of William McKinley,* 405. It is not entirely clear what was said between Roosevelt and Ida McKinley. It may be that he spoke to Mary Barber. Wellman wrote that Roosevelt went to the Milburn house to offer his condolence "to the representatives of the widow and the family." Wellman, "The Last Days of President McKinley," 425.

22. "Mrs. McKinley Bears Up," *WP,* Sept. 16, 1901; "McKinley's Life Insurance," *WP,* Sept. 16, 1901.

23. "Mrs. McKinley's Grief Is Uncontrollable," *NYT,* Sept. 16, 1901; "He is gone . . .": ISM's obituary, *NYT,* May 27, 1907.

24. Locke's prayer reference to Ida McKinley: "Tenderly sustain Thine handmaiden upon whom the blow of this sorrow most heavily falls. Accompany her, O God, as Thou has promised, through this dark valley and shadow, and may she fear no evil because Thou are with her." "At President's Bier," *WP,* Sept. 16, 1901.

25. "Mrs. McKinley's State Arouses Grave Fears," *NYT,* Sept. 15, 1901; "Sad Duties at White House," *WP,* Sept. 15, 1901.

26. "Proclamation of Mayor Van Wyck," *NYT,* Sept. 15, 1901.

27. "No Partner in Crime," *WP,* Sept. 8, 1901; "Polish Day at the Exposition Cancelled," *WP,* Sept. 10, 1901; the Italian immigrant suspected: "President

McKinley Shot," *Independent,* Sept. 12, 1901; "Death of the President," *Christian Observer,* Sept. 18, 1901; "Poles Repudiate Him," *Daily Picayune,* Sept. 9, 1901.

28. "The Assassin Sentenced," *Independent,* Oct. 3, 1901; Czolgosz on ISM: Henderson, *The Aristocracy of Health,* 543; "Emma Goldman 'Very Sorry,'" *WP,* Sept. 14, 1901; ISM on Czolgosz: Halstead, "Mrs. McKinley," Sept. 6, 1902.

29. "Labor Leaders Clash Over Buffalo Crime," *NYT,* Sept. 9, 1901; DAR, "President McKinley," *American Monthly Magazine,* Oct. 1901; "I cannot get her . . .": "President McKinley: What the World Thought of Him," *Outlook,* Sept. 21, 1901; "at least . . .": "Queen Margherita Words," *NYT,* Sept. 9, 1901; Harlan, *The Booker T. Washington Papers,* 6:201, 621; Nation, *The Use and Need of the Life of Carrie Nation,* 238, 245, 248.

30. "Favorable conditions": Wellman, "The Last Days of President McKinley," 427, 429; Rixey quoted in Rixey, Braisted, and Bell, *The Life Story of Presley Marion Rixey,* 247. "He really gave his life for Mrs. McKinley," a Cabinet wife concurred, declaring to Olcott: "He lived in close, stuffy rooms, for she was afraid of taking cold. He rode in closed carriages. He did not take sufficient exercise because all his leisure time was given to her. When he was shot there was not sufficient vitality to enable him to recover, as a man physically stronger might have done." Said Olcott, "This is confirmed by the testimony of Dr. Mann at the trial, who said that the patient was somewhat weakened by hard work and want of air and that this undoubtedly had something to do with the result." Olcott, *The Life of William McKinley,* 2:364–65; "Mrs. McKinley objecting . . .": Cattell, *Post-Mortem Pathology,* 5–6; no poison on bullets: "The Assassin Sentenced," *Independent,* Oct. 3, 1901, and *Bulletin of the American Academy of Medicine,* 672.

31. "Funeral on Tuesday," *WP,* Sept. 16, 1901; "Multitude Mourns as Train Speeds by," *NYT,* Sept. 17, 1901.

32. "Buffalo's Last Honors to Dead President," *NYT,* Sept. 16, 1901; Wilson, "*It Is God's Way,*" 21; "Trip of the Funeral Train," *WP,* Sept. 17, 1901; "Multitude Mourns as Train Speeds by," *NYT,* Sept. 17, 1901; "Only Once," n.p. [Ohio], Sept. 20, 1901, clipping, WMPL; Ellis, *From Tent to White House,* 225.

33. Everett, *Complete Life of William McKinley,* 345; Crook and Rood, *Memories of the White House,* 268; Pendel, *Thirty-Six Years,* 165–66; "Rests in East Room," *WP,* Sept. 17, 1901; "Alarm Over Mrs. McKinley," *WP,* Sept. 18, 1901.

34. "Service for the Dead in the Capitol Rotunda," *NYT,* Sept. 18, 1901; "Through the Night from the Capital to the Train," *NYT,* Sept. 18, 1901.

35. Harland, *Autobiography,* 469; Foraker, *I Would Live It Again,* 268.

36. "Grief at Old Home," *WP,* Sept. 19, 1901.

37. "Canton Streets Crowded with Hosts of Mourners," *NYT,* Sept. 19, 1901; "Mr. McKinley's Body in His Old Home," *NYT,* Sept. 19, 1901; "Climax of Sad Journey," *WP,* Sept. 19, 1901.

38. "Mrs. McKinley Doing Well," *NYT,* Sept. 20, 1901; "Dr. Rixey's Appointment," *NYT,* Sept. 20, 1901; Wilson, "*It Is God's Way,*" 37; "Last Service for the Nation's Dead," *NYT,* Sept. 20, 1901. On return from California, WM told Rixey,

"For your devotion to Mrs. McKinley . . . If you want to be Surgeon General of the navy you shall have the appointment when vacancy occurs." Witnessed by secretaries Long and Wilson. TR's note to ISM, *Munsey's Magazine,* 1902.

39. McKinley Memoir, "The Man & Husband," n.d., 19, Ohio Historical Society; *Heroic Life,* 42.

40. Rixey, Braisted, and Bell, *The Life Story of Presley Marion Rixey,* 244.

17. The Holding Vault

1. "Mrs. McKinley," *WP,* Sept. 21, 1901; "Mrs. McKinley at the Cemetery," *NYT,* Sept. 21, 1901; "Mrs. McKinley Improves," *NYT,* Sept. 21, 1901; "Mrs. McKinley Not So Well," *NYT,* May 23, 1901; Rixey, Braisted, and Bell, *The Life Story of Presley Marion Rixey,* 86, 243; "Benque, Dangerous Lunatic," *NYT,* Sept. 7, 1903; "Assassination Crank at Canton," *WP,* July 10 1902.

2. "President Roosevelt Has Many Callers," *NYT,* Sept. 22, 1901; "dearly prized . . .": Gilman, *Roosevelt,* 292.

3. "Dr. Rixey Leaves Canton," *NYT,* Oct. 2, 1901; "McKinley Estate Is Over $225,000," *NYT,* Sept. 28, 1901; "Zinc Ore from Illinois," *NYT,* Nov. 15, 1902. The exact amount of the appropriation approved by Congress was $39,809. "Salary Sent to Mrs. McKinley," *WP,* Sept. 16, 1902; "The Widows of Presidents," *NYT,* Dec. 12, 1901; "Pension for Mrs. McKinley," *WP,* Apr. 13, 1902; Mrs. McKinley's Condition," *New Orleans Daily Picayune,* Sept. 22, 1901; "Her Grief Is Intense—Doing as Well as Could Be Expected," n.p., n.d., [circa Sept. 1901], clipping, WMPL.

4. "Slippers Given Since Oct. 10, 1906," and "1906 Gifts Sent by Mrs. McKinley" list, both in unlabeled files in the WM Papers, WMPL.

5. GC to William Day, July 3, 1902; GC to Mary Barber, Oct. 5, 1901, WM Estate Correspondence, 1901–1902 Letter Press Book; GC to Farrond Organ Company, Oct. 3, 1901; GC to Mary Barber, Oct. 5, 1901; GC to Mrs. Stephen Rand, Oct. 19, 1901; GC to H. R. Jones, Dec. 14, 1901; GC to E. DeForest, Dec. 21, 1901; GC to Mary Barber, Jan. 24, 1902; GC to ISM, May 20, 1902; GBC to Judge Day, May 20, 1902; GBC to ISM, June 16, 1902, ISM Estate Correspondence, 1901–4; GC to Anna McKinley, Oct. 25, 1901; GC to Master A. Nashan, Nov. 21, 1901, WM Memorial Association Letterpress Book, 1901–4 file, Box 40, GBLC; "Much Work," *CR,* Dec. 26, 1902. Eventually the four secretaries at the local WM Memorial Association office who handled incoming contributions responded to continuing sympathy letters by sending out the printed card.

6. W. Chandler to ISM, Nov. 13, 1901, McKinley Papers, Container 5, Folder 7, WRH; Thomas Higgins to ISM, Sept. 30, 1901, WMPL. ISM sent a Richmond girl some slippers in appreciation for the child sending a picture of WM. "Slippers from Mrs. McKinley," *WP,* Dec. 27, 1901; "sad season": Sally Kneest to ISM, Dec. 27, 1901, WHPL; "Anarchy Text of Sermons," *NYT,* Sept. 23, 1901.

7. "Little Kate" poem and picture: *The Roller Monthly,* Canton, Ohio, Nov. 1901; postcard of "Little Kate" poem: author's collection; resolution for ISM: Methodist Women's Missionary Society, *Woman's Missionary Friend,* 436; *The School Journal,* 385; maid: Pettengill, *Toilers of the Home,* 142. Congressional eulogy was on February 27, 1902.

8. ISM to John Hay, Mar. 4, 1902, John Hay Papers, Brown Univ. Library. The artist was to be commissioned by a committee appointed by ISM, *Hearings Before Sub-committee of House Committee on Appropriations, consisting of Messrs. Cannon, Hemenway, Moddy, McRae and Bention, in charge of Sundry Civil Appropriations Bill for 1903,* 255; William Cook to GC, Sept. 26, 1901, "McK. Bio" Correspondence A-C file, Box 4, GCLC; "Mrs. McKinley Not to Be at Unveiling," *NYT,* Sept. 13, 1906; "Panic in Crowd at Unveiling," *WP,* Sept. 15, 1906; E. F. Siller to GC, Jan. 13, 1906, GBC Papers, LC; "Mrs. McKinley Annoyed," *WP,* Jan. 24, 1902.

9. Ohioan Walter Bradford argued that WM belonged to the nation, and that all four McKinleys should be buried in Washington. "Memorial to McKinley," *WP,* Nov. 20, 1901; "McKinley National Memorial," *The Chautauquan,* Jan. 1902; Dawes, *A Journal of the McKinley Years,* 290–91.

10. "Sketch of the Eventful Life of Mrs. McKinley," *CR,* May 27, 1907; "Mrs. McKinley's Christmas," *WP,* Dec. 26, 1901.

11. "I miss my . . .": ISM to CH, July 28, 1902; "I am not company . . .": ISM to CH, Sept. 29, 1902. Three months later, she again repeated this to Carolyn ("I realize I am not company for anyone"): ISM to CH, Dec. 13, 1902, and the sentiment is expressed in numerous other letters at that time, all in HWRH.

12. ISM to CH, Sept. 29, 1902, HWRH.

13. "Atlantic City Gaieties," *NYT,* Mar. 2, 1902; "Mrs. McKinley's Niece Weds," *WP,* June 5, 1902; ISM to CH, May 31, 1904, HWRH.

14. ISM to CH, June 27, 1902, HWRH.

15. ISM to CH, Sept. 29, 1902, HWRH; Bowen Brothers invoice, Mar. 24, 1903, WMPL.

16. "Very dear" and "her faith": 1902 Halstead interview; "I cannot . . .": ISM to CD, Mar. 23, 1903, EHS; "I feel as though . . .": ISM to CH, Aug. 16, 1904, HWRH; Foraker, *I Would Live It Again,* 259–60; Kohlsaat, *From McKinley to Harding,* 66–68; Bible reference, article on Mrs. McKinley: Chapple, "Affairs in Washington," 18.

17. ISM to CH, July 28, 1902, HWRH; ISM to CD, Apr. 18, 1904, EHS; Maud M. Healy to CH, Oct. 21, 1902, HWRH.

18. ISM to CH, Mar. 15, 1902, HWRH. Anthony wrote ISM: "it is for us who are left to . . . make the world better for our having lived." ISM had *Reminiscences of Mrs. Stanton* read to her. She again wrote Anthony, promising to send more slippers if the first pair wore out. Harper and Catt, *The Life and Work of Susan B. Anthony,* 1272; ISM to CH, Mar. 29, 1902, HWRH; Mitchell novel: 1902 Halstead interview.

19. "Social and Personal," *WP,* Feb. 23, 1902.

20. Halstead stated that Ida McKinley, as a widow, knitted only in blue and gray, but *The New York World* stated it was black and gray, more likely since she never used black before WM's death. "Mrs. McKinley's Love," *The New York World,* May 26, 1907; George Ernest McMurphy, "Is Always Faithful," n.p., n.d. [circa 1902], clipping, WMPL; slippers, ISM to CD, Apr. 18, 1904, EHS.

21. Wall hangings: State Univ. of Neb. Delegates to ISM, n.d., WMPL; McMurphy, "Is Always Faithful"; ISM to CH, Oct. 11, 1902, and ISM to CH, May 31, 1904, HWRH.

22. ISM to Caro Dawes, Apr. 27, 1907, EHS.

23. "Society at Home and Abroad," *NYT,* Oct. 20, 1901; "Pedigree and Smartness," *WP,* Jan. 20, 1902; Edith Roosevelt to ISM, n.d., WMPL.

24. "Secretary Root at Canton," *WP,* Sept. 1902; "Appeal for Funds," *WP,* Oct. 26, 1902; ISM to CH, Dec. 13, 1902, HWRH.

25. "McKinley Relative Married," *NYT,* Dec. 21, 1902; "Congratulations," *CR,* Dec. 31, 1902.

26. "Mrs. McKinley's Sad New Year," *WP,* Jan. 2, 1903; "The President's Eulogy of McKinley," *NYT,* Jan. 28, 1903; "Other Cities Keep the Day," *NYT,* Jan. 30, 1903.

27. *Southern California Practitioner,* 230; ISM to CH, Apr. 20, 1903, HWRH.

28. ISM to CH, Mar. 10 and 25, 1903, HWRH.

29. ISM to CH, Sept. 10, 1903, WRH; ISM to CH, Apr. 20, 1903, HWRH; ISM to CH, Oct. 22, 1903, HWRH.

30. GC to ISM, Apr. 22, 1903, GCLC; ISM to CD, Aug. 10, 1903, EHS.

31. ISM to CH, Sept. 10, 1903, HWRH; ISM to CH, Aug. 16, 1904, HWRH.

32. GC to ISM, Apr. 22, 1903, GCLC; "Mrs. McKinley in a Runaway," *WP,* Apr. 3, 1903.

33. Dawes, *A Journal of the McKinley Years,* 349–50.

34. "Mrs. McKinley's Niece Weds," *WP,* June 25, 1903.

35. ISM to CD, Aug. 10, 1903, EHS; ISM to CH, Sept. 26, 1903, HWRH.

36. William Day to GC, Nov. 9, 1903, GCLC; Austin Lynch to GC, Nov. 3, 1903, GCLC.

37. ISM to CH, Dec. 11, 1903, HWRH; ISM to CD, Apr. 18, 1904, EHS.

38. "Mrs. McKinley Attends a Concert," *WP,* Dec. 31, 1903; "Mabel McKinley to Sing," *NYT,* May 10, 1903.

39. ISM to CH, Feb. 12, 1902, HWRH.

40. ISM to CD, Mar. 28, 1904, EHS; "Cortelyou Goes West," *WP,* June 21, 1903.

41. ISM to CD, Mar. 28, 1904, EHS; Maud Healy to GC, Sept. 18, 1903, GCLC.

42. Edith Roosevelt to Emily Carow, Sept. 18, 1901, TR Collection, Harvard Univ.

18. The Comfort of Katie

1. ISM to CH, Aug. 16, 1904, HWRH. ISM also took an interest in Myron Herrick gaining the Republican nomination for governor of Ohio. "I am always glad to learn of the high esteem in which your husband is held by the people," she wrote CH.

2. ISM to GC, Aug. 23, 1904, GCLC; "Local Immigration Official Dismissed," *NYT,* Jan. 23, 1902; "Surveyorship Unsettled," *WP,* Feb. 23, 1907; "Mrs. McKinley's Plea," *WP,* Jan. 26, 1906; "An Ohio Postermastership," *WP,* Jan. 27, 1902; the appointment was made. "Capitol Chat," *WP,* May 24, 1902; "Mrs. McKinley's Friend Loses Government Place," *NYT,* July 4, 1902; "Mrs. McKinley Asks Favor," *NYT,* Jan. 27, 1906; Kittie Endsley Matthews to ISM Feb. 1906, GCLC; "President Back Home After His Record Trip," *NYT,* May 12, 1905.

3. Beer, *Hanna,* 105; "Visit to Canton Tomb," *WP,* June 24, 1902; "Filipinos," *CR,* July 1, 1904; "Filipinos Visit McKinley's Tomb," *WP,* July 2, 1904. Buencamino's visit to ISM drew notice in the House of Representatives. "Yesterday this man visited Mrs. McKinley and shed tears," said Jones of Virginia, "remarkable, because in a memorial to congress last year this miserable creature charged that the commencement of hostilities was due to the direct orders of President McKinley," "Lively Philippines Debate in the House," *NYT,* June 25, 1902.

4. "Hanna Dead: Mrs. McKinley Deeply Affected," *WP,* Feb. 16, 1904; "Death of Abner McKinley," *WP,* June 12, 1904.

5. ISM to CH, May 31, 1904, HWRH; ISM to CH, June 28, 1904, HWRH.

6. ISM to CD, Oct. 21, 1904, EHS; ISM to CD, Nov. 22, 1904, EHS; ISM to GC, Mar. 7, 1904, GCLC; Jessica L. Bailey to CD, n.d. [1904], EHS.

7. ISM to CD, Nov. 22, 1904, EHS.

8. "Mrs. McKinley at the Theater," *WP,* Sept. 17, 1904; ISM to CD, Oct. 21, 1904, EHS.

9. "A Box Party," *CR,* Jan. 13, 1905. By 1904, there were new faces in ISM's house. For a time her niece Mary's friend, Mary Cross, stayed with ISM, acting as a companion. Maud Healy returned for a time to Jennie Hobart in New Jersey. During her time away, her sister Gertrude assumed her job as lead nurse, assisted by Jessica Bailey and Mary Cross.

10. Dawes, *A Journal of the McKinley Years,* 17–18; ISM to CD, Feb. 14, 1905, EHS; "McKinley Banquet," *WP,* Feb. 1, 1905.

11. "[J]ust now I dread . . . ," ISM to CH, Aug. 16, 1904, HWRH; ISM to CD, Aug. 17, 1904, EHS.

12. Foraker, *I Would Live It Again,* 267–68; Groetzinger quote, EHPL, 6: 304.

13. Puerto Rico: Josiah Hartzell to ISM, Mar. 10, [no year], Box 23, WMPL; ISM to CD, Feb. 14, 1905, EHS.

14. Classmates: ISM to CD, July 18, 1905, EHS; "Stone Laid at Canton," *WP,* Nov. 17, 1905; "At Bier of President," *CR,* Oct. 3, 1905.

15. ISM to CD, Dec. 7, 1905, EHS; ISM to CD, Dec. 16, 1905, EHS.

16. ISM to CD, July 18, 1905, EHS; ISM to GC, Mar. 7, 1904, GCLC.

17. ISM to CD, May 1, 1906, EHS; "Mrs. McKinley's Memorial," *NYT,* July 10, 1906. She also enjoyed fall foliage: ISM to CD, Oct. 21, 1904, EHS.

18. "Music and Musicians," *WP,* Nov. 25, 1906; Jessie Bailey to Letter-Carriers Union, Dec. 8, 1906; ISM to Kitty Endsley, Mar. 12, 1906, private collection.

19. "Christmas 1906 Gifts Sent by Mrs. McKinley," WMPL; Jessie Bailey to Caro Dawes, Dec. 31, 1906, EHS.

20. Letters of Jessica Bailey to GC, Dec. 17, 1906; ISM to GC, Jan. 21, 1907. ISM sent GC a telegram saying she was "feeling much better and everything is well, but wish to speak with you." Within four days, when thanking him for the wreath sent on WM's birthday, which she brought to the vault, she added pointedly, "Wire when you will be here." ISM telegram to GC, Jan. 25, 1907; ISM telegram to GC, Jan. 29, 1907, all GCLC; ISM to CD, Jan. 9, 1906, EHS.

21. "Carnation Day at Canton" from "Current Topics," *Youth's Companion,* Jan. 26, 1905, 42, and Olcott, *The Life of William McKinley,* 2:392; "Mrs. McKinley's Gift," *NYT,* Feb. 22, 1907; "Keeping Death Vigil," *WP,* May 26, 1907; "Miss Eva Booth Ill," *NYT,* Apr. 11, 1907; ISM to GC, Feb. 2, 1907, GCLC.

22. ISM to GC, Mar. 13, 1907; Maud Healy to GC, Mar. 1907, GCLC.

23. ISM to CD, Mar. 15, 1907, EHS.

24. Telegrams from ISM to GC, Mar. 20, 1907; Maud Healy to GC, Mar. 20, 1907, GCLC.

25. ISM TO GC, Mar. 23, 1907, GCLC.

26. ISM to CD, Mar. 22, 1907, EHS.

27. ISM to GC, Feb. 22, 1906, GCLC; ISM to CD, Apr. 27, 1907, EHS; J. B. Parker to ISM, n.d. [circa early 1906], GCLC.

28. ISM to GC, Feb. 10, 1906, GCLC; "Around the Campus," *American Educational Review,* Feb. 1907.

29. ISM to GC, Apr. 1, 1907, GCLC; ISM to CD, Apr. 20, 1907, EHS; ISM to CD, Mar. 22, 1907, EHS; ISM to CD, Apr. 27, 1907, EHS.

30. "No Hope for Mrs. McKinley," *NYT,* May 24, 1907; "Mrs. McKinley Dying," *WP,* May 24, 1907; "No Hope for Mrs. McKinley," *NYT,* May 25, 1907; "Keeping Death Vigil," *WP,* May 26, 1907; "Mrs. McKinley Dies," *WP,* May 27, 1907; "Mrs. McKinley Dies in Canton Cottage," *WP,* May 27, 1907; "Mrs. McKinley Passes into Final Sleep," *CR,* May 27, 1907; "Surgeon Rixey's Account of Death of Mrs. McKinley," n.p., May 30, 1907, clipping, WMPL; Rixey's appointment: *Leslie's Weekly,* Oct. 24, 1901; Rixey, "Guarding the Health of Our Presidents"; *Record of Deaths, Probate Court, Stark County, Ohio, for the Year Ending March 31, 1909,* no. 499, 85–86.

31. "President McKinley Home Life," *NYT,* May 30, 1907; "8000 Honor Mrs. McKinley," *NYT,* May 29, 1907. Sickness prevented Taft, now war secretary, from attending as he had intended. "Cold Imprisons Secretary Taft," *WP,* May 28, 1907;

TR to Kermit Roosevelt, June 1, 1907, *Theodore Roosevelt Association Newsletter,* 5, 675–79; "Cantonians in Silent Tribute Gather at McKinley Home," *Canton Evening Repository,* May 28, 1907; "Mrs. McKinley," *The Outlook,* 261; "In the McKinley Tomb," *WP,* May 30, 1907; "Eulogy of Mrs. McKinley, *NYT,* June 3, 1907.

32. "Mrs. McKinley's Life Ideal," *WP,* May 27, 1907; "Mourning in Capital," *WP,* May 27, 1907; "Sketch of the Eventful Life of Mrs. McKinley," *CR,* May 27, 1907; *The Phrenological Journal and Science of Health,* 262; "Private Funeral for Mrs. McKinley," *NYT,* May 28, 1907.

33. "Move Mrs. McKinley's Body," *NYT,* Sept. 19, 1907; Phayre, *America's Day,* 209.

Bibliography

Manuscript Collections

Beer Family Papers: Yale University Library, New Haven, Conn.

Betsy Mix Cowles Papers: Kent State University, Kent, Ohio

California Register of the San Francisco Earthquake Scrapbook, 1893, 1898–1910: University of the Pacific Library, Holt-Atherton Special Collections, Stockton, Calif.

Charles G. Dawes Collection: Northwestern University Library, Evanston, Ill.

Charles G. Dawes Papers: Evanston Historical Society, Evanston, Ill.

Hanna Family Papers, Herrick Family Papers, William McKinley Papers: Western Reserve Historical Society, Cleveland, Ohio

John Hay Papers: Brown University Library, Providence, R.I.

McKinley Papers, Benjamin Montgomery Papers: Rutherford B. Hayes Presidential Center, Fremont, Ohio

Robinson Family Papers: New York Historical Society, N.Y.

Theodore Roosevelt Collection: Harvard University, Cambridge, Mass.

Various collections, including the twelve-volume "McKinley Biography" typescript by Edward T. Heald: William McKinley Presidential Library and Museum, Canton, Ohio

William McKinley Papers: Ohio Historical Society, Columbus, Ohio

William McKinley Papers, Hanna Family Papers, George B. Cortelyou Papers, Theodore Roosevelt Papers, Leonard Wood Papers: Library of Congress, Washington, D.C.

Web Sites

Alaska Yukon Pacific Exposition of 1909
  http://content.lib.washington.edu/aypweb/index.html

Documentary history of William McKinley's assassination
  http://mckinleydeath.com
The 1896 presidential campaign
  http://projects.vassar.edu/1896/1896home.html
Igorrotes of the Philippines
  www.encyclopedia123.com/I/Igorrotes.html
The Spanish-American War
  www.spanamwar.com

Selected Periodicals

The Advance Magazine, August 29, 1907, 255.
Arnold, Eugenia Hill. "Recollections of Mrs. Stonewall Jackson. *The Confederate Veteran Magazine,* November 1922, n.p.
"Around the Campus," *American Educational Review,* February 1907.
Baker, Ray Stannard. "General Leonard Wood." *McClure's Magazine,* February 1900.
Baker's Cleveland City Directory, 1864–1865. Cleveland: Ben Franklin Print, 1864.
Banks, Miss. "Sunday at the White House." *The Review of Reviews* 18 (July–December 1898): n.p. London: Horace Marshall & Son Publishers.
Barton, Frederick. "A Christian Gentleman: William McKinley." *Chautauquan* 34, no. 2 (November 1901): 134.
Bensley, E. W., and D. G. Bates. "Sir William Osler's Autobiographical Notes." *Bulletin of the History of Medicine* 50 (1976): 596–618.
Berrios, G. E. "Epilepsy and Insanity During the Early 19th Century: A Conceptual History" 9 (September 1984): 978–81. Archives of Neurology, U.S. National Library of Medicine, National Institutes of Health.
Borowitz, Albert. "The Canton Tragedy." *Cleveland Magazine,* July 1985, n.p.
———. "The Canton Tragedy." From "Crimes Gone by: Collected Essays of Albert Borowitz, 1966–2005," reprinted in *Legal Studies Forum* 29, no. 2 (2005).
Brotherhood of Locomotive Firemen. *Locomotive Firemen's Magazine.* Published by Brotherhood of Locomotive Fireman (U.S.), 1904.
Call, S. F. "A Love Story: The Courtship of Ida Saxton When She Was Major McKinley's Sweetheart." *The New England Home Magazine,* insert of the *Boston Sunday Journal,* June 2, 1901.
Cass, F. B. "Mrs. William McKinley: The Story of the Life of the Beautiful First Lady of the United States." *The New England Home Magazine,* insert of the *Boston Sunday Journal,* June 2, 1901.
Cather, Willa. "Two Women the World Is Watching." *Home Monthly Magazine,* September 1896, n.p.
Chapple, Jose Mitchell. "Affairs in Washington." *The National Magazine,* April–September 1905.

Cumming, Wallace. "Life in Manila." *The Century,* August 1898.

DeToledo, John C., Bruno B. DeToledo, and Merredith Lowe. "Epilepsy of First Lady Ida Saxton McKinley." *Southern Medical Journal* 93, no, 3 (March 2000): 267–71.

Fawcett, Waldon. "How the President Is Guarded." *Leslie's Weekly Illustrated,* September 21, 1901.

Frease, George B. "The Man McKinley, as Seen by a Personal Friend." *Our Day Magazine,* March 1, 1897.

"God's Hand in Recent American History." *The Interior,* November 24, 1898.

Hale, Edward Everett. *Social Service Magazine,* 4, July–September 1901. New York: The League For Social Service, A Monthly Magazine Devoted to Improving the Condition of the Employed.

Halstead, Murat. "Mrs. McKinley." *Saturday Evening Post,* September 6, 1902, 6–7.

Hamilton, J. W. "William McKinley." *The Contemporary Review,* October 1901.

Hawley, Mary K. [Willa Cather]. "Two Women the World Is Watching." *The Home Monthly,* September 1896, 4–5.

Hearings Before Sub-committee of House Committee on Appropriations, consisting of Messrs. Cannon, Hemenway, Moddy, McRae and Bention, in charge of Sundry Civil Appropriations Bill for 1903.

Hearing Before the Select Committee on Woman Su Vrage, United States Senate. On the Joint Resolution (S. R. 53) Proposing an Amendment to the Constitution of the United States Extending the Right of Suffrage to Women. Washington, D.C.: Government Printing Office, February 18, 1902.

Hearings Before the 537—Subcommittee of the Appropriations, United States Senate, on the It/1 Bill (H. R. 8347) Making Appropriations for the Legislative, Executive, and Judicial Expenses of the Government for the Fiscal Year Ending June 30, 1901, and For Other Purposes. Washington, D.C.: Government Printing Office, 1900.

Hirschhorn, Norbert. "Medicine Posthumous: Diagnosing the Illnesses of Famous Persons Long Dead." *The Writer* 8, no. 2 (Winter 2009–2010).

Hunt, Eva. "My Experiences as a Nurse to Mrs. McKinley and the Late President." *Sunday [San Francisco] Call,* January 19, 1902.

Indiana State Board of Agriculture Annual Report, 1900.

J. H. Williston & Co.'s Directory of the City of Cleveland to Which Is Added a Business Directory for 1861–2. Cleveland: Ben Franklin Print, 1861.

Jordan, E. G. "Appreciation." *Harper's Weekly,* September 21, 1901.

Kindergarten Magazine, November 1897–June 1898.

Kuhns, Dorothy. "My Favorite Character in History." *St. Nicholas: An Illustrated Magazine for Young Folks,* May–October 1903.

"Life Sketch of the Late Mrs. Ida McKinley." *Stark County Democrat,* May 28, 1907.

Logan, Mary. "The Gracious Lady of the White House." *Frank Leslie's Popular Magazine,* July 1899.

Lummis, Charles F. "In the Lion's Den." *The Land of Sunshine: The Magazine of California and the West* XIV (January–June 1901), 501–3.

The Manifesto: The Only Periodical Published by the Shakers, November 1897, 176.

Matthews, Franklin. "The President's Last Days." *Harper's Weekly,* September 21, 1901, 943.

"The Mentally Ill Ida McKinley." *Washington Times,* September 17, 2003.

Methodist Women's Missionary Society. *Woman's Missionary Friend,* December 1901. Methodist Episcopal Church, Woman's Foreign Missionary Society.

Mosher, Warren E., ed. *Mosher's Magazine: Organ of the Catholic Summer School and Reading Circle Union,* May–September 1899.

"Mrs. McKinley." *The Outlook Magazine,* June 8, 1907, 261.

"Mrs. McKinley's Lover: He Has Been Her Constant Admirer and Willing Slave for Many Years, and Now He Is the President." *The New England Home Magazine,* insert of the *Boston Sunday Journal,* June 2, 1901.

"Mrs. McKinley's Sorrow: Bereaved of Her Two Little Ones, Her Health and Strength Gave Way." *The New England Home Magazine,* insert of the *Boston Sunday Journal,* June 2, 1901.

"Mrs. McKinley's Wedding Card." *The New England Home Magazine,* insert of the *Boston Sunday Journal,* June 2, 1901.

Murray, Grace Peckham. "First Aid to the Injured." *Harper's Bazaar,* August 26, 1899.

The New England Home Magazine, insert of the *Boston Sunday Journal,* June 2, 1901.

Official Report, The Centennial Celebration. Of the Founding of the City of Cleveland and the Settlement of the Western Reserve. Compiled by Edward A. Roberts, Secretary and historian of the Centennial Commission, and Published Under Appropriation by the City Council. Cleveland: Bushing Co., 1896.

Papers Relating to the Foreign Relations of the United States, with the Annual Message of the President Transmitted to Congress December 5, 1898. Washington, D.C.: U.S. Government Printing Office, 1898.

Parish, Rebecca. "An Igorrote Kanyao." *Missionary Friend Magazine,* December 1911.

Philadelphia Commercial Museum Meetings of the International Advisory Board. *Opening of the Museum by President McKinley and Addresses Made at the Banquet.* Philadelphia: Avil Printing Company, June 1–4, 1897.

The Phrenological Journal and Science of Health, August 1907.

"President McKinley in War Times." *McClure's Magazine,* July 1898, 215.

Printers' Ink: A Journal for Advertisers, July 15, 1896, 52.

Reid, Babington. "A New Rear Admiral." *Munsey's Magazine,* April–September 1902.

Rixey, P. M., M. D. Mann, H. Mynter, R. Park, E. Wasdin, C. McBurney, and C. G. Stockton. "Death of President McKinley." *Journal of the American Medical Association* 37 (1901): 779.

———. "The Official Report on the Case of President McKinley." *Journal of the American Medical Association* 37 (1901): 1029.

Rixey, Presley Marion. "Guarding the Health of Our Presidents." *Better Health Magazine,* June 1925.

The School Journal, April 5, 1902.

Smith, Honorable James F. "The Philippines as I Saw Them." *Sunset Magazine,* February 1911.

Southern California Practitioner 18, no. 5 (May 1903): 230.

The Southern Workman and Hampton School Record, January 1899.

Speed, John Gilmer. "A Study of Major William McKinley." *Demorest's Family Magazine,* circa July–November 1896.

Taft, William Howard. "Why I Went to the Philippines." *National Magazine,* October 1908.

21st Annual Report of the Woman's Presbyterian Board of Missions of the Northwest Chicago. Chicago: C. H. Blakely & Co., April 1892.

United States Department of State. *Papers Relating to the Foreign Relations of the United States, with the Annual Message of the President Transmitted to Congress December 5, 1899.*

Wellman, Walter. "The Last Days of President McKinley: His Visit to Buffalo, the Tragedy, and the Nation's Mourning." *American Monthly Review of Reviews,* October 1901, 414–30.

West, Marian. "Our Four Year Queens." *Munsey's Magazine,* March 1901.

Wiemer, Andreas. "New Discoveries in McKinley Autographs." *Manuscripts,* Summer 2006.

Williams, C. S. *Canton & Massillon Directory, City Guide and Business Mirror,* vol. 1, 1859–1860. Canton, Ohio: C. S. Williams, 1859.

Woman's Missionary Friend. December 1901. Boston: Methodist Episcopal Church, Woman's Foreign Missionary Society.

Worchester, Dean C. "Knotty Problems of the Philippine." *The Century,* October 1898.

Selected Secondary Works

Adams, Henry, and Jacob Claver Levenson. *The Letters of Henry Adams.* Cambridge, Mass.: Belknap, 1988.

Adams, Myra Winchester. *Pathways and Other Poems.* New York: F. W. Orvis, 1903.

Albaugh, Thurlow K. *Canton's Great Tragedy—The Murder of George D. Saxton, Together with a History of the Arrest and Trial of Annie E. George, Charged with the Murder: With Biographical Sketches of George D. Saxton and Annie E. George: With Illustrations.* Wooster, Ohio: Press of Clapper Printing Co., 1899.

Anderson, Gerald H. *Studies in Philippine Church History.* Ithaca, N.Y.: Cornell University Press, 1969.

Anderson, Gerald H., and Thomas F. Stransky. *Christ's Lordship and Religious Pluralism.* Maryknoll, N.Y.: Orbis Books, 1981.

Anderson, Peggy. *The Daughters.* St. Martin's Press: New York, 1974.

Andrews, Byron. *One of the People: Life and Speeches of William McKinley, Citizen, Soldier, Congressman, Governor, and Presidential Candidate . . . to Which Is Added a Brief Sketch of Garret A. Hobart, Candidate for Vice-President.* Chicago: F. T. Neely, 1896.

Ashmead, Henry Graham. *History of Delaware County, Pennsylvania.* Philadelphia: Everts, 1884.

Bailey, Thomas Andrew. *A Diplomatic History of the American People,* 10th ed. Englewood Cliffs, N.J.: Prentice-Hall, 1980.

Baillie, Hugh. *High Tension: The Recollections of Hugh Baillie.* New York: Harper, 1959.

Banks, Louis Albert. *Windows for Sermons; A Study of the Art of Sermonic Illustration, Together with Four Hundred Fresh Illustrations Suited for Sermons and Reform Addresses.* New York: Funk & Wagnalls Co., 1902.

Barnes, James. *From Then Till Now.* New York: Appleton-Century, 1934.

Barrows, John Henry. *The Christian Conquest of Asia: Studies and Personal Observations of Oriental Religions: Being the Morse Lectures of 1898.* New York: Scribner, 1899.

Beer, Thomas. *Hanna,* 2nd ed. New York: Knopf, 1929.

Bemi, Samuel Flagg. *Diplomatic History of the United States.* New York: Henry Holt & Company, 1938.

Blount, James H. *The American Occupation of the Philippines, 1898–1912.* New York: G. P. Putnam's Sons, 1912.

Blue, Herbert Tenney Orren. *History of Stark County, Ohio, From the Age of Prehistoric Man to the Present Day.* Chicago: Clarke, 1928.

Briggs, Isaac G., *Epilepsy, Hysteria, and Neurasthenia: Their Causes, Symptoms & Treatments.* London: Methuen & Company, 1921.

Brogan, Hugh, and Charles Mosley. *American Presidential Families.* New York: Macmillan, 1993.

Bruce, H. Addington. *Handicaps of Childhood.* New York: Dodd, Mead and Co., 1917.

Butt, Archibald Willingham, and Lawrence F. Abbott. *The letters of Archie Butt, Personal Aide to President Roosevelt.* Garden City, N.Y.: Doubleday, Page, 1924.

Butterworth, Hezekiah. *The Young McKinley; or, School-days in Ohio; A Tale of Old Times on the Western Reserve.* New York: D. Appleton and Co., 1905.

Byars, William Vincent. *"An American Commoner"; The Life and Times of Richard Parks Bland. A Study of the Last Quarter of the Nineteenth Century.* Columbia, Mo.: E. W. Stephens, 1900.

Cain, Mary M. "Ida McKinley." In *American First Ladies,* edited by Robert P. Watson, 167–75. Ipswich, Mass.: Salem Press, 2002.

Canton First Baptist Church. *The Canton Favorite Cook Book.* Canton, Ohio: Canton First Baptist Church, 1896.

Cather, Willa, and William Martin Curtin. *The World and the Parish: Willa Cather's Articles and Reviews, 1893–1902.* Lincoln: University of Nebraska Press, 1970.

Cattell, Henry Ware. *Post-Mortem Pathology.* Philadelphia: J. B. Lippincott & Co., 1903.

Colman, Edna. *White House Gossip.* New York: Cosmopolitan Books, 1927

Conger, Emily Bronson. *An Ohio Woman in the Philippines; Giving Personal Experiences and Descriptions Including Incidents of Honolulu, Ports in Japan and China.* Akron, Ohio: Press of R. H. Leighton, 1904.

Corning, Amos Elwood. *William McKinley; A Biographical Study.* New York: Broadway Printing Co., 1907.

Croly, Herbert David. *Marcus Alonzo Hanna: His Life and Work.* New York: Macmillan, 1912.

Crook, W. H., and Henry Rood. *Memories of the White House: The Home Life of Our Presidents from Lincoln to Roosevelt, Being Personal Recollections of Colonel W. H. Crook.* Boston: Little, Brown, and Co., 1911.

Damon, Ethel M. *Sanford Ballard Dole and His Hawaii, with an Analysis of Justice Dole's Legal Opinions.* Alto, Calif.: Published for the Hawaiian Historical Society by Pacific Books, 1957.

Daniel, Peter, and Raymond Smock. *A Talent for Detail: The Photographs of Miss Frances Benjamin Johnston, 1889–1910.* New York: Harmony Books, 1974.

Danner, John. *Old Landmarks of Canton and Stark County, Ohio to Which Is Appended a Comprehensive Compendium of Local Biography—Memoirs of Representative Men and Women of the County, Whose Works of Merit Have Made Their Names Imperishable: Illustrated.* Logansport, Ind.: B. F. Bowen, 1904.

Davis, Richard Harding. *A Year from a Correspondent's Notebook.* London: Harper & Bros., 1898.

Dawes, Charles G. *A Journal of the McKinley Years.* Chicago: The Lakeside Press, Donnelley and Sons, 1950.

Dennett, Tyler. *Americans in Eastern Asia, a Critical Study of the Policy of the United States with Reference to China, Japan, and Korea in the 19th Century, by Tyler Dennett.* New York: Macmillan, 1922.

Dingley, Edward N. *The Life and Times of Nelson Dingley, Jr.* Kalamazoo, Mich.: Ihling Bros. & Everard, 1902.

Duffield, Isabel McKenna. *Washington in the 90's: California Eyes Dazzled by the Brilliant Society of the Capitol [sic].* San Francisco: Press of Overland Monthly, 1929.

Dunn, Arthur Wallace. *From Harrison to Harding, a Personal Narrative, Covering a Third of a Century, 1888–1921.* New York: G. P. Putnam's Sons, 1922.

Edgerly, Lois Stiles. *Give Her This Day: A Daybook of Women's Words.* Gardiner, Maine: Tilbury House, 1990.

Ellis, Edward Sylvester. *From Tent to White House; or, How a Poor Boy Became President.* Philadelphia: David McKay, 1901.

Everett, Marshall. *Complete Life of William McKinley and Story of His Assassination: An Authentic and Official Memorial Edition, Containing Every Incident in the Career of the Immortal Statesman, Soldier, Orator, and Patriot.* Memorial ed. Chicago: Historical Press/Marshall Everett, 1901.

———. *Exciting Experiences in Our Wars with Spain and the Filipinos.* Chicago: Book Publishers Union, 1899.

Fallows, Samuel. *Life of William McKinley, Our Martyred President, with Short Biographies of Lincoln and Garfield, and a Comprehensive Life of President Roosevelt, Containing the Masterpieces of McKinley's Eloquence, and a History of Anarchy, Its Purposes and Results.* Chicago: Regan Printing House, 1901.

Foraker, Julia Benson. *I Would Live It Again, Memories of a Vivid Life, by Julia B. Foraker.* New York: Harper and Bros., 1932.

Friedlander, Walter J. *The History of Modern Epilepsy: The Beginning, 1865–1914.* Westport, Conn.: Greenwood Press, 2001.

Furman, Bess. *White House Profile.* New York: Bobbs-Merrill, 1951.

Geary, Linda L. *Balanced in the Wind: A Biography of Betsey Mix Cowles.* Lewisburg, Pa.: Bucknell University Press, 1989.

Geer, Emily Apt. *First Lady: The Life of Lucy Webb Hayes.* Kent, Ohio: Kent State Univ. Press, 1984.

Gerlach-Spriggs, Nancy, Richard Kaufman, and Sam Bass Warner Jr. *Restorative Gardens: The Healing Landscape.* New Haven, Conn.: Yale University Press, 2004.

Gilman, Bradley. *Roosevelt, the Happy Warrior.* Boston: Little, Brown, and Co., 1921.

Gipson, Richard McCandless. *The Life of Emma Thursby, 1845–1931.* New York: New York Historical Society, 1940.

Goldman, Mark. *High Hopes: The Rise and Decline of Buffalo, New York.* Albany: State Univ. of New York Press, 1983.

Gould, Lewis L. *The Spanish-American War and President McKinley.* Lawrence: Univ. Press of Kansas, 1982.

Grammar, Punctuation, and Capitalization, Letter Writing with Practical Questions and Examples. Scranton, Pa.: The Colliery Engineer Co., 1899.

Hagedorn, Hermann. *Leonard Wood: A Biography.* New York: London, 1931.

Halstead, Murat. *The Illustrious Life of William McKinley.* Cincinnati, Ohio: M. Halstead, 1901.

———. *Life and Achievements of Admiral Dewey from Montpelier to Manila: The Brilliant Cadet—The Heroic Lieutenant—The Capable Captain, the Conquering Commodore, the Famous Admiral One of the Stars in the Class at Annapolis, Distinguished in Tremendous Battles on.* Chicago: C. W. Slauson Publishing Co., 1899.

———. *Victorious Republicanism and Lives of the Standard-Bearers, McKinley and Roosevelt.* Chicago: Republican National Pub. Co., 1900.

Halstead, Murat, Chauncey M. Depew, and A. J. Munson. *Life and Distinguished Services of William McKinley; Our Martyr President.* Memorial ed. Chicago: M. A. Donohue, 1901.

Halstead, Murat, John Sherman, Charles Henry Grosvenor, Albert Halstead, and Chauncey M. Depew. *Life and Distinguished Services of Hon. William McKinley: And the Great Issues of 1896: Containing Also a Sketch of the Life of Garret A. Hobart.* Philadelphia: Edgewood Publishing Company, 1896.

Harlan, Louis R., and Raymond W. Smock, eds. *The Booker T. Washington Papers, v. 6, 1901–2.* Urbana: Univ. of Illinois Press, 1977.

Harland, Marion. *Marion Harland's Autobiography; The Story of a Long Life.* New York: Harper & Brothers, 1910.

Harper, Ida Husted, and Carrie Chapman Catt. *The Life and Work of Susan B. Anthony; Including Public Addresses, Her Own Letters, and Many from Her Contemporaries During Fifty Years.* Indianapolis and Kansas City: The Bowen-Merrill Company, 1898–1908.

Harpine, William D. *From the Front Porch to the Front Page: McKinley and Bryan in the 1896 Presidential Campaign.* College Station: Texas A & M, 2005.

Hart, Craig. *A Genealogy of the Wives of the American Presidents and Their First Two Generations of Descent.* Jefferson, N.C.: McFarland, 2004.

Hartzell, Josiah *Sketch of the Life of Mrs. William McKinley.* Washington, D.C.: Home Magazine Press, 1896.

Heald, Edward Thornton. *The William McKinley Story.* Canton, Ohio: Stark County Historical Society, 1964.

Henderson, Mary Newton Foote. *The Aristocracy of Health; A Study of Physical Culture, Our Favorite Poisons, and a National and International League for Advancement of Physical Culture.* Washington, D.C.: The Colton Publishing Co., 1904.

The Heroic Life of William McKinley: Our Third Martyr President. Boston: DeWolfe, Fiske & Co., 1902.

Hobart, Jennie Tuttle. *Memories.* Paterson, N.J.: Hobart, 1930.

Hoover, Irwin Hood. *Forty-Two Years in the White House.* Boston: Houghton Mifflin Co., 1934.

Hopley, Georgia. *McKinley and His Campaign.* [No city or publisher], 1899.

Iredale, Andrew. *An Autumn Tour in the United States and Canada.* Torquay, U.K.: G. H. Iredale, 1901.

Iversen, Kristen. *Molly Brown Unraveling the Myth.* Boulder, Colo.: Johnson Books, 1999.

James, Edward T., Janet Wilson James, and Paul S. Boyer. *Notable American Women, 1607–1950: A Biographical Dictionary.* Cambridge, Mass.: Belknap Press of Harvard University Press, 1971.

Johns, A. Wesley. *The Man Who Shot McKinley.* South Brunswick, N.J.: A. S. Barnes and Co., Inc., 1970.

Johnston, Frances Benjamin, Pete Daniel, and Raymond Smock. *A Talent for Detail: The Photographs of Miss Frances Benjamin Johnston, 1889–1910.* New York: Harmony Books, 1974.

Jones, Alice Danner. *A McKinley Romance.* Canton, Ohio: Alice Danner Jones Company, 1901.

Jordan, Elizabeth G. *Three Rousing Cheers.* New York and London: D. Appleton-Century Co., 1938.

Kennedy, James Harrison, and Henry L. Burnett. *History of the Ohio Society of New York, 1885–1905.* New York: Grafton Press, 1906.

Kirk, Elise. *Music at the White House: A History of the American Spirit.* Champaign, Ill.: Univ. of Illinois, 1986.

———. *Musical Highlights from the White House.* Malabar, Fla.: Krieger Publishing Company, 1992.

Kohlsaat, Herman Henry. *From McKinley to Harding: Personal Recollections of Our Presidents*. New York: C. Scribner's Sons, 1923.

Kreisel, Martha. *American Women Photographers: A Selected and Annotated Bibliography*. Westport, Conn.: Greenwood Press, 1999.

Kuhns, William T. *Memories of Old Canton and My Personal Recollections of William McKinley*. Canton, Ohio: Kuhns, 1937.

Leech, Margaret. *In the Days of McKinley*. New York: Harper, 1959.

Littell, Eliakim. *Living Age*. Memphis Tenn.: General Books, 2010.

Logan, Mary S., and John Logan. *The Part Taken by Women in American History*. New York: Arno Press, 1972.

Logan, Mary Simmerson Cunningham. *Thirty Years in Washington; or, Life and Scenes in Our National Capital—Portraying the Wonderful Operations in all the Great Departments, and Describing Every Important Function of Our National Government . . . With Sketches of the Presidents and Their Wives*. Hartford, Conn.: A. D. Worthington & Co., 1901.

Long, John Davis, and Lawrence Shaw Mayo. *America of Yesterday, As Reflected in the Journal of John Davis Long*. Boston: The Atlantic Monthly Press, 1923.

Longworth, Alice Roosevelt. *Crowded Hours, Reminiscences of Alice Roosevelt Longworth*. New York: C. Scribner's Sons, 1933.

Lord, Walter. *The Good Years: From 1900 to the First World War*. New York: Harper, 1960.

MacNair, Harley Farnsworth, and Donald F. Lach. *Modern Far Eastern International Relations*. New York: Van Nostrand, 1950.

Marchesi, Blanche. *Singer's Pilgrimage*. New York: Da Capo Press, 1978.

Mattingly, Carol. *Well-Tempered Women: Nineteenth-Century Temperance Rhetoric*. Carbondale: Southern Illinois Univ. Press, 1998.

McCallum, Jack Edward. *Leonard Wood: Rough Rider, Surgeon, Architect of American Imperialism*. New York: New York Univ. Press, 2006.

McClure, Alexander K., and Charles Morris. *The Authentic Life of William McKinley: Our Third Martyr President: Together with a Life Sketch of Theodore Roosevelt*. Philadelphia: Globe Bible Publishing Co., 1901.

McElroy, Richard L. *William McKinley and Our America: A Pictorial History*. Canton, Ohio: Stark County Historical Society, 1996.

McKinley, Ida Saxton, Henry S. Belden, and Mary Saxton Barber. *Grand Tour of Ida Saxton McKinley and Sister Mary Saxton Barber, 1869*. Canton, Ohio: Henry S. Belden III., 1985.

The McKinley National Memorial. Canton, Ohio: McKinley National Memorial Association, 1907.

Melder, Keith. *Beginnings of Sisterhood: The American Woman's Rights Movement, 1800–1850*. New York: Schocken Books, 1977.

Miller, Nathan. *Theodore Roosevelt: A Life*. New York: Morrow, 1992.

Mitchell, Silas Weir. *Injuries of Nerves and Their Consequences*. Philadelphia: B. Lippincott Co., 1872.

Moore, Charles. *The Life and Times of Charles Follen McKim.* Boston: Houghton Mifflin Co., 1929.

Moore, Gay Morgan. *Canton.* Charleston, S.C.: Arcadia, 2009.

Morgan, H. Wayne. *William McKinley and His America.* Syracuse, N.Y.: Syracuse Univ. Press, 1963.

Morris, Clara. *The Life of a Star.* New York: Mcclure Phillips & Co., 1906.

Morris, Edmund. *Theodore Rex.* New York: Random House, 2001.

Morris, Sylvia. *Edith Kermit Roosevelt: Portrait of a First Lady.* Boston: Coward, Mc-Cann & Geoghegan, 1980.

Mott, Thomas Bentley. *Myron T. Herrick, Friend of France: An Autobiographical Biography.* Garden City, N.Y.: Doubleday, Doran & Co., 1929.

Mowbray, Jay Henry. *Representative Men of New York: A Record of Their Achievements,* vol. 1. New York: New York Press, 1898.

Murdock, Victor. *"Folks."* New York: Macmillan Co., 1921.

Musgrave, George Clarke. *Under Three Flags in Cuba: A Personal Account of the Cuban Insurrection and Spanish-American War.* Boston: Little, Brown, and Co., 1899.

Nation, Carrie Amelia. *The Use and Need of the Life of Carrie A. Nation.* Topeka, Kans.: F. M. Steves and Sons, 1908.

Newman, Angelia French Thurston. *McKinley Carnations of Memory: The McKinley Button of Two Campaigns.* New York: Mail and Express Job Print, 1904.

Olcott, Charles S. *The Life of William McKinley.* Boston: Houghton Mifflin Co., 1916.

Osborn, Albert. *John Fletcher Hurst: A Biography.* New York: Eaton & Mains, 1905.

Pearson, Francis Bail, and J. S. Harlor. *Ohio History Sketches.* Columbus: Pearson & Harlor, 1903.

Pell, Edward Leigh, James W. Buel, and James P. Boyd. *A Memorial Volume of American History: McKinley and Men of Our Times, Together with the Great Questions with Which They Have Been Identified and Which Are Still Pressing for Solution.* St. Louis: Historical Society of America, 1901.

Pendel, Thomas F. *Thirty-Six Years in the White House.* Washington: Neale Pub. Co., 1902.

Perrin, William Henry, ed. *History of Stark County, with an Outline Sketch of Ohio.* Chicago: Baskin & Battey, 1949.

Pettengill, Lillian. *Toilers of the Home: The Record of a College Woman's Experience as a Domestic Servant.* New York: Doubleday, Page & Co., 1903.

Phayre, Ignatius. *America's Day, Studies in Light and Shade, by Ignatius Phayre.* London: Constable, 1918.

Porter, Robert Percival. *Life of William McKinley: Soldier, Lawyer, Statesman.* Cleveland, Ohio: N. G. Hamilton Publishing Company, 1896.

Pringle, Henry F. *The Life and Times of William Howard Taft: A Biography.* New York: Farrar & Rinehart, 1939.

———. *Theodore Roosevelt: A Biography.* New York: Harcourt, Brace, 1931.

Raines, Cadwell Walton. *Year Book for Texas, 1901 Public Officials and Departments under the Republic and State, Institutions, Important Events, Obituaries of Distinguished*

Dead, Industrial Development, Statistics, Biographical Sketches, and History Never Before Published. Austin, Tex.: Gammel Book Co., 1902.

Ramsayer, Ralph King. *History of Christ United Presbyterian Church.* Canton, Ohio: Consolidated Graphic Arts Corp., 1971.

Reid, Whitelaw, and Howard Wayne Morgan. *Making Peace with Spain: The Diary of Whitelaw Reid: Sept.–Dec. 1898.* Austin, Tex.: Univ. of Texas Press, 1965.

Rhees, Harriet Chapin Seelye. *Laurenus Clark Seelye, First President of Smith College.* Boston: Houghton Mifflin Co., 1929.

Riley, B. F. *The Life and Times of Booker T. Washington.* New York: Fleming H. Revell, 1916.

Rivas, Mim E. *Beautiful Jim Key: The Lost History of the World's Smartest Horse.* New York: William Morrow, 2006.

Rixey, Presley Marion, William Clarence Braisted, and William Hemphill Bell. *The Life Story of Presley Marion Rixey: Surgeon General, U.S. Navy, 1902–1910: Biography and Autobiography.* Strasburg, Va.: Shenandoah Publishing House, 1930.

Robinson, Corinne Roosevelt. *My Brother Theodore Roosevelt, by Corinne Roosevelt Robinson.* New York: C. Scribner's Sons, 1921.

Robinson, Phyllis C. *Willa, the Life of Willa Cather.* Garden City, N.Y.: Doubleday, 1983.

Rosenfeld, Harvey. *Diary of a Dirty Little War: The Spanish-American War of 1898.* Westport, Conn.: Praeger, 2000.

Royster, Jacqueline Jones. *Profiles of Ohio Women, 1803–2003.* Athens: Ohio Univ. Press, 2003.

Russell, Henry B. *The Lives of William McKinley and Garret A. Hobart, Republican Presidential Candidates of 1896: An Authorized . . . History of Their Public Career and Public Lives . . . Containing Also the Complete History of the Republican Party from Its Rise to the Present.* Hartford: A. D. Worthington, 1896.

Samuels, Peggy, and Harold Samuels. *Teddy Roosevelt at San Juan: The Making of a President.* College Station: Texas A&M University Press, 1997.

Sawyer, Frederic Henry Read. *The Inhabitants of the Philippines.* London: S. Low, Marston, and Co., 1900.

Seale, William. *The President's House: A History.* Washington, D.C.: White House Historical Association with the cooperation of the National Geographic Society, 1986.

Shannon, T. W. *Eugenics.* Marietta, Ohio: S. A. Milliken, 1917.

Slayden, Ellen Maury. *Washington Wife (Journal of Ellen Maury Slayden From 1897–1919).* New York: Harper & Row, 1963.

Smith, Bessie White. *The Romances of the Presidents.* Boston: Lothrop, Lee & Shepard Co., 1932.

Smith, Ira R. T. *"Dear Mr. President": The Story of Fifty Years in the White House Mail Room.* New York: Julian Messner, 1949.

Snow, Jane Elliott. *The Life of William McKinley, Twenty-fifth President of the United States.* Cleveland: The Gardner Printing Co., 1908.

Stanton, Elizabeth Cady, Susan B. Anthony, Matilda Joslyn Gage, and Ida Husted Harper. *History of Woman Suffrage,* vol. 3. Rochester, N.Y.: C. Mann, 1887.

Sternberg, Martha L. *George Miller Sternberg; A Biography.* Chicago: American Medical Association, 1920.

Stout, Janis P. *Willa Cather: The Writer and Her World.* Charlottesville: Univ. Press of Virginia, 2000.

Tarbell, Ida M. *All in the Day's Work.* New York: The Macmillan Co., 1939.

Thompson, Charles Willis. *Presidents I've Known and Two Near Presidents.* Indianapolis: Bobbs-Merrill, 1929.

Tyler, John W. *The Life of William McKinley.* Philadelphia: P. W. Ziegler & Co., 1901.

Varon, Elizabeth R. *Southern Lady, Yankee Spy: The True Story of Elizabeth Van Lew, a Union Agent in the Heart of the Confederacy.* New York: Oxford Univ. Press, 2003.

White, William Allen. *The Autobiography of William Allen White.* New York: Macmillan, 1946.

Wilder, Marshall P. *The Sunny Side of the Street, by Marshall P. Wilder.* New York: Funk and Wagnalls, 1905.

Willard, Frances Elizabeth, and Mary Ashton Rice Livermore. *American Women: Fifteen Hundred Biographies with Over 1,400 Portraits: A Comprehensive Encyclopedia of the Lives and Achievements of American Women During the Nineteenth Century.* Newly rev. ed. New York: Mast, Crowell & Kirkpatrick, 1897.

Willets, Gilson. *Inside History of the White House.* New York: The Christian Herald, 1908.

———. *The Rulers of the World at Home.* New York: The Christian Herald, 1899.

Wilson, Edward Eugene. *"It Is God's Way." A Book Dedicated to the Memory of Our Beloved President, William McKinley, Consisting of the Story of the Assassination and Death, Funeral Services at Washington and Canton, Newspaper Editorials, Poems, and Eulogies from All the World.* Cleveland: E. E. Wilson, 1902.

Wilson, William L., and Festus P. Summers. *The Cabinet Diary of William L. Wilson, 1896–1897.* With an Introduction by Newton D. Baker. Chapel Hill: Univ. of North Carolina Press, 1957.

Winter, William, and Will Bradley. *The American Stage of To-day; Biographies and Photographs of One Hundred Leading Actors and Actresses.* New York: P. F. Collier & Son, 1910.

Wise, John S. *Recollections of Thirteen Presidents Illus.* New York: Doubleday, Page, 1906.

Wolf, Simon. *The Presidents I Have Known from 1860–1918.* Washington, D.C.: Press of B. S. Adams, 1918.

Wolff, Leon, and Paul A. Kramer. *Little Brown Brother: How the United States Purchased and Pacified the Philippine Islands at the Century's Turn.* Francis Parkman Prize, ed. New York: History Book Club, 1961.

Woman Suffrage Hearings Before the Committee on Woman Suffrage . . . on S.J. Res. 1, a Joint Resolution Proposing an Amendment to the Constitution of the United States

Extending the Eight of Suffrage to Women, and S.J. Res. 2, a Joint Resolution Propos-ing, Washington: Govt. Print. Off., 1916.

Wood, Eric Fisher. *Leonard Wood, Conservator of Americanism.* New York: George H. Doran Company, 1920.

Wright, G. Frederick. *Representative Citizens of Ohio Memorial-Biographical.* Cleve-land: Memorial Pub. Co., 1918.

Young, C. Howard. *Sunny Life of an Invalid.* Hartford, Conn.: Press of the Case, Lockwood & Brainard, 1897.

Ziff, Katherine. *Asylum on the Hill: History of a Healing Landscape.* Athens: Ohio Univ. Press, 2012.

Index

Sanford School (formerly Cleveland Female Seminary), 6

Saxton, Catharine "Kate" Dewalt (mother), 5; Ida's closeness to, 3–4, 16, 23; illness and death of, 24–25

Saxton, George (brother), 4, 45; Anna George and, 133, 178–79; Ida's response to murder of, 156–61; McKinley and, 28, 156, 158; murder of, 155–58, 178–79; scandals surrounding, 57–58, 68, 129, 156–57, 179; sisters' relationship with, 16, 156–57

Saxton, Hester B. Medill, 45

Saxton, James Ashbaugh (father), 2, 4, 38; businesses of, 8–9, 16–17, 34, 45; death of, 47; Ida and, 5, 16–17; on Ida's suitors, 8, 19; McKinley and, 17, 21, 28, 47; prosperity of, 8, 28, 47; real estate of, 23, 28, 238–39; support for women's rights, 9, 183

Saxton, John (paternal grandfather), 1–2, 10, 20, 23

Saxton, Joseph (uncle), 2, 269, 276

Saxton, Joshua (uncle), 3

Saxton, Margaret Laird (paternal grandmother), 2, 23

Saxton, Maria (aunt), 62–63, 117, 126, 150

Saxton, Mary. See Barber, Mary "Pina" Saxton (sister)

Saxton, Mrs. T. L., 69, 171

Saxton, Sam (cousin), 2, 145, 176

Saxton, Thomas, 3

Saxton Block Building, destroyed by fire, 219, 291

Saxton family, 258, 271; businesses of, 2–5; egalitarianism of, 9, 13; homes of, 3–4

Saxton House, 40; Barber family living in, 34, 128–29, 238, 266; George's funeral in, 157; Ida and, 132–33, 266, 282; McKinley avoiding George and, 57–58; McKinleys using, 34, 44–45, 128–29, 211; nieces' weddings in, 273, 276; rechristened "McKinley residence," 50

Scott, Henry T., 231

Semple, Letitia Tyler, 123

Senate, U.S., 176–77. See also Congress, U.S.; ratification of peace treaty by, 168, 171, 174

Seymour, Julius, 70

Shannon, T. W., 74

Shaw, Warren, 263

Shayne, C. C., 63

Sherman, Harriet, 6

Sherman, John, 49, 104, 125, 146

Sherman, William Tecumseh, 40

silver standard, 215

Sinclair, William T., 110, 169, 212

Slayden, Ellen, 201

slippers. See knitting, Ida's

Sloane, John, 136

Smith, Charles Emory, 84, 235

Smith, Ella, 228, 235

Smith, Ira, 119

Smith, Joe, 56, 79

Smith, M. E. T., 129–30

souvenirs: of assassination, 292; Ida collecting campaign ribbons and badges, 91; Ida's image on, 90; McKinley children used on, 91–92, 128, 264; McKinley giving boutonnières as, 110

Spain: McKinley trying to avoid war with, 133–34, 143; McKinleys entertaining ambassador from, 142; peace negotiations with, 154, 156, 162–63, 166, 168, 171; peace treaty with, 168, 174; Philippines ceded to US by, 159, 162–63; Roosevelt's eagerness for war with, 124–25, 134–35; US motives for war with, 124–25, 132–33, 144, 154, 159

Spanish-American War: in Cuba, 147; diseases in, 152, 154–55; end of, 154; Ida during, 149, 150–51; McKinleys visiting military camps in, 150, 153; nurses' corps in, 151–52, 184; in Philippines, 146–47; toll on McKinley, 146–48, 152; veterans anger at Alger for, 176; women's organizations in, 151–52

Speer, Robert, 166

Spratling, Edgar J., 199

staff, McKinley's, 52, 79–80. See also specific names

Stanford, Jane, 47

Sternberg, George M., 152, 187, 195, 236–37

Sternberg, Martha, 152

Storer, Bellamy, 64

suitors, Ida's, 8, 10–11; McKinley as, 19–21

Taft, William Howard, 175, 191, 197

Tarbell, Ida, 106

tariffs, 90. See also foreign trade; effects of, 52, 70, 89; McKinley's bill on, 51–52; McKinley's speech on, 47–49

technology, McKinley on, 241–42

temperance movement, xi, 28–29, 114–15

Tennessee Centennial Exposition, 122, 124–27

Terhune, Mary, 64–65

Tharin, Charles, 111, 212

Tharin, Clara, 66, 103, 111, 212, 262

theater, 182; acclaim for Ida while attending, 101, 144; Ida attending, 143–44, 171, 176, 218, 283, 287–88; Ida's participation in, 10; Ida's passion for, xi, 7, 112, 140; Ida's patronage of musicians and actors, 115–16, 140–41

Thompson, Charles Willis, 198

Thurston, John M., 143

Tod, John, 61

travel: friends encouraging Ida's, 266–67, 274, 284; Ida's, xi, 9, 41, 108, 227–28; Ida's health and, 47–48, 56–57, 58, 187–88; Ida's in Europe, with sister, 11–16, 230; Ida's wish for, 16, 68; McKinleys', 122, 169, 230; McKinleys' brief trips out of Washington, 152–53;